MUSIC AND SOCIETY IN CORK, 1700–1900

MUSIC AND SOCIETY IN CORK, 1700–1900

SUSAN O'REGAN

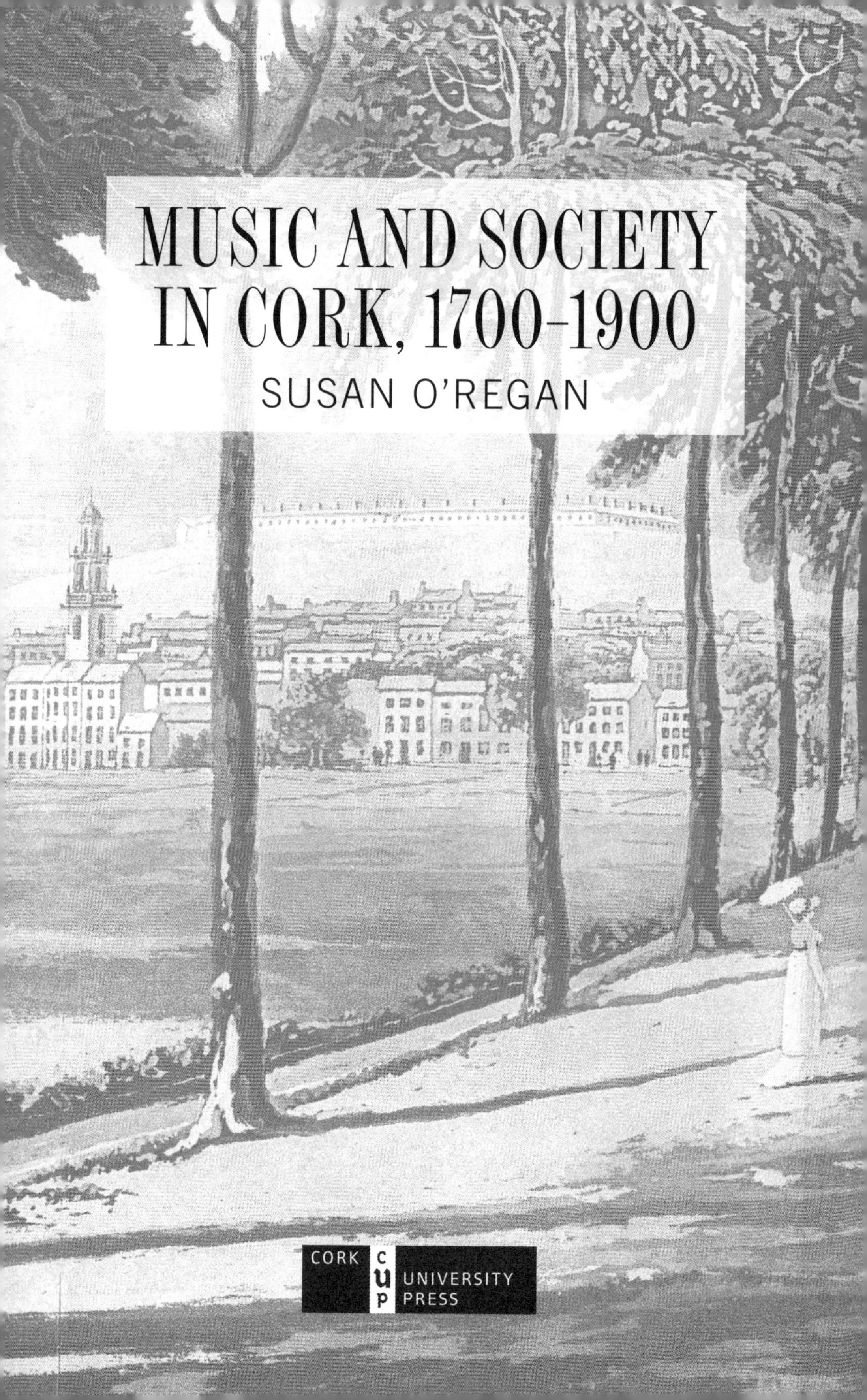

CORK UNIVERSITY PRESS

First published in 2018 by
Cork University Press
Youngline Industrial Estate
Pouladuff Road, Togher
Cork T12 HT6V, Ireland

British Library Cataloguing in Publication Data
A CIP catalogue record for this book is available from the British Library.

ISBN 978-1-78-205-2203

Typeset by Studio 10 Design
Printed in Poland by Hussar Books

CONTENTS

LIST OF TABLES

LIST OF ILLUSTRATIONS

ABBREVIATIONS

CJ	*Corke Journal*
CEP	*Cork Evening Post*
NCEP	*New Cork Evening Post*
HC	*Hibernian Chronicle*
CA	*Cork Advertiser*
CAG	*Cork Advertising Gazette*
CG	*Cork Gazette*
CMC	*Cork Mercantile Chronicle*
CMI	*Cork Morning Intelligencer*
SR	*Southern Reporter*
CEH	*Cork Evening Herald*
CS	*Cork Standard*
FJ	*Freeman's Journal*
CN	*The Constitution (Cork Constitution)*
CE	*Cork Examiner*
EMIR	*The Enclyclopaedia of Music in Ireland*, ed. H. White and B. Boydell (2013)
NGrove2	*New Grove Dictionary of Music and Musicians*, 2nd edition (2001)
JCHAS	*Journal of the Cork Historical and Archaeological Society*
NLI	National Library of Ireland, Dublin
NUI	National University of Ireland
BL	British Library
RAM	Royal Academy of Music, London
UCC	University College Cork
RCB	Representative Church Body Library, Dublin
IE CCCA	Cork City and County Archives
CSM	Cork School of Music

MUSICAL TERMS

cond	conductor, conducted by
sop	soprano
pf	pianoforte
vln	violin
vla	viola
vcl	violoncello
db	double bass
fl	flute
ob	oboe
cl	clarinet
tr	trumpet
hn	horn

CURRENCY

One pound (£1) = twenty shillings (20s)
One shilling (1s) = twelve pence (12d)
One guinea (1 gn) = £1 1s

NOTE: Irish name prefixes of 'O' and 'Mac' ('Mc') were not consistently applied during the nineteenth century. In quotations, they have been left unedited. Likewise, italics in quotations have remained unedited.

PRINCIPAL LOCATIONS FOR CONCERTS AND MUSICAL PERFORMANCES

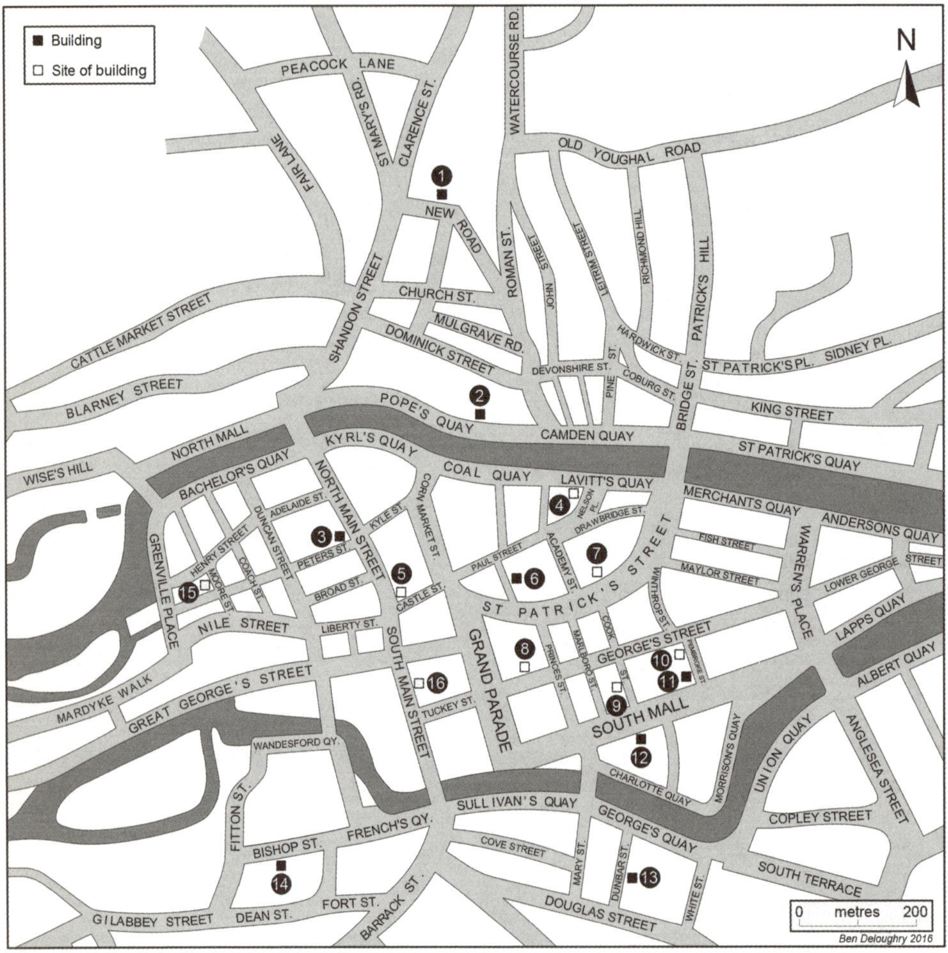

Key to locations

1. Cathedral of St Mary and St Anne (North Cathedral) (RC)
2. St Mary's Church, Pope's Quay (RC)
3. St Peter's Church (C of I)
4. Athenaeum/Cork Opera House (Site)
5. Council Chamber (Site)
6. St Peter and Paul's Church 1866 (RC)
7. Patrick's Street Theatre (Site)
8. George's Street Assembly Room
9. Victoria (Cook Street) Theatre (Site)
10. Theatre Royal 1760 (Site)
11. Imperial Hotel
12. Assembly Rooms (Protestant Hall)
13. St Finbarr's Church (South Chapel) (RC)
14. St Fin Barre's Cathedral (C of I)
15. Hammond's Marsh Assembly Rooms (Site)
16. Christ Church (Holy Trinity) (C of I)

INTRODUCTION

A thriving port and provincial city, Cork prospered during the eighteenth and nineteenth centuries due to its strategic location and vibrant commercial life. The musical culture that developed during the eighteenth century was the beginning of a new urban tradition that grew alongside other civic amenities. As an aspect of sociability, music emerged in many urban settings, prompting the development of professional structures and infrastructures, and serving multiple roles within the city's civic, religious and voluntary organisations.

By 1700, Ireland was a country of complex social and political divisions, brought about by aggressive incursions of English crown forces. Following the political and social upheavals of the previous century, the native Irish, the old English, and the new English settlers inhabited different worlds, of language, culture and religion. The patronage of harpers and poets by old Irish chieftains had all but vanished, as the new English settlers asserted their own order and way of life. The sophistication of Italian music appealed to Ireland's new Ascendancy, for whom music was part of social display, as an accompaniment to other forms of sociability, and as a personal pursuit, for which each household maintained provision of musicians, teachers, instruments and musical scores.

As urban centres developed, wealthy mercantile families adopted many of the social habits of the landed gentry, purchasing musical instruments for domestic use and employing musicians and teachers. New civic amenities such as theatres, assembly rooms and walks extended social interaction into civic settings, ensuring social cohesion. Towns and cities, and particularly the ports, were sites of mercantile transaction, negotiation, economic progress and communication, the centres in which modern Ireland took shape. Taverns and coffee houses catered for mercantile encounters, while assembly rooms and theatres facilitated evening social entertainment. Along with other leisure pursuits, music was commodified and assimilated into the new systems of commercial and professional exchange, influencing musical practices and repertoire. The European music that was introduced was never a single style, rather a series of fashionable idioms. The late Italian baroque, the *galant*, the Italian operatic style, exemplified in works of Rossini, English ballad opera and glees, and finally the German style, all achieved varying levels of popularity. The nineteenth century witnessed an intensification of organised musical life, moving from the small-scale environment of the assembly room to larger, purpose-built venues. Touring musicians from continental Europe as well as Britain brought new styles, and levels of virtuosity.

As larger works were performed, military bands supplemented the instrumental forces. Following Catholic Emancipation, the rapid development of music in Ireland's Catholic churches brought new traditions of liturgical performance.

The cultural fracture imposed by England's dominance of Ireland has formed the basis for scholarly discourse on music in Ireland. Harry White, in *The Keeper's Recital: music and cultural history in Ireland, 1770–1970* (1998), has emphasised the lasting effects of cultural dislocation of Ireland's music since the eighteenth century, the persistent Classical/Irish dichotomy of music, and Ireland's ultimate failure in the field of art music, particularly within the timeframe of this study. In addressing this and other historical issues, Martin Dowling's *Traditional Music and Irish Society: historical perspectives* (2014) explores a broad range of sources and methods to investigate music in Irish culture from early Irish societies to the present day, encompassing geographical, economic, political and religious considerations. Mary Louise O'Donnell's *Ireland's Harp: the shaping of Irish identity c.1770–1880* (2014) explores a range of literary and iconographical sources in articulating the role, both actual and metaphorical, of the harp in Irish cultural history.

The pioneering research of Brian Boydell into music in eighteenth-century Dublin, *A Dublin Musical Calendar* (1988) and *Rotunda Music in Eighteenth-Century Dublin* (1992), provides a foundation for subsequent explorations of public concert life in Ireland. The mapping of musical activity in Ireland's provincial urban centres began with Aloys Fleischmann's *Music in Ireland: A Symposium* (1952) and Ita Hogan's *Anglo-Irish Music 1780–1830* (1966). A recent publication of research by Roy Johnston with Declan Plummer, *The Musical Life of Nineteenth-Century Belfast* (2015), examines the structures of theatre and concert life and the pivotal role played by the city's musical societies. The publication in 2013 of the *Enclyclopaedia of Music in Ireland* (edited by Harry White and Barra Boydell) has provided an indispensible resource of biographical and historical detail concerning music in Ireland.

Cork's political and economic history is examined in depth in David Dickson's *Old World Colony: Cork and south Munster* (2005). As a feature of the city, religious divisions are key to understanding the city's social structures. These are examined in Ian d'Alton's *Protestant Society and Politics in Cork, 1812–1844* (1980) and John B. O'Brien's *The Catholic Middle Classes in Pre-Famine Cork* (1979). Patrick O'Flanagan and Cornelius G. Buttimer's *Cork: history and society: interdisciplinary essays on the history of an Irish county* (1993) represents a wide scope of scholarly work, including folklore, art institutions, Gaelic literature and urban development. In exploring music in Cork's urban settings during the eighteenth and nineteenth centuries, the present work fills a gap in current knowledge and understanding of Cork's social and cultural history. In examining the structures and practices of music in Cork's civic, religious and commercial settings, this study will provide a basis for understanding the social conditions, interactions, taste preferences and musical activities of the city's inhabitants.

This examination of music in Cork's urban setting uses a number of perspectives and approaches. The first are the channels – civic institutions, societies, churches and theatres – through which musical performances were generated. Following from this are the particulars of organisation such as the occasion, the event, the venue, the performers and their audiences. The repertoire that was performed reflected fashion, taste preferences, canonic traditions. Biographical approaches are useful in some cases. As key figures in shaping Cork's musical culture, the local musicians feature in all chapters of this book.

This study is based largely on contemporary newspapers. The sparse information given in eighteenth-century newspapers contrasts sharply with the level of detail encountered in those of the nineteenth century, when commentary on matters of cultural interest became commonplace. This becomes particularly interesting when the socio-political standpoints of Cork's liberal and conservative newspapers are compared. Throughout the nineteenth century, the local newspapers were both reporters and influencers, and their reviews of musical events provide valuable insights into prevailing values. Exclusive use of this source has its own drawbacks, however, and it is clear that many important issues never reached the local press. Memoirs, travel writing, church records and contemporary journals also provide important sources. The immediacy and transience of musical experience is not always captured in words. But this is one of the challenging aspects of music history and musicology.

This book is organised into ten chapters, on a broadly chronological basis, each dealing with an aspect of the city's musical life. Chapters 1 to 4 are rooted in the eighteenth century, and Chapters 5 to 10 feature nineteenth-century developments. As a prelude to the work, Chapter 1 outlines the developing urban environment of eighteenth-century Cork, its inhabitants, and patterns of social life. Chapter 2 takes the public concert as the focus for a survey of Cork's emerging musical infrastructures during the eighteenth century, investigating the nature of concert life, the social bases of locally organised concerts, and the status of Cork on the itineraries of touring musicians. Concert repertoire and performance practices are examined in the light of wider contemporaneous developments. Chapter 3 traces the development of musical provision at St Fin Barre's cathedral and the city's Anglican parish churches during the eighteenth century, which was a period of consolidation of its structures. Chapter 4 provides a detailed survey of music in Cork's theatrical life from the 1730s to 1840, focusing on repertoire, organisation and reception, and considering the theatre's influence on urban popular musical taste.

The changes that occurred in socio-political life following the failed rebellion of the United Irishmen in 1798 brought new political awareness and sectarian tensions. The period of prosperity in Cork during the early nineteenth century led to a strengthening of the music trade, and the range of musical platforms diversified to include some large-scale charitable performances. More intimate concert settings facilitated vocal concerts, the appearance of the piano and harp, and performances by touring Irish harpers and pipers. These developments are explored in Chapter 5.

Developing the theme of the musical profession, Chapter 6 focuses on the careers of three young Cork musicians who travelled to England in search of professional opportunities, demonstrating the influence of London's musical world and its commercial opportunities. In a survey of concerts during the 1830s, Chapter 7 illustrates the emergence of new patterns in touring itineraries, professional networking, repertoire, concert organisation and reception. During the latter half of the nineteenth century, voluntary associations were a dynamic element in urban life, effective vehicles for change and improvement, as well as being important means of sociability. Chapter 8 surveys the range of new amateur societies and educational initiatives that emerged during the years 1840 to 1870. From temperance bands to choral societies, these developments extended the scope for amateur musical participation and altered the musical landscape of the city.

It was not until Catholic Emancipation was gained that an overt musical tradition was established in the city's Catholic churches, further energised in the momentum of the 'devotional revolution' in the latter half of the nineteenth century. The development of music in Cork city's Catholic churches is examined in Chapter 9, constituting a case study of music's role in the resurgence of the Catholic Church in nineteenth-century Ireland.

The last quarter of the nineteenth century saw the consolidation of the city's cultural institutions, which will be examined in Chapter 10. Amateur musical societies, both choral and instrumental, continued to flourish, and amateur operatic societies emerged in the last decade of the century. The founding of the Cork Municipal School of Music in 1878 was a notable achievement. By the end of the nineteenth century, the city's public musical infrastructures embraced a wider section of the population than at any previous time in its history, under the direction of a dedicated core of music professionals. In examining these developments, and setting them within wider cultural contexts, this book provides new light on a hitherto unexplored aspect of the cultural fabric of eighteenth- and nineteenth-century Ireland.

1

IRELAND'S SECOND CITY

Detail from 'Cork from the Mardyke Walk'.

Small vessels only can approach the city, which stands seven miles up the river Lee. According to my recollection, this is the chief port of merchants: and in truth, there is more beef, tallow, and butter shipped from hence, than from all the other ports of the kingdom put together.[1]

By the early eighteenth century, Cork was a major Atlantic port. With a large natural harbour and rich agricultural hinterland, it grew rapidly within the trading culture of early merchant capitalism, following the English settlement of Ireland in the previous century.[2] Cox in 1685 referred to it as 'the second best citty of Ireland', its commercial development accelerated by the increased involvement in the colonial Atlantic economy, in particular that with North America.[3] Exports of beef, pork and butter soared during the latter half of the eighteenth and early nineteenth century, as Cork became an important centre for provisioning the British naval and military forces during the French wars. Tanning and textile production ensured continued economic growth in the last quarter of the eighteenth century, when linen exports also rose dramatically.[4] The city's population increased from 17,500 in 1706 to 40,000 in 1750, and by 1800 it had grown to 60,000, brought about by inward migration of English and Protestant Irish, Huguenots, and of Catholics from the surrounding regions.[5] In 1786, a visitor to the city noted that 'some of the merchants in Corke far exceed in opulence any others in the nation'.[6]

The marshy islands which gave the city its name (*corcach* = marsh), and on which the original settlement was founded, developed into a compact urban centre, surrounded by the two streams of the River Lee and bounded by medieval walls. In the 1750s, the city's physical structure remained within the bounds of its medieval walls, containing the main street, enclosed on either end by the north and south gates. Numerous narrow lanes led off the main street in a distinctive fishbone pattern. A visitor in the latter half of the century wrote of dirty, unpaved narrow streets, and a stand of fifty sedan chairs,[7] one of which was captured in a drawing by Nathaniel Grogan. Scarcity of available land prompted the reclamation of adjacent marshes from the 1670s onwards. The filling-in of marshes by developers, who leased tracts of land from the corporation, led to the construction of public and commercial buildings, such as the Exchange (1710), the Custom House (1724), the Corn Market (1740) and the Butter Market (1750). From early in the century, coffee houses such as the Turk's Head (1713) were important meeting places for the mercantile community, where London and Dublin newspapers were circulated.

Events during the politically turbulent years of the mid-seventeenth century had radically reconfigured Cork's social structure. Aggressive territorial incursions by successive English crown forces altered the balance of power, creating a new administrative structure, with the establishment of Anglicanism as the official religion. After a rebellion against Cromwell and his plantation policies in 1641, Catholics were perceived as a threat to Protestantism. Mistrust was exacerbated when the Irish besieged Cork city in 1642, and by 1644 all of the city's Irish and Old English Catholic inhabitants were expelled and replaced by new English Protestants, who gained municipal control of the city by a charter granted by Cromwell in 1656.[8] The defeat of the Jacobites by the Williamite forces at the Siege of Cork in 1690 quenched the last hopes for Catholic claims on the city, finally securing Protestant political privilege. The new Protestant inhabitants of Cork, like those of other Irish towns, viewed themselves as agents in the creation of a stable Protestant society, with notions of 'superiority, improvement and civility' evident in their lifestyle and attitude.[9] They adopted social patterns that emulated elite society of Dublin and London, which included balls, private parties, theatre and concert attendance.

The enactment of penal legislation against Catholics in Ireland between 1695 and 1709 further asserted the dominance of the Protestant minority. These Penal Laws included the expulsion of regular clergy in 1697–8, restrictions on Catholic priests and bishops, and a prohibition on carrying arms, purchasing land or procuring long leases. The expulsions from the city did not remain unchallenged. By January 1704, however, a decision was made by the Corporation to make an application to parliament, expressing concern that the trades of the Protestant inhabitants were being encroached upon by 'the great numbers of Irish flocking into this City, to the great damage and danger of the Protestant inhabitants'.[10] The request was not granted and in 1737, Alexander the Coppersmith, a local pamphleteer, complained that the Catholics of Cork had commandeered the bulk of the city's provision trade. For the remainder of the century, Catholic merchants and traders prospered without ostentation, gaining formidable economic power.[11] Irish was still much spoken among the city's inhabitants in the 1790s.[12]

The relative stability of the eighteenth century brought radical transformation of the urban infrastructures and a rising commercialism, as the new Protestant English settlers sought to create a new society. While Gaelic culture was not entirely absent from Cork city, political power was firmly in the hands of the city's Protestants. Catholic merchants gained increasing economic power as the century progressed, and liberal, patriotic Protestants contributed to the city's social mix.

At the centre of the city's politics was the Corporation, consisting of a mayor, two sheriffs, aldermen, burgesses and freemen. The sheriffs, who were elected annually, were the most powerful members, with the power of nomination of other key offices. The existence of the 'Friendly Club' maintained the Corporation as a 'self-perpetuating oligarchy' of Protestant merchant families, a means of guarding their own economic interests.[13] This was a major point of contention within the increasingly prosperous community of Catholic merchants during the early nineteenth century, who were excluded from the Corporation before the Municipal Reform Act of 1840.[14]

Among the city's inhabitants was a community of Huguenots, having settled since the late seventeenth century as refugees following religious wars in France. A Huguenot church between French Church Street and Carey's Lane was in use in the early years, but they were gradually accommodated within the Anglican parish churches. Their relative wealth and level of skill in areas such as silversmithing ensured their contribution to the productivity of the growing affluent city. The Methodists gained strength in the city during the eighteenth century. Open-air meetings were held at Hammond's Marsh in 1748, and Charles Wesley spent several weeks in the city in 1752. John Wesley proposed the building of a chapel at Hammond's March, which he subsequently visited many times. A new Wesleyan chapel on Patrick Street was opened for worship in 1805.

In addition to generating surplus wealth as a major port, Cork, as the county town, was a centre for commercial, social, legal and administrative affairs, and attracted wealth through the provision of goods and services for the gentry of the entire region. By the mid-eighteenth century, specialist shops such as drapers, tobacconists, perfumers, jewellers, silversmiths and booksellers were located in the centre of the city.[15] Castle Street was the location of a number of booksellers. The establishment of the city's first regular newspaper from the mid-eighteenth century provided a focus for the new urban society, its advertisers prospering through the supply of material luxuries, and through the promotion of commercialised leisure pursuits such as dancing, music and theatre-going, becoming, in Borsay's words, 'a channel of communication for the leisure industry'.[16] The earliest regular provincial newspaper that represented Cork interests was *The Limerick Journal* (1739–49), continuing from 1749 as *The Munster Journal*, a Limerick publication. Aimed at a Munster readership, it published the earliest advertisements for musical supplies in Cork, such as an advertisement by Cork bookseller Cornelius Sullivan for 'a variety of music by the best masters, for the Violin, German Flute and Harpsichord, with the newest songs set to music'.[17] In 1750–1, this newspaper published an advertisement by bookseller Phineas Bagnell for the sale of German flutes, in addition to music for the German flute, violin and harpsichord.[18] The establishment of the city's first regular newspapers, the twice-weekly *Corke Journal* in 1753, owned by Catholic printer Eugene Swiney, and Phineas Bagnell's *Cork Evening Post* in 1755, provided an important channel of communication for musicians and their intended audiences. William Flyn, also Catholic, established the *Hibernian Chronicle* in October 1769, a twice-weekly publication that continued under his proprietorship until 1802.[19]

A significant aspect of social organisation and control was display and exhibition. Fleming has noted the importance of public events in eighteenth-century Ireland as 'displays of the state's power and pre-eminence', reminding 'those who participated in them of the danger of a defeated Catholic population and to be ever on guard for any stirrings of danger'.[20] Such displays recorded in Cork were the firing of canons, ringing of bells, bonfires, and illuminations that were organised on important commemorative days such as royal birthdays, accessions, anniversaries of battles, etc., that were popular public entertainments. Concerts were frequently organised to mark such celebrations.

A feature of the growth of urban culture in British towns and cities during the eighteenth century was the appearance of leisure facilities for the middle and upper classes, leading to a physical and social transformation of urban landscapes and infrastructures.[21] Assembly rooms, bowling greens, walks, and Cork's 'new and imposing theatres, blessed by royal patents, sprang up in the provinces in the decade 1755–65'.[22] Cork's urban advancement kept apace, with each of the above established by 1760. The majority of the twenty-eight shareholders of the new theatre built in 1760 were based in Cork city, and included four or five Catholic merchants.[23] Assemblies, balls and 'drums' were regularly organised:

> There were weekly Drums, which were said to have been extremely social and agreeable, the admission was trifling, the company danced, played

> cards, talked or promenaded without restraint, and the attendance was generally numerous and respectable. These Drums were much resorted to by the military [...][24]

A distinctive feature of eighteenth-century urban life was 'associational culture'. Voluntary membership of clubs, societies and associations was widespread in Ireland throughout the century, and was a dynamic force in culture, philanthropy and politics.[25] From the early decades of the eighteenth century, loyal societies, charitable societies and convivial societies flourished in Cork city. Although private, many of these societies enacted public displays such as processions, or charitable events, welcoming press attention and thereby maintaining a public profile. Charitable events organised by these societies included concerts, balls, plays and sermons, bringing them into the public sphere.

The city's Freemasons were a prominent convivial organisation throughout the eighteenth and nineteenth centuries, part of a wider network that extended across Ireland.[26] In 1771, there were thirteen lodges in Cork, meeting at a range of taverns and members' homes.[27] Their primary concern was social security, provided through fraternal support, and charity, for members and their families, and for civic charitable organisations. One of their public ceremonies was the annual St John's Day procession, accompanied by a band, from Christ Church to the theatre, where they attended performances with bespoke Masonic music.[28] By the late eighteenth century, the city's Freemasons were a broad-based society, organised into lodges, inclusive of Catholics, despite papal denunciations of membership of such societies.[29] Mirala argues that cost of admission and annual fees may have been a barrier to membership, and that the various city lodges catered for particular social classes or groups. A number of Cork's prominent musicians were members, including many of the organists and lay singers associated with St Fin Barre's cathedral, and also theatre managers Tottenham Heaphy and Francis Seymour.[30] A society with broadly similar aims of mutual benefit and sociability was the Friendly Brothers of St Patrick. Established initially as an anti-duelling society, the Friendly Brothers established 'knots' countrywide during the eighteenth century. Sir Richard Cox established a knot in Cork city in the 1750s.[31] The requirement for membership was that one was a Christian.

Since the mid-seventeenth century, the city's demographic included a sizable number of military troops, billeted within the city walls. By the 1760s, there was a large city garrison and seventeen barracks in the Cork region.[32] Advertisements for military musicians appeared in the local press from the late 1750s, specifying trumpeters, fifers, drummers and Irish pipers.[33] A recruitment party that appeared in Cork city in 1775, led by Major Boyle Roche, included 'an elegant band of Music, consisting of French Horns, Hautboys, Clarionets and Bassoons, playing "God save the King"'.[34] This range of instruments corresponds to that of *Harmonienmusik*, the Austro-German band model, common across mainland Europe and used in British military bands until the end of the eighteenth century.[35] The sight and sound of military bands was always a remarkable feature of city life, whether to attract young recruits or to enhance civic or social occasions. Regimental culture strengthened from the late eighteenth century, becoming the most effective organisational military unit, encompassing different ranks and classes.[36] Funded directly by military officers, bands enhanced the status of the regiments to which they were attached. A report of a visual exhibition entitled *Eidophusikon* at the Theatre Royal in 1792 noted that 'these grand and magnificent scenes are wonderfully enhanced by the Music of the Band, belonging to the 28th regiment, which, in itself, is a feast for voluptuous ears'.[37] A new barracks northeast of the city (now Collins Barracks) was opened in 1806, which accommodated 156 officers and 2,000 men.[38] By 1811, almost a third of the region's garrison was billeted in the city's seven barracks, totalling almost 5,000 men.[39] The regiments were thus numerous and conspicuous and the presence of their musical bands was a ubiquitous feature of city life. The military bandsmen were part of the oldest and most extensive professional network of musicians in the British Isles. As part of the regiments' duties involved the enforcement of public order, however, they changed location regularly, to avoid over-familiarity with local communities.[40] Hence, the involvement of specific military musicians or bands in civic music was always of a transient nature.

A number of civilian armed societies were established as a means of local defence during the early years of the American War. Some of Cork's new Volunteer companies of the 1770s were revivals of earlier local militia groups, such as the True Blues, formed in 1745 and re-established in 1776. Among the local companies were the Cork Boyne, the Cork Union, the Royal Cork Volunteers, the Loyal Cork Legion, the Blackpool Horse, the Glanmire Union, the Cork Cavalry and the Culloden Volunteers.[41] Initially filled by Protestants, as the Penal Laws prohibited the carrying of arms by Catholics, a network of Volunteer companies grew up countrywide.

After 1779, Catholics were admitted to some of the south Munster companies. The Volunteer movement became politicised, emerging as a nationwide force, 'sons of liberty', according to Fitzgerald.[42] Inspired by ideals of patriotism and solidarity, the movement provided a pathway for political assertion and action, notably in the campaign for free trade and legislative independence.[43] The appearance of Volunteer songs and medleys on concert and theatre bills over the following decades indicated the extent of the wide popularity of this movement, and some of the songs subsequently appeared among the publications of the Young Ireland movement.

Music featured in the ideology and in the public display of the Volunteers. Many of the Volunteer flags and emblems incorporated the symbol of the Irish 'winged-maiden harp'.[44] A visitor to Cork in 1790 described shop signs depicting St Patrick inciting the Volunteers to play in praise of liberty on the Irish harp.[45] The Volunteers used songs to promote their ideals, setting new words to traditional Irish melodies. A trumpeter and fife and drum pair were part of several of the Munster companies, and a few of the companies featured military-style bands that participated in a range of civic occasions. The Band of the Cork Union performed at local events, such as parades, balls and at the theatre, in a distinctive scarlet uniform. Francis Gould, a Catholic merchant, was Captain of the Loyal Cork Legion in 1797, a company that included many of the Catholic gentry of the city and surrounding region.[46] The legendary status of this company's band was recalled in 1840 at a meeting of the Cork Literary and Scientific Society, noting that its members were

> universal performers on every military musical instrument, using them all in common as taste or necessity dictated. […] Indeed so proficient were the Irish militia bands that they formed a nursery for future band masters who extended the knowledge of good music and true taste […][47]

The eighteenth and nineteenth centuries witnessed the widespread commercialisation and commodification of music – publishing, instrument-making, professional concert organisation – and the music profession flourished. Commercialisation brought the practice of paying to hear music, paying to learn music, and purchasing musical goods. All of these were endorsed by the new civic society that flourished during the late eighteenth century. Concerts enhanced the leisure time of an increasingly affluent society, and the professional musician became a significant figure in urban cultural life.

Typical newspaper advertisements during the 1760s and 1770s listed violins, guitars and accessories such as strings and reeds. In 1762, Richard Byrne, a general shopkeeper at the 'Raven and Sugarloaf' opposite Christ Church, supplied 'a fresh assortment of the finest Roman strings for violins, silver fourths and best London bridges for ditto', and also 'setts of strings for bass, violins, reeds for hautboys and ruled paper for music'.[48] In 1762 Phineas and George Bagnell received 'a large parcel of English guitars made by the most noted London makers' and also accepted commissions for the construction of guitars by Gibson of Dublin.[49] In 1768, Thomas Lord, bookseller, with premises under the Exchange coffee house, advertised the sale of 'a large assortment of the newest music for the violin, German flute and harpsichord, strings for the violoncello' and also 'hautboy and bassoon reeds.'[50] Local military band musicians would have required supplies of oboe and bassoon reeds. In the same year, John Bardin, bookseller in Castle Street, advertised 'genuine Roman fiddle strings, harpsichord wire, brass, steel and silver strings for the guitar, directions for all sorts of instruments, simple songs', the latter clearly aimed at an amateur market.[51]

Education for society was a preoccupation of the urban middle and upper classes in the eighteenth century. Social accomplishments such as dancing, singing and instrumental performance were valued for children, and particularly for girls, improving their marriage prospects.[52] Dancing masters were a clearly defined professional group who travelled widely, bringing new styles and steps from the metropolitan centres of London and Dublin to provincial towns and cities, issuing press advertisements on their arrival. Masters for Irish step dancing did not generally advertise in the press. Hugh O'Brien, in 1754, made it known that he was not the Brien that 'kept a Jigg house near North Gate', adding that 'he is not a man of that step'.[53] Gleaning from memoranda dating from the early decades of the eighteenth century, Tuckey states that quarterly fees of between 10 and 15 shillings were paid for lessons in dancing and playing the violin, the latter entailing three lessons per week.[54] In addition to teaching privately at either their own or their pupils' homes, music and dancing, together with art and literature, consitituted a set of 'accomplishments' which were offered as additional subjects at privately run boarding and day schools. In 1756 Mrs Johanna Donovan's school offered 'French, Musick, Dancing and Writing, by some of the best teachers in this City'.[55] From the turn of the century, some boys' schools began to feature music on their curricula. In 1810, Mr Upton's School in Nile Street offered tuition in 'Classics, science, etc., accompts, music, fencing, dancing and drawing'.[56] In 1816, an advertisement for Glanmire School for boys listed music masters for both the violin and flute among its staff.[57] In addition to attending schools, the dancing masters and music professors taught at their own rooms in the city or at pupils' homes. The abundance of newspaper advertisements published during the second half of the eighteenth century for private tuition by peripatetic music masters and dancing masters indicates that these professions had begun to flourish.

Musical instrument makers featured among press advertisements of the later eighteenth century, among whom were Thomas Flanagan of Broad Lane, and James Brealsford Stephens, harpsichord maker. One of the most colourful figures in the late eighteenth century music trade was Marsden Haddock, organ-builder, repairer and mechanical inventor. In 1793, he issued a novel trade circular, later described by Cork antiquarian Robert Day (1836–1914), written 'In Hudibrastic verse, upon old handmade paper, 12 inches long by 6 inches wide, in a floral border, and with an organ as a heading'. It begins as follows:

> Haddock's Umbrella Manufactory, Earthenware, Glass Shop, etc.
> No. 15 Castle Street
>
> Whilst Marsden Haddock greets his friends,
> With gratitude his heart distends,
> At No. fifteen Castle Street,
> Those who to visit him incline
> Will find an organ for his sign,
> Where on the most improved construction
> He makes and sells at great reduction
> Organs for church and chamber use –
> Barrel or finger, which you chuse;
> Aeolian harps, whose soothing strings
> Are touched by Zephyr's trembling wings;
> Guitars, whose soft enchanting air
> Invites the fingers of the fair;
> And shrill-toned pipes may here be found
> For such as love a martial sound.
> He tunes and puts in good repair
> All organs put beneath his care ...[58]

During the latter part of the eighteenth century, specialist music shops appeared as local professional musicians undertook direct music retailing. The earliest to advertise in the local press was Patrick Reynolds, a professional violinist whose music shop was located in Fish Street, a lane off the Long Quay (developed as Patrick Street since 1783). In April 1769 he advertised 'a few Gibson and London guitars, violins, with choice strings of all sorts, and a great collection of new songs and other music'.[59]

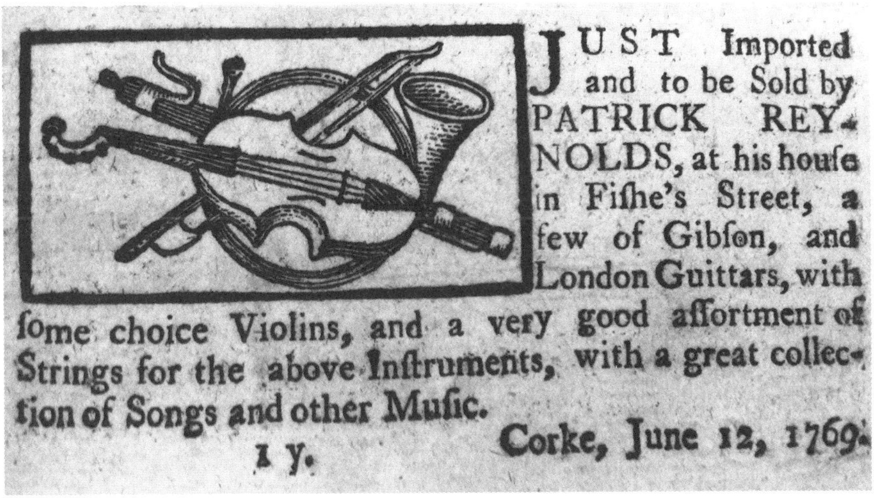

Figure 1.1. Advertisement for Patrick Reynolds' music shop, *Corke Journal*, 1769.

In December 1769, he offered 'a right good Fortepiano to be sold [...] price fifteen guineas'.[60] This appears to have been one of the earliest references to such an instrument for sale in Ireland, and is remarkable in that Henry Walsh's performance on a forte piano in Dublin the previous year, in May 1768, is the earliest recorded instance of such a performance in the British Isles.[61] James Magrath, singer and teacher of singing and guitar, ran a music shop in Castle Street from 1777, when he offered for sale 'Concert French horns upon a new construction, trumpets, violins, guitars and sundry other instruments'. In 1779 his shop was located on the Mall,[62] and in 1783 it was on the Grand Parade.[63] Press advertisements and trade directories indicate that specialist music shops increased towards the end of the eighteenth century, and the location of so many music shops in the new and fashionable areas of Patrick Street and the South Mall was an indication of the increasingly high status of the music business at the turn of the nineteenth century.

The marketing of patented pianos surged from the last decade of the eighteenth century. The first local dealer to participate in an escalated piano boom was organist James Roche, who in 1792 advertised the supply of 'an elegant assortment of small patent forte pianos; [...] also a very fine toned Grand forte piano, and a remarkable fine toned harpsichord, with a swell cover and crescendo pedal'.[64] In 1795, Roche advertised Southwell's new Sonovent pianos, sourced in Dublin, and some fine-toned English patent pianos by the best makers, 'with and without additional keys'.[65] Southwell's Sonovents were also stocked that year by James Haly, printer, and in 1796 by William Lewis, general shopkeeper and bookseller.[66] Over the next decade a succession of new Cork piano dealers emerged, the majority of whom were music professors entering this lucrative market.

A humorous poem published in a local magazine, *The Rover*, in 1796 describes Daniel Fitzpatrick and his thriving music shop:

BRAVE IRISH DANIEL AND HIS HARP

There is a man in fair Cork town,
Fitzpatrick at the harp,
A choice musician of renown,
Can play a flat and sharp.

He can tune a Violin or Tenor,
And sweetly blow his flute,
A jolly soul of gay demeanor,
Which no one can dispute.

He can play the Harpsichord,
Guitar or Hurdy Gurdy,
To sound a Dulcimer, by the Lord!
Not one alive more sturdy.

He sells instruments of ev'ry sort,
And music of all kinds,
The ladies fair his shop resort,
To harmonise their minds.

For he can play the Union pipes,
And nobly squeeze his bags,
His sweet hautboy can cure the gripes,
And yet he never brags.

Now there are two damn'd imposters,
Mere John Bulls of fellows,
Two rascally imposing Forsters,
Want to damn his Violincellos.

Being jealous of Irish fame,
Now look with envious eyes,
They give his music a bad name,
And encourage cursed spies.

Let these John Bulls now scold and carp,
And vainly advertise,
Success to Daniel and his harp,
May Irish merit rise.[67]

The poem draws on the literary metaphor of the harp, and notes the commercial rivalry between the city's music dealers as a metaphor for Irish political tensions and aspirations. Fitzpatrick was likely to have been one of the city's many successful Catholics involved in retail trade. An advertisement of 1791 locates his business at 18 Paul Street, when he imported from London 'the most new and elegant assortment of Music for the Piano Forte, German Flute, Violin, Tenor and Violincello [*sic*]; likewise a variety of fine-tuned violins, made by the best makers in London'.[68] He relocated his music shop to Daunt's Bridge in 1793 and, two years later, to the fashionable South Mall.[69] Fitzpatrick is portrayed in the poem as a congenial businessman, a multi-instrumentalist whose abilities spanned different musical traditions. His competitors, the two 'John Bulls', were probably James Magrath and James Roche, both Anglican church musicians, who also ran music shops.[70]

The play on commercial rivalry is not the only issue raised in the poem. By the end of the eighteenth century, a sense of Gaelic identity had been formed. With the antiquarian explorations of the late eighteenth century, a discourse on Ireland as a nation began to emerge. The publication of Joseph Cooper Walker's *Historical Memoirs of the Irish Bards* (1786) and the Belfast

Harp Festival of 1792, which attempted to recover the last remnants of the ancient harp tradition, provide tangible evidence of a distinctive Gaelic musical past. Its history, its legends, and particularly its music, or even the idea of its music, defined Gaelic identity. The iconography of the harp went from being associated with the Ascendancy in Ireland to being a symbol of Irish identity, a literary metaphor and a political and cultural icon. It appeared on the publications of the United Irishmen, whose periodical *The Harp of Erin* was published in Cork in 1795–1796. Mary Louise O'Donnell asserts that during the 1790s, the harp became for the Irish a 'utopia' – representing hope for a people who saw themselves as dispossessed,[71] a sonic and visual metaphor for a free Ireland, where hope of things being different and better could survive.[72]

The music dealer 'Brave Irish Daniel' in the poem accommodated all of the city's musical tastes, carrying out his business with liveliness and good humour, his musical fluency a metaphor for his mental flexibility and ease with 'music of all kinds'. The harmonising potential of the musical arts is alluded to, though not without a hint of satire. The musician's ability to 'play a flat and sharp' may be a more specific reference to the writing of French political theorist Jean Louis de Lolme in 1787, articulating the contribution of the Volunteer movement to the transformation of Irish politics, using the metaphor of the harp:

> Ireland was now expressing herself in a different tone which she had not used at any former time. The Irish Harp had passed into a different modulation, it had left the *flat*, or minor, *Mode* or Key – the musical *Mode* of Plaint. It had passed into the *Mode* of reproach and demand, and the Irish Harp was sounding with the Third *sharp*, or *Tierce majeure*.[73]

Penned by an anonymous writer, the poem presents an assertive outlook for Irish aspirations. What is remarkable is that the central figure is not primarily a performer, but a music shop owner, a robust and multi-dimensional man of the new commercial world, who commands public respect, admiration and patronage. The scene also captures Cork's lively commercial environment of the early 1790s, its prosperity and patriotism, prior to the upheavals of the rebellion of 1798 and the Act of Union in 1800.

2

PUBLIC CONCERTS IN THE EIGHTEENTH CENTURY

The Exchange, at the corner of Main Street and Castle Street.
CORK CITY AND COUNTY ARCHIVES

*On Hammand's-marsh [*sic*], is a large pleasant Bowling-green, planted, on its margin, with trees kept regularly cut [...] and on it, a band of music has been supported by subscription, for the entertainment of the gentlemen and ladies who frequent it; adjacent to it, is the Assembly-house, where assemblies are held two days in the week; as also a weekly concert, which is maintained by a subscription, for the support of the Infirmary. Here is an organ, the other performers play on violins, German flutes, &c. with vocal music, and are sometimes assisted by gentlemen, who play to encourage this charity.*[1]

This extract from Charles Smith's account of mid-eighteenth-century Cork portrays an urban elite engaged in musical activities that displayed taste and accomplishment. The society in question, the Charitable Musical Society, pledged its 'surplus funds' towards the establishment of the North Charitable Infirmary in 1744.[2] Modelled on a society of the same name that was established in Dublin some years previously, this society, by 1750, held regular concerts at the Assembly Rooms on Hammond's Marsh, combining charitable support with convivial musical activity.[3] Such were the earliest concerts in Cork, sparsely documented, in which gentlemen amateurs performed alongside local professionals in concerts that usually concluded with a ball.

Engagement in refined recreation such as music denoted civic authority and superiority among the city's elite of the eighteenth century, whose musical preferences were 'a social and cultural locator'.[4] Many of the city's social elite were accomplished amateur performers. An earlier reference to a musical society in Cork appears in a letter dated 1710, written by one of its members, Philip Crofts.[5] Addressed to Sir John Perceval in London, the letter refers to fortnightly meetings 'for the best gentlemen to perform' and requests 'the best and newest music' to be sent from London.[6] According to music historian Grattan Flood (1859–1928), two Cork musical societies met at the Joiners' Hall in Cork on 22 November 1733 to celebrate St Cecilia's Day, when they performed 'several celebrated pieces of musick of Corelli, Vivaldi, Valentini, and Handel'.[7] Grattan Flood also refers to a Grand Concert held in Cork in 1747 commemorating the anniversary of the Battle of Culloden, when the evening concluded with the singing of 'the National Anthem' and 'Long live the King', 'the chorus joined by all the Gentlemen and Ladies present'.[8] There is also a reference to a weekly 'academy of music' at the old theatre at Dunscomb's Marsh.[9] Little documentary evidence has survived of a performance of Handel's *Messiah* at St Fin Barre's in 1744, directed by William Smith, the cathedral organist.[10] It was likely to have been organised for the benefit of the North Charitable Infirmary, which was established in that year, possibly the first major venture of the Charitable Musical Society.[11] A poem inspired by the performance was published in *Faulkner's Dublin Journal*.[12]

The phenomenon of the touring professional performer emerged in Ireland during the early to mid-eighteenth century, an outgrowth of London's flourishing cultural consumption, referred to contemporaneously among its fashionable elite as 'the rage for music'.[13] By mid-century, rapid expansion of metropolitan musical institutions led to saturation levels of professional musicians, estimated to have been in the region of 1,500.[14] Outside of the winter social season, large numbers of these musicians, many of them Italian and German, sought work in the provinces.

Dublin's viceregal court and its fashionable entourage sustained a vibrant cultural environment during the eighteenth century. Its theatres and concert rooms attracted leading performers from Britain and the continent, mainly during the 'winter' season, from November to March.[15] Foremost among Dublin's musical traditions during the latter half of the eighteenth century was the annual season of concerts at the Rotunda Room, built at the New Garden in Great Britain Street, which flourished from 1749 to 1791, organised by the governors of Dr Mosse's Lying-in hospital. Held three times a week from April to September, these concerts ran for almost fifty years, employing a regular band of around twenty musicians, and visiting soloists from prestigious London venues.[16] At the conclusion of their Dublin engagements, many of these musicians took the opportunity of touring Ireland's provincial cities and towns, where, with assiduous planning, concerts held during assize and race weeks could attract optimum audience numbers. Cork's late summer assizes, held in August or early September, co-ordinated well with the Dublin season.

Concert activity in Cork during the first half of the eighteenth century is largely undocumented. Among the earliest noted touring professionals was an Irish harper, David Murphy, well known to London and Dublin audiences, who performed in Cork in 1721.[17] From the late 1750s, local newspaper printers were a point of contact for visiting musicians, for the publication of advertisements and the printing of handbills and tickets. The handbills, which were circulated in great quantities, have not survived. Advertisements customarily included the source of tickets, the admission cost and partial or, rarely, full programme content. The notices provide evidence that professional public concerts were organised and publicised by the performers themselves as one-off events, usually involving the collaboration of local amateurs and professionals.[18] From the late 1750s to the 1780s, concert tickets were sold at the Exchange Coffee House and the Turk's Head Coffee House. The printers of the newspapers, who most likely also printed the handbills, acted as ticket sellers; and the performers usually sold tickets at their lodgings. By the end of the century, the music shops supplied tickets.

Early sources indicate a number of key locations for public musical performances in eighteenth-century Cork. The Council Book records several instances of musical entertainments at the council chamber, situated next to the Exchange on the Main Street (see page 21), and an entry dated 1717 refers to a music chamber.[19] Details of public concerts held at this location appeared in press advertisements dating from 1757 until 1767,[20] but it is likely that it was used as a public concert venue prior to this date. Up to mid-century, Hammond's Marsh, to the west of the city, was the location of an assembly room and bowling green. Dunscombe's Marsh, to the east, which became George's Street, was the site of a theatre built by His Majesty's Company of Comedians in 1736. A new assembly room built in 1751 on George's Street became the focal point of the social life of the city's fashionable elite during the second half of the eighteenth century.[21]

The popularity of Italian music among elite audiences in early eighteenth-century Ireland has been noted by writers of the period.[22] Both Bishop Robert Clayton (Bishop of Cork from 1735 to 1745) and Bishop George Berkeley of Cloyne (1734–1752) were renowned for their love of all things Italian.[23] Italian music dominated two of the earliest full programmes by touring professionals published in the Cork newspapers. In December 1754, a notice appeared in the *Corke Journal* announcing a concert at the new Assembly Rooms to be performed by Mr Russwurm, a horn player in the employment of fourth Viscount Kenmare of Castlerosse, Killarney.[24] The three-act programme, also published in the *Corke Journal*, shows a plan of alternating overtures and Italian concertos and, unusually, features no vocal items.[25]

ACT I

The Overture in *Pastor Fido*	[Handel]
The fourth concerto of Geminiani by Signor Lava	
The Overture in *Samson*	[Handel]

ACT II

The Overture in *Richard*	[Handel]
A concerto on the German flute to be performed by Mr Murphy	Sig. Morigi
An Overture of Sig. Palma	

ACT III

A concerto solo on the French Horn, never performed in this Kingdom by Mr Russwurm

A contrast del Sig. Tessarini

By particular desire of the Ladies and Gentlemen, Mr Russwurm will perform a Musette on the French-horn [26]

Concerts by touring musicians entailed social exchange with local musicians, either professional or amateur, to augment the performing forces, and provide additional musical items of their own. One of the supporting musicians on this occasion, Mr Murphy, German flute, was probably Thomas Murphy (d. 1759), a local musician who had appeared at the Cork theatre with the Smock Alley company earlier in the year.[27] Russwurm's notice also referred to a ball after the concert, a custom that endured until the 1820s. Handel overtures and Italian concertos also featured on the programmes of two concerts given at the new Assembly Rooms at Dunscombe's Marsh by violinist Francis Woder in February and April 1755.[28] Woder was billed as 'one of his Majesty's State Musicians from Dublin'.[29]

In April 1760 Mr Mahony, an Irish harpist, presented a 'Grand Concert of Instrumental Musick' performed by gentlemen, with 'several Irish and Scotch favourite airs on the Irish harp'.[30] Information was often sparse, such as a notice in the *Corke Journal* in 1760 announcing 'two noted masters lately arrived from London' to give a concert which included 'several pieces performed on the French Horn', and a solo on the 'chileman [*sic* – *chalumeau*], an instrument which imitates the human voice'.[31]

An early exponent of the guitar in Ireland was thirteen-year-old German girl Gertrud Schmeling (1749–1833), later known as singer Madame Mara. Her two concerts at Cork's Council Chamber in May 1762 were part of a tour that included Dublin and London.[32] Her programme featured 'several select pieces on the violin and guitar [...] and favourite Italian and English songs'.[33] Her Dublin concert at the Fishamble Street Music Hall the previous February has been noted as the earliest reference to the guitar in concert performance in Ireland.[34] The 'English' guitar, fashionable at the time among amateur female players, was in fact a type of wire-strung cittern. Schmeling's Cork performances appear to have generated commercial interest in the instrument, as the arrival of a consignment of 'English' guitars was announced the following December by printers Phineas and George Bagnell, the earliest Cork newspaper advertisement for such instruments. The Bagnells also invited commissions for instruments by the Dublin guitar maker William Gibson. Local businesses thus developed their music retailing interests in association with visiting concert performers.

A few touring musicians attempted to organise performances on a more ambitious scale, without advance preparation, with varying degrees of success. Italian musicians Giuseppe Passerini (fl.1750–) his wife Christina (fl. 1750–1776) and their son Francis (fl. 1760s, d.1809) had popularised Handel's oratorios in the English provinces and in Dublin for over a decade before settling in Dublin in 1762.[35] They arrived in Cork in July 1762 and advertised a concert at the Assembly Rooms.[36] They also issued appeals in the *Corke Journal* for subscriptions for an oratorio performance featuring selections from Handel's *Judas Maccabeus* and *Messiah.*[37] There is no documentary evidence that this event took place, however, but in October they presented *Acis and Galatea*, 'a pastoral [...] in the manner of an Oratorio, with Chorusses [*sic*], as composed by Mr Handel'.[38] The Passerinis returned to Cork in October and announced a concert assisted by local gentlemen. The programme centred on vocal solos by Signora and Master Passerini, and the final item, 'See the conquering hero comes, with the Duke's March', was to be 'accompanied with drums and French horns', presumably by local musicians.[39]

A number of concerts during these years were organised by local amateur musicians for the support of individuals in financial distress, appealing to public sympathy in discreetly worded press notices. Visiting performers frequently contributed to these concerts. In September 1757 Signor Ferdinando Arrigoni conducted a concert performed 'chiefly by gentlemen for the relief of an unfortunate and distressed son of a late and much regarded merchant of this city'.[40] Formerly active in Edinburgh, this is an early reference to Arrigoni's musical activities in Ireland. The following year he was appointed as conductor of the band of the Great Britain Street concerts in Dublin, remaining there until 1762.[41] A concert held for the benefit of the Widow Bastable in 1773, performed by gentlemen, featured a solo on the 'vax humana' [*sic*] by a Mr 'Patrea'.[42] Gregorio Patria (1753–*c.* 1793) was a member of Dublin's Rotunda band from 1771 until 1782, performing on the oboe, flute and vox humana.[43]

Founded in 1744 to support the North Charitable Infirmary, the Charitable and Musical Society, often referred to as the Musical Society, was a highly organised body.[44] William Smith, organist at St Fin Barre's cathedral, was a member of the committee. An abstract of the Accounts of the Infirmary from March 1749 to March 1750 verifies the high proportion of income generated by musical means.[45]

Received by Subscriptions	£275 - 12 - 10
Received from the Musical Society	£100 - 00 - 00
Received from the Grand Jury of the City	£006 - 12 - 09
Received by a Charity Play	£034 - 01 - 02
Received from Thomas Parker, esq.	£014 - 15 - 09
Balance in the Treasurer's Hands last Year	£343 - 15 - 10
	£774 - 18 - 04

The Trustees of the Charitable Infirmary remained active throughout the century, and through membership subscriptions, and performances by the Musical Society, remained an effective and prominent charitable organisation, and a regular organising body for concerts. In 1766, the trustees took a lease on the George's Street Assembly Rooms, which had opened in 1751, where regular assemblies, card drums, concerts and balls were held in support of the charity. An assertive approach was taken: notices published in the local newspapers requested that no private parties be held on dates that would conflict with its fundraising events. Visiting musicians were prevailed upon to contribute by holding a benefit concert, or participating in the society's annual benefit concert, which was a highlight of the city's social calendar.

Over the next three decades, the city's most prestigious musical events were the annual charity performances for the benefit of the North Charitable Infirmary, featuring the Musical Society and visiting musicians. In his *Musical Memoirs*, oboist William T. Parke (1762–1847) refers to a solicitation made by members of the organising committee during his visit to Cork with the theatre company in 1796:

> During the time I remained in Cork I was waited on at my lodging by a deputation from the committee for managing the annual benefit for the hospital, to request me to play a concerto on that occasion, which I did with unfeigned pleasure.[46]

The Musical Society members were well disposed to supporting visiting musicians in their benefit concerts. On one unusual occasion, a celebrated visiting musician was the recipient of local benevolence when, in June 1767, the Musical Society members participated in benefit concerts for Giusto Ferdinando Tenducci (*c.* 1735–90), an Italian castrato singer, who found himself in financial difficulties following his alleged elopement with a daughter of Thomas Maunsell, a prominent barrister and Chief Justice of County Cork.[47] A prominent Protestant Ascendancy family, the Maunsells had an estate in County Limerick. Thomas Maunsell's legal duties brought him and members of the family to Cork for the assizes. Tenducci had been engaged at the Crow Street theatre in 1765.[48] While on a theatre engagement in Dublin, he had befriended Maunsell's daughter, Dorothea, then fifteen or sixteen years of age, at the family's new town residence on Molesworth Street. In defiance of her father's wishes for her to marry an arranged suitor, Dorothea declared her love for Tenducci, and the couple were secretly married by an aged Catholic priest, Patrick Egan, at Mallow Lane in Cork in August 1766.[49] Tenducci was pursued by members of the Maunsell family and placed in Cork jail, but released on bail by the end of August, due to the intervention of a Cork relative of Dorothea at her behest. After months of persecution by the Maunsell family, with a further imprisonment, charges against Tenducci were finally dropped.[50] He recommenced his provincial concert touring, arriving in Cork in late May 1767.

In its alternation of vocal and instrumental works, the programme of Tenducci's first concert exemplifies a typical 'miscellaneous' structure[51] (see below). More remarkable is the inclusion of seven overtures, by Johann Christian Bach (1735–82), Carl Friedrich Abel (1723–1787), Thomas Arne

(1710–1778), 'Lord Kelly' (Thomas Erskine, 6th Earl of Kellie, 1732–1781), and Tenducci. All of these composers had enjoyed recent successes in London with newly-composed overtures, which were in effect prototype symphonies. Two of the overtures by J.C. Bach were from his operas *Orione* and *Zanaïda*, composed for the King's Theatre in 1763. Erskine had published a set of six three-movement overtures (sinfonias) in Edinburgh in 1761, and in 1765 his overture to *The Maid of the Mill* quickly became a favourite with London audiences. Thomas Arne's overture to his opera *Artaxerxes* (1762) was already popular as an independent concert piece.[52] The ballad song, 'Ellen a Roon', variously described as being of Irish, Scottish and English origin, had featured in Charles Coffey's *The Beggar's Wedding* (1729), and was one of Tenducci's favourite concert pieces.

ACT THE FIRST	
Mr Back's Overture, in orien [*Orione*]	[J.C. Bach]
Mr Tenducci will sing by particular desire 'Ellen a Roon'	
Mr Tenducci's first overture	[Tenducci]
'Water parted from the sea' by Mr Tenducci [*Artaxerxes*]	[Arne]
The Overture to Artaxerxes	[Arne]
'What means that tender sigh' by Mr Tenducci	[Arne?]
Lord Kelly's Overture	[Erskine]
ACT THE SECOND	
Mr Back's Overture	[J.C. Bach]
Mr Tenducci's song 'See the purple morn arise'	[Tenducci]
Mr Abel's overture	[Abel]
Mr Tenducci's song 'Oh how shall I in language weak'	[Arne]
Mr Tenducci's trio	
Mr Tenducci's song 'When my Chloe smiles upon me'	[Tenducci]
Mr Back's overture, in Zanaida [*Zanaïda*][53]	[J.C. Bach]

For Tenducci's second concert twelve days later, the admission cost was raised from three to five shillings, 'in consideration of the many distresses falled [...] upon Mr Tenducci'. It was similarly structured, and included a harpsichord concerto by J.C. Bach and sonatas by Mattia Vento (1735–76) and Baldassare

Galuppi (1706–85). Tenducci sang 'Ellen a Roon' and several songs from *The Royal Shepherd*, linked to his current theatre performances, and performed two duets with John Martin, a local singer.[54] Having departed Cork, Tenducci presented a benefit concert during the assize week at Clonmel, in late August,[55] and a fortnight later at the Assembly Rooms in Mallow.[56] He returned to Cork and gave a Grand Concert at the Theatre Royal, followed by a Ridotto 'as done at the opera house in London'.[57] Despite the generous support he received in Munster, his financial difficulties persisted. He went on to perform concerts in a number of English provincial towns, followed by an engagement in Edinburgh.

By 1769, another musical society was in existence, identified in the *Cork Evening Post* as the Philharmonic Club, also known as the 'Thursday Musical Society' (the Musical Society was known as the 'Tuesday Musical Society').[58] Dining and the drinking of toasts were customary, and Cork historian John Windele notes that the new club was 'much given to water parties in the summer season'.[59] In November 1769 members of this society performed a concert to raise funds for the planting of the Red-House Walk, a tree-lined promenade to the west of the city, later known as the Mardyke Walk.[60] Tickets for the concert were available from Rev. Richard Pigott, vicar of Christ Church, Henry Sheares, Henry Wrixon (City Sheriff in 1764), physician Bayley Rogers, Thomas Burnett and Richard Kiely, all of whom were likely to have been members of the society. The society held its meeting at the new assembly room on the newly developed Tuckey Street.[61] Although Gibson described this as being larger than the George's Street Assembly Rooms,[62] it did not supersede the latter as a concert venue, but was hired occasionally by visiting performers throughout the remainder of the eighteenth and early nineteenth centuries.

To meet the demands of such amateur activity, a number of local businesses supplied printed music. William Flyn, Catholic printer and bookseller in Castle Street, had specialised in Catholic religious publications from early in his career. In October 1769, he established a new newspaper, the *Hibernian Chronicle*.[63] In November, he advertised a supply of the following:

> Handel's sixty overtures, complete with all their parts
>
> Corelli's twelve concertos
>
> Corelli's twelve solos made Concertos, by Geminiani
>
> Vivaldi's Select Harmony

Geminiani's twelve concertos
Two setts of Alberti's concertos
Humphries's Concertos
Tessarini's Concertos
Morigi's Concertos
Corelli's twelve sonatas, in four books
Six sonatas for two violins, by Battino
The music of the Magdalen Chapel
The Beggar's Opera, Maid of the Mill, Thomas and Sally,
Daphne and Amintor, set for German Flute, violin or guitar
Instruction books, for different instruments, variety of songs,
and good fiddle strings.[64]

The availability of sixty of Handel's overtures reflected current concert repertoire, requiring high levels of amateur instrumental proficiency and musical literacy. Such items would have been aimed at musical connoisseurs from among Flyn's readership that extended to the surrounding counties. By 1772, the newspaper was circulated to twenty-six towns in counties Cork, Limerick, Waterford and Kerry.[65] The predominantly Italian Baroque idiom represented on this list had been popular in London and Dublin since the 1730s, but was already being replaced by newer German music in the galant style.

The plight of debtors was a key humanitarian concern during the eighteenth century, and prompted many small-scale charitable endeavours. In 1774, the Cork Society for the Relief and Discharge of Persons confined for small debts was established.[66] Among its founder members were Rev. Richard Pigott, Henry Sheares and William Flyn, who acted as secretary for several years. The committee was unusual for its time in constituting 'a model of religious co-operation'.[67] The following year a concert was organised by this charity 'for the relief of a family once in a very respectable situation in this town, now in distress', which was performed by gentlemen.[68] From 1780, this charity incorporated the Charitable Loan Society, for poor tradesmen, and was supported by Catholic Bishop Moylan during his episcopacy from 1787 to 1815.[69]

For a variety of performers, provincial touring became essential to earning a livelihood. These musicians introduced new repertoire and performance practices and, occasionally, novel instruments. A visiting dulcimer player, Mr Isaac, advertised a number of breakfast concerts at the Assembly Rooms from September to December 1768, for a fee of 'three British sixpences'.[70] He may be identified as Isaac Isaacs, a German-born Jew who spent many years under the patronge of Mrs Margaret Leeson in Dublin.[71] He returned in 1773 and advertised a 'breakfast ball' at the new Assembly Rooms in Tuckey Street, to include a performance of 'several favourite pieces of Music, which were never performed here before'.[72] Although Mrs Crow (*née* Rachael Baptist, fl. 1750–73) had sung at several concerts in Dublin during the 1750s, her concert at the George's Street Assembly Rooms in July 1770 was billed as her first Cork appearance.[73] A month previously, she held two concerts in Bandon, 'assisted by the best performers from Cork',[74] who also would have provided support for her Cork concert. An African woman, she had studied with Bernardo Palma in Dublin, and sustained a successful singing career in Britain and Ireland.[75] Her husband, Mr Crow, advertised lessons in violin and guitar during the couple's stay in Cork. In 1777, Mr Cartwright held exhibitions on the musical glasses on several days between the hours of twelve and three, for an admission fee of 1s 1d.[76] This type of 'daily exhibition' by performers was also popular in London in the late eighteenth century.[77] In January 1771 French-born composer and theorist Antonio Borghese (fl. late eighteenth century) announced a concert 'on the Great Harpsichord-Fortepiana [*sic*], an instrument of very particular harmony, and never exhibited in public in this city'.[78] This was probably the first public performance on a fortepiano in Cork. The earliest known Dublin concert featuring this instrument had been in May 1768.[79] Borghese performed his own fortepiano compositions and Madame Borghese sang several of his vocal compositions in French. The programme included two overtures, two symphonies and a concerto. The instrument was offered for raffle at the end of Borghese's stay, a practice not uncommon at this time. In March of the following year, the *Corke Journal* published a request for 100 subscribers to the raffle, at half a guinea each, valuing the instrument at 50 guineas.[80]

A touring musician who was to have significant influence on the city's concert life was Michael Arne (*c.* 1740–1786), who visited Cork several times during the 1770s with the Dublin theatre company. Son of Thomas Arne, he was a key figure in the promotion of glee singing in concerts and theatre in London.[81] A concert under his direction in 1770 featuring the Musical Society concluded with a performance of Handel's Coronation anthem.[82]

On a visit in 1777, he directed a concert for the benefit of the North Charitable Infirmary, featuring the Gentlemen of the Choir of Cloyne cathedral.[83] The programme included four glees, and each act concluded with a Handel chorus, 'Oh, the pleasures of the plains' from *Acis and Galatea*, and the 'Coronation' anthem, respectively.

ACT THE FIRST

Overture

Glee 'Adieu to the Village delights' [Josh Baildon]

Song, Mrs. Arne 'In this shady blest retreat' [J.C. Bach]

Italian Glee 'Viva tutti la Vizzose', by the Gentlemen of the choir [Giardini]

Concerto on the harpsichord by Mr Arne

Song, Mrs. Arne 'Adieu [thou] dreary Pile' [*The Duenna*] [Linley]

Chorus, 'Oh, the pleasure of the plains' [*Acis and Galatea*], by the Gentlemen of the choir [Handel]

ACT THE SECOND

Glee 'Fill the bowl with rosy wine' [Henry Bowman]

Song, Mrs. Arne, 'Come, come live with me and be my love' [Arne]

A glee, by the Gentlemen of the Choir

A concerto

Song, Mrs. Arne, 'Sweet passion of love' [*The Padlock*] [M. Arne]

A Glee by the Gentlemen of the choir

Song, Mrs. Arne 'The soldier tir'd of war's alarms' [*Artaxerxes*] [T. Arne]

To conclude with Handel's celebrated Coronation Anthem, by the Gentlemen of the Choir.

This is the earliest concert performance by a specified choir, with prominent placing of choral items on the programme. Traditionally associated with church choirmen, the singing of glees and catches was already established in private circles. Lord Orrery referred to singing catches in the company of Robert Clayton, Bishop of Cork from 1735–45.[84] A performance of *The Beggar's Opera* at the Theatre Royal 1776 had included a scene featuring glees, 'as performed in London under the direction of Dr Arne', and announced as the earliest such performance in Cork:

First glee: 'Gently touch the warbling lyre' by Geminiani
Second glee: 'You ask me dear Jack' by Dr Arne
Catch: 'Jack thou'rt a Toper' by Purcell
Third glee: 'Which is the properest day to drink' by Dr Arne
Last glee: 'Beviamo tutti tre' by Giardini [85]

Local singer John Martin, who had sung in Tenducci's concerts in 1767, held a benefit night in 1779 entitled 'A Musical Entertainment, consisting of catches and glees'. The performance was followed by a ball, in which catches and glees were performed between the 'minuets and country dances'.[86] In 1782, the Widow Mahony's Tavern was the meeting place for 'members; of a singing club'.[87] In January 1792 a vocal group known as the Guidonian Club featured in a benefit concert for visiting cellist Joseph Reinagle (1762–1836), with members of the Musical Society and pupils of Henry Delamain.[88] By the turn of the nineteenth century, glees had become standard concert items, and were to remain popular for over a half-century. In 1782 William Flyn advertised a three-volume collection of songs entitled *The Vocal Magazine or Compleat Songster, consisting of such English, Scotch and Irish Songs, Catches, Glees, Cantatas, Airs, Ballads, as are deemed most worthy of being transmitted to posterity*, a reprint of *The Vocal Magazine or Compleat British Songster*, which was published in London the previous year.[89]

Organist, composer and dancing master Henry Delamain came to prominence in this society in the late 1770s as Master of Ceremonies at the Assembly Rooms, presiding at concerts and at the Annual Fancy Ball. Identifying a need for an improved Assembly Rooms band, he proposed a musical apprenticeship scheme, outlined in the following notice:

> The Master of Ceremonies is induced from the frequent complaints made of the Assembly Music, to propose a mode whereby a proper band may be established. 1st, a subscription is requested for the purchasing of musical instruments, and half a year's maintenance and cloathing of six boys, who, at the expiration of said time shall perform at the Assembly room. 2nd ly, These boys are to be indented as apprentices to the master of the ceremonies for seven years, the last year of their servitude they are to instruct a new set of boys, by which means the Band will always be kept up.[90]

He directed a benefit concert for the North Charitable Infirmary in July 1778 featuring the renowned operatic singer Anne Catley (1745–89), with instrumentalists Mr Valentine and Mr Smyth, and the gentlemen of the Musical Society. The programme was weighted heavily in favour of instrumental music, with 'overtures' (sinfonias) by Ignaz Holzbauer (1711–1783), Carl Ditters (von Dittersdorf) (1739–1799), Antonio Sacchini (1730–1786), Gaetano Pugnani (1731–1798) and Johann Vanhal (1739–1813).[91] These were early examples of the concert symphony performed by local musicians, influenced by London publications such as *The Periodical Overture in 8 Parts*, which featured three-movement overtures by four of the above composers.[92] Also featured in the concert was a quartet by Haydn, an early reference to his music on a Cork concert programme. London-born Catley had featured on the Smock Alley stage since 1763, appearing at the Cork theatre to great acclaim in 1765 and 1768, and since 1767 she had featured regularly at Dublin's Rotunda concerts.[93] Her songs included the florid aria 'The soldier tir'd of war's alarms', a coloratura aria from Thomas Arne's *Artaxerxes*, one of the most popular pieces sung at concerts by female vocalists in the late eighteenth century.

Table 2.1. Benefit concerts of local music professors, 1771–92.

YEAR	MONTH	PROFESSOR	INSTRUMENT
1771	November	John Martin	voice
	December	Mr Reynolds Jr	violin
1777	November	John Martin	voice
1778	January	James Magrath	voice
	November	Henry Delamain	organ, harpsichord
1779	October	Mr Gray, Mr Brown	violin, voice
	November	John Martin	voice
1780	January	James Magrath	voice
1781	February	Mr Morgan	violin, cello
1782	May	James Magrath	voice
1784	June	Mr Connell	
1787	March	Mr Grundler	
	April	John Martin	voice
1788	June	Benjamin Hallahan	German flutes
		John Buckley, Isaac Varian	
1792	February	Edward Nagle	

As the local music professors consolidated their practices during the 1770s and 1780s, notices of musicians' benefit concerts began to appear in the local press (see table 2.1). Customarily an annual event, the benefit concert was a professional showcase featuring self-display as a performer, and promotion of one's teaching practice, which could lead to employment opportunities at private homes in the city and county. Financial gain from a benefit depended on the gratuitous assistance of fellow musicians.[94] Attended by the families of the professor's students and open to the public, the advertising for the majority of these concerts by the Cork musicians was minimal; the only full programme published in the newspapers being that of Messrs Gray and Brown in 1779.[95] The list in Table 2.1 is a representative section; in addition to gaps in newspaper runs, not all professors may have chosen to advertise in the local press.

James Magrath, parish clerk at Christ Church, advertised instruction on the guitar for ladies from 1773, and continued to teach guitar and singing over the ensuing decades, becoming a popular figure in the city's musical life.[96] Isaac Varian was active in the latter decades of the eighteenth century, described as 'a good musician, and sustained a circle of amateur theatrical and musical friends by his general and kindly manners'. His father, also Isaac Varian, was a musician and dancing master resident in Cork around 1723.[97] The notice for the joint benefit listed above was among the earliest references to him. In May 1790, he held a theatrical benefit at the Theatre Royal featuring local amateurs, in a performance of Arne's *Love in a Village*.[98] In 1793 he advertised as a Professor of the German Flute, and also tuned harpsichords and pianofortes.[99] John Buckley, also a flautist, was listed as a professor of music in trade directories of the early nineteenth century, and composed duets.[100] Mr Morgan, violinist and cellist, was typical of many eighteenth-century music professors in offering tuition in a range of instruments. In addition to strings, he taught the German flute and the guitar, and was the instructor to the band of the Cork Union, who performed a selection of pieces at his benefit concert in 1781.[101] All musicians earned their income from more than one source. Mr Grundler, who held a benefit in 1787, was a former bandmaster of the 15th Regiment. Many of the military musicians during this period were civilians who did not reside at the military barracks.[102] Many of them advertised musical tuition at their own residences.

Military bands became a regular feature of concert life during the 1780s. The earliest advertised concert featuring a military band in Cork took place in May 1780 to celebrate the Queen's birth night, organised as a benefit evening for the North Charitable Infirmary.[103] In 1786, a concert was held 'by desire of several Ladies and Gentlemen of this city' for the benefit of the Band of the 20th Regiment, 'in consideration of their attendance to all balls, assemblies and drums, gratis, since their residence in town'.[104] From this time onwards, military bands constituted one of the city's principal musical resources, and participated in a range of public events.

Throughout the 1780s musicians who had concluded engagements at Dublin's Rotunda concerts toured the provinces and arrived in Cork in late summer or autumn. The length of their stay was subject to local opportunity. If prospects were favourable, additional concerts were organised at short notice. An advertisement for a concert at the George's Street Assembly Rooms by Dublin violinist Thomas Pinto in 1782 offered gallery tickets costing 2s 2d, in addition to the regular tickets at 4s 4d.[105] The use of the gallery was again referred to in 1784, when a concert advertisement provided the information that 'The Gallery will be open for the reception of such Ladies and Gentlemen who do not chuse to dress for the room, at 1s 7d each.'[106] For the majority of concerts held at this venue between 1784 and 1787, there was a two-tier price system, gallery tickets offered at between half to two-thirds of the full ticket price.

Frantisek Kotzwara (*c.* 1750–91), Czech viola player and composer, who arrived with the Crow Street theatre band in 1783, presented new instrumentation and repertoire in his programmes. No details of a morning concert at the Assembly Rooms on 13 September have survived.[107] Two weeks later singer and actress Mary Jameson (fl. *c.*1770–86), also with the company, took a benefit concert, in which she was joined by singers Pietro Urbani (1749–1816) and Giusto Ferdinando Tenducci, the latter on his first visit to Cork since 1767. Jameson had performed for several seasons at the Rotunda between 1776 and 1789 in addition to being engaged by the Crow Street theatre company, and the rival Smock Alley company for the previous two seasons. The instrumentalists listed for this concert were Mr Erskine, oboist, and Mr Rakeman, clarinettist, and Messrs Bartoli, Stevens, Gani and Lockhart, all members of the theatre band.[108] Mr Rakeman, a clarinet player and Master of the Band of the 32nd Regiment of Foot, had performed a clarinet concerto at Cork's Theatre Royal the previous year, and composed (or arranged) the music for a 'new volunteer medley', performed as a theatre interlude in that season.[109] The unusually large number of wind players present in Cork in that season was due to the requirements for Arne's opera *Artaxerxes*, currently in production at the Theatre Royal.

These instruments were also featured in Kotzwara's dramatic and colourful pieces, 'Thunder and Shipwreck' (overture) and 'Turkish Music', which concluded the programme of Mary Jameson's benefit.

ACT I

Solo on the Vln by Mr Kotzwara

Song 'Why ask my fairest' in *Amintas* composed and to be sung by Mr Urbani

Concerto on the Hautboy, by Mr Erskine

The celebrated Duette of 'For thee I live my dearest' [*Artaxerxes*] by Miss Jameson and Signor Tenducci [Arne]

Solo on the Tenor, by Mr Kotzwara

The much admired song of 'Adieu thou dreary Pile', [*The Duenna*] Miss Jameson [Linley]

ACT II

Solo, Mr Kotzwara

Italian song, composed and to be sung by Mr Urbani

Song of 'Molly Astore' Miss Jameson

Duetto on the Vln and Tenor, by Signor Urbani and Mr Kotzwara

'Queen Mary's Lamentation' by Signior Tenducci [Tomasso Giordani]

And an overture called Thunder and Shipwreck, by Mr Kotzwara

To finish with original Turkish Music, with all the Turkish instruments, composed by Mr Kotzwara.[110]

Kotzwara returned to Cork in the autumn of 1784 and held a concert at the Assembly Rooms, featuring Miss Jarrett, who had performed at the Rotunda in 1781 and 1782.[111] The programme featured a septet for flute, oboe, violin, viola, horn, bassoon and violoncello, likely to have been composed by Kotzwara, and an overture by J.C. Bach for two orchestras.[112] The programme included a quartet by Luigi Boccherini (1743–1805), whose string quartets had already appeared in nine publication sets, the most recent published in 1781.

Kotzwara remained in the city over the winter months and advertised a series of subscription concerts to commence in January 1785.[113] Subscription concert series were a feature of larger cities during the eighteenth century, such as London, Dublin and Bath, centres with a core of professional musicians and a strong leadership figure, with potential to sustain audiences over several weeks or a season. Cork society had not supported such arrangements up to this time. In April he advertised a benefit concert 'in a stile [*sic*] never attempted before',[114] featuring 'an Overture representing a Battle, with drums, trumpets and cannon', possibly his composition *The Battle of Prague*, published as a 'Sonata' for piano in London by G. Walker *c*. 1780.[115] In the same month, he appealed for subscriptions for another series of concerts, a 'Musical Academy', to begin on 13 May. As no further details appeared in the press, it is difficult to estimate the success of this venture. Having dominated Cork's concert life for over a year, he had left the city by 1786.

English violinist Charles Weichsel (1767–1850) divided his time between London and Dublin, directing the Rotunda concerts from 1786 to 1788. He performed two concerts at the Cork Assembly Rooms in 1786, the first featuring 'his Chace and battle piece, which was so universally admired at the Rotunda in Dublin'.[116] Brian Boydell has suggested that the former may refer to Haydn's 'New Overture (La Chasse)', which was performed twice at the Rotunda concerts during the previous June as Haydn's Symphony No. 73, 'La Chasse'.[117] In May 1787, English violinist John Abraham Fisher (1744–1806) gave two concerts, as part of an extended Irish tour, the first a benefit for the North Charitable Infirmary.[118]

Another performer who toured extensively was flautist Andrew Ashe (1759–1838), who arrived in Cork in 1788. Born in Lisburn, County Antrim, he commenced musical training at Woolwich, which abruptly ended due to his family's financial misfortune. As a protégé of a Count Bentnick, he received training in violin and military instruments, and travelled widely, residing for several years in Holland. Acquiring a Potter 'improved' flute, he made remarkable progress on this instrument, and in 1778 was appointed as first flautist in the Brussels Opera. He moved to Dublin in 1782 and performed at the Rotunda concerts.[119] His first Cork concert, supported by the Musical Society, featured several of his own compositions, including 'a concerto for two flutes, both instruments to be performed by himself'. Ashe had performed a 'duet upon two flutes' on several occasions in 1780 at Dublin's Rotunda, the flutes presumed to have been two recorders.[120] He performed this 'Double Concerto for two flutes' again a month later at a benefit concert for the North Charitable Infirmary, joined by singers Wright

Bowden (1752–1823) and John Henry Johnstone (1749–1818), both of Covent Garden, who were currently engaged at the Theatre Royal. He held a third concert in September prior to his departure, and returned to give another concert in November.[121]

Although performances of Handel oratorios had been a feature of Ascendancy social life in Dublin since the 1740s, Cork's concert-going population did not support such a tradition. After the *Messiah* at St Fin Barre's in 1744, there were no locally organised performances of sacred choral music until the 1780s, when a confluence of events stimulated interest in the medium. Michael Arne's direction of choral performances in 1777 featuring the choir of Cloyne cathedral demonstrated the potential of cathedral choirs in a public concert setting. In July 1780 a choral service at Cloyne cathedral was held for the benefit of the Cloyne Infirmary, performed by the gentlemen and boys of the choir. In addition to full cathedral service, the performance included Richard Woodward's (1743/4–77) *Te Deum* and *Jubilate*, and selections from Handel's *Messiah*, *Judas Maccabeus* and *Esther*.[122] In 1784, the London Handel Commemoration concerts at Westminster Abbey inspired similar performances across Britain and Ireland. Dorothea Herbert described oratorio performances at Cashel cathedral.[123] In December of that year, local singer John Shaw directed a performance of *Acis and Galatea* at the George's Street Assembly Rooms. A preview in the *Hibernian Chronicle* reflected the influence of the Handel revival, commending the 'novelty and spirit of the undertaking' and asserting that 'any production that can boast the immortal Handel in the composition possesses everything requisite to insure universal admiration'.[124]

In January 1788, organist James Roche issued an appeal for subscribers for a forthcoming performance of *Messiah* at Christ Church.[125] Held during Lent, on 20 March, as was customary in England, the performance featured local professionals and the choirs of the cathedrals of Cashel, Cork and Cloyne.[126] Although the event was not reviewed in the local press, the organisers subsequently announced that £24 19s 10d had been raised for the poor of the parish.[127] Just over a month later, the Cork KNOT of the Antient and most Benevolent Order of the Friendly Brothers of St Patrick presented another performance of sacred music at Christ Church, featuring local gentlemen and directed by James Roche.[128] On a smaller scale, it consisted of a sermon framed by sacred music including Purcell's *Te Deum and Jubilate* and a selection from Handel's *Messiah*, listed as an 'anthem':[129]

Chorus, 'For unto us a Child is born', &c
Song, 'He was despised and rejected', &c
Rec and Song, 'Thy rebuke hath broken his heart', &c
Song, 'But thou didst not leave his soul in Hell', &c
Chorus, 'Lift up your heads, O ye gates', &c
Song, 'I know that my Redeemer liveth', &c
Chorus, 'HALLELUJAH'

A subsequent press notice announced that £32 10s 2d had been collected for the 'distressed poor' of the parish of Christ Church.[130] *Messiah* was performed at Cloyne cathedral the following June, featuring the choirs of Cloyne and Cork, with a band 'at least as numerous as that at the late performance at Cork'. A brief report given in the *Cork Evening Post*, reprinted in the *Dublin Chronicle*, stated that the instrumentalists numbered about thirty, and the combined choirs of the cathedrals of Cloyne and Cork numbered about twenty.[131] James Magrath and John Shaw were listed among the solo singers.

A Lenten oratorio performance was again undertaken at Christ Church in 1789, with the comment that 'no trouble has been spared by the conductors in collecting the best performers, to render it as agreeable to the public, and as beneficial to the Poor of the Parish as possible'.[132] The programme was in three parts, the first two comprising a repeat of the previous year's programme, and the third consisting of a further selection from Handel's oratorios, concluding with his Coronation Anthem:

Song 'Tears such as tender fathers shed' *Deborah*
Song 'The Lord worketh wonders' *Judas Maccabeus*
Select parts of the *Te Deum*
Song 'Shall I in Mamre's fertile plain' *Joshua*
Song 'Return O God of Hosts' *Samson*
Chorus 'To dull his glory they would tread' *Samson*
Song 'Arm, arm, ye brave' *Judas Maccabeus*
Chorus 'But thanks be to God' *Messiah*
Coronation anthem[133]

In August 1790, an oratorio was performed at Cloyne cathedral for the benefit of the Cloyne Infirmary, beginning at 11 o'clock.[134] Tickets at 5s 5d were available from Anthony Edwards' bookshop in Castle Street.[135] This series of events in Cork and Cloyne marked the beginning of the public ritual of the oratorio in the region, auspicious occasions on which the nobility and gentry attended in great numbers, some travelling from a distance, to support a local charity. It brought sacred and secular together in a civic ritual, centred around a musical canon of large-scale works by deceased composers, the beginning of the historically based musical canon of 'great works'.[136]

The influx of musicians from Dublin and further afield continued during the early 1790s. In July 1791 Louisa Gautherot (d. 1808), French *émigrée* and female professional violinist, arrived in the city to give a concert, following an engagement at the Rotunda in Dublin.[137] In September she was joined by cellist Joseph Reinagle (1762–1836), clarinettist John Mahon and violinist Mr Fontaine, for a concert featuring all four players, eagerly anticipated in the *Cork Gazette* as 'not only a feast, but a perfect luxury to the lovers of music'. This new radical newspaper, edited by Denis Driscol, maintained a keen interest in contemporarary developments in France. The programme, which it published, commenced with a Haydn symphony and included a double concerto for two violins played by Gautherot and Fontaine, solo concertos by Reinagle, Mahon and Gautherot, all unidentified, and a string quartet by Pleyel. The finale was 'a Grand Piece (now performing in Paris) entitled The Taking of the Bastille', one of many new pieces inspired by recent revolutionary events in Paris.[138] A brief report in the *Cork Gazette* expressed concern that 'from the number of performers, and other expences [*sic*] attending such an exhibition, Mr Fontaine must be considerably out of pocket'.[139]

Another French refugee, flautist Louis Vogel (fl. 1781–98), arrived in Cork in June 1793 and gave two concerts.[140] His first advertisement described him as 'Musician to the late King of France'.[141] In an appealing notice for his second concert, he informed the public of

> his loyal exertions, the late amiable tho' unfortunate Louis on the 10th August, at the Tuileries (where, covered with wounds, he lay for many hours near his slain father, and other deceased sufferers) occasions his being at present expatriated, infirm and almost friendless.[142]

Supported by local professionals and amateurs, Vogel's first concert featured a concerto and sonata composed by himself, and Bucher's Variations on 'Malbrook' Op 37, 'in which he will sing and play at the same time'. James Roche performed a 'Grand Concerto' on the piano.[143] Roche had by this time established a music shop and had begun importing pianos, and he was the first local musician to pioneer concert performances on the piano.[144]

In December, Count Joseph Boruwlaski (1739–1837), a Polish dwarf, performed on the guitar with the support of the Gentlemen of the Musical Society and Catch Club.[145] Born in Polish Russia, Boruwlaski toured widely throughout Europe before settling permanently in Durham in 1800.[146] In his published memoirs, he noted the elegance of the parade, and expressed gratitude for the warmth of the reception he received from the Musical Society members:

> Among other instances of their bounty, the gentlemen, who were amateurs in music, graciously offered their assistance at my concert; and, to prove the extent of their good dispositions, performed themselves on that night. This act of generosity, which I did not expect, rendered my benefit brilliant and numerous.[147]

The following evening he dined by invitation with his Worshipful the Mayor. From Cork, he travelled to Kinsale, where he held a private concert under the patronage of Lord and Lady Kinsale,[148] followed some days afterwards by 'an overflowing concert of the best society' in Youghal.[149] During his stay, he was received by his fellow Freemasons of Lodge 28 (Cork).[150]

Although there is no documentary evidence of concerts having taken place in the city during 1795,[151] an exceptionally large number of visiting musicians arrived in Cork in late summer of 1796, all associated with the theatre. Andrew Ashe and violinist Felix Yaniewicz (1762–1848) arrived in August, having completed engagements at the Dublin and Limerick theatres. Interspersed with a comedy and farce, they performed two concerts at the Cork theatre 'at Play-House prices'.[152] Their benefit concert at the George's Street Assembly Rooms two weeks later featured 'several new concertos for violin and flute' and 'a Concertante for Flute and Violin, composed for the occasion by Mr Janiewicz'.[153] According to his *Musical Memoirs*, oboist William Parke, who was currently engaged at the theatre, joined them for three concerts.[154] The theatre band that year included Dublin-based instrumentalists violinist John Bianchi (d. 1802) and cellist Robert Haigh.[155]

In September they performed at a benefit concert for the widow and children of the late James Brealsford Stephens (d. 1796), a local harpsichord maker of some fifty years' standing, organised by Henry Delamain, in which they were joined by Martha Poole. Following a concert at the Assembly Rooms in Youghal on 21 September with Haigh and Bianchi, Martha Poole returned to Cork in October and advertised a benefit concert, modelled on Harrison and Knyvett's celebrated vocal concerts in London.[156] Her programme featured 'the celebrated Cantata, composed by Dr Haydn, never performed in Ireland'.[157] Bianchi and Haigh concluded their sojourn in the south with a concert at the Assembly Rooms in late October.[158]

Bianchi returned to Cork as leader of the theatre orchestra in 1797 and directed the annual benefit concert for the North Charitable Infirmary, one of the few advertised concerts of that year.[159] There is no record of concerts during 1798, the year in which the United Irishmen staged uprisings in several locations, leading to restrictions on travel and evening entertainment.[160] The only concert advertised in 1799 was organised by the Society for the Relief and Discharge of Persons confined for small debts, coinciding with the spring assizes, to assist thirty-one debtors, currently confined to the city gaol.[161]

The last years of the century witnessed a lull in concert activity by independent touring professionals, and theatre became the principal channel of musical provision. The reduced number of professional touring musicians during these years reflected a wider trend. The Rotunda concerts in Dublin had ceased since 1791, replaced by smaller-scale ventures. Derek Collins refers to the 'decline and revival of concert life' in Dublin during the years 1792–1814. William Weber refers to the period 1790–1813 as 'a hiatus in presentations',[162] and Rohr has also noted the decline in London concert activity during the years of the French wars.[163] During these years, concerts organised by Cork's charitable societies were the principal frameworks for musical performances, drawing musicians, audiences and patrons together in congenial public settings.

3

MUSIC AND THE ESTABLISHED CHURCH TO 1820

David Weyman's *Melodia Sacra*, vol 1 (frontispiece).

Excellent certainly the music was. The organ was a noble instrument and as yesterday, I remember the fine voice of Magrath, 'old evergreen' as Magrath was called, filling with mellow tones, a magnificent anthem of Delamain's.[1]

Throughout Western history, the churches were important centres of musical activity. Religion was problematic in Ireland, however. Henry VIII's break with Rome and the imposition of a vernacular liturgy created a distinctive Anglican Church. Amidst aggressive attacks on native and local communities, Protestant landlords chose conformity to the reformed English Church from 1660, which became the legal inheritor of the medieval Christian tradition in Ireland. The Act of Uniformity (1666) affirmed its position, and over the following decades its privileges increased, reflecting its role as an agent of anglicisation.[2] The subsequent wars of succession of the seventeenth century between supporters of Protestant Prince William and Catholic James II confirmed Protestant dominance of Ireland, the basis of social and political tensions in Irish culture over the ensuing centuries. By the early eighteenth century, two strong religious identities, Catholic (both Irish and 'old English') and the Church of Ireland, both regarded themselves as inheritors of the tradition of St Patrick. While the Catholics and Dissenters endured a series of repressive laws, the period of relative stability from 1770 to 1820 was one of reform and regeneration for the Church of Ireland, which saw building or restoration of physical structures, liturgical regulation, the installation of organs and the establishment of choirs.

The cathedral of the Diocese of Cork and Ross, St Fin Barre's, was built on a rocky outcrop to the south-west of the walled city, on the site of earlier churches, the earliest allegedly of St Fin Barre. Documentation of musical activity at the cathedral dates back to the early seventeenth century.[3] From 1591, records indicate that a college of four vicars choral had been founded and endowed by some of the predecessors of the Bishop of Cork.[4] The number fluctuated during the early seventeenth century, however, and many of the appointees simultaneously held offices of prebendiary, treasurer or vicar choral at Cloyne cathedral.[5]

In 1633, the Dean of Cork cathedral ordered the adoption of the practice of daily choral service 'in imitation of the laudable custom observed in the Metropolitan Church of Cashel'.[6] In the same year, the Dean and Chapter sanctioned the payment of ten pounds 'for the completion of a musical instrument, called in English, *organs*, as is the custom to have in Cathedral Churches'.[7] Among the four vicars choral appointed to fill vacancies in 1669 was William Love, who first appears as organist in the records of 1677.[8] The appointment of Bishop Edward Wetenhall in 1679 brought ecclesiastical reform. Records indicate a move towards consolidating the cathedral's musical personnel. In November of that year, Thomas Bennett was appointed as 'Master of the Song' at a salary of £30 per annum, and Robert Northall and Charles Boulton were appointed as 'choristers' at £5 each per annum.[9] However, indiscipline seems to have continued. The visitation books of Bishop Edward Synge of 1684 express concern that

> both by the general complaint of people, and by our owne observacion it appreareth to us, that the publiq service of God is grossly neglected by the Vicars Chorall of the Cathedral Church of St. ffinbaries, Corke, and through their example (or as wee have reason to believe, through the advice and approvement of some of them) by the organist, and others of the quire, contrary to orders made and provided in our primary visitacion, in the year 1679.[10]

As organist, William Love was granted a quarter of the rents of the vicars choral in 1691, and entitlement to part of their benefits was included in 1694. An account dated 1700 describes the financial structure of the parish of St Fin Barre's:

> The parish of St Barry's contains sixteen plowlands. All the tythes of corn of the sixteen plowlands in this parish belong to the oeconomy of St Barry's. All the rest of the tithes of these sixteen plowlands belongs to the Vicars Choral of St Barry's. [...] The tyth belonging to the oeconomy in this parish is worth about £40 per an. The tyth belonging to the Vicars Choral is worth about £30 per an.[11]

Gentlemen 'choristers' received an annual payment of £10, and Master of the Song £12.[12] During the episcopacy of Bishop Dive Downes (1699–1709), William Toole was appointed as organist in 1703, and Edward Broadway was appointed as chorister in 1704 and Master of the Song in 1707.[13] Liturgical music consisted of metrical psalms, either from the older Psalter by Sternhold and Hopkins (1584), or the version of 1696 by Nicholas Brady and Nahum Tate.[14]

The episcopacy of Bishop Peter Browne from 1710 brought further changes, prioritising building and repair and the consolidation of church infrastructures, including the building or rebuilding of the parish churches of Christ Church (Holy Trinity), St Ann Shandon, St Paul's and St Nicholas'.[15] In 1710, a new organ was commissioned for the cathedral with Dublin-based organ builder John-Baptiste Cuvillie.[16] The choir of St Fin Barre's was discharged 'and all the servants belonging to it, from further attendance, receiving their salaries to 24th June, and their means to be applied to the service of the Church'.[17] On completion of the new organ in 1712, Edward Broadway was appointed as organist, at an annual salary of £20, succeeded eight years later by William Smyth, former organist at Cloyne cathedral. With Broadway appointed as 'Master of the Song' in November 1723, new terms for the choir were issued:

> Mr Broadway, and his successors, Lay Vicars, are ordered to sing a Solo Anthem every Sunday, in the afternoon, and provide a variety of them, and that he instruct two boys to join in singing said Anthems; that he observe such fines as the Masters of the Song of this Cathedral were formerly subjected to.[18]

Brown also supervised plans for the rebuilding of the cathedral. The medieval building was demolished and a modest new building in the Doric style was completed in 1735, shortly after Brown's death.[19] The Cuvillie organ was reinstated in 1739,[20] and the following year an application was made to Bishop Robert Clayton (1735–45) for £150 for the purchase of a chair organ for the use of the choir.[21]

An account of an oratorio performance at St Fin Barre's dates from 1744, when *Faulkner's Dublin Journal* reported a performance of Handel's *Messiah* at the Cork cathedral.[22] It is likely that it was organised by the Musical Society in support of North Charitable Infirmary, which was established that year. William Smith was a member of the committee.[23] By mid-century, a viable structure was in place. Charles Smith (1750) reported 'a good organ' and 'choristers and singing boys'.[24] From 1752, Rev. Richard Piggott was nominated as a 'Reader' (Deputy) by the then vicars choral,

> as some of them have cure of souls in different parishes, or through their infirmities cannot without great difficulty attend to their duty in the Cathedral, and in order that the service on them incumbent may regularly be performed in case of their necessary absence.[25]

Figure 3.1. Tower and steeple of old St Fin Barre's cathedral (1735–1865).
CORK CITY LIBRARY

Also in that year, a steeple with a new set of eight bells was completed, and the 'bells of St Barry's' became a feature of the city's soundscape.[26] In 1763, Dublin-based keyboard instrument maker Ferdinand Weber (1715–84) was commissioned to supply two new stops for the Cuvillie organ,[27] and a new bellows four years later.[28] Weber continued to tend the organ until 1772 and, thereafter, William Smith received an annual sum of £8 for tuning and cleaning the organ in addition to his organist's salary.

A reference to a sub-organist towards the end of William Smith's tenure was possibly due to the latter's ill-health, and it appears that Lewis Gibson was the appointed organist at St Fin Barre's for a short time from 1778 until 1781, until his alleged dismissal from his position. There appears to have been some controversy regarding the appointment in 1782 of Henry Delamain, as Lewis Gibson believed he himself had already been appointed, and in the same year published a letter expressing his grievances in *A Letter to the Revd., the Dean and Chapter of the Cathedral Church of St. Fin-Barry, Cork.*[29] In May 1782 Gibson advertised his availability 'to instruct a certain number of ladies on the Harpsichord' at 'his lodgings, the Library, St. Barry's'.[30] During the following year, however, he was appointed as organist at St Colman's cathedral, Cloyne, a position he retained until 1837.[31]

Although not formally united until 1835, the diocese of Cloyne was linked to that of Cork and Ross, in terms of clerical transfers, promotions and exchanges.[32] Situated some twenty miles to the east of Cork city, the diocesan cathedral of Cloyne had a choral tradition that surpassed that of Cork in expertise and organisation during the eighteenth century. From a fund bequeathed by Bishop Crow, who served at Cloyne from 1702 until 1706, a diocesan school for boys was established, which, from 1729 extended to provision of musical education for six choristers. The 'Crow foundation' continued to flourish through the episcopacy of Bishop George Berkeley.[33] Bishop Charles Agar, appointed to the Cloyne diocese in 1768, zealously oversaw further improvement of the cathedral's musical establishment.[34] In addition to continued expenditure on the organ, the vestry book records the acquisition of printed music, much of it purchased personally by Agar. From 1771, music purchased for the choir included Green's Anthems, Handel's Overtures and church music by Boyce, Purcell, Crofts, Boyce, Blow, Baily, Bond and Woodward, indicating the building of a substantial choral library. The purchase of copies of Handel overtures and a spinet 'for the use of the boys' indicates an interest in instrumental music. The Cloyne choir contributed to oratorios in Cork on several occasions from 1788 onwards, continuing during the nineteenth century. James Roche had been organist at Cloyne cathedral for a short time in 1782, prior to his appointment at Christ Church in Cork.

Having previously served as organist at Christ Church, Henry Delamain (d. 1796) held the post of organist at St Fin Barre's from 1782 until his death in 1796. His father, Lawrence Delamain, an immigrant Huguenot, married Alice Boland in 1733 and inherited a property at Red Island in Rochestown, to the south-east of the city, formerly owned by Mr Boland, dancing master. The name 'Hop' island was used by locals, referring to the occupation of its owners, 'hop' being a commonly used term for dance. Henry Delamain combined the professional roles of cathedral organist, music professor, composer and dancing master. He was elected as Master of Ceremonies at the Assembly Room from the late 1770s and retained the position until his death. Delamain used the Tuckey Street room as a dancing academy from about 1782,[35] which on his death in December 1796 was taken over by dancing master John Bernard.[36] Delamain's *Six New Psalm Tunes in Score,* dedicated to Rev. Richard Pigott and the parishioners of Christ Church, were published by J. Blundell of London in 1781, but many more of his compositions remained unpublished.[37] Crofton Croker later wrote that

> the name of De la Main, many years organist at the Cathedral, ought to be more generally known from the merit of his compositions, particularly of his church music, and it is a reproach to Cork, that no effort has been made to collect and publish his works; inaccurate copies of some of which are to be found in print.[38]

Delamain was succeeded by James Roche, who duly resigned his post at Christ Church and continued to serve as organist and Master of the Boys at St Fin Barre's from 1797 until his death in 1811.[39] In addition to the organist's salary of £30, Roche received an annual payment of fifteen guineas for keeping the organ in repair. James Magrath, parish clerk at Christ Church, also contributed to choral music at the cathedral and, in 1801, the Dean and Chapter granted him an annual salary of ten pounds 'for his long services in the Choir'.[40] In 1808, an account of a visitation by the Archbishop of Cashel reported that:

> The vocal performance of the Choir did very great credit to Mr Magrath, the master. The organ, one of the best in the kingdom, which underwent

> a perfect repair and tuning, by Mr Haddock, the organ-builder, gave great satisfaction by the performance of Mr Roche, organist; the Church was never known to be so crowded. His grace was so much satisfied with the respectable manner in which the whole of the musical service was conducted, that he was pleased to express his acknowledgements to Mr Magrath and the other gentlemen on the occasion.[41]

In 1817, a new organ built by the London firm Flight and Robinson was installed, at a cost of 500 guineas,[42] and the old Cuvillie organ was advertised for sale in the *Cork Advertiser.*[43]

Throughout Ireland, cathedral musicians of the Established Church formed the earliest networks of professional musicians, operating within their own provinces. This is illustrated in a description of a performance by the cathedral choir in an account written in 1867 by Richard Caulfield of the consecration of the chapel of the Cork Foundling Hospital in 1811:

> The Chapel attached to this Institution was consecrated on Tuesday 14 May 1811 by the late Hon. Thos St. Lawrence Bishop of Cork and Ross. A choral service was performed on the occasion by the members of the cathedral choir consisting of the late Mr James Magragh, Master of the boys Cork Cathedral, Mr John Magragh, master of the boys at Cashel, Mr Roger Bertridge, Mr Joseph Gibbs and the late Mr Edu Moeran. The boys of the choir were Master William Connell afterwards organist of St. Ann's Shandon, Frederick Daly, late organist of Cloyne Cathedral, Edward Paul (now Sep 6 1867) organist of St Paul's Cork and his brother Andrew Paul (now 1867) clerk of St. Peter's, Cork.[44]

This account indicates the subsequent career paths of this group of church musicians. Of the choirboys listed, Frederick Daly became organist at Cloyne cathedral in 1838 and John Magrath (son of James Magrath) was appointed as organist at Cashel cathedral in 1840.[45] In addition to those listed above, John Carroll, choir member from 1817 to 1824, was appointed as organist at St Peter's church in 1830. Edward Moeran was appointed as organist at the Catholic North Parish chapel from 1813 and remained in the post until the 1850s.

References to the repertoire in use at St Fin Barre's appear in several documentary sources. Caulfield's report of the 1811 performance by the cathedral choir specifies the music performed on the occasion:

> The anthem was Dr Green's 46 Psalm 'God is our hope and strength' – Kent's service in C and the Bristol chant in E, the 100 Psalm by the Foundling children. Mr William Gillespie, later organist of Christ Church, Cork, presided at the Piano Forte, the Rev. Thos Cole, Chaplain to the Institution, preached from 66 Psalm v.13.

The loose usage of the term 'anthem' occurs in this and other sources. A collection of music books presented to the cathedral by James Magrath in 1813 contained the following:[46]

Manuscript:

1 Organ Contraction Service
2 Organ Anthem
3 Organ Anthem
4 Service Books Score
5 Smith's Score

Printed:

1 Messiah, Handel
2 Croft's Score
3 Woodward's Score
4 Nare's Score
5 Page's Anthems, 6 vols
6 Psalms, Weyman
7 Psalms, Magrath
8 Kent's Anthems
9 Boyce's Anthems, 3 vols
10 Haydn's Creation

This collection represents a range of up-to-date Anglican church repertoire by prominent English and Irish cathedral composers, consisting mainly of anthems and metrical psalm settings, in addition to the two most popular oratorios of the early nineteenth century. David Weyman (1771–1822) and Richard Woodward 'the younger' (1743/4–77) held half vicar choral posts at St Patrick's cathedral, and Weyman was a stipendiary singer at Dublin's

Christ Church and Woodward served as organist there. The first volume of Weyman's collection of psalms, hymns and anthems, *Melodia Sacra or the Psalms of David*, published the previous year, included seven psalm settings by Henry Delamain (see page 45).[47] Over 38 Cork subscribers to this work were listed, including St Fin Barre's cathedral and the parishes of Christ Church and St Peter's, and two Cork booksellers had placed subscriptions for multiple copies. With the publication of further volumes over the ensuing years, Weyman's *Melodia Sacra* became the standard collection of the Church of Ireland during the nineteenth century, in which he sought to 'build up hymn tunes on the plan of little anthems, with "verses" and chorus, and with some rude counterpoint'.[48] Woodward's small output of sacred music consisted of *Veni creator spiritus* Op 2 (Dublin, 1767) and *Cathedral Music* Op 3 (London, 1771).[49] William Boyce's *Fifteen Anthems, together with a Te Deum and Jubilate* were first published in 1780, and Winchester Cathedral organist James Kent's *Twelve Anthems* were first published in London *c.* 1790.[50] Anthems by Greene and Croft were listed in the Chapter acts at this time.[51] Entries in the Oeconomists Accounts indicate a system that insured the management of the library, by means of discretionary payment made to an individual, often a junior choir member, for 'the care of books' or 'caring for the anthems'. John Carroll received such a payment for two years from 1817 to 1819 and Charles Daly received this annual payment of £1 2s 9d continuously from 1820 to 1824.[52]

Although the stipendiaries formed the core of the cathedral choir, there was some flexibility in occasionally accommodating extra singers. In 1817, Frederick Daly was appointed as a 'Supernumerary Singer' and William Connell as countertenor.[53] In 1827 it was agreed that Henry Allen and John McCarthy, former outstanding boy singers, be retained in the choir at an annual salary of £25.[54] Richard Keays entered the choir as a tenor in 1821[55] and continued to receive an annual salary of ten pounds until 1839.[56] In 1837, the boys of the choir were requested to 'attend on Week Days when Divine Service is performed'.[57] Alexander Roche, on his return from London in 1838, offered to sing in the choir without payment.[58] In 1842 vacancies arising on the death of Joseph Gibbs and Richard Keays were filled by James Roche and James W. Keays, and Robert Orr was appointed as countertenor.[59] In 1843, Finny's *Almanac* lists six stipendiaries and, in 1844, Jackson's *County and City of Cork Almanac* lists five men.[60]

James Roche's successor James Brealsford Stephens (d. 1860) remained in the post from 1811 until 1860. During his forty-nine-year tenure, he contributed occasionally to local music activity, and there were no significant public musical events held at the cathedral. Although the lay choirmen were active as professional singers in local concerts and musical societies, the poor reputation of the absentee vicars choral endured. In 1845, an article entitled 'Music in Cork' in *The Musical World* stated that:

> Cork possesses a cathedral, St. Finn Bars, [*sic*] which ought to possess a good choir, but we fear the revenues of the vicars choral are appropriated to other purposes than the legitimate uses of the choir. There is above one thousand per annum (by law established), under the superintendance of the dean and chapter; this is sadly perverted, and instead of the choir receiving that sum we should say they hardly receive one-fourth of it. Parties who never visit the cathedral except to receive the amount enjoy the salary, while paying a miserable stipend for a deputy or professional. Such a state of things should be remedied. Service commences at eleven and three o'clock, on Sundays. The musical service of the cathedral differs very little from that of a parish church, the only characteristic of a cathedral is the singing of an anthem, in rather a different manner from what it ought to be – no service being sung, except in the manner I have stated, as in a parish church. They have rather odd notions of anthem singing in this cathedral; we have heard Dr. Smith's 'Nunc Dimittis' in B flat sung as an anthem, instead of occupying its legitimate place in the afternoon service [...][61]

The Anglican parishes formed the basis of the city's social cohesion during the eighteenth century. Since the expulsion of Catholics in the previous century, the area within the city walls contained the highest concentration of Protestants and was served by two parishes: Christ Church near the south gate, and St Peter's further north along the main street. With a rapidly growing population during the eighteenth century, the city parishes and the suburban parish of St Mary Shandon expanded, and their churches underwent structural improvements, with the installation of organs, the appointment of organists and the establishment of choirs.

Christ Church (also named Holy Trinity) was the older of the city parishes, dating back to medieval times, when it was the parish church of the twelfth-century Hiberno-Norse settlement of Cork. A church on this site was damaged during the 1690 siege and demolished in 1717. A new church, designed in neo-classical style by John Coltsman, was completed in 1725,[62] 'with good pews and galleries', capable of containing 3,000 people.[63] A visitor to the city described it in 1786:

> Christ Church is the largest and most magnificent in the city, being accounted one of the largest modern parish churches in the kingdom: It is said to contain three thousand people. The building is of hewn stone, in an elegant, though plain style.[64]

The parish was partially financed by the city Corporation, whose members regularly attended service there. The tower of this new church began to lean, a feature which frequently provoked comment by visitors such as Philip Luckcombe: 'I went to the new Church, near the South-gate, the steeple of which exactly answered Shakespeare's description in sloping "to its foundation", which argues the fenny bottom whereon it stands.'[65] The leaning steeple was taken down in 1814, and the side wall was rebuilt.[66]

Council records indicate progressive changes at Christ Church from 1760, when a committee was appointed to oversee the installation of an organ by Ferdinand Weber of Dublin, at a cost of £482 15s.[67] The front of the organ casing consisted of a screen 'of most elaborate and graceful design'.[68]According to Grattan Flood, a recital was given on the new organ at the Dutch Church, Lazar's Hill, Dublin in 1761, prior to its installation in Cork.[69] In the same year, Cork City Council resolved to pay an annual salary of £20 to the newly appointed organist, Henry Delamain.[70] The installation was completed by 1765.[71]

Prior to the introduction of church organs and choirs, congregational singing in Anglican parish churches was led by the parish clerk. Christ Church's parish clerk during this period was James Magrath (d. 1824), who brought exceptional vocal expertise to his duties, in both choir training and liturgical performances, and he also served as 'Master of the Boys' at St Fin Barre's from 1811. An early reference to music at Christ Church dates from 1779, in an account by traveller Philip Luckcombe, reporting that 'the service was, throughout, performed with the utmost decency and propriety; they had a good organ, and the singing was remarkably good'.[72] A choir was not formally established however until 1787, when the vestry book recorded that 'the establishment of a choir by voluntary subscription would be of essential service to the poor of the parish by inducing greater congregations and of course larger contributions'.[73] In addition to religious ceremonies, the Anglican parish churches in Ireland assumed responsibility for caring for the poor, in the absence of statutory provision such as the English Poor Law of 1601.[74] This law distinguished between the 'deserving' poor, the orphaned, infirm, blind, and disabled, and the 'undeserving' poor, the idle and vagrant.[75] The linking of church music with charitable provision accords with the eighteenth-century association of public music with charity, and underlines the significance of the Church of Ireland parishes as agents in administering to the poor in eighteenth-century Ireland. It also provided justification for significant expenditure on musical provision.

The enhancement of the liturgy with music and the improvement of church interiors were important means of heightening the experience of church attendance as a civic as well as religious ritual. Records indicate considerable expenditure on the provision of music and the upkeep of the organ. In 1796 the vestry book records an additional payment of £11 7s 6d to Magrath 'for better assisting in the performing [of] Divine service'. He received this amount again in 1797, with a supplementary payment 'for instructing boys to sing'.[76] The vestry book records several payments to Magrath for 'singing anthems' in 1808, in addition to his £20 salary. By 1802, the organ was in need of repair, necessitating the services of Marsden Haddock, for which the sum of £63 11s 3d was levied on the inhabitants of the parish.[77]

Henry Delamain was appointed as cathedral organist in 1782 and was replaced at Christ Church by James Roche, who had officiated as organist at Cloyne cathedral for a short time earlier that year.[78] In April of the following year, the council agreed to pay him an annual salary of £20.[79] A typical parish church organist in Dublin at this time would have been paid £30.[80] The organisation of an oratorio at Christ Church in 1788 by Roche and Magrath was an indication of their commitment to a high standard of musical performance, as well as confidence in attracting an audience. In 1797 Roche tendered his resignation at Christ Church to take up the post of organist at St Fin Barre's cathedral, on the death of Delamain, and the vacant post at Christ Church was filled by James Magrath's son, Terence,[81] who held the post until April 1804,[82] and was replaced by William Gillespie.[83]

The particular contribution of Magrath's role, as parish clerk, in the teaching of the choirboys at Christ Church was noted in several vestry entries of the early nineteenth century. From 1810, a payment of £9 2s 0d was recorded to 'the four choirboys for attending evening service'. This sum appears to have been an annual amount, shared by the four choirboys, awarded for a service that was regarded as extra to their regular duties. At a meeting of the parishioners of Christ Church in 1813, it was agreed 'that our thanks be given to Mr James Magrath, for his care and attention, at all times, of the boys of his choir'.[84] Following general practice, the choirboys were recruited from the poor school of the parish, and were taught singing by the parish clerk. There are no records of payments to adult choir members until 1821, when the minute book records the payment of £5 9s 3d for five men attending the church at 11s 1½d per week.[85] In 1815 James Magrath was paid twenty guineas for instructing the girls of the Christ Church parish school in singing.[86] This annual payment was recorded up to 1818 and in 1821 he was paid £22 15s for instructing the boys of the parish school.[87]

From 1776 until 1788 Magrath received an annual salary of £10 from the city council for teaching singing to the boys in St Stephen's Hospital, a role previously held by the parish clerk of St Mary's Shandon. Also known as the Bluecoat Hospital, St Stephen's was established in 1699 for the 'maintenance, clothing, and education of 22 boys, the sons of reduced Protestant citizens [...] under the superintendence of the Mayor and Council', located in the yard of Shandon church.[88] On reaching the appropriate age, the boys were apprenticed to various trades; three are recorded as having been apprenticed to organists. Roger Bertridge (b. 1768) is recorded as having been apprenticed to Henry Delamain, then organist at Christ Church. Jonathan Fenn (b. 1787) and James Tomkins, both of St Stephen's Hospital, were apprenticed to James Roche in 1797.[89] Magrath served as parish clerk until his death in April 1824. His funeral was recorded in *The Freeholder*:

> On Wednesday last, we followed to the grave the remains of James Magrath. He was reckoned the best looking man of his age in Cork – and he lived to that age in the respect and regard of his fellow-citizens. We trust that the Vestry of the Holy Trinity, on Easter Monday, will manifest a generous recollection of his length of services.[90]

In April 1824 the vestry book recorded a payment to Mrs Aphra Magrath for instructing the boys of the parish school to sing until the appointment of a parish clerk.[91] A pension of twenty guineas a year was voted to his widow at the Easter Vestry in 1824, which, however, was discontinued a year later.[92]

By February 1824, plans for restoration of the church interior were under way, and the vestry minutes record a plan for the dismantling and storage of the organ by local organ tuner Richard Gillespie.[93] Day recounts that the ornate screen was destroyed at this time.[94] In March, however, it was resolved 'that the organ be advertised for sale in the Cork papers and that proposals be secured for the same'.[95] According to Day, it was divided in two, half of it sold to the church in Tralee, the other half to either Kinsale or Skibbereen.

The construction work was completed in 1832, consisting of a remodelling of the interior and the removal of the spire and tower. William Gillespie was reinstated as organist, and also served as parish clerk, a contraction of church personnel that reflected tighter budgetary constraints as the nineteenth century progressed.[96]

St Peter's was the second parish within the city walls, located a short distance along the main street from Christ Church. References to this church date from as early as AD 1199. Concerns for its structural condition were noted in several sources from the 1760s onwards.[97] In 1763, the Corporation applied to parliament for a grant of £5,000 to rebuild the church, a project that did not commence until 1782, when an appeal was issued for public contributions.[98] Over the next five years a systematic programme of building was carried out, and the church re-opened for daily service in May 1787.[99] In July, a notice was published in the *Hibernian Chronicle* for proposals and plans for furnishing the interior of the church, with the specification that a place was to be left over the mayor's gallery for the installation of an organ.[100] In September 1788 the City Council sanctioned the payment of fifty pounds for the installation of an organ, which was supplemented by private subscriptions by 'Gentlemen of the parish'.[101] This instrument, built by William Gibson of Dublin, was completed in 1790. The inaugural performance by the newly appointed organist, John Shaw, was reported in the *Hibernian Chronicle*:

> On Sunday last was opened for the first exhibition, the new organ in St. Peter's church, made in this city by Mr Gibson from Dublin, when two select pieces from Handel's *Messiah* were performed, viz. 'I know that my redeemer liveth', and 'He shall feed his flock', which were very agreeably accompanied by the vocal performance of a promising young girl (Rosetta Edgcombe) from the Foundling Hospital in our City. The organ met with universal approbation, and was done great justice by Mr Shaw, whose performance both in the voluntary and accompaniments were excellent, particularly on the swell stop, he showed the greatest taste and expression; the young girl was much distressed, it being her first appearance, yet acquitted herself without mistake, and bids fair to be a capital singer.[102]

The *Hibernian Chronicle* reported that it was 'entirely executed in the modern stile, and the front is perhaps the most beautiful in the kingdom'. As with its counterpart in Christ Church, the newly acquired organ was an object of civic pride, promising larger congregations to support the Sunday collections:

> The Poor of said Parish (who are a very numerous list) will no doubt benefit very considerably by the encrease of the Sunday Collections, as much larger congregations will henceforth be induced to frequent that Church, which in every respect is most elegantly finished, and is by much the handsomest in Cork.[103]

By December proposals were sought for gilding the organ pipes.[104] In 1791 a newspaper advertisement for a parish clerk was published, which specified that 'a person qualified to accompany an organ with an unblemished character will meet with good encouragement'.[105]

In the early years of the new century, records indicate increased efforts to improve church singing at St Peter's. Thomas Nugent was listed as parish clerk in 1811. A vestry book entry for that year notes that an additional sum of £5 per annum was to be paid to John Shaw and Thomas Nugent 'for their trouble in instructing the boys that sing in the church',[106] and from 1814 Nugent was paid an additional annual sum of £10 'for teaching the children of Deane's Charity School to sing the Psalms'.[107] In 1817 provision for improving church singing was further increased, with the proposal

> that the sum of thirty six pounds sterling yearly be at the disposal of the Minister and church Wardens for the purpose of improving the children that sing in the church of which sixteen pounds are to be applied to the use of the children and the remaining twenty pounds to be equally divided between the organist and parish clerk to be paid by an order from one of the clergymen.[108]

Records of the city's other Anglican churches indicate similar programmes of rebuilding, installation of organs and appointment of organists during the latter part of the eighteenth century. The suburban parish of Shandon was the largest of all the Cork parishes.[109] An organ was installed at St Mary Shandon in 1760 or 1761:

> The parishioners having contributed towards buying and erecting an organ in the new-built church in the parish, which has regularly accompanied Divine Service for several months past, but is now in bad order; it is agreed that the sum of £11 7s 6d be raised on the inhabitants of the parish by a rate for the repairing of the organ.[110]

The organ, having been recently restored by William Gibson of Dublin, was featured at a charity sermon in October 1789 in the performance of an anthem by Delamain.[111] Further details of expenditure on the organ included an annual payment of £8 to Gibson for maintenance and, in 1803, a new trumpet stop was added at a cost of twenty pounds. A new organ was purchased from London for the church in 1840, and the existing instrument was offered for sale 'on very reasonable terms', being suited to 'a tolerably-sized Church'.[112] The church of St Anne Shandon was built in 1722 on the site of an older church, and gained parochial status in 1772.

The Established Irish church, as a cornerstone of eighteenth-century provincial musical culture, was an important musical institution with a strong community base, providing a professional pathway for church musicians. The training system of St Fin Barre's cathedral and the two principal city parishes provided a core of professional musicians that served the city and extended into a wider network of Anglican church musicians. These singers and organists provided civic musical leadership and, by the late eighteenth century, several of the cathedral choral stipendiaries were members of singing clubs, a tradition that was to endure throughout the nineteenth century. The majority of them were also music professors. The city's parishes were involved in charity schooling, where the parish clerk, who also possessed some level of musical expertise, provided tuition in singing, and from which choirboys were recruited.

The development of music in the Church of Ireland from 1770 to 1820 established it as a standard element of religious worship, raising its civic importance. In the city's Protestant churches, the use of music was viewed as a means of attracting larger congregations, which would in turn generate more substantial collections to benefit the poor of the parish. With its central location and skilled musicians, Christ Church was the setting for oratorio performances from the 1780s to the early decades of the nineteenth century, gaining favour among the elite of the region and blending charitable support with heightened aesthetic experience.

4

'SPIRITED LESSEES': OPERA AND THEATRE MUSIC TO 1840

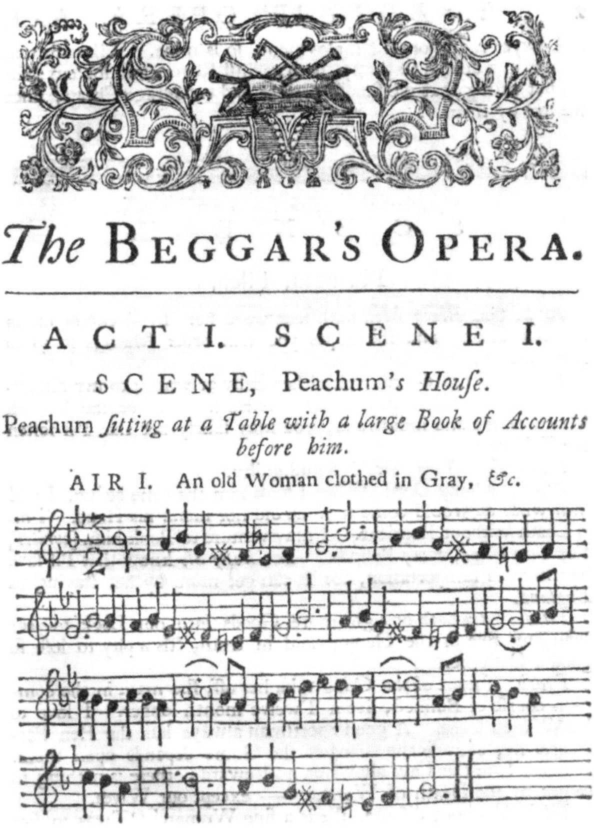

The BEGGAR'S OPERA.

ACT I. SCENE I.

SCENE, Peachum's *Houſe.*

Peachum *ſitting at a Table with a large Book of Accounts before him.*

AIR I. An old Woman clothed in Gray, *&c.*

The Beggar's Opera score: opening of Act 1.

At the several halts of a dramatic company in Ireland, the great variety of personages assembling at the inn-door made the circumstance whimsical enough: the post-chaise, the gig, the whiskey, the noddy, the single horse, the double horse, the car, the St Francis's mules: yet all the travellers were cheerful and comfortable.[1]

From the mid-eighteenth century, professional theatre in Ireland commanded wide public patronage on its provincial circuits. The Cork season was part of a circuit from a centralised patent theatre in Dublin, which engaged actors, actresses and producers from London's Covent Garden and Drury Lane theatres.[2] Although there was some selectivity in the touring repertory, Cork audiences enjoyed the best of contemporary theatre from Dublin and London.

The theatre was an important urban social space, attended by members of differing social class, occupation and creed, facilitated by its tiered pricing structure and seating arrangements. The annual arrival of a professional company from Dublin's Theatre Royal in late summer was a highlight of the city's social calendar, coinciding with the late summer assizes. Whether in the private boxes, the pit or the gallery, citizens attended theatre to see and to be seen. Drama, music, dance and visual spectacle all formed part of the experience. Theatre was thus a prominent aspect of the public sphere, discussed in the press, and noted by visitors to the city.

On an operational level, music and theatre had a synergic relationship throughout the eighteenth and nineteenth centuries. From the late 1750s, songs, dance spectacles and processionals enlivened spoken drama in tragedies and comedies.[3] Allardyce Nicoll attributes such increased use of 'pageantry and show' to the need to entertain audiences in increasingly large venues.[4] Hitchcock commented on the 1762–3 Dublin season:

> Music, at this time, began to make some progress in this kingdom. It had always been cultivated, but in an inferior degree. Hitherto, it had been considered as an auxiliary to the Theatre, but we shall soon find it beginning to take the lead, and constituting a principal feature in its amusements.[5]

Theatre programmes typically consisted of a main piece and an afterpiece.[6] The bills usually included at least one of the many 'illegitimate' dramatic sub-genres that featured music. These have been variously classified as musical farce, operatic farce, ballad opera, comic opera, prelude, burletta and masque.[7] The phenomenal success of John Gay's *The Beggar's Opera* in 1728 placed English opera on a decidedly popular base, with its characters of London low-life set alongside parodies of Whig politicians (see p. 63). Musically, its settings of London street ballads set it apart from both Italian opera and the English courtly masque. Although it endured on professional bills for the remainder of the century, it had no significant successors, but its legacy of short, straightforward melodies with simple accompaniments, interspersed with spoken dialogue, defined English eighteenth-century opera.

The most frequently performed musical mainpieces of the mid-eighteenth century were collaborations between Dublin-born librettist Isaac Bickerstaffe (1733–1812) and English composer Thomas Arne. Two of their collaborative works, *Thomas and Sally* (1760) and *Love in a Village* (1762), were particularly successful as new models of English pastiche opera, featuring newly composed songs by Arne, along with adaptations of his earlier pieces, and also music and songs by other composers such as Baldassare Galuppi and G.F. Handel.[8] Other popular stage works were Bickerstaffe and Samuel Arnold's *The Maid of the Mill* (1765) and Charles Dibdin's *Lionel and Clarissa* (1768) and *The Padlock* (1768).

Apart from the repertory of English operas, theatre productions featured music in a variety of ways. Both spoken plays and operas could incorporate interpolated material, in the form of songs, dances and instrumental music from diverse sources. The 'suitcase' aria was commonplace, as leading singers performed their own showpieces regardless of the composer's original score. The interval between the main piece and the afterpiece provided another opportunity for musical entertainment, vocal or instrumental, often extended to form a short concert. With popularity and variety as key considerations, these performances may be regarded as the beginnings of popular music traditions, linked to sales of songbooks by local printers. In 1766 and 1767, Cork printer Eugene Swiney supplied a series of comic operas,[9] and William Flyn in 1769 advertised Charles Dibdin's comic opera *The Padlock* and 'Nancy Dawson – a new song-book [...] containing all the newest songs, and particularly those sung by herself at Ranelagh, Vauxhall, Theatres, etc.'[10] The following year, he advertised 'Miss Ashmore's collection of favourite songs as sung at the Theatres and gardens in London and Dublin, containing near 300, in which are many originals [...]'.[11] Frances Ashmore (later Mrs Sparks) had appeared at the Cork Theatre in August 1769.

PROVINCIAL TOURING

The beginning of provincial touring in the south of Ireland can be dated to 1713, when the directors of Dublin's Smock Alley Theatre, Joseph Ashbury, Thomas Elrington, John Evans and Thomas Griffith, procured a lease on a disused building in Dingle Lane (off the main street) in Cork city from builder John King for conversion to a theatre.[12] A notice appeared in *Lloyd's Newsletter* of 14 March 1713 seeking subscribers from among the 'Nobility and Gentry in and about the city of Cork', to contribute to the fitting up of the new theatre.[13] The company presented a summer season of productions in that year, but the venue appears to have fallen into disuse as a theatre thereafter. A theatre subsequently set up in Broad Lane remained in use for some years.[14] Dublin's Aungier Street Theatre Royal replaced its rival Smock Alley company on the Cork tour, and in 1736 this company established a permanent theatre in a lane off George's Street, which came to be known as Playhouse Lane (now Prince's Street), frequently referred to as the 'Theatre Royal on Dunscombe's Marsh'.[15]

From this time onwards, the stock company from Dublin's Theatre Royal that entertained the capital's fashionable society during the winter arrived in Cork for an extended season commencing with the summer assizes week.[16] Performances were normally staged three nights a week, on Mondays, Wednesdays and Fridays, beginning at 7 o'clock, and on each night during the assizes. Admission prices matched those of Dublin, consisting of Boxes 4 shillings, Pit 3 shillings and Gallery 2 shillings.[17] The manager and troupe operated on a shareholding arrangement, whereby each player earned an equal share of the profits of a performance after expenses had been cleared. At the conclusion of the season, the leading performers, the manager, the box-keeper and first violinist were each granted a benefit night, which entitled these individuals to the takings after the deduction of expenses.[18] A full house on this occasion could significantly augment a performer's seasonal earnings. The annual round of benefits generated at least two additional weeks of performances to the season, which then concluded with benefit performances for one or two of the principal local charities.[19]

The investment in a new theatre in George's Street in 1760 by the Crow Street managers Spranger Barry and Henry Woodward reflected the company's confidence in Cork's increasingly sophisticated theatre-goers.[20] Ireland's first purpose-built provincial theatre,[21] it was modelled on the Crow Street Theatre, reconstructed by Barry from the existing Crow Street Music Hall two years previously.[22] Based on Rocque's Survey of 1771, Clark estimates the dimensions of the Cork Theatre to have been 136 feet long by 60 feet wide, making its external dimensions larger than those of Crow Street, which measured 131 feet by 50 feet nine inches,[23] though it had a single gallery, whereas the Crow Street theatre had two.[24] Robert Sillard, writing in 1910, stated that it was 'internally about the size of the London Haymarket previous to its alteration twenty years ago'.[25] As the Crow Street theatre is estimated to have had an audience capacity of about 1,000[26] and the Haymarket's pit and two galleries accommodated a similar number,[27] it is likely that the Cork theatre also had this capacity. According to Hitchcock, a full house yielded £150, based on the current admission prices of 4s, 3s and 2s, for boxes, pit and gallery, respectively.[28]

STAGE IRISHMEN

Although eighteenth-century Irish theatre was a colonial institution, it provided a locus for the convergence of conflicting cultural perspectives.[29] Since 1770, Irish comic actor John O'Keeffe (1747–1833) had performed short comic interludes featuring local scenic settings such as *Harlequin in Derry* and *The Giant's Causeway; or, A Trip to the Dargle*, staged in Belfast.[30] In 1773, his performances brought a new 'Irish' and local dimension to the Cork stage. He presented a 'comic musical interlude' called *Tony Lumpkin's Ramble thro' Cork, with a view of the Mall, Red-House Walk, Sunday's Well, Tavern, Coffee Houses, etc.*[31] From a dispossessed family, O'Keeffe brought aspects of the native perspective in these humorous sketches, in which he delivers a satirical commentary that demonstrates his ability to blend seemingly opposite perspectives, his dual-cultural performances representing emerging Irish modernism.[32] On his next appearance that season Cork harbour was the theme of 'A local interlude called *The Humours of Cove* or the Smugglers' Return, with an exact representation of the town of Cove, the harbour's mouth, Ardbowling Island and Castle' painted by Dublin scene painter John Vandermere (1743–86).[33] An English visitor, in a letter to the editor in the *Hibernian Chronicle*, described a performance in 1780:

> When the tragedy ended, Mr O'Keeffe made his appearance as Tony Lumpkin, in which character for nearly half an hour, without any auxiliary or stage assistance, he amused a very brilliant audience, with a most laughable interlude on the follies of Dress.[34]

Although not a musician, O'Keeffe incorporated indigenous Irish music in his performances.[35] Several of his comic operas (spoken dramas with music) featured the music of Turlough Carolan (1670-1738). In July 1774, he introduced Cork theatre audiences to performances of Carolan's airs by local piper James McDonnell. *The Poor Soldier* (Covent Garden, 1783), performed three times in 1784 and several times thereafter, included airs, mainly by Carolan, from an earlier entertainment entitled *The Shamrock, or St Patrick's Day* (Crow Street, 1777). Another of O'Keeffe's comic operas, *The Castle of Andalusia*, performed in Cork in 1783 and on several occasions during the 1790s, featured Carolan's music and airs 'Voorneen Deelish' and 'Erin go bra', known only by their Irish words at that time.[36] The first Irish staging of Richard Brinsley Sheridan's farce *St Patrick's Day*, in August 1776, featured colourful pageantry in the form of an opening procession of 'Hibernians' featuring 'Irish Kings, Milesians, Druids, Bards, Dermod Roderick O'Connor, Bryan Borro, Sitric O'Neal, Strongbow Earl of Pembroke' with a concluding chorus 'Carolan the Irish Bard', sung by all the characters.[37]

The vocal performances of Robert Owenson (1744–1814) presented an authentic representation of Irish song on the Cork stage during the years 1778 to 1781.[38] Born in County Mayo, then an Irish-speaking region, Robert McKeown (Owenson) was a strolling player for several years. Using his anglicised name, he took his professional début at Covent Garden in 1774, and afterwards settled in Dublin. A rare stage performer in the Irish language, his stage acts during the 1780 season in Cork included a prelude entitled 'Darby Mulroony, an Irish actor', in which he sang 'several favourite songs and planxties of true Irish manufacture [and] a new humorous medley, adapted to the most favourite Irish lilts, called "the Humours of Patrick's Day" or Manus Mc Whackum's Journey to Cork, &c. &c. and his Ramble to the Mardyke Field, to see the Review, with a new song in honour of the Volunteers, adapted to the occasion'. The local Volunteer reviews were a popular spectator event. Owenson's interpolated songs were also Irish: as the character of Teague in George Farquhar's comedy *The Twin Rivals*, he sang 'the old favourite song of 'Dhrimunduh' in English and Irish, and in Kane O'Hara's *Midas* he sang 'The Dublin Cries' and 'Planxty Connor', composed by Carolan.[39] A letter published in the *Hibernian Chronicle* by 'an Englishman' commented on his role in Tobias Smollett's farce *The Reprisal* later in the season: 'Here Mr Owenson in the character of Captain O'Clabber highly entertained us, and introduced a song to the much-admired air of Ellen-a Roon, which pleased me much better than if sung by a Tenducci.'[40] Returning to the Cork Theatre in 1781, Owenson presented a prelude billed as 'several new Songs and Planxties' including 'Ple Raca Nah Riurough', by Carolan the Irish bard, and a new humorous song, called 'Teagues Ramble to Blarney, to see the Review'.[41] In his performances, he aimed to portray the 'national mind'.[42] Owenson's obituary in the *Freeman's Journal* in 1812 referred to his 'exquisite mode of singing his native airs, with their original words'.[43] In these dramatic and musical acts O'Keeffe and Owenson, according to Burke, used the setting of the English stage as 'a site of negotiation between this tradition and a no less vital though subordinate native Irish performance tradition'.[44]

THE RISE OF OPERA

Early newspaper reports of Cork theatre performances reflect a particularly warm reception for leading vocalists. In 1765, although the 'Theatrical Intelligence' published in George Busteed's *Cork Evening Post* was harsh and derogatory towards the current management and dramatic productions, twenty-year-old Anne Cately (1745–89) as Rosetta in Arne's *Love in a Village* was singled out as 'a lovely Syren, indeed perfection', and her benefit performance at the end of the season drew a capacity house at George's Street, filled two hours before the performance commenced.[45] In a season dedicated mainly to operatic works the following year, the castrato singer Giusto Ferdinando Tenducci and soprano Clementina Cremonini (fl. 1763–66) featured in the first Cork performance of Thomas Arne's *Artaxerxes* (1762).[46] Unique within English operatic repertory of the period, this work was all-sung, modelled on Italian *opera seria*, and set to a text by Pietro Metastasio (1698–1782), with elegant tuneful melodies sung in English that became popular as concert pieces.

Opera featured increasingly on theatre bills during the 1780s. Major expansion of the Drury Lane and Covent Garden theatres in 1780 and 1782 created greater audience capacity, and an escalation of production, which influenced its provincial circuits.[47] This was reflected in the repertory brought on tour to Cork. Performances by leading female singers generated substantial editorial commentary in the local press. In 1780, for example, Irish-born contralto Mrs Kennedy's (d. 1793) performance in *The Beggar's Opera* inspired a glowing review in the *Hibernian Chronicle*:

> The sanguine expectations which Mrs. Kennedy's fame had raised in the lovers of music were transcendently gratified by her excellence last

> Saturday, in the songs of Macheath. Her voice is sonorous and clear, and with a dulcet sweetness (particularly in the duet which ended the first act) imparted an idea of what we may imagine seraphic harmony! A peculiar beauty in singing this lady possesses, which capital singers in general too much disregard; she conveys the words of her songs to the auditor, with a distinct articulation; and by this combination of sense and sound (by doing justice to the composer, without robbing the poet of his laurel) she does very great honour to her own judgement.[48]

Mrs Kennedy specialised in singing male roles, and had first sung at Covent Garden in 1776.[49] Tenducci returned in 1783 to sing the role of Arbaces in a revival of Arne's *Artaxerxes*. One of his signature pieces from this opera was 'Water parted from the sea', which he sang at Richard Daly's benefit.[50] At another benefit, he sang 'Sweet Echo', from Arne's masque, *Comus*, accompanied on the viola by František Kotzwara. The latter was one of a large number of instrumentalists employed that year, including several wind players, specifically required to perform the score of *Artaxerxes*. The band performed Kotzwara's 'Turkish music', featuring 'Turkish instruments', after the main play at Mrs Kennedy's benefit in September.[51] This novel piece featured in a concert performance at the Assembly Rooms the following week.[52]

For the 1791 season, Daly announced the engagement of 'the most capital Company in the British Dominions', which featured two of Covent Garden's most eminent singers, tenor Charles Incledon (1763–1826) and soprano Elizabeth Billington (1765–1818), the latter at a nightly fee of £50, supported by Joseph Kelly (d. 1817) and Miss George (b. *c.* 1768).[53] Billington's powers were extolled in the *Cork Gazette*:

> Mr Daly certainly deserves well of the public, when he entertains them with that fascinating siren, Mrs Billington, whose powers can soften rocks, and rend the knotted oak. Six nights are only six ecstatic fits, for the sons of harmony, who must sink into apathy when Billington is gone.[54]

The series of productions had been presented at Dublin's Crow Street in June and July. An augmented orchestra in Cork that year featured cellist Joseph Reinagle and clarinettist John Mahon (1749–1834), both of Oxford, who had recently completed an engagement at Dublin's Rotunda concerts.[55] The season concluded with Cork's first staging of Gluck's *Orpheus and Euridice*:

> The present theatrical season, the most brilliant and successful hitherto experienced, is now nearly concluded. Friday evening next is, perhaps, the last time we shall ever have an opportunity of gratifying our eyes, ears, taste and understanding, with the performance of the unrivalled Billington. Never yet has she (captivating as she is) appeared to such an advantage, as in the charming, elegant Musical drama of Orpheus. Her Euridice is acknowledged to be the most capital exhibition ever yet performed.[56]

For her benefit performance, Billington chose Arnold-Bickerstaffe's *The Maid of the Mill*, incorporating extra musical material, including the popular soprano aria 'The Soldier Tir'd' from *Artaxerxes*.[57]

A touring troupe from London's Haymarket Theatre provided Cork audiences with a taste of Italian opera in September 1808 after the conclusion of the main summer season. Following a successful run at Crow Street,[58] the troupe, headed by Madame Angelica Catalani (1780–1849), arrived in Cork for a three-night engagement. Catalani was the latest sensation on the London stage, having made her début at the King's Theatre at the Haymarket in 1806 in Marcos Portugal's (1762–1830) *La morte di Semiramide*. She was supported on this Irish tour by tenor Giuseppe Siboni, bass Carlo Rovedino (1751–1822), bass Nicolò Miarteni, his wife Maria Miarteni, and Irish tenor Michael Kelly (1762–1826), who both sang and directed the performances.[59] Son of Thomas Kelly, a Catholic Dublin wine merchant, Michael Kelly was concurrently engaged as stage manager at the King's Theatre at the Haymarket.[60] Thomas Cooke led the theatre band.[61]

The programmes consisted of scenes from current Italian operas. The opening performance on 27 September consisted of Johann Mayr's comic opera *Il fanatico per la musica* (1798) and the first act of Portugal's *La morte di Semiramide*. The reviewer found much to commend in Catalani's vocal delivery:

> The various excellencies of a Singer are almost miraculously combined in M. Catalani. We do really think that nature has not withheld one single gift from her, nor science an attainment which could form a perfect singer. Her voice is full, round, and clear; her execution inconceivable; there is a richness of feeling and expression in her delivery which carries her song to the heart; its effect is not describable. Her shake excels for its closeness and regularity anything we have ever heard – and the rapidity and distinctness with which she executes it, are incredible.[62]

Figure 4.1. Madame Catalani; drawing by Adam Buck.

The second performance, on 29 September, consisted of the first act of Giovanni Paisiello's *Didone abbandonata* (1794), and the second act of Valentino Fioravanti's *Il furbo contro il furbo* (1797). The *Cork Mercantile Chronicle* observed that 'there were not any distinct songs in the Opera – but the music was admirable, and she sung with inexpressible skill and sweetness'. The Irishmen Michael Kelly and Thomas Cooke were commended:

> The genius and talents of Mr Cooke are really an ornament to his country, and we have no little gratification in calling him an Irishman. It is a flattering thing to observe two of our countrymen connected in the same performance, so eminently distinguished by ability and science – in a school where it is difficult to excel – and not the characteristic music of the country. The Orchestra, generally speaking, is admirably well filled – better than any we ever recollect before in this City.[63]

Support for Michael Kelly's benefit was particularly advocated by the *Cork Mercantile Chronicle*, not only for his 'musical excellence', but also for possessing 'every good quality of an Irishman'.[64] In his account of the tour in his *Reminiscences*, Kelly recounted that 'The Cork audiences are passionately fond of music; and Catalani's reception was enthusiastic.'[65]

ENTERTAINMENTS

Spoken drama was interpolated with music and dancing. These 'entertainments' provided novelty and variety on all theatrical occasions; their detailed listing on eighteenth-century playbills and newspaper advertisements were a feature of the 'benefit' season. A typical attraction was a selection of vocal items by one of the leading singers, which could be non-theatrical in origin. In 1772 Mrs Pillion's benefit consisted of a performance of the tragedy *The Orphan*, at the end of the second act of which 'Gra ma chree' [*sic*] was sung, and at the end of the fourth act 'a new cantata, composed by Dr Arne, to be sung by Miss Shewcraft'.[66] In 1775, the local lodges of Freemasons sponsored a benefit night for the completion of the Linen Hall, a project of importance to the mercantile members of the brotherhood. It was the first Masonic night of Brother Heaphy's managership. The evening commenced with a typical Grand Masonic Procession to the theatre in full regalia. Between acts of Farquhar's *The Recruiting Officer* and Murphy's *The Old Maid*, Masonic songs were sung, and the evening included Signor Comorelli performing 'a Favourite song' from Piccinni's opera *La buona figliuola* (1760).[67] In 1791 Joseph Kelly's benefit night commenced with 'a Prelude, entitled *The Anacreontic Catch Club*, which featured Kelly singing 'The Anacreontic Song' and three glees.[68] An even more elaborate presentation of glees at Catherine Gough's (1765–1829) benefit in September 1797 consisted of a grand finale to the afterpiece, *The Maid of the Oaks*, consisting of a procession of masqueraded gentlemen singing catches and glees by Callcott, Danby, Michael East and Stephens.[69]

Instrumental music also maintained a place on the bills of entertainments, providing audiences with a taste of contemporary repertoire and performance practice. The range was rich and varied. In August 1776, after the main play, Mr Walsh performed 'a celebrated lesson on the harpsichord, concluding with the favourite Irish air of Loghaber with variations'.[70] This was probably Henry Walsh, organist at St Patrick's Cathedral, Dublin, until 1769, and resident organist at the Rotunda in 1767 and 1768.[71] Michael Arne performed a harpsichord concerto 'between the operas' in August 1777.[72] By the late eighteenth century, solo concertos had become standard *entr'acte* material, particularly on the violin or clarinet. In September 1795, Martha Poole (*c.* 1774–1833) performed two piano concertos at her benefit night at the Theatre Royal, the earliest reference to a piano concerto performance at the theatre.[73]

Stage spectacle with music featured increasingly during the 1790s, when dramatic themes and musical works evocative of revolutionary France appeared on bills. As early as September 1789, an entertainment entitled *The Triumph of Liberty; or the Destruction of the Bastille* was presented at the Cork Theatre Royal, only a month after its premiere in London.[74] In 1792 Mr Holden's benefit included a musical battle piece 'adapted by himself, called *The Bastille*, to be executed by above sixty performers'.[75] The British war with France, which began in 1793, provided further musico-dramatic inspiration. For Charles Kemble's benefit night in 1797, *King Henry the Fifth or, The Conquest of France* was performed with 'the overture, marches, and music, incidental to the piece […] by The Full Band of the Elgin Fencibles'.[76] An overture by François-Joseph Gossec (1734–1829) performed by the 'full band' in 1793[77] was likely to have been one of this composer's forty symphonies that had been published by this time.[78] Works such as these remained a colourful addition to the Crow Street Company's programmes for at least another decade, demanding skilled wind players, who featured increasingly from the late 1790s. Among these were English oboist William T. Parke, who performed in 1796, and clarinettist and military bandsman James Tutton (1761–1817), who performed with the theatre band in 1800.[79] Trumpeter Henry Willman and his brother Thomas, a clarinettist, appeared with the theatre band in the early years of the nineteenth century.[80]

As rank-and-file musicians were seldom listed, it is difficult to determine the constitution of the Cork theatre band. The leaders, who performed solos between the acts, usually appeared on the bills, and were customarily granted an end-of-season benefit. John Bianchi, Thomas Cooke (1782–1848) and James Barton (*c.* 1785–*c.* 1850) were successive leaders of the Crow Street band, but the list shows that the leader did not always travel to Cork for the season, and would have been replaced by a local such as Mr Reynolds (see table 4.1). English cellist Francis Attwood (b. *c.* 1775) arrived in Cork in the summer of 1800 and joined the theatre band for two successive seasons.[81] Thomas Simpson Cooke, Dublin-born tenor, violinist and composer, led the theatre orchestra for the Cork season from 1802 until 1805.[82]

The state of Irish theatre was the subject of John Wilson Croker's satirical work entitled *Familiar Epistles to Frederick E. Jones, Esq. on the Present State of the Irish Stage* (1804), calling for more dramatic material from Irish sources.[83] Scathing in reference to Cooke, Croker criticises the theatre publicity system that 'with shameless puff will tell ye/That Cook is equal to Corelli'. He describes Cooke as 'the modest and diffident Mr Tom Cooke, who played on *eight* different instruments for his *own* benefit; I am sure it was neither benefit nor pleasure to any one else. The person writes *new* overtures, to all the operas which are imported to our stage, beginning generally with *chords*, and ending with an Irish *jig*, and this he calls composition.'[84]

Robert Bowden came to Cork with the theatre band in 1804.[85] During the 1805 and 1806 seasons at Crow Street, his solo violin performances had incorporated Irish airs, and his 'Grand Irish Medley' was performed on several occasions.[86] He returned to Cork in the autumn of 1806 and took up permanent residence there, becoming one of the city's foremost professional musicians during four decades.[87] As leader of the theatre band from 1806, he frequently performed *entr'acte* violin concertos. In 1808, his benefit performance included several of his songs and '*A Grand Irish Medley Overture* [...] in which will be introduced *The Original Irish Funeral Dirge*'.[88] This overture was a rare example for the time of new orchestral music based on Irish themes.

Table 4.1. Band musicians at Cork Theatre Royal, 1748–1811.

YEAR	FIRST VIOLIN	OTHER MUSICIANS
1748	Mr Delahoyd	
1754		Murphy (German fl)
1769	Mr Reynolds	
1770	Mr [Charles] Clagget?	
1772	Mr Reynolds	
1773	Mr Reynolds	
1774	Mr Reynolds	
1776	Mr O'Neill ('conducted')	
1777	Mr Valentine?	Arne (harpsichord)
1778	Mr Valentine?	
1779		Crawford (guitar)
1781	Mr Gray (?)	
1782	Mr Kelly	Rackaman (cl)
1783		Kotzwara (vla), Bartoli, Stevens, Gani, Lockhart, Erskine (ob), Rakeman (cl)
1790	Mr Mountain (?)	
1791	Charles Weichsel	Reinagle (vcl), Mahon (cl), Billington (db)
1796	John Bianchi	Haigh (vcl), Parke (ob)
1797	John Bianchi	Haigh (vcl)
1800		Attwood (vcl), Tutton (cl)
1801	John Bianchi	Attwood (vcl) – Spring season
	Mr Smith [Aug]	Attwood (vcl) – Summer season
1802	Tom Cooke	
1803	Tom Cooke	
1804	Tom Cooke	R. Bowden (vln, vla), H. Willman (tr), T. Willman (cl)
1805	Tom Cooke	H. Willman (tr)
1806	Robert Bowden	
1807	Robert Bowden	Barron (cl), Sardo (hn)
1808	Robert Bowden	
1811	[James] Barton	

AMATEUR THEATRE

From the late eighteenth century, advertisements for amateur theatrical productions in support of local charities occasionally appeared in the press, generally involving a core of gentlemen amateur actors, together with a few professional actresses. In February 1783, the 'Gentlemen's Theatre on the Long Quay' (Patrick Street), for example, was the venue for a performance of O'Keeffe's *The Agreeable Surprise* 'for the benefit of a Gentlewoman in distress'.[89] An intensification of charitable activity during the early years of the nineteenth century prompted the founding of the Apollo Society in 1805. Among those active in its establishment were Richard Milliken, actors Charles Connor (1788–1826) and Frank Seymour (d. 1854), and grocer and wine merchant Edward A. Scott, who was the secretary of the original committee.[90] Other amateur members included Michael Rogers, Master of Ceremonies at the Assembly Room from 1814, Dr Bernard, Dr Mann, Daniel Connell (attorney), John Toleken (jeweller), and Catholic dentist Daniel Corbett (*c*.1785–1855).[91] Among the local professional actresses-singers who featured in the society from its early years was Miss Webb, who had arrived in Cork in 1799 and was a student of Francis Attwood.[92] Peter Smith directed an amateur orchestra, consisting of members of the Musical Society.[93] An announcement of the society's first production in October 1805 sought 'Theatrical and musical amateurs' and welcomed donations of costumes.[94]

Beginning with a performance in aid of the House of Recovery, nineteen charitable performances were given at the Theatre Royal, George's Street, followed in April by a round of benefits for the professional actresses, before a final charitable performance (see Table 4.2) The schedule of performances for the inaugural season provides evidence of the vigour and productivity of the society. In addition to its major charitable role in the city, the society filled a gap in theatrical entertainment during the winter/spring season. Much of the repertory demanded substantial musical input, such as O'Keeffe's *The Castle of Andalusia*, with airs from Handel, Vento, Giordani, Bertoni, Arne and Carolan, and an overture and new airs by Arnold.

The society achieved due prominence in the local press: its advertisements appeared regularly in the *Cork Mercantile Chronicle*, and its activities received ample attention from John Boyle in his satirical journal *Boyle's Magazine*.[95] He published a poem 'To the Apollo Society' in February 1807, one verse of which lists the recipients of its proceeds:

Table 4.2. Apollo Society performances for 1805–6 season.

DATE	TITLE	BENEFICIARY
28 Oct	*The Merchant of Venice* (Shakespeare)	House of Recovery
	The Agreeable Surprize (O'Keeffe)	
2 Dec	*The Way To Get Married*	Lying-in Hospital
	The Deserter (C. Dibdin)	
	[*The Padlock* listed in 2nd advertisement]	
17 Dec	*She Stoops To Conquer* (Goldsmith)	Schools of Industry
	Netley Abbey (Pearce/Shield)	
13 Jan	*The Inconstant*	Lock Ward
	The Deserter (C. Dibdin)	
10 Feb	*The Busy Body* (Centlivre)	Dispensary and Humane Society
	The Farmer	
3 March	*The Weathercock*	North Infirmary
	The Lying Valet (Garrick)	
	The Flitch of Bacon (Shield)	
20 March	*The Castle of Andalusia* (O'Keeffe/Arnold)	Debtors' Charity
	The Weathercock	
7 April	*The Beggar's Opera* (Gay/Pepusch)	House of Industry
	The Weathercock	
12 April	*The Busy Body*	Benevolent Society
	Sprigs of Laurel	
19 April	*The Will*	Mrs Johnston's Benefit
	The Farmer	
21 April	*The Dramatist*	
	Rosina (Shield)	
29 April	*The Farmer* (afterpiece)	Mrs Johnston's Benefit ?
12 May	*Love in a Village* (Arne)	Miss Webb's Benefit
30 June	*The Heir at Law* (Colman)	Charitable Institutions of the City
	Matrimony (Kenney/King)	

First, grateful females raise your thankful voice;
You, from contagious burning fever freed;
Debtors, in new-born freedom who rejoice;
Ye myriads succoured in the hour of need;
Ye poor, by industry from want preserved;
Abandoned orphans saved from guilt and shame –
'Tis yours to tell how well they have deserved,
Sing grateful P[…]s and their work proclaim.[96]

Established during the 1780s by English equestrian performer Philip Astley (1742–1814), the Amphitheatre Royal, Patrick Street, was reopened in 1803 as a theatrical venue following major alterations,[97] and used for the Apollo Society's first two productions of its second season in November and December 1806.[98] In March 1807, a Mr Clarke leased the Patrick Street theatre for a season of plays, and the Apollo Society returned to the George's Street theatre to continue its season.[99] Having been active as one of the society's professional members since its inception, singer John Magrath was granted his first benefit in May 1807, for which he enlisted the Cork Catch and Glee Club, of which he was a member, to sing between the play and the afterpiece.[100]

In April 1810 the society staged a benefit play for its musical director Peter Smith, 'driven by the pressure of Bad Times', due to the failure of his music retail business.[101] In May 1810, Apollo Society members took the lead roles in a benefit performance sponsored by the Freemasons, which included O'Keeffe's comic opera, *The Poor Soldier* (1783), which, in addition to its Irish songs arranged by William Shield (1748–1829), featured a song composed by Robert Bowden.[102] English actress and singer Miss Macauley (d. *c.* 1836) featured in the society's productions in 1810, and her benefit in December of that year was the last performance before the society lapsed.[103]

The society was revived in September 1814[104] and presented a substantial winter season at the George's Street Theatre Royal.[105] Renewed support for the society included donations of 'two suits of silk clothes' by William Beamish and 'a suit of embroidered silk' by George Atkins.[106] Towards the end of the season, benefit nights were held for Mr McCarthy, in acknowledgement of his 'active and gratuitous professional exertions' in directing the society's productions, and for box-keeper Felix Daly.[107] A performance of the Arnold/ Coleman's comedy *The Mountaineers* in April featured members of the Harmonic Society, playing the parts of the muleteer and goatherds, singing several glees during the course of the play, and Miss Webb also sang a solo by popular demand.[108] One of the professional actresses engaged during the season was Harriet Smithson (1800–54), daughter of the manager of a strolling theatre company based in Ennis, County Clare. She was later to be the wife of Hector Berlioz (1803–69), who admired her Shakespearian performances on the Paris stage. Her benefit night in April included a one-act burletta by William Barnes Rhodes, *Bombastes Furioso* (1810).[109]

The Patrick Street theatre had in the meantime changed hands. There is no record of performances during the first half of 1812, and in July 'all the scenery, machinery, lustres, properties, timber work, iron work, etc.' were advertised for sale by auction, with the advice that 'the entire of the above articles are new, and well worth the attention of Managers'.[110] In June 1815, the building was offered for lease 'during a minority of 15 years, either as a Theatre, or with permission to the tenant to turn it to whatever other use he may think proper'.[111] By December 1815 it was owned by a Mr Deane, renamed as 'the Apollo Theatre', and re-occupied by the society.[112] A press notice reported that

> an Artist of the first abilities has been employed on its decoration for several weeks, and that in point of comfort, convenience, and elegance of appearance, they challenge the Theatres of the United Kingdom to present a more tasteful and splendid coup d'oeil.[113]

The refurbishment was also commented on in *The Freeholder*:

> This valuable Association resumes its labours to-morrow evening – and we take upon us to say, in as tasteful and splendid a Theatre, for its size, as any in the United Kingdom. Too much praise cannot be given to the Proprieter, Mr Deane, for the spirit and liberality with which he went to a vast expense in this fitting it up for the public – and also for his benevolence in giving it to the Society at the very moderate and inadequate charge of only ten guineas a night.[114]

A performance of John O'Keeffe's comic opera *Fontainebleu* received an enthusiastic review in the *Cork Mercantile Chronicle* in January 1816.[115] In the same year, the society held a benefit night for its new musical leader, Robert Bowden, featuring his setting of Walter Scott's narrative poem *The Lady of the Lake* (1810).[116] By this time, the taking of benefits by professional members had begun to cause tensions within the society. A correspondent in the *Southern Reporter* in March 1817 noted that the society's performers had agreed not to support benefit nights by actors or actresses.[117] Nonetheless, Harriet Smithson took another benefit night in March 1817.

In 1818, local auctioneer John McDonnell became proprietor of the George's Street Theatre, and introduced new arrangements for a series of productions during the spring assizes,

> the Corps to consist of the gentlemen of the Apollo Society, aided by some excellent Amateurs from Dublin, and a selection of Ladies from the Crow Street Boards, Miss Whitaker, Miss L. Kelly, Miss Johnson and others. For supplying the latter, and a Leader and other Principals for the Orchestra, together with the free use of the House, the Patentee receives one half of the Receipts, the other half to go, as the fruits of this laudable Society have always gone, to the use of the Public Charities.[118]

This commercial arrangement in effect eroded the Apollo Society. In 1822, the gentlemen of the 'juvenile Apollo Society' participated in a benefit play for Miss Stanfield at the Theatre Royal,[119] and, apart from a brief revival in 1834, there are no subsequent records of its activities.[120] In November 1818 the Patrick Street theatre building was leased by the Society of Arts, another of Milliken's initiatives, and converted to an exhibition area for its recently acquired collection of Canova casts.[121] It was subsequently acquired by John McDonnell, whose Great Auction Rooms and City Mart were based at this location from the 1830s, and it later became the publishing office of the *Cork Examiner*.[122]

The level of amateur dramatic activity in the years from 1805 until 1818 indicated a dedicated and accomplished core of performers. Frank Seymour, one of its members, later reflected on its contribution to the city:

> At no period of our local history was Cork so replete with social and elegant exhilaration, as during the existence of the Apollo Society, when the histrionic genius and talent of the elite of its inhabitants diffused a spirit of unalloyed gratification, together with rational and sentimental instruction among all its classes [...][123]

Its operational difficulties and ultimate demise arose, however, from the realities of theatre logistics and the demands of professional actors and actresses.

As a flourishing performing society that gained wide popular admiration, the Apollo Society survived in memory and was subsequently written into the city's cultural history, recollected by Cork-born writers Denny Lane (1818–95) and Thomas Crofton Croker (1798–1854).

PROFESSIONAL THEATRE

The repertory of professional companies began to show a clearer distinction between operatic and dramatic productions, and several seasons were dedicated primarily to opera. The Crow Street company presented both spring and summer seasons in Cork. Having featured in the 1816 winter season at Crow Street, English tenor John Braham (1774–1856) and Irish soprano Mary Byrne headed the bills in a theatre season during the spring assizes in 1817 that included Henry Bishop's *Guy Mannering* (1816), Thomas Dibdin's *Family Quarrels* (1802), Braham's *Narensky* (1814), Cobb and Storace's *The Haunted Tower* (1789) and *The Siege of Belgrade* (1791), and Cherubini's *Lodoïska* (1791).[124] From one of Dublin's wealthiest Catholic families, Mary Byrne had made her début at the Crow Street theatre the previous December, following study with Giovanni Liverati (1772–1846) in London. Her grandfather, Edward Byrne (d. 1804), was a wealthy Dublin merchant and prominent member of the Catholic Committee. Her father, also named Edward Byrne, had recently lost his fortune, prompting her to take to the Dublin stage as a protégé of Daly's successor, Frederick Jones (1759–1834).[125] *The Freeholder* reported on the extensive refurbishment of the interior of the theatre, including 'an entire new ceiling representing the seasons', painted by Chalmers and Marinari.[126]

FRANCIS (FRANK) SEYMOUR

Frank Seymour, a founder member of the Apollo Society, had in the meantime launched his professional acting career.[127] For his first engagement at Crow Street in 1818, he played the role of Octavian in *The Mountaineers*.[128] A review of his part in Sheil's tragedy *Bellamira* the following June noted that he had 'much to unlearn as well as to learn'.[129] He announced a benefit night, with the assistance of gentlemen amateurs at the Cork Theatre Royal in April 1818, adding the explanation that he was 'from particular circumstances, being obliged to make the Stage a temporary profession'.[130]

In 1821 he returned to Cork and established his own professional company, who performed the following May at the Tuckey Street Assembly Room, newly fitted-up, featuring Seymour, Montague Talbot (1774–1831), Mr M. McCarthy, Mr James, Miss Walpole and Mrs J. Kelly.[131] Montague Talbot was another Irish provincial actor-manager, who had sublet his theatre in Belfast the previous year, and also relinquished his involvement with the Derry theatre.[132] For the late summer season, the company performed at the George's Street Assembly Room, headed by Mary Byrne, opposite the new company from Dublin's Hawkins Street Theatre at the Theatre Royal.[133] Byrne's end-of-season benefit consisted of Dibdin's *Lionel and Clarissa*, followed by the 'Musical Entertainment' of *The Marriage of Figaro*,

> as performed with the most unbounded applause upwards of one hundred nights at the Theatre Royal, Covent Garden, partly taken from Beaumarchais's celebrated Comedy of *La folle journee*, and partly from the Italian opera of *Le Nozze di Figaro*, the music composed by Mozart, and adapted to the English stage by H.R. Bishop.[134]

The Freeholder commented that:

> Too much praise cannot be bestowed on Seymour, for the highly effective Corps he has before the Public, to meet the very heavy expenditure, must require, what he so richly deserves, the best patrons from the Lovers of the Drama. The season, strictly speaking, is a musical one – and who has not the ear for the dulcet tones warbled every night at the Assembly rooms?[135]

Despite its initial success, Seymour's company was short-lived.[136] He moved to Glasgow, where he was actor and stage manager at the Theatre Royal, and in 1825 he acquired a lease on the Caledonian Theatre, which under his management became the city's minor theatre, featuring musical productions and equestrian displays.[137] This theatre was destroyed by fire in January 1829,[138] and later that year Seymour moved to Belfast, where he became manager of the Theatre Royal.

Financial difficulties continued to frustrate the promoters of professional theatre in Cork. By the end of the 1821 season, despite the productions of a remodelled company from Dublin's new Theatre Royal at Hawkins Street, *The Freeholder* reported that 'notwithstanding the Theatre presents high attraction, it does not draw houses'.[139] A solution was again sought in the provision of a major musical attraction the following year, 1822, with the engagement of Mary Anne Wilson (1802–67) for the spring season at the Cork Theatre Royal. This young stage and concert singer had made her début at Drury Lane in 1821, earning a total of £10,000 in that year.[140]

A shift in public taste for opera spread from London during the 1820s. The enthusiastic reception of William Ayrton's production of Mozart's *Don Giovanni* at London's Haymarket Theatre in 1817 precipitated a vogue for adaptations of foreign operas.[141] London critics had begun to comment on the disparity between English and Italian operas, viewing the native genre unfavourably.[142] From 1824, William Abbott's Hawkins Street company performed at the Cork Theatre Royal under the musical directorship of Alexander Lee (1802–51).[143] In 1825, Lee directed the first Cork performance of Weber's *Der Freischütz*, for which the orchestra was 'considerably enlarged'.[144] *The Constitution* reported that 'for brilliancy and splendour we have never witnessed the like before', praising 'the effective strength and ability of the Orchestra, under the direction of Mr Bowden'.[145]

Over the next five years, *The Freeholder* reported ongoing difficulties encountered by the theatre manager in drawing houses, despite the engagement of contralto singer and actress Lucia Vestris (1797–1856) in 1826 and 1828,[146] and the introduction of 'second' (late entry) prices of 3s, 2s and 1s at half past nine in 1827.[147] Catalani's engagement during the spring season at the Theatre Royal in 1829 reversed the trend. Her first performance was a 'Grand Miscellaneous Concert' for which the orchestra was 'considerably augmented', followed by a performance of the comedy *The Taming of the Shrew*.[148] A similar arrangement was adopted on her second and third nights: short dramatic pieces framed a 'Grand Musical Intermezzo, in 2 parts' consisting of glees, Italian operatic solos and duets, ballads and national airs sung by Catalani, with Miss Hamilton, Mr Shuter and Mr Latham. After a fourth concert, Catalani's benefit, the *Southern Reporter* announced her re-engagement for four more performances.[149]

On the closing of the season in May, the writer in *The Constitution* reported 'a longer and a more successful season than is usual in Cork', provided 'at great risk and heavy expense'.[150] Frank Seymour resumed his connection with Cork theatre during the 1830s. As manager in Belfast from 1829 to 1831, his repertory had included a high proportion of musical mainpieces and afterpieces, featuring leading singers, a strategy that had proved effective in drawing audiences.[151] Having relinquished this involvement in 1831, he arrived in Cork in October 1832, formed a new company, and leased the

Theatre Royal from John McDonnell for a short season. The theatre had served as a venue for a succession of successful concerts since 1831. Seymour appointed William Forde as musical director and established an orchestra, led by Dublin violinist Robert Mackintosh. For William Forde's benefit on 15 November three theatrical pieces were staged, preceded by a 'Vocal and Instrumental Concert', including the overtures to *Der Freischütz* and *Oberon*.[152] A list of the orchestra members published in 1835 indicated that at least five of the players – Mackintosh, Powell, Harrington and the Griesbachs – were Dublin professionals. Promoted as a concert venue by McDonnell and William Forde since the 1820s, the Theatre Royal enjoyed a heyday as a concert venue during the 1830s, an environment that facilitated the enrichment of theatre music (see chapters 6 and 7).

Table 4.3. Cork Theatre Royal Orchestra, 1835.

Violins	Mr [Robert] Mackintosh, leader
	Mr Griesbach
	Mr Smith
	Mr Warde
	Mr Kelly
Principal tenor	Mr Forde
Principal flute	Mr W. Forde
Principal hautboy	Mr Griesbach
Principal clarinet	Mr Tigh
Principal horn	Mr Edwards
Second horn	Mr Edmonds
Principal violoncello	Mr Powell
Second violoncello	Mr Musgrave
Principal double bass	Mr [Thomas] Harrington
Double drums	Mr Scott
Director of the Musical Dept.	Mr W. Forde

Following their Cork spring season, Seymour and his company toured the principal towns of the south and west of the country. This arrangement continued over the following years, and Seymour became a well-known figure in provincial life, managing theatres in Waterford, Limerick, Tralee and Galway. Among his leading names during the 1834–5 season and again in 1838 was actor Ira Aldridge (1807–67), 'the African Roscius', who headed the company's bills for several extended periods.[153] Seymour's contribution to Cork's theatrical life was acknowledged in an editorial piece in the *Cork Standard* in 1837:

> Mr Seymour, the Lessee of George's street takes his benefit tonight, and deserves a good one. This gentleman is the only one spirited enough to bring down a dramatic Company of any kind to Cork to enliven the dullness, and occasionally to animate the numbed state of our Theatrical world here. He is an untiring public servant in the most precarious and most task-begetting walk of public servitude. His efforts are at the best, but indifferently remunerated, taking to account the deep mental responsibility, and high intellectual power his profession demands.[154]

The arrival in November 1834 of an Italian opera company led by Italian baritone Giuseppe de Begnis (1793–1849) was welcomed in the local press.[155] Having concluded a season at Dublin's Hawkins Street Theatre the previous month, the company performed six nights of Italian operas, 'in the same style as at the King's Theatre'.[156] De Begnis had directed operas at Bath from 1823, and performed in Dublin in 1829.[157] The opening performance was Rossini's *Tancredi*, for which 'books of the opera, in Italian and in English', were available at Bowden's Music Shop and at the theatre. The performances also included *Il barbiere di Siviglia*, *Otello* and *Il fanatico per la musica*, and several of the performances incorporated 'Grand Concerts'.

Opera dominated the late summer theatre seasons by the Hawkins Street Company at the Theatre Royal throughout the 1830s, who now availed of the professional orchestra. In September 1834, John McDonnell announced the arrival of a 'first-rate Operatic Company', headed by Miss Byfield, George Stansbury (1800–45) and soprano Jane Shirreff (1811–83), who played Susanna in the opening production, *The Marriage of Figaro*, billed in *The Constitution* as an 'Unprecedented Combination of Musical Talent'. The *Cork Mercantile Chronicle* writer opined that 'If our spirited Lessee produces such entertainments as these, he will be sure to bring crowded houses, for there is nothing tells in Cork, like Opera.'[158] In the same month, the company presented Bellini's *La sonnambula*, 'the first time it has been attempted out of London'.[159] This was its first Irish performance; it was not staged in Dublin until the following February, with Shirreff, Byfield and Stansbury in the leading roles.[160] *The Constitution* reported that 'The melodies throughout the Opera are refined, without being abstruse; it has all been arranged from the piano-forte score for the Orchestra by our talented fellow-citizen, Mr William Forde.'[161] In August 1838, under the management of George Bennett, the Hawkins Street company featured Michael Balfe (1808–70), Emma Romer (1814–68) and John Templeton (1802–86), in a season of opera that included a performance of Balfe's *The Maid of Artois* (1836), its first Irish performance.[162]

The inclusion of concerts with theatre performances had become commonplace in the 1830s, and the range of admission prices undoubtedly widened the social spectrum of the audience. Informality and good humour appear to have prevailed. In September 1833, in a preview to a benefit for William Forde, the *Cork Evening Herald* advised patrons that 'The frequent calls for encores have a considerable effect in retarding the entertainments to a late hour, which the Deities of the Gallery should not forget'.[163] In August 1838, reporting on a benefit performance for Jane Shirreff, which concluded with a concert, the writer in the *Southern Reporter* reported that:

> After the Concert there was a call for the old favourite 'I'm over young to marry yet', which was, however, unheeded, and the Orchestra was directed to play 'God save the Queen'; but loyalty itself was forgotten in the enthusiasm, not alone of the Olympic inhabitants, but even of those in the more lowly regions, and we doubt if even the Trumpet or Big Drum, heard a note of its own music.[164]

THEATRICAL RIVALRY

In January 1837, Watkins Burroughs, actor and manager of the Belfast theatre, leased the George's Street theatre for his company. Despite lowering of admission prices to 1s 6d for boxes, 1s for the pit and 6d for the gallery, the houses were poor.[165] His principal guest performer was the Norwegian violinist Ole Bull (1810–80), who performed between minor dramatic pieces. Seymour and his company leased the theatre again in May, joined by the young actor Barry Sullivan (1821–91), who became one of Seymour's key players.[166]

Theatrical rivalry intensified in the early weeks of 1838, when John Collins, a Dublin actor and strolling player, set up a rival theatre in George's Street. His 'Pavillion' was a circus-like tent, in which he staged melodramas and occasional Shakespearian performances. Collins's wife was a rope dancer, who added further novelty to the bills. As his fit-up thrived, Collins erected a small wooden theatre at Nelson Place, retaining the name of 'Collins's Pavillion'. Opened in October 1841 under licence from the mayor, the new venue enjoyed overflowing audiences, at the highly competitive rates of one shilling for the boxes, 6d for the pit, and 3d for the gallery.[167] A letter to the editor of the *Cork Examiner* in 1844 written by Charles Beamish noted that Collins had constructed 'an apparatus to manufacture gas' to supply his theatre, whereby his weekly expense for 60 lights burning for five hours each night was only eight shillings.[167] By 1847, however, his theatre no longer functioned.[168]

Collins's successes had not augured well for the George's Street Theatre. Early in 1838, following conflict between Seymour and McDonnell over rent, Seymour relinquished his lease, and with financial assistance from Kyrle Alleyne Deane, a local solicitor, he refurbished a disused diorama in Cook Street for use as a theatre.[169] For the inaugural season, beginning in April, he engaged the celebrated harpist Nicolas-Charles Bochsa (1789–1856), whose five performances on successive nights were framed by minor theatrical pieces from Seymour's stock company (see page 159). The following account appeared in the *Southern Reporter*:

> The performance at this very beautifully fitted up place of amusement last night was highly gratifying. The very great improvement which the Theatre has undergone during the Easter Recess deserves to be noticed. The Boxes are very tasteful and most comfortable, the Pit equally so, and the Gallery larger and capacious. We should say that at the present prices it would hold very near the George's street house. The scenery is excellent and the stage large and well proportioned. Indeed on the whole we are greatly pleased at the interior of the house and have no doubt but when the comfort of the Public is so strictly attended to, Mr Seymour will reap the benefit of it.[170]

In June, the first performance of 'a local drama', *The Groves of Blarney*, composed by Alexander D. Roche, to a libretto by Anna Maria Hall, was presented at the benefit night of Mr and Mrs Martyn and Scottish soprano Elizabeth Inverarity (1813–46).[171] Over the next three years, Seymour's bills of melodramas and minor theatrical pieces were animated by the appearances of a number of celebrated musical performers. The 1839 spring season saw the return of Bochsa to the theatre, with Mrs Bishop and Miss Riviere, followed by a series of performances by the Distin family of brass players and guitarist Trinidad Huerta (see page 162). Reference to the theatre band rarely appeared in advertising notices, but in 1838, a preview of a benefit night for band leader Peter Smith described him as 'our very clever fellow citizen [...] the able leader of the band at the Royal Victoria Theatre. For many years Mr Smith has occupied a prominent position as a profound musician and excellent performer on the violin'.[172]

Full-length opera was received with renewed fervour during the 1838 summer season at the George's Street Theatre Royal, when Michael Balfe (1808–70) made his first Cork appearance, with Emma Romer (1814–68) and John Templeton (1802–86). The season opened in late July and consisted of a number of full-scale operatic performances, including *La Sonnambula*, *Il barbiere di Siviglia* and *Der Freischütz*. *The Constitution* noted that 'the present season is one of the most prosperous remembered for years. The houses have been throughout nightly crowded with the rank and beauty of the city and county'.[173] A performance on 8 August of Balfe's *The Maid of Artois* (1836) was announced as 'the first time in this Kingdom'.[174] *The Constitution* asserted that 'the attendance at the Theatre has fully evinced the high estimation in which Miss Romer, Mr Templeton and Mr Balfe are held in Cork, as the best operatic artists that have ever appeared here'.[177] A review in the *Southern Reporter* showed some discernment in questioning Balfe's introduction of a song in *La Sonnambula*, stating that this opera 'is so rich in musical beauties that it is difficult to ingraft anything on it which can bear the contrast'.[176] The new full-length operas, in both Italian and English, were establishing new conventions, moving away from the patchwork offerings of previous decades. But some old favourites lingered among a week-long series of performances headed by the veteran tenor John Braham in 1839, consisting of *The Devil's Bridge*, *Love in a Village*, *Fra Diavolo*, *The Siege of Belgrade*, *Masaniello* and concluding with *Der Freischütz*, the orchestra led by Dublin violinist Richard Levey.[177]

It was clear by this time that concerts and operas occupied the foreground at the theatre, as musical content had all but eclipsed spoken drama, whether in the grand productions at George's Street, or in Seymour's Victoria theatre. Fluid and ever-changing, theatre bills represented the managers' best efforts to fill houses by providing dramatic entertainment across a wide range of taste categories. Struggling to gain patronage for drama, management cloaked the majority of bills with items of musical interest. By 1840, theatre had been given over to opera and music to such an extent that the boundaries between theatre and concert performance had become blurred. Following the burning of the Theatre Royal in April 1840, however, the Victoria theatre was elevated, as the Royal Victoria Theatre, to the status of principal venue for theatre, hosting both local and touring companies for several seasons each year.

5

'A REFINED PUBLIC': MUSIC FOR CHARITY AND AMUSEMENT

'View of South Mall', by Alphonse Dousseau (1796–1876).
LLYFRGELL GENEDLAETHOL CYMRU/NATIONAL LIBRARY OF WALES

The dissolution of the Irish parliament in Dublin, which transferred legislative power to London, under the Act of Union (1800), altered the geo-political landscape of Ireland. Although Cork's elite had been pro-Union, a growing sense of alienation emerged among the city's middle classes during the post-Union years. The number of boroughs had been drastically reduced, excluding all but the most powerful local contenders from the political arena. The withholding of Catholic Emancipation led to a growing political agitation among the city's Catholic middle classes, who also sought repeal of the Act of Union, heightening tensions between a Protestant state and a national Catholic Church. The emergence of Daniel O'Connell (1775–1847) as a leader of the newly formed Catholic Association (1823) amplified the demand for Emancipation by constitutional means, and Munster quickly became an O'Connell stronghold. A strong voice for the Catholic perspective was provided in the *Cork Mercantile Chronicle*, a continuation of William Flyn's *Hibernian Chronicle*

Figure 5.1. Cork from the Mardyke walk. CORK CITY LIBRARY

from 1802, which from 1812 was under the editorship of Rev. John England, becoming the city's first overtly Catholic newspaper.

Cork and its surrounding region continued to prosper economically in the years following the Union. The demand for military and naval provisioning during the French and Napoleonic Wars (1793–1815) generated substantial trade for Cork suppliers and contractors, and a surge in the construction of barracks and naval fortifications generated high demand for building materials.[1] Physical expansion at the turn of the nineteenth century led to the filling in of many of the city's remaining waterways. Although the city centre continued to sustain a high population density, many of its merchants built houses in the fashionable new suburbs of Blackrock, Sunday's Well and Montenotte.

In addition to Emancipation, Cork's Catholic middle classes and liberal Protestants sought reform of the Corporation, which remained subject to the control of the Friendly Club, retaining civic authority among a close circle of Protestant families. The city's Catholic merchants wielded considerable economic power, however, and in 1819, the Chamber of Commerce was founded to provide a business forum that was independent of the Corporation-dominated Committee of Merchants. By the 1820s, a defensive stance was evident among the city's conservative Protestants. Religious societies became more active, among them the Church Missionary Society and the Religious Tract Society, which was the southern branch of the Irish Evangelical Society.[2] An anti-Catholic and anti-Emancipation society, the Cork Brunswick Constitutional Club was founded in 1827.[3]

The emergence of several new societies and associations based on intellectual and cultural pursuits during the early decades of the nineteenth century led to the term 'cultural renaissance' being used in relation to Cork.[4] A few of these were to have lasting significance, such as the Cork Library Society (1792), the Royal Cork Institution (1803),[5] the Society for Promoting the Fine Arts (1815), the Philosophical and Literary Society (1819), and the Cork Literary and Scientific Society (1820), which flourished under strong intellectual leadership and patronage by merchants, bankers and businessmen.[6]

MUSIC AND CHARITY

Widespread poverty among the city's lower classes prompted several new charitable initiatives around the turn of the century. Public health was a major concern. A prominent figure in charitable provision was Unitarian minister Rev. Thomas Dix Hincks (1767–1857), who in 1799 was involved in the establishment of the Cork Society for Bettering the Condition and Increasing the Comforts of the Poor, linked to a wider network of similar organisations in Dublin and London established the previous year.[7] Pioneering local doctor John Milner Barry (1768–1822) was a key figure in its activities. Under his supervision, and under the auspices of the Benevolent Society (formed in 1795, associated with the Dispensary and Humane Society), the Fever Hospital and its associated House of Recovery were established in 1802, serving a vital role in the city.[8] Martin Farrell's Academy, a prominent private school for boys, staged charity plays in 1801 and 1802 for the proposed House of Recovery.[9] The performance in 1801 featured visiting musicians John Bianchi and Francis Attwood, who led a local orchestra for the event, raising £177 2s 6d for the charity.[10]

To counteract the high level of petty crime and idleness among the poor children of Cork, a School of Industry was founded by the Society for Bettering the Condition and Increasing the Comforts of the Poor in 1801, described in the *Cork Advertiser* as

> an Institution entirely new […], the nature of which is, to educate the children of the poor to habits of Industry, by employing and feeding them during the day, and allowing them at night to return and lodge with their friends. The number of these children, now on the lists, considerably exceeds one hundred; and though the undertaking is quite an infant one, the progress they have already made in the different occupations taught them, and particularly in the making of Straw hats, is such as to suggest hopes, that the Institution will, one day, be able to maintain itself.[11]

Involvement in the running of the school became fashionable among the upper-class ladies of the city.[12] In August 1801, a 'Grand Sacred Oratorio', consisting of excerpts from Handel oratorios and Haydn's *The Creation*, was organised to raise funds, directed by James Roche and James Magrath. *The Creation* was first performed in London the previous year and excerpts from the work had featured in a Dublin oratorio performance in April 1801.[13] A report of the Cork performance in August affirmed the heightened aesthetic value ascribed to oratorio:

> The Oratorio of yesterday, performed in Christ Church, far exceeded any musical effort ever made in this city. It must have convinced the numerous and polite audience, of the progressive improvement in this country, of that delightful Art, which excites all the noble, the generous, and tender passions, and is so powerfully conducive [*sic*] to soften the asperities of disposition, and to civilize the manners of mankind.[14]

The appearance of women amateurs drew press commentary:

> The Female Performers particularly arrested attention, and their fascinating powers were universally felt and acknowledged. Respectful delicacy to these truly amiable Ladies, is an additional motive for not mentioning them by name. They were all dressed in a white uniform, emblematic of their virtues; and displaying that elegance in their attire, which was in such perfect union with the unaffected sweetness of their Syren voices.

> Their respective merits were, indeed, pre-eminently impressive; their natural diffidence, perceptible to every observer, gave additional grace to all their charms, and occasioned a thrilling melody in their sweet warbles, which vibrated to the very soul.[15]

The *Cork Advertiser* reported 'an orchestra of nearly one hundred persons, composed of a number of Ladies and Gentlemen, amateurs, of this city and neighbourhood, the choirs of Cashel, Cloyne and Cork, and all the eminent professors in this part of the country'.[16] A Mr Miller led the band and Francis Attwood was the principal cellist. The reviewer noted that 'the superior excellence of Schmidt, on the trumpet, was felt, and acknowledged, by everyone'. Johann Gunther Schmidt, a member of the West York Band, had participated in several concerts in Dublin earlier in the year.[17] As several supporters of the charity had been unable to attend due to 'Assizes Business', a repeat performance was announced for 14 August.[18] The ample press writing that surrounded this event indicates that it engendered a strong sense of common purpose among the upper classes of the city and surrounding region.

An oratorio performance featuring selections from Handel and Haydn was organised for the School of Industry at Christ Church the following August.[19] The choirs of Cashel, Cloyne and Cork again participated, with vocal and instrumental performers from the Theatre Royal, including Thomas Cooke, who led the orchestra, which included 'double trumpets and drums'. Francis Attwood's cello accompaniment was noted as being 'distinguishedly fine'. Lewis Gibson performed on the organ, and Terence Magrath on the piano. Vocal soloists Thomas Phillips (1774–1841) and John Spray (*c.* 1768–1827), both from Dublin, were supported by local singers James Magrath and Mr Swiney.[20] Renewed interest in oratorio performance was short-lived, however. In 1803 and 1804 Grand Balls were the chosen modes of fundraising events.[21] For the ball in 1804, held at the Patrick Street Theatre, music was supplied by 'the two yeomanry bands', probably the bands of the Royal Cork Volunteers and the Loyal Cork Legion.[22] From 1805 the School of Industry was among several local charities that were supported by the amateur theatrical productions of the Apollo Society (see page 77).

According to Keogh, Catholic education in Cork at this time was more advanced than at any other location in Ireland.[23] Since 1776, the Presentation Sisters, founded by Honora Nagle (1718–84), from a wealthy north Cork family, had established a school in the South Parish to educate poor girls, supported by Francis Moylan (1735–1815) while he served there as parish priest.[24]

His appointment as Catholic Bishop of Cork in 1787 brought further progress, with his support for the initiatives of the Catholic Poor Schools Committee. From 1793, under the title of the Cork Charitable Society,[25] this organisation launched a vigorous programme of Catholic school building and educational provision. Edmund Rice's community of Christian Brothers commenced teaching in Chapel Lane in 1811.[26] Contrary to the prevailing charitable disposition towards the 'undeserving' poor, Catholic charities embraced all forms of need from the city's poorest inhabitants, forging strong links between clergy and people.

Charity sermons, enhanced by musical performances, were an important means of fundraising for the city's Catholic charities, and became significant social events for the emerging Catholic middle class.[27] Military bands compensated for the scarcity of musical resources and were an effective means of attracting audiences. In 1810, a charity sermon at the North Parish chapel in aid of the Magdalen Asylum, founded in 1809 by Nicholas Terry, featured the band of the Kilkenny Militia,[28] and the following year, a sermon held there featured the band of the Kerry Regiment, raising two hundred pounds for the Catholic Poor Schools.[29] The tradition consolidated, with musical performances as a standard feature, each charity holding an annual sermon in one of the city's three principal Catholic chapels, usually during Advent or Lent.

While details of music performed at these sermons were seldom published in the early years, there is sufficient evidence to indicate a sacred repertoire selection that was meaningful to both Catholic and Protestant audiences, featuring anthems, oratorio selections and organ voluntaries. Publicity notices indicate that musicians from the city's Catholic and Protestant churches participated. In December 1814 a sermon held at the North Chapel featured the choir with Edward Moeran at the organ in the following short programme:[30]

Grand Overture – Oratorio of the Messiah	Handel
Anthem – Mr Bowden – recitative and song, 'Thus saith the Lord, and who shall abide';	Ditto
Grand Voluntary, Mr Moeran, organ	
Anthem – Mr Moeran and choir, 'My song shall be in Mercy'	Kent
After the sermon, A Grand Symphony, Mr Moeran, organ	

An important figure in the promotion of these events was the Rev. John England, editor of the *Cork Mercantile Chronicle* from 1812 to 1816, and a noted public speaker.[31] His lengthy, eloquent appeals to the public on behalf of the city's poverty-striken communities were published prior to the events.

Over the next decade, full and partial programmes for music at sermons in the city's Catholic churches published in the local newspapers indicate that airs, recitatives and choruses by Handel and anthems by James Kent were regularly featured. Works by Robert Bowden were performed at the South Parish Chapel in 1816 and 1817, and a sermon at the North Cathedral in 1818 featured works by Handel, Haydn, Kent and Delamain.[32] Giovanni Pergolesi's four-voiced motet, 'Gloria in excelsis', was the only Latin piece performed. An Advent Charity Sermon in aid of the Poor Schools of the City was held at the North Parish Chapel in December 1822, newly rebuilt after a suspected sectarian arson attack two years earlier. Edward Moeran directed performances of music by Handel, Pergolesi and Kent.[33] There is a reference to the 'professional exertions' of the 'Gentlemen of the choirs of the Carey's Lane and South Parish Chapels' in a press notice following a charity sermon at the South Parish Chapel in 1823, at which £84 was raised for the Roman Catholic Poor Schools.[34] The Peacock Lane and Sullivan's Quay schools for boys were consolidated in 1821, and an annual charity sermon was held thereafter at the North Parish Chapel on the fifth Sunday in Lent.[35] By this time, the tradition of annual charity sermons with sacred music performances was well established as a means of fundraising for the city's Catholic educational and charitable institutions.

EXPANDING MARKETS

Even though professional concerts were few, amateur involvement in music increased. Music shops were among the businesses that were established in the new fashionable locations of the South Mall and Patrick Street. The stock advertised by violinist Peter Smith, who opened a music shop in Patrick Street in 1807, confirms a buoyant market, offering 'musical instruments, military instruments, and all the fashionable new songs and operas'.[36] Later that year, he added Callcott's *Musical Grammar* to his stock, and a consignment of 130 violins from London.[37] In January of the following year, he advertised a list of such diverse items as Shield/Dibdin's new opera *Two Faces under a Hood*, Mazzinghi's *Airs Grotesque*, and *O'Farrell's Collection of National Irish Music for the Union Pipes* (London: McGow, 1804).[38] O'Farrell's *Collection of National*

Irish Music for the Union Pipes had been published in London around 1804. In February 1808, Smith announced the arrival of Stevenson and Moore's *Irish Melodies*, claiming to be the first supplier of this publication in the county.[39] He also aimed to take advantage of the seasonal surge of genteel customers in advertising 'new music for the assizes'.[40] In August, Smith advertised 'a great variety of new music, particularly all the hymns and anthems sung at the Methodist Chapel'.[41] He apparently lacked the necessary skills to sustain his business, however, and in 1809, he published the following notice:

> For one guinea, the Nobility and Gentry of this City and County will have an opportunity, on the 5th of June, of supplying themselves with Grand, Square and Patent Cabinet Piano-Fortes, Lute guitars, Violins, Violincellos, Patent Flutes, Tambourines, a Complete set of Military Musical Instruments, and all the New Musical Publications of London and Dublin.[42]

In 1810, the Apollo Society staged a benefit play for Smith, their musical leader, stating that he had been 'driven by the pressure of Bad Times'.[43] Despite the closure of his business, Smith continued his career as a performer. In July 1811 Peter Smith held a benefit concert for his prodigy son at the Bath Rooms, Blackrock, assisted by Bowden and Gillespie.[44]

The market for musical instruments continued to expand. Makers listed in the early nineteenth century trade directories included Richard Tobin, Musical Instrument Maker, E. Kenny, harp and pianoforte maker and Thomas Flanagan, flute maker.[45] Since the late eighteenth century, the city's artisan instrument makers competed with an escalating supply of patented instruments from London's manufactories, and there was a surge in music retailing. The earliest imported patented instruments were flutes, in demand by military bandsmen, music teachers and gentleman amateurs. In 1783, Alexander Fitton's music shop in Paul Street offered for sale 'elegant bassoons, German flutes of Tacet and Florio's construction, with all the additional joints and keys of silver'.[45] In 1806 Isaac Varian offered 'Six-keyed patent flutes' direct from Potter of London,[46] and the following year Daniel Fitzpatrick's music shop stocked 'Scott and Purkis's Delecta Harmonia, or Patent Double Flageolets, by which instrument one Performer may play Duetts with much ease and correctness'.[47]

Of all the market trends in musical goods, it was the trade in pianos by London makers that grew most rapidly from the last decade of the eighteenth century. From the turn of the nineteenth century, general shopkeepers and music retailers established dealerships with London piano firms, and their retail businesses expanded at an unprecedented rate. At the centre of an emerging pedagogical and social transformation of domestic music-making, the piano became an essential accomplishment for middle-class young women. The amateur market stimulated the publication of sheet music arrangements, principally of operatic excerpts, which could be studied and enjoyed in the private, domestic sphere, shaping middle-class musical taste.

Advertising notices from the early nineteenth century confirm the widespread teaching of both harp and piano at private schools for girls, such as Madame de Lestang's French, English and Drawing Academy at Duncan Street, which in 1800 provided tuition in forte piano, harp and singing.[48] Notices from the second decade of the century provide the identities of Cork's first female music professors. In 1816, Miss Thomas advertised herself as Professor of the Pedal Harp, Pianoforte and Flageolet, in addition to being the principal of a French and English boarding school at Wellington Place,[49] and in 1817, Mrs Herbert, with an address at Miss Stack's boarding school, advertised herself as Professor of the Harp and Piano Forte.[50]

The provision of specialised piano teaching became a concern during the second decade of the nineteenth century, prompting professionals to look towards London and, to a lesser extent, Dublin. In 1816, John Roche, son of James Roche, having studied in London with 'Russel, C [Charles] Neate, Sexto Perez and Kalkbrenner', returned to teach piano in Cork, bringing with him a Clementi grand piano for the purpose.[51] By the following summer, he had also studied at Logier's Academy in Dublin,[52] one of at least six that have been identified in Dublin at this time.[53] Johann Bernhard Logier (1777–1846) was a German-born musician who moved to England in 1791, where he joined the Duke of Abercorn's regimental band as a flautist, later becoming director. He arrived in Ireland with this band and by 1808 was appointed as director of the band of the Kilkenny militia. From 1810, he began to diversify his musical activities in Dublin, as theatre musician, concert promotor, teacher and music shop owner.[54]

Logier's fame as a piano pedagogue rested on two innovative features. His 'chiroplast', patented in 1814, was essentially a mechanical hand-directing device, for elementary teaching, an invention which remained highly controversial among his fellow music professors. The other distinctive element of his pedagogy was group piano teaching, whereby concepts of chords, harmony and ensemble were actively developed from the earliest stages. In this he was relatively successful. In December 1818, John Roche announced the first public examination of his pupils by Dublin organist Jonathan Blewitt.[55] An account was published in the *Cork Advertiser*:

> The first examination of Mr Roche's pupils took place at his Academy, South Mall, on Thursday last, and was attended by a most numerous assemblage of the first rank and consequence in our city. The performance commenced with 'Handel's Occasional Overture', which was exceedingly well performed; and although eight pianofortes were employed, they had the effect of one only, from the accuracy with which the time was kept. The junior class, some of whom were not more than five years of age, were then examined in the first principles of music, time, key, major and minor, enharmonic changes, chords, fundamental basses, and transposition. Their answer and writing on the lecture board displayed a quickness and intelligence really astonishing, and proves how well calculated Mr Logier's system is to simplify to the lowest capacity subjects hitherto almost entirely confined to professional musicians. The Chiroplast lessons with accompaniment, followed by the class in the best manner – 'Haydn's Grand Symphony', 'Clementi's Sonata' and the 'Rondo of Steibelt's Storm Concerto' were also performed with the greatest precision and neatness, particularly the latter, the solos of which were performed by one of the young Ladies in the first style, the Tutti parts had a peculiarly grand effect from the number of Instruments employed.
>
> The senior class were examined in minor chords, inversions, dissonances and composition, with all which they seemed perfectly acquainted. The specimen which they gave of the latter manifested much knowledge of the subject, the time and key (major and minor) being left to the choice of a professional Gentleman who was present; one of the pupils immediately composed an air, which was then harmonized for three voices in a most pleasing and correct style. The manner in which Mr Blewitt conducted the examination, as well as the performance of the pupils, gave the greatest satisfaction to all present.[56]

A school that invested heavily in pianos was the Catholic Ursuline Convent boarding school for girls, founded in 1771, which in 1825 was relocated from the city centre to Blackrock.[57] On a visit to the school in 1842, writer William Makepeace Thackeray noted that 'there were pianos all over the educational part of the house',[58] and Asenath Nicholson, who visited the school in 1844, noted that 'Pianos were in every room, and in some we found two'.[59] This practice continued at the school, where James Roche Jr continued to teach Logier's system following the death of his brother. A piano quartet performed at an award ceremony in 1852, and a report of a similar ceremony in 1857, included performances by 'nine young ladies on three pianos, which had all the brilliancy of a full orchestra'.[60]

AMATEUR SOCIETIES

Ever since the late eighteenth century, glee clubs based on male conviviality flourished among the city's elite. The Guidonian Club was in existence in 1791–2.[61] Probably a continuation of this was the Cork Catch and Glee Club, which lasted until around 1807.[62] Its president, Sir Richard Kellett, of Lota, was an alderman of the city, and vice-president John George Newsom was sheriff in 1801 and mayor in 1816. The Harmonic Society, which succeeded the Catch and Glee Club, published notices of its dinner meetings from 1810, held regularly during the winter season at the Bush Tavern in George's Street.[63] Its members were also drawn from the city's merchant class, supplemented by a few core music professionals. Singers Roger Bertridge, James Magrath, Edward Moeran, William Gillespie and John Shaw, all Protestant church musicians, featured regularly in its meetings and concerts.

Central to the activities of many clubs and societies was the drinking of toasts, a custom introduced from England. Charles Étienne Coquebert de Montbret noted its popularity during his visit to Cork in 1790.[64] An account of a meeting of the Harmonic Society published in the *Cork Morning Intelligencer* in 1821 describes this social ritual, whereby each of the toasts was linked to the performance of specific songs and glees:

> Cork Harmonic Society
>
> This Society held its fourth Meeting this season, on Wed the 21st inst. at the Commercial Tavern, which was most numerously and respectably attended. Among the visitors we noticed some of the first rank. The Dinner was, as usual, excellent without profusion, and the countenances of the party denoted, that the gratification of the ear in vocal harmony, combined with a taste and feeling to encourage and patronize that delightful science was more their object, than the gratification of the palate. The Toasts and Glees were appropriately selected. After *Non nobis*, as usual, 'The King',

> which was immediately followed by our National Anthem, 'God save the King', and both were received with the most marked applause. Sir John Stevenson's Glee, 'Give me the Harp', accompanied by two performers on the Piano Forte, identified itself with the next toast, 'The Cork Harmonic Society'.
>
> To proceed *Seriatim*, would exceed our limits; but we cannot avoid noticing some of the Glees which made their due impression on the auditory: 'Great Father Bacchus', 'How merrily we live', 'Here in cool grot', 'Faithless Emma. Harmonized by Banks', 'La mia Dorabella', 'Ask me why', 'Oh Nanny', and though last not least in excellence, that admirably composed Glee by Stevens, 'Some of my Heroes are low', a tribute of feeling to departed worth, after the President had announced a standing toast in solemn silence, promising that it was the first day the Society met since the Anniversary of that event, 'The Memory of our Reverend Sovereign Geo. the Third'.[65]

The society meetings were held in local taverns and hotels. Members of the Harmonic Society occasionally sang in concerts and contributed to the productions of the Apollo Society. In May 1810 the musical societies of the city combined in a 'Grand Concert of Vocal and Instrumental Music', namely, the Musical Society and the Harmonic Society. The concert was to commence with 'a highly esteemed overture', and the music of the witches' scene in *Macbeth* was to be sung 'with full chorusses' by the vocalists.[66] A short review of the concert noted that 'the fine band of the Kilkenny Militia played several excellent tunes, and some of them performed in the orchestra'.[67]

During the 1820s, the Harmonic Society held its meetings at the Commercial Hotel and Tavern, a new development completed in 1819,[68] designed by architect Sir Thomas Deane as part of the Commercial Buildings in Pembroke Street, and renamed the Imperial Hotel from 1824 (see page 142). A report of a dinner meeting at Lloyd's Hotel in George's Street in 1834 refers to the violin playing of Mr Travers, the singing of Mr Keays, with William Gillespie at the piano.[69] The society appears to have lapsed after 1834,[70] although briefly revived by Alexander D. Roche in 1838.[71] This mixture of conviviality, gastronomy, and professional and amateur music-making remained a standard form of male sociability and such groups, under various names, were a part of Cork society until the end of the nineteenth century. The subservient role of professional musicians within these societies was noted in an article entitled 'Music in Cork' published in *The Musical World* in 1845:

> There are one or two musical clubs – if they may be so designated – the Albert and the Beefsteak, which meet once a month to dine and sing glees, and the principal citizens and merchant traders and shopkeepers belong to it; but how much music or the musical profession benefit by it requires no prophet to make known – the reverse being the case in most institutions of the kind. Unless the professor be paid he should never exercise his talent in such places.[72]

Having endured since the early decades of the eighteenth century, the Musical Society remained active as a charitable body, presenting regular concerts for the benefit of the North Charitable supervised by the Master of the Ceremonies at the Assembly Rooms. George Ware, music professor and dancing master, formerly of Woolwich Academy,[73] was elected Master of the Ceremonies at the Assembly Room in 1811 and continued in that role until his resignation in 1814.[74] Balls were a prominent mode of fundraising for this charity. As part of a revitalisation of the city's public amusements in 1813, the Assembly Room was refurbished at the mayor's expense, and a series of eight subscription balls for the benefit of the North Charitable Infirmary was announced.[75] Ware published notices in the press seeking 'three good fiddlers, dulcimer, tambourine and violoncello' for the season.[76] In 1824, plans to close the Assembly Room were announced, which left the Musical Society without a base. *The Freeholder* announced that:

> The Tuesday-night's Club, after standing for a century, has ceased to exist. Another, called the Anacreontic, has risen from its ashes. At its meeting on Monday night last, the Committee made their report of the Rules – one of which was, denying the professional men a vote in the procceedings of the Club. This, where the professional men are paid for their services, is very fair – but where they pay their admission money (three guineas) and every thing else, the same as the amateurs, and equally with them give their services gratis, it was most preposterous. The Rule was put forward at the instance of two of the young Beamishes. 'I am glad that I had not been there,' says Jack Shaw, 'for such would have been the barm of my indignation at the frothy pretensions of these brats, that it would be impossible I could beguile my feelings.[77]

CONCERTS

Musicians' benefit concerts accommodated changes in public taste. For his benefit concert in 1803, Peter Smith capitalised on the current vogue for military spectacle, featuring the bands of the Royal Cork Volunteers and the Loyal Cork Legion in a large-scale concert.[78] The performance, given by a total of seventy players, concluded with Daniel Steibelt's (1765–1823) *Battle of Alexandria*, which was previewed as 'the first thing of the kind which has ever taken place in this city'.[79] This descriptive piece was composed to commemorate the British victory over the French at Alexandria in 1801 under General Ralph Abercromby. It was the first of several newly composed 'battle' pieces for military band which were popular during the years of the Napoleonic Wars. In May 1812, John Shaw held a benefit concert, under the patronage of the Harmonic Society, who performed several glees, and the band of the Kerry regiment also performed.[80] Theatrical entertainment by the newly formed Apollo Society eclipsed James Magrath's annual benefit in 1806, leading to its postponement from January to June,[81] and in 1807, in deference to the society, he replaced his annual concert with a benefit play, which consisted of *The Curfew*, with the musical afterpiece of *The Padlock*, assisted by the Apollo Society.[82]

Musicians' benefit concerts had the dual function of self-promotion and financial gain, so it was essential that music professors cultivated good relationships with patrons and fellow musicians. This topic proved irresistible to John Boyle in a piece in his satirical journal *The Freeholder*, who reported that John Shaw's benefit concert in 1822 attracted 'the nobility and gentry of the city and county, including the Marques and Marchioness of Thomond and the Ladies O'Brien, who came to town specially'. The writer also noted the last-minute withdrawal of the support of dancing master William Hickey ('a tolerable violin player').[83] An account of George Ware's benefit concert in 1823 is another example of this magazine's relish for local gossip:

> Mr Ware's Concert was neither fully nor fashionably attended. We thought that this gentleman stood better with the upper folk. But no such thing. His manner, they say, is very offensive. We like to see a man independent of his movement – but, beyond this, is not the thing. Mrs Beamish, it seems, made a large party that evening at Beaumont, in opposition to it. The cause of the lady's hostility, we are told, is this: Some time ago, she said to him, 'Mr Ware, I'd be glad you'd take Miss Beamish in hands, and see what you can do with her voice'. '*Her* voice, Madam, *her* voice', replied

> Ware, 'Why, her voice is only fit *to cry oysters*'. This, certainly, is not easily to be forgiven. There were, notwithstanding, in the house some excellent judges in music [...]' [84]

While the commercialisation of music had escalated, and a market boom in pianos was under way, a disrupted continuity of concerts had been evident from the mid-1790s, due to a number of external forces. The demise of Dublin's Rotunda concerts fractured the strong provincial circuit of performers that, since the 1760s, had provided Cork with its most illustrious concert performers. A corresponding downturn in concert performances in London during the 1790s has been attributed both to the French war (from 1793) and to the popularity of London's Vocal Concert.[85] In Ireland, the 1798 rebellion had shaken society; the certainties of the eighteenth century were crumbling, and society was becoming more openly sectarian. Although there were a few notable exceptions, small-scale concerts were favoured by touring musicians during the ensuing years.

The emergence of the pedal harp as a concert instrument during the early nineteenth century was reflected in concert advertisements. Joseph Elouis (1752–*c.* 1817), a Swiss harpist resident in Edinburgh, visited Cork in October 1806. For reasons that remain unclear, he was refused support by the usual ensemble musicians, and he was obliged to rely on pianist William Gillespie, and the band of the 82nd Regiment, who performed at short notice.[86] On a return visit in 1810, Elouis included 'several favourite Irish airs' in his programme.[87] The only two advertised concerts in 1809 also featured the harp, given in April by a visiting group of Italians, Signora and Signore Morasca, 'from the Italian Opera House, Lisbon, and Signore Pucci, professor of the Pedal harp'.[88] A week later, the Italian musicians joined the Musical Society in a shared benefit concert for themselves and the North Infirmary.[89]

Three 'vocal concerts' given by Dublin musicians Mr and Mrs Willis, Miss Cheese and Madam O'Moran in May also featured new repertoire for piano and harp.[90] The first concert received great acclaim in a review in the *Cork Mercantile Chronicle*:

> It was that description of musical entertainment which we are not here much accustomed to, where so few individuals depend upon their own talents for gratifying auditory; and it was certainly the most successful effort we ever recollect, upon any scale, to convey enjoyment and delight.[91]

Piano solos by Woelfl and Latour, piano duets by Steibelt and Latour, a piano and harp duet by Dussek, and an arrangement of Mozart's Overture to *Die Zauberflöte* constituted a major portion of the programme for the third concert. Both instruments accompanied a Stevenson glee.[92]

The 'miscellaneous' programmes by the Ashe family represented current developments in Italian opera in London. On his first visit to Cork since 1796, Andrew Ashe arrived in August 1813, with his singer wife, Mrs (Mary) Ashe, formerly Mary Comer of Bath, whom he had married in 1799, and their daughter Miss H. Ashe. Ashe's career in the intervening years had brought him to London and Bath. He had been principal flute player at the Italian Opera, London, and directed concerts at Bath from 1810 until 1821.[93] A concert given by the family in October featured music from the operas of Vincenzo Pucitta (1778–1861),[94] a scena and aria from *La vestale* and, as a finale, the chorus 'Viva Enrico' from *La caccia di Enrico IV*. This chorus, with its loyalist sentiments, was to become a favourite finale piece on Cork concert programmes. Introduced to London by Angelica Catalani, Pucitta was then employed as composer and music director at the King's Theatre.[95] Mrs Ashe was a keen exponent of his music in Cork, along with other Italian operatic repertoire. Miss H. Ashe performed a piano concerto by Dussek, a genre as yet rare in provincial concert programmes of the period.[96] On a visit in August 1815, the Ashe family were joined by another of their daughters, performing on an Érard new patent double action pedal harp, 'selected by Mr Ashe at Broadwood's for this occasion', to be sold afterwards 'at the London price'.[97] The Ashe sisters presented additional new repertoire for harp and piano, demonstrating the accompanying and ensemble potential of these instruments, including a Steibelt duet for harp and piano. The *Cork Mercantile Chronicle* reported an audience of almost five hundred, 'comprising all the rank in this city and vicinity'.[98]

The vocal concert was a new concert model that achieved popularity in the first two decades of the nineteenth century. Often termed an 'Entertainment', it featured a selection of vocal items interspersed with recitations or readings given by one or two singers, performed with minimal musical or dramatic support, relying usually on piano accompaniment. It also satisfied audience taste for dramatic and literary subjects. The earliest of such concerts was given by Martha Poole at the Assembly Rooms in October 1796, billed as an entertainment after the manner of Harrison and Knyvett's celebrated vocal concerts in London.[99] Most of the touring acts originated in the Crow Street theatre. Having recently given four performances of 'Melologues' in Dublin,

Charles Incledon presented 'The Wandering Melodist – an entertainment (entirely new)' in July 1803.[100] A 'Theatrical Bouquet' performed at the Assembly Rooms by Messrs Putnam and H.P. Warren in September 1804 consisting of 'readings, recitations and comic songs' was on a similar model, and was subsequently performed at Bandon and Mallow.[101]

Miscellany was the basis of these programmes, in which Irish melodies invariably found a place. A surviving handbill of Rosemond Mountain's (*c.* 1786–1841) entertainment in August 1805 at the George's Street Assembly Rooms shows the programme's design and content.[102] It was 'recited and sung' by Rosemond Mountain,[103] and accompanied on the violin by her husband, John Mountain,[104] and on the piano by George Kollmann (1789–1845). It featured a performance of a concerto on the Grand Piano Forte by Kollmann, believed to be that of his father, A.F.C. Kollmann,[105] and a song 'Nature and Melody', billed as 'National Harmony', by Carolan, the Irish bard. In August 1815, Charles Incledon and his co-performers from the Theatre Royal, Covent Garden, presented an 'Entertainment' at the Assembly Room entitled 'Minstrels, or a Summer's Tour – a miscellaneous performance, entirely new, in three parts' consisting of

> interesting oral matter, embracing a variety of subjects, and introductory to a number of the best selected songs, duets and glees, composed by the most eminent masters, with many ancient National and Scots melodies.[106]

Vocal concerts given by Messrs Vincent and John Spray in 1811 were of a literary rather than theatrical character. On tour in the southern part of the country, these Dublin musicians arrived in February, supported by singers Mrs Vincent, Miss Spray, and John Spray's nephew John Smith (1797–1861).[107] They presented lectures on elocution and literary readings together with selections of vocal music. The concert on 6 February received unprecedented coverage in the *Cork Mercantile Chronicle*. The reviewer eulogised Mr Vincent's delivery of his subject matter, and the inordinate length and level of detailed description suggests the pen of Rev. John England.[108] The group's second presentation, 'An Attic Evening's Entertainment', was given at the Theatre Royal, Patrick Street, in late February, consisting of a three-part presentation of recitation and music, the music categorised as 'Sacred music, Irish melodies and miscellaneous music.'[109] After engagements at Limerick, the group returned to Cork at the end of March and performed 'A Grand Selection of Sacred Music' at the Theatre Royal, Patrick Street, in which they were assisted by a number of amateurs, and for which the stage was to be occupied by an orchestra 'fitted up as the Theatre Royal, Covent Garden.[110] The success of these concerts reflected the current vogue for solo vocal delivery, both spoken and sung.

By 1826, press reports of concerts by veteran tenor John Braham reflect further changes in public taste. He arrived in Cork in January, giving three Grand Concerts at the Theatre Royal on the 'entertainment' model, featuring recitations and comic singing, accompanied on the piano by Alexander Lee and supported by three singers from Dublin's Theatre Royal, Mr Brough, Miss Hallande and Mr Smollett.[111] The entertainment consisted of four parts – the first and third presenting 'the comic and vocal powers of Mr Smollet'; the second and fourth, vocal music performed by Braham, Brough and Miss Hallande.[112] This event received extensive coverage, in both the *Cork Mercantile Chronicle* and *The Constitution*, the latter reporting that 'he sang the different songs, with an expression that really electrified and enraptured his auditory'.[113] The editorial commentaries were not without criticism, however, on two points. The writer in *The Constitution* remarked:

> Had a good Orchestra been established, under the direction of an experienced leader, to supply the vacancy in the performances which Mr Smollet's 'Trip by the Mail' is endeavouring to make up for – we should have no hesitation in giving the Concert our most unqualified approbation.

Concerts featuring comic recitation, so popular during the previous decade, it appears, had declined in public favour. The reviewer in the *Cork Mercantile Chronicle* also criticised the choice of songs, stating that 'it occurred to none of these singers that an Irish audience would be pleased with an Irish melody. We think that they cannot well account for this disregard of the national partiality.'[114]

NATIONAL MUSIC

The 'national partiality' was increasingly evident in instrumental programmes since the first decade of the nineteenth century, represented primarily by the music of Carolan, who by this time had become an iconic cultural figure. Already established as an urban professional group, Irish pipers gave theatre and concert performances with increasing frequency. In 1809 and 1810, William Talbot (b. 1780), 'professor of the Union pipes', spent time performing and teaching in Cork. Talbot was a blind piper from Roscrea,

County Tipperary, who appeared at theatres in London and Dublin, and was reputed to have performed before George IV.[115] In 1810, he advertised performances from 12 to 4 each day for three days at the Assembly Rooms, at an admission cost of 1s 8d.[116] An alternative to the standard concert, this 'exhibition' setting would have attracted a wider, less formal gathering of listeners, which, especially in the case of Irish music, may even have included other players.

Since the 1790s, the patronage of harpers became an important means of patriotic expression. Urban-based societies for the preservation of Irish harp music and the training and patronage of young performers on the wire-strung instrument were established in Belfast (1808) and Dublin (1809).[117] In December 1812, William O'Gorman, of Ballymena, County Antrim, student of the Belfast Harp Society, advertised his availability to attend at 'Taverns, balls, etc' during his stay in Cork city. The editor of the *Cork Mercantile Chronicle* advocated public support:

> [...] we are convinced they will not withhold their patronage from him, when they consider that by encouraging his exertions they contribute to the revival of that admired melody, which, in the best days of Ireland, swelled the song of her joy, and in the time of disaster was the solace of her sons.[118]

O'Gorman appears to have been the first performing member of the Harp Society to travel south to Cork, despite his dismissal from the society's school in June 1810, being deemed 'incapable by nature of learning the Harp'.[119] In February 1814 two leading students of the Belfast Harp Society, Valentine Reany (Rennie) and Edward McBride, announced a concert at the Assembly Rooms, billed as 'Irish Harmony Reviv'd'. Two previews and a full programme were published in the *Cork Mercantile Chronicle*.[120] Carolan's concerto was played on two harps in the first act, and the second act featured 'several planxties of Carolan, not yet published'. Thomas Willman and his wife, who were on a visit from Dublin, participated, Mrs Willman with the songs 'Savourneen Deelish' and Thomas Moore's 'The Meeting of the Waters', and Thomas Willman with a clarinet concerto by Jean-Xavier Lefèvre. Mr Stevenson performed a flute concerto by Ignaz Pleyel and Mr Kelly performed a duet on the 'double flageolet'.[121] The concert ended with a performance of 'God Save the King', and was followed by the customary ball.[122]

Over the next two decades, the *Cork Mercantile Chronicle* continued to promote Irish native music, and art music derived from it. In 1827, visiting pianist Carl Schunke's performance of 'Recollections of Ireland' prompted a lengthy commentary in the *Cork Mercantile Chronicle*:

> A paroxysm of delight pervaded, and strongly evinced itself in all parts of the House at his 'Recollections of Ireland', that delightful mélange of bravaura and pathos – truly descriptive of the passions of Irishmen. The soft, plaintive strain in which this exquisite piece of Music commenced, reflected as it were through a mirror the sensitiveness of the Irish heart, and called back the mind to those scenes of former days which were well nigh lost in the dark vista of the past, the darkness of oblivion; and threw around them a light which will shine steady and unflickering, while Ireland groans in the menacies of disgraceful but unmerited slavery – and again, the light strain of St Patrick's Day dropped the curtain on the past, and brought forth a new and opposite, but peculiar feeling of our Countrymen, a species of jollity, that compromises with sorrow, and allows itself to be absorbed in the sentiment exquisitely expressed in that song to the air of St Patrick's Day.[123]

Unattributed in the programmes, the title and description point to *Recollections of Ireland* Op 69, composed by Bohemian virtuoso pianist Ignaz Moscheles (1794–1870) following a visit to Dublin in 1826.[124] Moscheles had performed this piece at London's Argyll Rooms the previous April, and again in June 1827.[125] Schunke's performance may have been a free adaptation of it, or simply unattributed. The press review presents a striking example of emerging nationalistic sentiments, evoking 'remembrance' of Ireland's past, recently articulated in the poetic texts of Moore's *Irish Melodies*,[126] represented here in a modern pianistic idiom. The review was the most extended piece of writing on a single piece of music that had appeared in a Cork newspaper up to this time, penned, perhaps, by radical journalist Thomas Sheahan (1797–1836), who had taken over editorship of the *Cork Mercantile Chronicle* the previous January.[127] In the final sentence, the writer, in response to this music, articulates the sense of reconciliation of conflicting emotions communicated in the work's transcendent finale.

LARGE-SCALE PERFORMANCES

Concerts by visiting musicians predominated in 1814, a year of diverse and remarkable musical events. In February, a spectacular performance of Johann Bernhard Logier's Grand Characteristic Military Symphony called 'The Battle of Vittoria' took place at the Assembly Room. This work had been given four performances at Dublin's Rotunda the previous August,[128] one of which attracted an audience of over 2,000.[129] The work was composed to commemorate the Duke of Wellington's defeat of Joseph Bonaparte's forces at the Battle of Vittoria, Spain, in June 1813. Beethoven's Op 91, which also commemorated this event, proved to be an extremely popular (and lucrative) work in this medium. The concert was advertised as a benefit for Mr and Mrs Willman. Thomas Willman had featured as a clarinettist in Cork theatre productions from 1802 to 1804, but this was his first concert appearance. The band, led by Robert Bowden, was 'composed of all the Military Musicians in the Garrison, with the addition of string instruments, comprising upwards of one hundred performers',[130] probably the largest instrumental ensemble featured in a public concert up to this time. The principal singers were Mrs Willman, Roger Bertridge, James Magrath and a Mr Alcock. Advertised as a benefit for Mr and Mrs Willman, the concert, attended by the mayor, Sir David Perrier, and Lady Perrier, was 'more crowdedly attended than any thing of the kind ever before witnessed in this City'.[131] A rare account of the audience at the concert and the ensuing ball was published, in the characteristic witty style of *The Freeholder*:

> We shall not enumerate the names of any who were there, as, in short, every body was there. On that night every little Tea Table gave up its scandal votaries – the Street and the Ale-House their Jack-a-napes and Buckeens – there was assembled the Taylor and Tinker – the Horse-Milliner and the Man-Milliner – the Barber and Baker – the Grocer and Chandler – the Clerk and the Shop-Boy – all, all had dedicated the night to the soul-ravishing sounds of harmony, and the pleasures of the 'light fantastic toe'.
>
> When the Ball commenced, the better orders sat down to witness the graceful movements of the Dancers. Mr Hide, the Sadler of Patrick-street, and his newly-espoused Consort, attracted universal admiration. Mr Hide was dressed in a new white dimmitty pair of loose over-alls and nankeen spaterdashes and Mrs Hide to give her a due elevation, wore her Sunday High-Heel Shoes. The hoppers kept it up until shop-opening

> time in the morning, and then, stupid after the night, dispersed to their daily labour. We should have mentioned that, at the close of the dancing, there was a general cry from the Ladies for the Cushion; & it is but justice to Mr William Butterfield to say, that he opened it with all that fashionable humour and gaiety, which the Crown Tavern records of him – and we farther [*sic*] omitted to mention in its proper place, that, when the Concert finished, Merchants Cogan, Bellew, and Maurice Hore, at the special request of the Misses Cremin, Parade, sung in their best stile, Caulcort's [*sic*] celebrated glee, 'The Three Loggerheads'.[132]

In August 1814, a Grand Musical Festival was announced in the press, consisting of operatic concerts at the Theatre Royal and oratorio performances at Christ Church and St Mary's Cathedral. Since the late eighteenth century, provincial music festivals were an integral part of English provincial musical life. Established as triennial events in major towns and cities such as Norwich, Birmingham and Salisbury, they were locally organised, and centred around major Anglican cathedrals, employing London-based soloists in addition to local professionals. Since 1801, members of the Ashley family developed the speculative touring festival, usually aligned with local celebrations or commemorations.[133] Although not advertised as such, the company of ten singers and seven instrumentalists who arrived in Cork in late August showed all the features of an Ashley festival. The company had already performed in Dublin as part of a civic festival, announced as 'the Dublin Jubilee Festival, to celebrate the happy coincidence of the Centenary of the reign of the Illustrious House of Hanover, with the Birth Day of His Royal Highness the Prince Regent, and the Celebration of the Glorious and Honourable Peace'.[134] The 'peace' referred to the restoration of the Bourbon monarchy in France, and Napoleon Bonaparte's first exile to Elba. The Jubilee was not emphasised in the Cork publicity notices, but was signalled in *The Freeholder* in a reproachful address to the theatre manager:

> The Public of Cork are to be amused, it seems, this season, with the powers of Madame Catalani's Voice; whilst the Instruction and Entertainment afforded from the production of the Masters of the legitimate Drama are rigidly excluded. The People are to be amused in a Language they do not understand, and the mere faculties of sound are to be substituted for the gratification of sense and information. We know not whether this will redeem the penalty in the Contract of the Patentee with the original

> Subscribers to the Theatre; but this neglect and the ruinous way he has left the Theatre for a Number of Seasons back manifest an evident disrespect and disregard of the Interests of the People of Cork. There seems to be a general disposition, at this Season of Hilarity and Rejoicing to amuse the Gentry, to the exclusion of the middle and humble ranks. The Feasting, the Dancing, and the Theatrical Exhibitions, are all directed to this object, whilst nothing but *new* Taxes and *new* Penalties, are held out to the lower Orders. If Madame Catalani's Music be the only Amusement afforded to the Citizens this Season, we trust, the *Prices* to the *Theatre* will not be raised, so as to prevent the Majority of them from partaking in the only Jubilee afforded to them in these Centenary times.[135]

As anticipated in *The Freeholder*, the admission costs were high, clearly aimed at the upper classes. Tickets for the inaugural performance at Christ Church cost ten shillings, and the admission prices to the concerts at the Theatre Royal on the following evening were boxes 10s, pit 6s 8d, gallery 4s 2d. Current concert prices ranged from seven down to five shillings. The Dublin festival had consisted of three sacred concerts at St Werburgh's Church and four secular concerts at the Rotunda.[136] The Cork festival consisted of three secular concerts at the Theatre Royal and five sacred performances – three at Christ Church and two at St Mary's Cathedral (North Chapel). The schedule of performances is shown in Table 5.1.

Table 5.1. Schedule for the 1814 Grand Musical Festival.

DATE	DAY	TIME	VENUE	PROGRAMME
22 Aug	Monday	morn	CC	Oratorio of the Messiah
23 Aug	Tuesday	eve	TR	Grand Miscellaneous Concert
24 Aug	Wednesday	morn	CC	Oratorio The Creation
25 Aug	Thursday	morn	N Ch	Selection of Sacred Music
25 Aug	Thursday	eve	TR	Concert and Opera
26 Aug	Friday	morn	CC	Oratorio selections: Handel, Mozart
27 Aug	Saturday	morn	N Ch	Sacred Music
27 Aug	Saturday	eve	TR	Opera and Concert (Catalani's benefit)

TR = Theare Royal; CC = Christ Church; N Ch = North Chapel

The initial advertisement included a declaration of the safety of the building at Christ Church following the recent removal of the steeple. The singers, all of whom had performed in Dublin, were:

> Madame Catalani
> Madame Ferlendis, Principal Singer at the Opera House, London
> Madame Bianchi Lacy, from the King's Concerts and Carlton House
> Miss Hughes, from the Nobility's Concerts, London
> Master Stansbury, from the King's Chapel
> Mr Garbett, Mr Tinney and Mr Lacy, from the Oratorios, London
> Mr Tett, Mr Chiodi

Madame Ferlendis and Madame Bianchi Lacy were currently active in London, as were the instrumentalists.[137] The instrumental performers were:

Mr Loder	leader
Mr Mori	second violin
Signor Ferlendis	oboe
Mr Lindley	cello
Mr C. Lindley	tenor
Mr Willman	clarionet
Mr H. Willman	trumpet
Mr Jenkinson	double drums
Madame Gerbini	solo violin

Luigia Gerbini (*c.* 1777–*c.* 1819), the solo violinist, had studied with virtuoso violinist and composer Giovanni Battista Viotti (1755–1824).[138] The choruses were led by the celebrated Lancashire Singers, a small professional group of female choral leaders who performed at English festivals and oratorios. Programmes for two of the concerts have survived, and there were a number of press reviews.[139] Although it was a commercial venture, a notice in the *Cork Mercantile Chronicle* announced that a 'considerable portion of the receipts of the sacred music' would be given to a committee for charitable purposes.[140] The opening night featured Catalani in *Messiah* at Christ Church, in which she 'captivated her auditory almost to distraction; the whole contributed so much delight as we are convinced was never enjoyed on any public occasion in our city'.[141] A review in the *Cork Advertiser* noted that 'the effect of the Chorusses, and the Sacred Bravura, on the Church, was electrifying! The power of the concurring harmony of the instrumental and vocal performers, may be felt, but not described.'[142]

A concert presented the following evening at the theatre featured a selection of predominantly Italian operatic arias, duets and trios, interspersed with instrumental concertos. A review in the *Cork Advertiser* referred to oboe concertos by Alessandro Ferlendis (1783–*c.* 1833) and a violin concerto played by Madame Gerbini. It was Robert Lindley's (1776–1855) cello solo, however, which drew the highest praise:

> To say that Mr Lindley excels on the violoncello, would be too cold an expression only applicable to ordinary abilities, and the exertions of ordinary men which daily occur, and are forgotten. Mr Lindley stands alone – above criticism and independent of praise; while his powers astonish, we are lost in admiration at the facility with which he executes such difficult passages and produces such inimitable tones.[143]

The third performance, again billed as an oratorio, held at Christ Church on Wednesday morning, consisted of the first part of Haydn's *The Creation*, followed in the second part with a selection of sacred music by Handel and Mozart, at which a 'respectable' attendance was reported. Catalani's performance was again praised:

> [...] what filled every heart with rapture and overwhelmed with extace [*sic*] and wonder was Catalani's 'Angels ever bright and fair' but who may describe the beauties of this exquisite song, or its effects on the audience, when Catalani's sweet countenance, in unison with her angelic strains, gave a bewitching sweetness that almost would induce one to indulge in the delusion that one of the happy spirits was breathing strains from Heaven.[144]

On Thursday morning, a performance of sacred music was given at the North Chapel consisting of music 'from Handel, Mozart, and other authors'. The *Cork Advertiser* reported that 'the attendance generally is not proportionate to the ability employed, or to the high feast which is layed [*sic*] before the public'. However, Thursday evening's performance at the theatre, described as a 'Concert and Opera', was well attended.

On Saturday morning, the last day of the festival, a selection of 'the most admired songs and choruses from the *Messiah* and *The Creation* was performed at the North Chapel, at reduced prices. The report of this concert gives an indication of a possible cause of the previous ailing attendance:

> This morning the North Chapel was filled a considerable time before the performance began, those whom the idle report of the dangerous state of Christ Church kept from the performances there, had an opportunity of enjoying the entertainment in supposed security, and many Gentlemen and families from the country, who had not previously arrived in town, attended on this occasion, indeed the attendance here at reduced prices, gave a sufficient proof that the original admission at the Church was injudiciously high. The pleasure of the audience could not be concealed, satisfaction and delight beamed on every countenance.[145]

The admission prices charged on this occasion were 5s and 2s 6d, considerably less than the prices for the earlier concerts at Christ Church and at the theatre. The company departed for Limerick in early September.[146]

In 1818, an oratorio held at Christ Church was an event on an unprecedented scale, in aid of the Fever Hospital and House of Recovery, which were under considerable pressure following the fever epidemic that raged in 1816. William Beamish chaired the managing committee for the event. Ten stewards were in attendance, and the treasurers of the hospitals acted as doorkeepers. Robert Bowden directed the hundred-strong performing forces, which included musicians from Cashel cathedral.[147] Twenty-six ladies from Cork city and county participated in the choir, and several local women were listed as soloists: Miss Travers, Miss Roche, the Misses Jervois and the Misses Noblett, all of whom impressed the reviewer in the *Southern Reporter*:

> In truth, altho' it was well known that the City could boast of much vocal talent of the first order among its fair residents, it could scarcely be conjectured that its combination on a Public display could be productive of so extraordinary an effect, as not only to stand the test of the severest criticism, but to rival with success some of the most eminent Professional Singers in the Empire.[148]

Reference was made in a review to 'the grandeur and fullness of the choruses, now swelling in all the "strength of sweetness", and then in silence hanging upon the dulcet tones of a single voice'.[149] The performance, which was reported to have lasted four hours, was in three acts: the first, a Grand Selection from Haydn's *Creation*, the second, a Grand Selection from *Messiah*, and the third, a Grand Miscellaneous Selection of Sacred Music from Handel, Haydn and concluding with Beethoven's 'celebrated chorus from *The Mount of Olives*', its first performance in the city. Vocal solos were performed by James Roche Jr and Edward Moeran, and by Mr Dorian of Cashel cathedral. Dorian's singing was commended: 'Mr Dorian gave the songs of "Comfort ye", etc and "Total Eclipse" with that degree of professional excellence that stamps him of the first order of vocal performers',[150] a view that was echoed in the *Southern Reporter*.[151] William Gillespie was the organist and James Brealsford Stephens the pianist.

The performance was repeated five days later 'with several additions'. Donations from a number of listed patrons were expected to supplement the proceeds from ticket sales and, in total, the *Cork Mercantile Chronicle* reported that £600 was raised for the Fever Hospital, although Tuckey gives the figure as 'nearly £800'.[152] The list of donations received from patrons shows the regional ambit of the venture.[153]

His Grace the Archbishop of Cashel	£5	0	0
His Grace the Duke of Devonshire	£5	13	9
Earl of Bandon	£3	8	3
Earl of Kingston	£5	0	0
Viscount Ennismore	£11	7	6
Sir Benjamin Hallowell	£5	0	0
Honourable Richard Hare	£5	13	9
Colonel Longfield	£10	0	0
Lord Arden	£10	0	0
Lord Riversdale	£5	0	0

Two donations were later acknowledged:[154]

Viscount Doneraile	£10	0	0
Richard Aldworth	£4	0	0

The review in the *Cork Mercantile Chronicle* concluded with the hope that 'an annual repetition of this most delightful Union of Charity and Amusement may take place, and that it may be equally productive'.[155] It represented the most ambitious locally led musical event to date in the city, offering a medium of expression of class identity and philanthropy for the city's upper and middle classes. Such an aspiration was not to be realised, however, and this was to be the last full-length oratorio to be staged in Cork for another fifteen years.

Although the fever crisis had abated by 1821, the city had reached an economic nadir. The end of the French wars had resulted in an economic decline that was felt at all levels of society. The collapse of the Roche bank in that year had repercussions that extended far beyond the city. Although the boom years of the early nineteenth century had brought significant new organisations for civic engagement in science and art, little had changed for music. As an urban social pursuit, music underwent some advancement, through the broadening of its commercial base, and expansion of its public role as a means of charitable support. It remained an amusement, not gaining the type of intellectual or artistic interest that was already shown in art and science. The fledgling music profession, as yet, saw its role as a praxial one, working without the potential benefits of a learned or professional society.

6

'TALENTED TOWNSMEN': MOBILITY AND OPPORTUNITY, 1820-1840

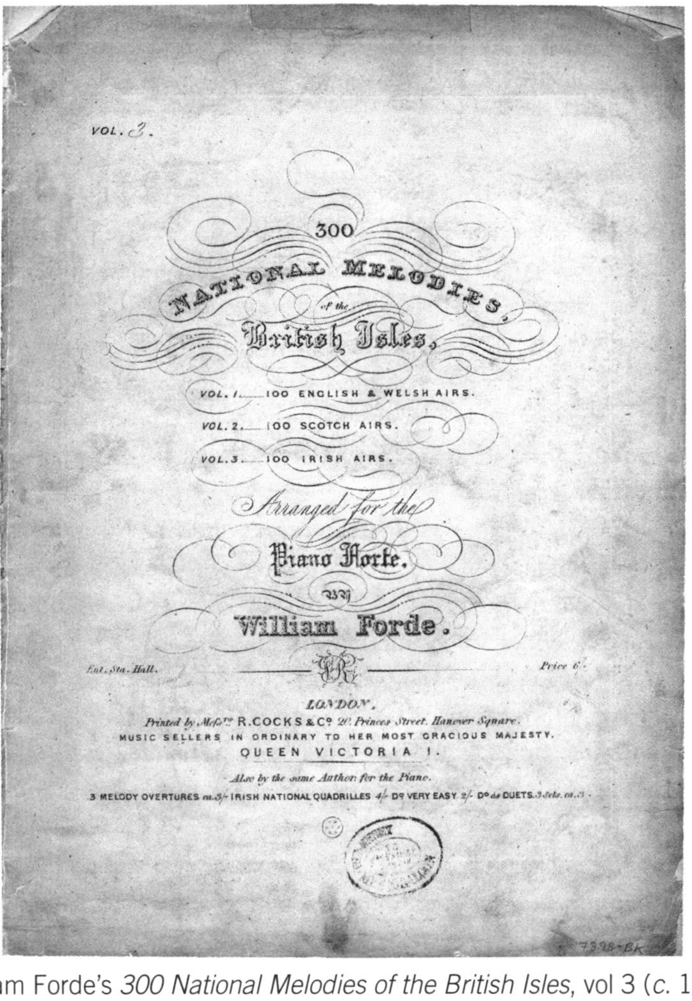
VOL. 3.

300

NATIONAL MELODIES,

of the

British Isles,

VOL. 1. 100 ENGLISH & WELSH AIRS.

VOL. 2. 100 SCOTCH AIRS.

VOL. 3. 100 IRISH AIRS.

Arranged for the

Piano Forte.

BY

William Forde.

Ent. Sta. Hall.

Price 6/-

LONDON.

Printed by Mess.rs R. COCKS & Co 20, Princes Street, Hanover Square.

MUSIC SELLERS IN ORDINARY TO HER MOST GRACIOUS MAJESTY.

QUEEN VICTORIA !.

Also by the same Author for the Piano.

3 MELODY OVERTURES ea. 3/- IRISH NATIONAL QUADRILLES 4/- Do VERY EASY 2/- Do as DUETS. 3 Sets, ea. 3/-

William Forde's *300 National Melodies of the British Isles*, vol 3 (*c.* 1841).

The Superb arrived in our River yesterday, after a short and agreeable passage, bringing with her the staff of the musical talent of London, accompanied by Mr Forde, preparatory to our splendid Concerts. Many of those persons are now in Ireland for the first time, and speak rapturously of the urbanity and attention they have already experienced.[1]

The establishment of the St George Steam Packet Company in Cork in 1823 heralded a new era in the cross-channel passenger trade. Designed for speed and passenger comfort, the *Superb* provided links to London via Bristol, one of the new routes facilitating the professional movement between the two islands that had commenced with the Act of Union. As well-developed centres of musical activity, London, Bath and Edinburgh attracted professionals from abroad seeking performance opportunities in theatres and concert halls. According to Fergal Gaynor, Cork had not honed the 'raw creative energies' of its boom years into anything of artistic or cultural significance. A number of talented and well-educated young men saw their best opportunities in emigration. Gaynor poses 1822 as a year that marked the coming of age of a generation well educated in the classics, and he states that 'to be educated in the early nineteenth century into the classical tradition was […] to be introduced into European culture, to be given its language, models, and frames of reference'.[2] Among them were William Maginn (1793–1842), Francis Mahony and artist Daniel Maclise, who sought professional advancement initially in London, a path already chosen by numerous Irish writers.[3]

British literary interest in Ireland grew during the early nineteenth century. The novels of Sidney Owenson represented a new literary form, the 'national tale', articulating a post-Union view of Irish life, set amid ruined castles, focusing on the figure of the bard, appealing to Romantic sensibility while articulating political sentiments. Thomas Moore's patriotic poetry, set by Sir John Stevenson to melodies from Bunting's collections, brought Irish patriotism 'from the podium to the parlour', proving immensely popular among English listeners.[4] Published in ten volumes between 1808 and 1834, Moore's Irish Melodies evoked 'remembrance' of Ireland's past, particularly through the symbolism of the harp.[5] Rekindled after a twenty-year lapse following the 1798 Rebellion, the work of Irish antiquarians also appealed to English readership. An early explorer of the antiquities of the Munster region was Cork-born Thomas Crofton Croker (1798–1854), who moved to London in 1818, where he published his seminal work *Researches in the South of Ireland* in 1824. Waterford-born Samuel Carter Hall (1800–99), who had lived in Cork during his youth, left Cork for London in 1821 to begin a career in journalism, while sustaining a keen interest in the antiquities of Ireland.

An escalation in music publication in London saturated the market with new compositions, adaptations and arrangements of operatic and dance selections for amateur use. Journals such as the *Quarterly Musical Magazine and Review* (1818–28) and *The Harmonicon* (1823–33) circulated up-to-date commentary on a broad range of topics relating to music events, personalities and new works, metropolitan and provincial musical life, together with copious advertisements for the major music publishing houses.[6]

TERENCE MAGRATH (1780–1865)

One of Cork's promising young musicians at the turn of the nineteenth century was Terence Magrath, son of singer, music teacher and parish clerk James Magrath. In 1797, at the age of seventeen, Terence replaced James Roche as organist at Christ Church. An account of an oratorio held there in September 1802 contains a reference to his piano playing in the orchestra,[7] when he was reported to have 'displayed taste, execution, and feeling, in a manner highly creditable to his talents'.[8] However, his ambitions lay in vocal music, and in 1803 he resigned his organist's post and departed to study singing with the much sought-after teacher and castrato singer Venanzio Rauzzini (1746–1810) of Bath.[9]

During the eighteenth century, Bath had developed into a sophisticated spa resort, visited annually by London's nobility and gentry. Musical performances of a high standard were organised at venues such as the Pump Room and the New Assembly Room, and the city sustained a strong core of professional musicians. As concert director, Rauzzini introduced his new student to the town's professional music circle, and within months of his arrival, Magrath was selected to fill a vacancy in the Bath Catch Club.[10] From Febraury 1805 until 1810, he was listed on Rauzzini's concert programmes, both as a soloist and ensemble singer.[11] He featured as a soloist at a musical festival at Exeter in 1813, and in 1814 at Bristol, Winchester (the Hampshire Musical Festival), and Bath (the Fifth Bath and Somersetshire Grand Musical Festival).[12] In 1813, he was among the principal vocal performers at a performance of *Messiah* for Andrew Ashe's benefit at the Pump Room.[13] From 1814 onwards,

Magrath appeared at prestigious London venues.[14] As an ensemble tenor singer, he performed at five of the Philharmonic Society concerts in the spring of 1815.[15] Among his performance venues in 1816 were the Holywell Music Room in Oxford,[16] and London's Argyll Room.[17]

On a vacation visit to Edinburgh, Magrath was introduced to Walter Scott (1771–1832), who persuaded him to move there, and from 1817 he taught singing to Scott's daughters, also becoming immersed in the city's musical life, performing with prominent local musicians such as Felix Yaniewicz.[18] In a letter dated 2 October 1817 to the 5th Duke of Buccleuch (1806–84), Scott wrote:

> I have an inimitably good songster in the person of Terence Magrath who teaches my girls. He beats almost all whom I have ever heard attempt Moore's songs and I can easily cajole him out to Abbotsford for a day or two. In jest or earnest I never heard a better singer in a room though his voice is not quite full enough for a concert and for an *after-supper* song he almost equals Irish Johnstone.[19]

At the Duke of Buccleuch's household, Magrath was introduced to the Rev. Charles Lindsay (1760–1846), Bishop of Kildare and Dean of Christ Church, Dublin, who offered him the next vacant post of Vicar Choral at Christ Church.[20] In 1823, at the age of forty-three, Magrath became a stipendiary at Christ Church cathedral and was listed in Pigot's 1824 trade directory as Professor of Music at Lower Mount Street, Dublin.[21] He was appointed as vicar choral at Dublin's Christ Church cathedral on 19 April 1830.[22] He was appointed as full vicar choral at St Patrick's on 15 October 1833, on the death of John Stevenson (1767–1833), having previously been a 'half vicar'.[23] He retained both positions until his death in 1865. The annual salaries for both vicars choral and stipendiaries at the Dublin cathedrals, at £222 and £150 respectively, were remarkably high, exceeding those at the Chapel Royal, London.[24]

Unlike their Cork counterparts, the vicars choral in the Dublin cathedrals were employed on the basis of being primarily musicians rather than churchmen.[25] In February 1825, Magrath and his fellow stipendiaries William Robinson, Francis Robinson, and Simeon Buggine (d. 1842) presented a series of four vocal concerts at the Rotunda, modelled on those of the London vocal concerts at the Hanover Square Rooms.[26] In May, the group arrived in Cork to present two vocal concerts at the Theatre Royal.[27] A preview in *The*

Constitution referred to the great expense of the admission cost, which at 6s 8d, 3s 4d and 2s 6d exceeded the local standard rate, although admission to the Rotunda concerts had been 8 shillings.[28] This was a rare appearance by Magrath in his home city.

Magrath's career as a concert singer in Dublin continued to flourish and his involvement on committees of some prominent musical societies indicates his position at the core of Dublin's musical establishment. He was listed as a committee member and trustee of the Dublin Choral Society from its commencement in 1837 until at least 1843,[29] and sang in the choir of Trinity College until 1840.[30] He was active on the committee of the Irish Musical Fund Society for several years from 1839 onwards,[31] and was Vice-President of the Dublin Glee Club in 1853.[32] His musical contributions at Masonic meetings were reported in the Dublin newspapers in the 1840s and 1850s.[33] Copies of half a dozen of his vocal compositions and arrangements are held at the National Library of Ireland. His death in March 1865 was marked by an obituary in the *Evening Mail*, reprinted in the *Cork Examiner*, describing him as 'a keen, though charitable observer, with a relish for the humorous and eccentric', a man 'of great conversational power', who 'lived in the best society in the three kingdoms'.[34] His circuitous route to a high-status professional role in Dublin highlights the relatively weak musical connections between Cork and Dublin at this time. Not only his performing ability, but his social adeptness enabled him to move in an upward trajectory and to spend his later years among the echelons of Dublin's musical circles.

WILLIAM FORDE (1795–1850)

Born in Cork, William Forde was the son of a tradesman who lost his business and abandoned his young family for America. William and his younger brother Samuel (1805–28) both 'manifested talent at an early age: one a talent for music, the other for painting'.[35] Samuel Forde subsequently gained a reputation as an artist before his untimely death. William's early musical training was not acquired within a church environment. He studied flute in Cork with James Gillespie before moving to London in 1818 at the age of twenty-three. One of his earliest publications was a three-part glee setting of Thomas Moore's text 'When freshly blows the northern gale', published around 1819 by John Green of London,[36] who was also agent and publisher for piano pedagogue Johann Bernhard Logier.[37] Green ran an academy on Logierian principles at Soho Square, where Forde would have encountered the novel pedagogical approaches of Logier and Friedrich Kalkbrenner (1785–1849). In 1821, a notice was published in a Cork newspaper for William and Ann Forde's Academy at 35 Grand Parade, offering piano tuition based on the latest methods of Logier and Kalkbrenner.[38] Forde also secured a position as principal flautist at the English Opera House, the name given to the former Lyceum in 1816 under the management of Samuel John Arnold (1774–1852). This theatre gained a reputation for its operatic productions and its impressive orchestra.[39] Although the precise length of his engagement is unclear, Forde would have gained valuable orchestral experience in the pit of this minor but significant London theatre.

The richness of London's musical life would have appealed to the youthful Forde. The flute, in particular, was entering a new phase of technical development and artistic expression. Charles Nicholson (1795–1837), the leading English virtuoso flautist of the early nineteenth century, performed regularly at the Philharmonic Society concerts, and featured in the city's major theatre orchestras. The performances of flute virtuosi associated with the Paris Conservatoire, established in 1795, also captured public interest. Although Louis Drouet (1792–1865) did not study flute at the Paris Conservatoire, he performed there at the age of seven, and later became renowned for his tone. He visited London in 1817, where he established a flute-making business, which, however, was subsequently eclipsed by the popularity of Nicholson's model of instrument.[40] He commenced a publication agreement with Robert Cocks at the same time as Forde, the two names frequently appearing on the publisher's advertisements. Drouet's older compatriots Jean-Louis Tulou (1786–1865) and Antoine Benoit Tranquille Berbiguier (1782–1835) also gained public attention in London with their distinctive style and techniques. In 1830, Cocks advertised *The Beauties of Berbiguier for the Flute, extracted from the author's works by William Forde*. It was in such work that Forde quickly established an income, supplying pedagogical materials, arrangements, adaptations and editions for flute, piano and violin for a new amateur public.[41] In addition to works by noted composers of the day, Forde produced arrangements of Irish airs, country dances, quadrilles, and operatic selections. In discussing the proliferation of such material in London during this period, Rohr suggests that 'the temptation to churn out as many works as possible for the publishers must have been strong, particularly given the dim prospects of achieving performance or publication, let alone money or fame, in the realm of church music, theatre, or orchestral composition'.[42] Forde did not invest all of his time and efforts in such work, however, and his frequent returns to Cork brought opportunities for performance. His wife Ann continued to live in Cork, with a growing family, in addition to instructing students on the harp and piano.[43] In March 1820, Forde was admitted as a Freeman of Cork city, a status not previously held by a professional musician.[44]

In January 1823, Forde arrived in Cork ahead of his début concert at the Assembly Rooms, previewed in *The Freeholder* as 'one of the most delightful bills of fare for a Concert that we have seen for years', introducing 'sublime selections from Mozart, Beethoven and Cherubini – the brilliant beauties of Drouet, Tulou, and Kalkbrenner'.[45] The programme was certainly a new departure in repertoire, with its emphasis on instrumental virtuosity. Originally planned for 16 January, the concert was deferred due to 'the arrangement for a performance on so large a scale requiring a longer period to complete than was anticipated'.[46] The programme was presented in three acts, rather than the customary two (see below). Apart from glees sung in each of the acts, the programme was instrumental in focus. Robert Bowden led the orchestra in performances of three overtures, opening with Beethoven's *The Creatures of Prometheus*. A sextet by Kalkbrenner featured John Roche at the piano. Forde performed Tulou's Fantasia 'Durandarte and Bellerma' and Drouet's variations on 'God save the King', a choice which underlines the equal merit given to an original composition and an arrangement of a well-known melody, the latter an undeniable crowd-pleaser. The reviewer commented that 'all was harmony in its utmost perfection, gratifying the most refined ear, and leaving an impression of the evening's entertainment, the recollection of which will be dwelt upon with reiterated pleasure'.[47]

PART FIRST

Overture to *The Men of Prometheus*	Beethoven
Glee 'Faithless Emma', 4 voices, Messrs Magrath, Bertridge, Moeran and Keays	Banks
Solo 'Introduction and Polonaise' Vln, Mr Bowden	Rosquellas
Song, 'Spring Song' (*Lalla Rookh*) Moeran, acc by himself	Dr Clarke
Solo 'Durandarte and Bellerma' Fl, Mr Forde	Tulou

PART SECOND

Overture to *La Clemenza di Tito*	Mozart
Song, 'The Troubadour' Mr James Roche	Horn
Grand Sestetto, Pf principal, Mr Roche	Kalkbrenner
Glee 'Tell me Mary Dear', Magrath, Bertridge, Moeran, Keays	Bowden
Solo, Introduction and French Air, with Vars, alto viola	Bowden

PART THIRD

'God save the King' with vars, Fl, Mr Forde	Drouet
Song 'Love's delightful hour', Mr Keays	Emdin
Duet 'Borne in yon Blaze' Moeran, Keays	Dr Clarke
Divertimento, two Fls, Mr Forde and an amateur	Forde
Glee 'By Celia's arbour all the night' Magrath, Bertridge, Moeran and Keays	Horsely
Overture to *Anacreon*	Cherubini

The arrival in Cork of London violinist Antonio James Oury (1800–83) in September may have been on Forde's invitation. Oury's first concert was held at the Great Room in Conway's Hotel, George's Street.[48] Carlo Rovedino (1751–1822), singer and Spanish guitar player, also performed.[49] Oury performed Joseph Mayseder's 'Irish air and le petit Tambour' and an 'adagio and polonaise' by Kreutzer/Mayseder.[50] Austrian virtuoso violinist and composer Joseph Mayseder (1789–1863) was among the first continental composers to feature Irish works in solo instrumental compositions and arrangements. Among the glees sung by a local group was Forde's 'When freshly blows the northern gale'. A second concert given by Oury over a fortnight later at the Assembly Rooms featured Frederick Mathews, organist of Cashel cathedral,[51] on the piano, and eighteen-year-old local singer Henry Allen (1809–76), making his first named appearance.[52]

Oury's concert was to be the last full concert to be held at the Assembly Rooms. The building was offered for sale or to let the following June,[53] and for his next concert, in October, Forde chose the Theatre Royal, much to the delight of the writer in the *Southern Reporter*, who anticipated a considerably larger audience, adding that:

> We can also promise, that, from the arrangements which have been made, the Theatre, on this occasion, will differ in no respect from a private Saloon, except in the extent and superiority of the accommodations. The rere [*sic*] of the stage, a few feet beyond the first drop scene, has been enclosed, which, while it will produce a good optical effect, will also add to the comfort of the audience. The Orchestra, too, has been thrown forward into the body of the house, by which, without injury to any, the full advantage of the music will extend to all parts; and at the banquet thus prepared, we hope to see a fashionable and numerous assemblage.

The writer welcomed 'an entertainment from which more is expected, and more, we are sure, will be realised, than from any other of the same kind that has taken place in this City for many years'.[54] A lengthy preview in the *Southern Reporter* announced the performers, who were to include Oury and the Ashe family, who had recently arrived in the city.[55] Admission to the concert was at the standard tiered theatre prices of 5s 5d, 3s 6d and 2s 6d.[56] These prices compared favourably with Forde's previous concert at the Assembly Rooms, for which admission had cost 6s 8d. Forde announced another concert in late November, for the benefit of the Mendicity Asylum. Oury, Rovedino and Mr and Mrs Ashe were again to participate.

With the six concerts of 1823, Forde emerged as an effective concert director, animating a mediocre provincial concert tradition. The six programmes presented a new concert model, which brought instrumental music to the fore while maintaining the 'miscellany' principle of alternating vocal and instrumental genres. Framed by orchestral overtures, each section of the programme featured a balance of instrumental and vocal items. Italian operatic ensemble featured prominently, and glees continued to feature in all programmes. The music of Mozart, both orchestral overtures and operatic vocal ensemble, was a notable addition to Cork's concert repertoire. These concerts represent a move from the assembly-based model to a formal setting. Despite the successes of this year, however, Forde did not return again in 1824 and 1825. By 1825, the local musical scene in Cork had reached a nadir. The Musical Society disbanded in 1824, along with the cessation of activities at the Assembly Rooms. Forde's absence left a vacuum in local musical leadership, which was, however, soon to be reactivated.

On his next visit to Cork in July 1826, Forde announced an extended musical festival, featuring a large company of English musicians and singers. Pre-dating the Dublin Festival of 1831 by five years, the event was a collaborative speculative venture between Forde and John McDonnell, proprietor and manager of the Theatre Royal.[57] Designated variously as the Grand Musical Meeting, the Grand Cork Concerts, and the Grand Cork Concerts and Oratorios, it was the most ambitious music undertaking in Ireland up to this time. The Theatre Royal had suffered poor houses for a number of years, a fact that may account for McDonnell's interest in the venture, which was timed to coincide with the summer assizes, when the city's population was augmented by an influx of the county gentry. The Theatre Royal was the established venue for the annual season of the visiting Hawkins Street company at precisely this time of year. As the Grand Concerts had now been given prior claim to the theatre, manager William Abbott was obliged to arrange an alternative venue for his company's performances in the disused Assembly Rooms, which were refurbished specially for the theatre season, and reopened on 22 July as the 'New Theatre Royal', featuring Madame Lucia Vestris, one of the most celebrated contemporary singing actresses, on her first Cork appearance. Nonetheless, *The Constitution* welcomed the prospect of rival events:

> A fair and honourable competition will always meet with our warmest support, and we are gratified from the character of the party engaged in this undertaking, no other feeling will be manifested. We have a population fully equal to the support of both establishments, and without detracting in the slightest degree from the attraction of either party, we must say that the name of Madame Vestris is a tower of strength.[58]

In addition to the offerings of both theatres, George Aspull was due to give a second morning concert on Thursday 3 August, at the Imperial Hotel.[59]

Musical meetings had a long tradition in English provincial cities, and were being organised with renewed vigour after the end of the French wars.[60] When the London theatre and concert season concluded in July, many performers took up engagements at the provincial festivals, which were held in August and September. Unlike the major English festivals, and the Cork Astley-run touring festival of 1814, which were three- or four-day events, combining daytime and evening performances, this Cork Festival was to continue for over a week, commencing with six Grand Concerts, on consecutive evenings, beginning on 31 July. The intention to continue the festival into a second week was not fully disclosed in the advance advertising, but was indicated by a heading in an earlier newspaper advertisement entitled 'The Grand Cork

Concerts and Oratorios',[61] and plans for operatic performances emerged in subsequent publicity notices during the first week.[62] The local newspapers provided extensive editorial coverage of the events and appealed to the public for support:

> With such inducements, we have no doubt that the enlightened and liberal portion of our city, proverbial for musical and scientific taste, will come forward and support the public spirited individual who has so manfully stood up, in the absence of all other entertainments, to cater on such an expensive and extended scale for their amusement.[63]

The performers, mainly from London, represented the largest non-theatrical group of musicians to visit the city up to that date. They travelled to Cork on the newly operating steam packet, the *Superb*, which carried passengers to and from London via Bristol, on a 65-hour voyage.[64] Forde's contacts in London yielded a large and distinguished company, numbering forty-five, although one advertisement stated that 'the number of persons engaged amounts to nearly one hundred'.[65] This may have included singers from the local church choirs to augment the chorus. The initial advertisements listed:

> Mr Keiswetter [*sic*], the celebrated performer of the violin
> Mr Schunk [*sic*], Principal pianist to the King of Wirtemburg
> Madame Cornega, of the Italian Opera
> Madame de Kolli, Theatre Royal, Covent Garden
> Mr A. Sapio, Principal Bass Singer, Royal Academy of Music, London
> Mr Lucas, Principal Violin, Royal Academy of Music, London
> Mr Forde, Professor of the Flute, Royal Academy of Music, London[66]

An extended list published a week later added nine more names:

> Miss Cubitt, of the Theatre Royal, Covent Garden
> Seignor [*sic*] Giovanola, of the Italian Opera
> Mr Byng, of the Theatre Royal, Bath, Bristol, etc
> Mr Christian Schunk, of the Italian Opera, Berlin and the Philharmonic Society, London, French Horn
> Mr Taylor, Double Bass

Mr Harper, the celebrated trumpeter
Mr Godwin, tenor, 'arranger of the music'
Mr Keays, of Cork [singer and cellist]
Mr Bowden, of Cork, leader of the Band[67]

Links with London's newly established Royal Academy of Music permeate the notices and biographies of the performers. The claim made in several of the advertisements that Forde was professor of the flute at London's RAM cannot be substantiated by reference to the academy's records. He may, however, have been engaged as a performer at some of the academy's concerts, or have been one of the academy's 'sub-professors', who, according to Ehrlich, were widely employed but received no payment.[68] Pianist Carl Schunke and violinist Christoph Gottfried Kiesewetter (1777–1827) had both participated in academy concerts in 1826.[69] According to Sainsbury's *Dictionary*, Antonio Sapio (1792–1851) was 'unquestionably the most promising tenor singer that has for many years appeared in this metropolis'.[70] He was listed as an Associate of the Royal Academy of Music for the years 1825–6.[71] The academy's Committee Minutes of 20 July 1826 record an 'agreement with Mr Forde for Sapio signed by the chairman in the name of the Committee'.[72] Cellist Charles Lucas (1808–69) was listed as 'sub-professor and student' of the Royal Academy of Music in 1826, and later became Principal of the Academy.[73] Mr Godwin, 'arranger of the music', may have been Mr Goodwin, librarian at the academy in 1826.[74]

Christoph Gottfried Kiesewetter was described in Sainsbury's *Dictionary* of 1825 as 'a very celebrated violinist, and has spent much time in England since the winter of 1821, when he performed at the Philharmonic Society concerts in London'.[75] Thomas Harper was Britain's most celebrated trumpeter at this time. An entry in Sainsbury's *Dictionary* describes him as 'first trumpet at the King's Theatre, Ancient and Philharmonic Concerts, [...] engaged within the last sixteen years at most of the other principal concerts and music meetings both in town and country'.[76] Sapio, Godwin and Taylor were also listed as performers at several English provincial festivals during the 1820s.[77] A seven-octave piano, manufactured by Érard and valued at 200 guineas, was imported for the occasion.[78] Its arrival on the *Superb*, along with 'Double Drums and other instruments', was reported in the *Cork Mercantile Chronicle*.[79] Unlike many such festivals, there was no stated charitable aim, and no list of patrons, whose donations would offset some of the expense. As a festival, this musical event was apparently self-styled, lacking a strong community base, such as the choral societies that were at the core of many of the English festivals.

The fact that less than capacity audiences attended the Grand Concerts was noted in successive editions of *The Constitution*.[80] The cancellation of the sixth concert may not have been surprising, but plans for the second week's events continued, which included benefits for Kiesewetter, Schunke and Forde, and a Sacred Oratorio in which Madame Cornega, Miss Sampson and Signor Giovanola were to feature.[81] It was also announced that Rossini's *Il barbiere di Siviglia* was in preparation for production the following week.[82] On 12 August, the *Southern Reporter* bluntly stated the position:

> It is already known that the Concert, for the effective support of which so many performers of eminence had been brought from England to this city at great expense, and which had been patronized for one or two nights, with a tolerably fair prospect of continuing success, were subsequently so deserted that they were obliged to be given up, to the great loss of the spirited projectors of the undertaking. Whether the failure arose from the competition of the little Theatre fitted up by Mr Abbott, whose career has been very prosperous, or from any deficiency in the Concerts, we cannot decide; but it is likely both causes contributed to it. Madame Vestris was evidently more attractive than Mr Keiswetter [*sic*], and we doubt if Mr Schunke was preferred to Miss Noel. This may be an imputation on the taste of the fashionables of our City, or it may be an exposure of their pretentions to be considered patrons and lovers of an accomplishment without which modern education cannot be said to be completed. The fact is, however, as we have stated, and those who were deluded with the notion that the people of Cork were a musical people, and speculated accordingly, will have to pay dearly for their credulity.[83]

The attempt to extend the festival into a second week was a serious miscalculation, and the proposed extra performances were abandoned. A lack of experience on the part of the organisers may have been the cause. The clash with the theatre company's annual season was an obvious contributory factor, although assize week was the only time when sizable audiences could be sustained. Moreover, the scale of the event was mismatched to its intended audience. The five extant concert programmes were similar in format, each featuring the same performers with slightly varied repertoire. It is unlikely that, in a provincial city, audience interest could be sustained over a week of such concerts. Furthermore, the patrons of the pit and gallery, whose absence was noted, may simply not have afforded to attend on several nights. At any rate, Forde had overestimated the support that the venture would receive from the Cork public, despite much promotional newspaper coverage.

The Grand Concerts were a testament to Forde's courage and idealism. However, the motivations behind this major initiative may not have been entirely personal, or indeed local. A publicity campaign on behalf of the Royal Academy of Music had already been under way since the publication and circulation of Sainsbury's *Dictionary*, for which subscription books were to be established in the provincial music shops.[84] Cork's new steamship connections with England would have facilitated travel by intending students.[85] It is quite plausible that the Musical Meeting had broadly similar aims, seeking provincial support for the academy in a city that already had strong commercial links with London. This hypothesis would provide answers to some of the questions posed by the circumstances of this event. The presentation of a predominantly secular festival comprising vocal and instrumental concerts would have been an appropriate showcase for the talents of the academy's professors, students and associates. Continued references to Forde as a professor at the academy suggest an informal link, and a writer in the *Southern Reporter* anticipated possibilities of a more enduring connection:

> In general reference to the orchestra, we can say that the overtures and accompaniments were admirably and efficiently executed, and afford the most satisfactory evidence of the advance of Musical Science, under the fostering care of the Royal Musical Academy, of which several of the performers are members and students.[86]

Returning to Cork in September 1828, and resuming his promotion of concerts, Forde's interest centred initially on his pupils. He arrived in time to participate in a benefit concert for brothers John, Boyle and Walter Travers, sons of Captain John Travers, an event which attracted much press publicity.[87] Already well known to the public, and now 'on their first onset in life, to make a profession of that which they had heretofore studied for amusement',[88] the brothers presented this concert as a prelude to their first musical tour. Boyle Travers was a student of William Forde. Walter Travers was listed as a violinist at the Dublin Musical Festival of 1831,[89] and would hold his own benefit concert at William Hickie's Rooms in Bridge Street in 1833.[90] This concert included a début performance by William F. Gillespie, a young member of a family of musicians, music dealers and organ and piano tuners and repairers, who was to feature prominently in the city's musical life in subsequent decades. His performance of Schunke's fantasia on 'Hope told a flattering tale' was pronounced as 'excellent' in a review in *The Constitution*.[91]

Two weeks later, Forde held a benefit concert which was heralded in *The Freeholder* as 'rich in the music of the greatest composers; to which the most numerous and effective orchestra that we ever had in Cork, will give us an effect splendid in the extreme'.[92] The Travers brothers had delayed their departure in order to participate, and the band of the 34th Regiment was engaged.[93] The instrumental content of the programme was previewed as being 'full and more effective than we have known on any former occasion'. The overtures commencing each of the three acts were, respectively, Winter's *Maria de Montalbert*, Rossini's *The Italian in Algiers* and Méhul's *The Two Blind Men of Toledo*, none of which had appeared on previous Cork programmes. The first and third acts concluded with choruses: the first from Pucitta's *Henry IV* and the third with the Grand Military Chorus 'The Warrior's Welcome' from Weber's *Euryanthe*. The second act concluded with a grand march for double orchestra composed by Robert Bowden. A review in *The Constitution* commended the violin solos of Walter Travers, noting that 'this young gentleman bids fair to have no rival in his profession'. William Gillespie's performance of Moscheles's fantasia 'Recollections of Ireland' was deemed 'exquisite', and the review concluded that:

> It would be well if performances of this description were got up at intervals throughout the Winter – they would add much to the pleasures of the long nights, and what would be more satisfactory, would enliven the drooping funds of some of our charitable institutions.[94]

The latter comment indicates an enduring view of public music as a means of serving charity. An overarching comment in this review noted that 'the science of music has arrived at such perfection in Cork', acknowledging Forde's achievement in concert organisation.

Forde presented three concerts in Cork in October 1829, the first 'on a scale of magnitude unprecedented in this city' according to *The Constitution*,[95] featuring Mrs Ashe and her three daughters and Dublin cellist Samuel Pigott.[96] These concerts feature continuing adjustments with the public in mind, such as half-price tickets for children, and the inclusion of guest performers.

Orchestral discipline was also a concern. A review of the second concert in the *Southern Reporter* paid particular attention to the orchestral performance, stating that 'the Overtures were performed with more smoothness and precision than on the former evening, and an additional number of Violins rendered them considerably more effective'.[97]

The following week many of the county gentry were in the city for a sitting of the Special Commission for the Doneraile conspiracy trial.[98] It was a major social occasion, a display of solidarity among the gentry. 'Several distinguished families' prevailed upon William Forde to present a Grand Concert at the Theatre Royal, which he devised on his characteristic lavish scale. The concert featured the first Cork appearance of Dublin pianist and guitarist William Conran, and the Band of the Scots Greys, directed by Mr Owen.[99] Walter Travers performed a violin concerto 'with great execution' and the orchestra demonstrated 'remarkable precision and unity of effect'.[100] His innovative concerts had clearly gained favour among the elite of the region, and were featured annually over the following decade.

By the 1840s, Forde, in tune with current Romantic representations of Irish music, developed a scholarly perspective on Irish musical heritage and sought to accommodate both Irish indigenous music and European art music in a series of concerts and lectures. In July/August 1844, he sought subscribers for a series of three 'Entertainments of National and Artistic Music', during the assizes, featuring 'a combination of concert and lecture on the National Music of the British Islands'.[101] He presented a series of lectures on Irish music at the Imperial Hotel in 1844 and 1845. Between 1840 and 1850 he undertook a major project of folk song collection and transcription, drafting a prospectus for his 'General Collection of the Music of Ireland', and seeking 250 subscribers. The publication did not proceed, and after his death in 1850, the collection was acquired by John Edward Pigot (1822–71), a collector and friend of Forde's, a native of Kilworth, in County Cork.[102] Nineteenth-century Cork historian John Windele credited Forde with influencing taste, stating that: 'The beauty of the subjects he has chosen and the style in which they are arranged have effected a considerable change in the taste for this species of music.'[103] His broad range of published works was also acknowledged by his inclusion in Brown and Stratton's *British Musical Biography* of 1897.[104]

ALEXANDER DEANE ROCHE (1807–1870)

Alexander Deane Roche was the youngest son of cathedral organist James Roche. His mother, Agnes Deane, was daughter of David Deane.[105] His older brothers, James and John, had already established themselves as professional musicians. John Roche studied piano in London in 1816. The young Alexander was acclaimed at the age of eleven as 'a young Gentleman of great promise' at an oratorio at Christ Church in 1818 with his performance of 'There were shepherds abiding in the fields' from *Messiah*.[106] In 1822, at the age of fifteen, he left Cork for London, where, according to Gilbert, he studied singing with Macfarren and others, and commenced a prolific phase of song composition.[107] Among his early collaborators was poet and antiquarian Cork-born Thomas Crofton Croker, who had also arrived in London in 1818. One of his earliest songs was 'Long Summers have smiled', on words from *Blackwood's Magazine*, now held in the British Library. The ballad 'We met and we parted', set to a text by Croker, was first published in London in 1823 by James Power. Power had already published some of Thomas Moore's melodies. He also composed a song featured in the comedy *Love's Victory* by George Hyde, dated 1825. Another ballad resulting from the collaboration with Crofton Croker was 'Oh Twine me a bower', published in 1827 by James Power.[108] This song evidently remained popular for over eighty years, as it was alluded to in James Joyce's *A Portrait of the Artist as a Young Man*, which first appeared in 1914.[109] English soprano Elizabeth Rainsforth (1814–77) sang Roche's 'A coronet may gild thy brow' at a *fête champêtre* at Regent's Park, London, in 1836.[110] From 1825 to 1828 Alexander's brother, James Roche, studied singing in London with Giovanni Liverati (1772–1846).[111]

During these years Alexander's brother John also visited London at least twice,[112] and a reference to the singing of Miss Susan Roche was made in the *Quarterly Musical Magazine and Review* in 1826 noting that it was her first time being heard in London.[113] In 1831, she moved to Edinburgh, where her début performance at Felix Yaniewicz's concert in March 1831 was reported in the *Edinburgh Literary Journal*, stating that 'her voice is fine and just, although perhaps, scarcely powerful enough for a public singer'.[114] In 1833, following a performance in Cork in August, Alexander and his sister planned a concert tour of several English cities.[115] In September, they embarked on a voyage from London to Leith on the single-rigged smack the *Earl of Wemyss*, which ran aground at Brancaster on the Norfolk coast. Susan Roche was among the female passengers who were drowned, along with her nephew. The tragedy was reported in several English newspapers, and several accounts identified the child as the son of Eugenius Roche (1786–1829), former editor of the *New Times*.[116]

Accounts in London newspapers and journals suggest that this ill-fated concert tour occurred at the beginning of a new phase in Roche's performing career, as his engagement at the Festival of Northampton in 1833 was cancelled shortly afterwards.[117] A reviewer in *The Court Journal* commended his 'rich voice and just expression' in a performance of Beethoven's 'Adelaide' in 1833.[118] In 1835, he made several more London concert appearances. At the sixth concert of the Society of British Musicians at the Hanover Square Rooms, he sang John Blockley's (1800–82) ballad 'Sweet Village Stream' in a 'most impressive and finished style'.[119]

Among the new literary works inspired by Ireland and its people was *Lights and Shadows of Irish Life*, a three-volume set of stories written by Irish novelist Anna Maria Hall (née Fielding, 1800–81), published in London in 1838. Wife of antiquarian Samuel Carter Hall, she stated in the book's introduction that her aim in this work was 'to make the character of the Irish more extensively known and better understood, to excite a generous sympathy for their sufferings, a kind indulgence towards their faults, and a just appreciation of their virtues'.[120] As such, it may be regarded as an amplification of the national tale. The leading story in Hall's collection, 'The Groves of Blarney', was set as a three-act drama by the author and performed in London's Royal Adelphi Theatre in April 1838.[121] It was performed at the Royal Victoria Theatre in Cork the following June.[122] The Overture, composed by William Forde, and the songs in the drama, composed by A.D. Roche to Hall's texts, were published separately by Duff.

Roche's ballad from *The Groves of Blarney*, 'Aileen Mavourneen', achieved wide popularity, being also published that year in a version for guitar. Like the earlier 'O twine me a bower', it endured in concert and parlour repertoire for many decades. It was republished in America during the 1840s and was sung at the Music Hall in Dublin in 1842 by Miss Land,[123] and by Miss Elizabeth Birch in Dublin in 1845.[124] A reference to this song appears in Mark Twain's short story *A Dog's Tale* (1902): the dog was named 'Aileen Mavourneen' by his mother, who had heard it in a song. Roche's ballad 'Gilla Machree', set to a poem by Gerald Griffin, was sung by Elizabeth Rainsforth at Dublin's Rotunda in July 1842, and on her subsequent concert tour throughout England later that year.[125] Major library catalogues currently hold copies of some fifty ballads and songs by Roche, most of which were first published in London between 1823 and 1840, including poems by Mrs

S.C. Hall, Thomas Crofton Croker, Felicia Hemans (1793–1835), Thomas Haynes Bayly (1797–1839), Eugenius Roche (1786–1829) and Limerick-born poets John Francis Waller (1810–94) and Gerald Griffin (1803–40). Reviews were not always positive. Two songs written by Roche on the death of Felicia Hemans (1793-1835) were published in 1835.[126] One was 'How many have loved and honoured thee?' on a text by Letitia Elizabeth Landon (1802–38). A critic in *The Court Journal* commented:

> We know not in what mood Mr Roche was when he attempted to compose music for the above delightful poem: but we do know that the composition is unworthy the subject, and our critical notice [...]

With regard to 'My gentle child', Roche's song based on a poem by Felicia Hemans, the same writer found it to be 'a piece of scarcely any merit. It may rank among the common-place productions of the day'.[127]

Despite his moderate professional achievements, Roche chose not to remain in London. Having spent sixteen years there, he returned to Cork in July 1838.[128] His career took a new direction, focusing on concert promotion, and occasional performances of his own. His new Musical Repository at 5 South Mall in the former premises of Richard Gillespie's Music Warehouse rivalled the most prestigious of the city's principal music warehouses, his retail capacity later expanding to include art and photography supplies. In 1839, J. Duff of London published his book *A New Introduction to the Art of Singing*, but, after 1840, he appears to have lost interest in composition.

As case studies in the music profession, the early careers of these three Cork men validate Rohr's findings concerning the precarious nature of the music profession during the early nineteenth century. All three musicians had sought status as well as musical and monetary fulfilment. Magrath achieved all three, gaining entry to the most coveted professional circles in Bath and Dublin. Roche's song composition was relatively successful, but, having performed on the tedious English provincial circuits for over a decade, he returned to Cork, turning increasingly to his music business. He maintained status in the musical world in his role as an impresario for the celebrated foreign artists who arrived in the city. Although Forde's Cork–London travel was to continue throughout his career, his work in Cork remained central to his artistic and cultural aspirations, his professional adaptability being a key attribute in his role as a provincial musical leader and teacher.

7

'CULTURAL EXPLOSION': DIVERSITY ON THE CONCERT PLATFORM, 1830-1840

Detail from 'Debut in London of Niccolò Paganini'.

As middle-class concert-going increased in the provinces, touring professionals across continental Europe extended their ambits. The term 'cultural explosion' has been applied to the sudden increase in the concert phenomenon in London, Paris and Vienna,[1] which rippled outwards to European cities and larger towns. In examining concert life in Cork during the 1830s, this chapter will focus on concert management, repertoire and reception.

Following the closing of the Assembly Rooms in 1823, larger venues were favoured by most performers. In his use of the theatre from that date, William Forde had initiated a new model of concert presentation. Conway's Hotel on George's Street was used occasionally as a concert venue from 1823 until 1830. From 1824, the ballroom of the Imperial Hotel became a select venue for touring musicians. Lewis described the room as '70 feet long and 36 feet wide, elegantly fitted up, with a refreshment room adjoining, 50 feet long, and 36 feet wide'.[2] Holland gives the dimensions of the ballroom as 72' x 32' x 26', 'decorated by German artists' and 'one of the grandest rooms in Ireland', with a 'gallery at one end for musicians, and a stage 20 feet deep at

Figure 7.1.
Imperial Hotel, 1843,
Illustrated London News.
CORK CITY LIBRARY

the other'.[3] The organisation and promotion of concerts were facilitated as links with the local press were regularised, with an increase in the publication of full programmes, previews and substantial reviewing. *The Constitution* led the way in this regard, providing detailed writing on concerts since 1822. The *Southern Reporter* and the *Cork Mercantile Chronicle* followed; the writers in all remained anonymous.

From 1830 onwards, European folk groups included Cork on their tours, providing a novel concert model. In March of that year, the Tyrolese Rainer family gave four concerts over three days at Conway's Hotel,[4] presenting 'twelve of their most popular national melodies, appearing in the dresses presented to them by the King, [...] concluding their performance with a specimen of their national dance'.[5] Reputedly singing by ear, this family of singers, Maria Rainer and her brothers Felix, Anton, Joseph and Franz, from Fügen in Austria, had successfully toured Britain in 1827 and 1828, inspiring the publication of arrangements of their melodies by Ignaz Moscheles.[6] The group returned to Cork to give three concerts at the Imperial Hotel in late March during the spring assizes, after an intervening visit to Limerick.[7] For all of their concerts, a reduced admission fee of 2 shillings was available for children and 'members of school establishments'. Another folk group, the Bohemian Brothers, presented four concerts at the Imperial Hotel in early August of the following year, appearing, like the Rainer family, in national costume and singing national airs.[8] These concerts introduced the phenomenon of performing family groups, encouraging attendance by families with specially tailored admission rates.

The Russian Horn Band that arrived in the spring of 1832 had already toured widely throughout the United Kingdom. The performers, numbering twenty-six, used a method similar to hand-bell ensembles, each performer playing only a single pitch.[9] Developed from indigenous Russian hunting horns, the instruments were described in a preview in *The Constitution*:

> [...] they are Horns made entirely of Brass; the largest of which is eight feet in length and nine inches in diameter, the smallest two and a half inches long and one in diameter, the others (the number of which is fifty five) are all larger and smaller in proportion. Another set of Reeds, of various sizes and proportions, each instrument producing only one note, but of the most melodious sounds, though not so powerful and grand as those of the Horns, the Band also sing in Chorus their original National Songs, with accompaniments on the Clarionet, Cymbals and Tambourine.[10]

The advertisement also drew attention to the 'moderate scale of prices' which, at 3s, 2s and 1s, for boxes, pit and gallery, compared favourably with those of the Imperial Hotel concerts, and even those of the Rainers or the Bohemian Brothers.[11] Concerts by folk groups were not usually reviewed in the local press. However, recent performances provided a point of comparison in a vivid description of an Anti-Tithe meeting at Schull, County Cork, the following July, given in the *Southern Reporter*:

> Nor was the aid of musical minstrelsy wanting on the occasion; the fiddle and bagpipe, and the drum vied in the expression of the most obstreperous merriment, and were responded to by such a choral symphony of yells, cheers and sympathetic flourishes of the voice, as to excel the combined efforts of 'the Russian horn band' and 'Bohemian brothers' [...] [12]

William Forde continued to develop the local concert scene with innovative repertoire and programme planning, on an expanded version of the 'miscell-aneous' concert. His student, flautist Boyle Travers, held a benefit concert in June 1830, featuring an orchestra led by Robert Bowden.[13] Boyle's brothers, John and Walter, played violin, and Mr F. Smith was the cellist. The young Cork singer Henry Allen (1809–76), who had recently commenced study at London's Royal Academy of Music,[14] sang three solos. Mr Pentland, a new name on Cork concert programmes, performed a concerto on the corno bassetto.[15] The three Travers brothers' engagement as orchestral musicians for the Dublin Grand Musical Festival in August of the following year was a rare opportunity to perform alongside the capital's leading players.[16]

Young musicians again appeared at a concert organised by Forde in November 1830, featuring Master Reeves, harpist, Master Smith, guitarist, and Masters Coghlan and Gamble, both piano pupils of Bowden. Mr Pentland, corno bassetto player, made another appearance and 'displayed musical skill of a high order', and Mr Macalaney performed on the clarinet.[17] Boleyne Reeves (1821–1905) was the son of a Cork paper manufacturer, Peter Reeves. The young Reeves subsequently left Cork for London, distinguishing himself as a harpist and establishing a literary career.[18] In three acts, the programme was long and varied. Rossini's overtures *Semiramide* and *William Tell* commenced the first and third acts. A grand march and waltz, composed and 'newly arranged' by Bowden, opened the second act. A novel feature was the inclusion of four recitations by actor Nicholas Moore Stack (1798–1854),[19] one of which was Thomas Moore's *Melologue on National Music*

(1811), 'with characteristic musical accompaniment'. The adjustment of admission prices to 2s 6d and 1s 6d, in comparison with the regular prices of 3s and 2s, was evidence of Forde's policy of promotion of concerts for a wider section of the public. The gallery price of 1s 6d was the lowest-priced concert admission ticket offered in Cork up to this date, apart from folk group concerts. However, a report in *The Constitution* noted that the attendance was less than optimal and criticised the excessive length of the programme.[20]

Following his appearances at the Dublin Musical Festival in August 1831, Niccolò Paganini (1782–1840) arrived in Cork in mid-September, with pianist Pio Cianchetini (1799–1851) and singer Costanza Pietralia (*c.* 1770–*c.* 1830).[21] The performers were at the beginning of a five-month tour of England, Ireland and Scotland that would feature sixty-five concerts. On Saturday 24 September the Theatre Royal was 'crowded to excess, by a most fashionable audience' for the first concert. The *Southern Reporter* captured the mood of the gallery occupants, as the performer made his first delayed appearance on stage:

> The Gods were rather unceremonious in their first salutation, and, as if to banish the diffidence of the Signor, they gave him a truly Irish reception. Loud cries of 'don't be bashful', 'hand him out in a wheelbarrow'. &c., &c. went through the house, succeeded by loud laughter. At length Paganini appeared, and in a moment the noisy shouts of the gallery were lost in the enthusiastic plaudits and acclamations of the entire audience. He acknowledged this kind reception in a warm and good humoured manner.[22]

For the second concert, on the following Tuesday, *The Constitution* reported that 'upwards of one hundred and fifty Ladies and Gentlemen were obliged to accommodate themselves in the orchestra, and on the stage, there not being room in the boxes, so crowded was every part of the house'.[23] Paganini's third concert, two days later, was not so well attended 'in consequence of a generally received opinion that he had left town'.[24] This was probably due to a press announcement that he was to leave for Killarney on Wednesday.[25] The fourth and final concert on Saturday 1 October necessitated alterations to the stage 'to accommodate a great number of persons'.[26] Paganini's financial arrangement for two-thirds of the receipts applied during this tour rendered his Cork visit lucrative.[27]

Figure 7.2. Debut in London of Niccolò Paganini (1831): drawing by Daniel Maclise.

Paganini performed four times in each of the acts, interspersed with performances by Cianchetini and Pietralia. The writer in *The Constitution* described Paganini's entry on stage on the first night:

> When the moment for his coming forward arrived, all eyes were turned to the stage, and a solemn silence prevailed until he was seen issuing forth in one of his *echellon* movements. This was the signal for the burst of loud and general applause, which continued for several minutes, and such was the warmth of his reception, that numbers rose in the pit and galleries to give greater vent to their feelings. At the musical flourish of the Signor's bow, the plaudits instantly subsided.[28]

The third concert featured a performance of variations on 'St Patrick's Day', a piece which Paganini had premiered in Dublin.[29] Feeling unequal to the task of precise technical description, the reviewer focused on the audience response:

> To convey a proper idea of the display of his unrivalled powers of execution in the Irish Air of Patrick's Day, with variations of his own composition on one string, would be a difficult task for the most accomplished and experienced proficient in the science of Music. The raptures of the audience, the loud and vehement calls of encore, and the enthusiastic cheering that followed, when Signor Paganini responded to the call, were tests of the delight which his performance imparted![30]

Less than a month after Paganini's departure, *The Constitution* published an advertisement for a concert featuring London violinist Isaac Collins (1797–1871), 'the English Paganini', organised and directed by William Forde.[31] He was first introduced to the London public by Samuel Arnold at the English Opera House,[32] where Forde was an orchestra member. Collins's six-year-old son, Viotti Collins (1822–99), a prodigy violinist, was his co-performer. Forde saw a concert-touring opportunity in the wake of Paganini's successful concerts, arranging a formidable line-up of musicians, including Dubliners Samuel Pigott, cello, Thomas Harrington, double bass, and Mr and Mrs Haydn Corri.[33] Outside of theatre season, Dublin professional musicians rarely appeared in Cork for one-off engagements. Forde appears to have prompted such exchanges, which were to be of mutual benefit to the performers. Born in Edinburgh, Haydn Corri (1785–1860) held the post of organist at Dublin's Marlborough Street church (later known as the Pro-Cathedral) from 1825 until 1860.[34] His wife Ann (née Adams) (1800–67) was a singer at the Theatre Royal in Dublin. The first concert featured Haydn and Ann Corri, in a buffo duet, which 'amused the house exceedingly'. Thomas Harrington had studied at the RAM from 1824 until 1826, and was most likely an acquaintance of Forde. Samuel Pigott (*c.* 1790–1853) was a well-known Dublin cellist, who had played in the Dublin theatre orchestras.[35] Local instrumentalists included Robert Bowden, Mr Smith (second violin), Boyle Travers and William Forde, flutes. Henry Allen sang and Nicholas Moore Stack delivered three recitations. The reviewer in *The Constitution* attempted some technical description:

> In all those points which constitute musical perfection, Mr Collins is not surpassed. His taste and feeling are excellent, his tone is pure and rich, his intonation is singularly correct, and his execution at once clear, firm, and brilliant. After an introductory movement, formed of a most delightful alternation of the majestic and the plaintive styles, Mr Collins proceeded to a display of the most exquisite harmonics, in a series of popular airs. An arpeggio, exhibiting an extraordinary command of the bow, followed; then, that beautiful air 'Sweet Home'. As a quartett on one violin; and his first piece concluded with a variation in the style denominated pizzicato, which we do not hesitate to assert is unequalled by any violinist; a unanimous encore burst from all parts of the house. Mr Collins, in his solo on one string, completed his triumph.[36]

After four more performances, father and son continued their tour, with William Forde and Henry Allen as supporting musicians. Samuel Pigott directed their Dublin concert at the Rotunda in November, billed as Allen's first Dublin performance,[37] and the group appeared at the Belfast Assembly Rooms in early December.[38] Before they departed Cork, the Corris performed at the South Parish chapel to support a charity sermon in aid of the Orphan Asylum. Haydn Corri presided at the organ and performed 'an extempore medley of sacred airs'. Ann Corri sang two Handel arias, and joined the chorus in 'The marvellous works' from Haydn's *The Creation*.[39]

From the early nineteenth century, the harp had emerged as a concert instrument, featuring on programmes given by the Ashe family on their tours. Mrs Ashe and her daughters returned to Cork in September 1832, undeterred by a cholera epidemic in the city since the spring, which had devastating effects on the city's poorer communities. With James Roche as the only listed local support, their first concert was held at the Imperial Hotel. Miss C. Ashe's performances of 'Imp's March' introduced Nicholas Bochsa's 'New Harp Effects', apparently for the first time in Ireland.[40] Bochsa's publication *New Harp Effects* (Goulding & D'Almaine, 1832) was his latest contribution to the developing technique of the instrument, involving various harmonic and damping effects.[41] The groups gave a second concert five weeks later at William Hickie's New Ball Room, part of his recently opened 'Dancing Academy and Gymnasium' at 14 Bridge Street.[42] Occasionally listed as principal second violin player for concerts, Hickie had been active as a dancing master in the city since 1814, with previous academies located at the George's Street Assembly Rooms and at 2 Academy Street. This concert opened with Beethoven's *Fidelio* overture, presumably in arrangement, either by the string performers, or by a military band.

A concert was given in August by two members of the Roche family, Alexander and Susan Roche, which also featured their brother, James Roche, with William Gillespie, Jr, and William Forde. Since their concert in Cork in 1827, Alexander Roche and his sister had subsequently performed in Dublin and London.[43] Susan Roche had been professionally active as a singer in Edinburgh for a number of years.[44] It was to be Susan Roche's last concert in Cork before the ill-fated tour of England that ended with her tragic drowning. (see pages 137–138). The band of the 28th Regiment performed overtures to Rossini's *La gazza ladra* and Auber's *Fra Diavolo* to open each of the two acts, and Forde presented a flute solo. In addition to Italian vocal repertoire by Mercadante and Donizetti, Susan Roche sang 'The Last Rose of Summer' and Alexander Roche sang his own ballad 'We met and we parted'.[45] *The Constitution* reported a less than capacity audience, and gave the performers moderate praise.[46]

The visit of Italian singer Signora D'Alberti in October was announced in all of the city's newspapers, including the recently established *Cork Evening Herald*. Billed as 'prima donna de la Scala de Milan et première Cantatrice du Roi de France', she had been engaged by Calcraft at the Hawkins Street Theatre Royal during the previous winter. Her three performances at the Imperial Hotel featured an orchestra which was 'numerous and complete', conducted by Robert Bowden and led by Walter Travers. D'Alberti's arias by Rossini, Nicolini, Mayer and Donizetti, and duets with James Roche were sung with full orchestral accompaniments. *The Constitution*'s reviewer was highly impressed with her first concert:

> Never do we remember anything in the Musical line in our City that caused so great a sensation among the lovers of good Music as did the Concert given by Signora D'Alberti on Tuesday evening [...] And we candidly admit, that we never were more at a loss for words wherewith to express ourselves, than when asked for a description of her performances, to do anything like justice to her perfections with the pen is totally impossible and any attempt must fail to convey an adequate conception of her richness of intonation, her power and extent of voice, her sweetness of expression, or the wonderful effects of her Contre-alto and Soprano notes, which she blends together in such a manner as to excite the amazement of her hearers.[47]

The *Cork Mercantile Chronicle* presented an equally brilliant review:

> When first she came forward, she appeared as if but trying her voice, and then burst out as one exulting in the discovery of a new and delightful power, producing a thrilling effect upon the audience. This bubbling and, as it were, welling out of music (so peculiar to the Italian school) has an enchanting effect. Signora D'Alberti has a very captivating appearance, and the cheerful acquiescence with which she executed the encores, won almost as much as her musical powers upon her audience. Her face is English, but her singing is perfectly Italian, and of the very purest and best school.[48]

D'Alberti's use of an orchestra provided opportunities for concerto and ensemble performances. William Gamble, a member of a local family of dancing masters, displayed 'much brilliancy of execution and elegance of style' in a piano concerto by Kalkbrenner 'with obligato violins, violincello, and horns',[49] and Mr W. Fisher, probably a military musician, gave what was likely to have been the first Cork performance of Mozart's clarinet concerto.[50] Together with harp solos by Mrs Harrington and flute solos by William Forde and his student, Boyle Travers, the three concerts provided exceptionally rich content and variety.

A charity sermon was preached at the South Parish chapel in November 1833 in aid of St Patrick's Orphan Asylum, which had been set up as a hospital during the cholera epidemic of the previous year, and now catered for fifteen children orphaned as a result. Edward Moeran performed on the organ, with performances by the choir. £83 4s was raised for the charity.[51]

Further sermons followed in December, January and February for the Lancastrian Free Schools, SS Peter and Paul Female school, and the schools of the Presentation Monastery in Douglas Street, respectively, each featuring selections of sacred music by organist and choir. A sermon with a sacred music performance at the South Chapel in April 1834, for the benefit of the Lying-in Hospital, attracted an unusually high level of press attention. The programme consisted of a selection of sacred music 'principally from the collection of the treasurer', Richard Beamish.[52] The programme featured solos and choruses by Handel, Haydn, Clifton and Zingarelli. The solo singers were Richard Keays, Edward Moeran and James Roche, A.P. Herrmann, Mr Seymour, Mr McCarthy. The choir, conducted by William Forde, included singers selected from both the Protestant and Catholic cathedrals and the South Chapel. William Gillespie presided at the organ.[53] The contribution of Forde was praised in the *Cork Mercantile Chronicle*:

> The combined effort of the Organ, and the singers in the Choral parts were magnificent. Accuracy and precision in taking up the contrast in the points were attained to a degree we have seldom heard in similar performances. These perfections are manifestly to be attributed to the appointment of the Conductor, Mr Forde, by whom the measure was visibly marked, and signals given which insured unity of effect.[54]

It was a prominent social event comparable with the oratorios of the early nineteenth century. The *Cork Evening Herald* noted that 'the Chapel was crowded by all sorts and parties, and the attendance of officers was very numerous'.[55]

The Spanish guitar provided one of the novel sounds on concert platforms across Europe during the mid-1830s. In July the guitar prodigy Giulio Regondi (*c.* 1822–72) visited Cork, having given ten concerts in Dublin.[56] Accompanying him was Signor A. Regondi, a buffo singer who was his manager and foster father.[57] He gave several concerts over a two-week period at the Imperial Hotel and one at the Theatre Royal, where his concert formed a theatrical interlude.[58] Although guitarist and singer Carlo Rovedino had performed in Cork in 1823, Regondi is generally regarded as the earliest exponent of this instrument in Ireland, the earlier 'English guitar' being a type of cittern.[59] Giulio's concerts also featured vocal duets with Regondi senior and promotional performances on Wheatstone's patent concertina, which included 'The Last Rose of Summer' with variations.[60]

After a week of concerts in Limerick, he returned to Cork and gave at least six more performances, both morning and evening, at the Imperial Hotel.[61] The retention of audiences for such a lengthy succession of concerts may have been partly due to the low admission price of 2s 6d (with further concessions for children and families), which was considerably less than the standard concert admission price of five shillings.[62] The programmes show the preponderance of arrangements of operatic and popular airs, in the form of duets and variations by Mauro Giuliani (1781–1829), Ferdinando Carulli (1770–1841), Matteo Carcassi (1792–1853) and Hippolyte Loüel (fl. 1830–46).[63]

Up to this time, musical societies in Cork were either philanthropic or convivial, involving mainly amateurs, supplemented by a few professional musicians. Established in 1831, the Philharmonic Society was the first of its kind, centred on professional activity, aspiring to 'the more general cultivation and extension of the Art than at present exists in this City'. In 1831 and 1832, meetings were held on Tuesday evenings at the Imperial Hotel, during which time local merchant William J. Sheehy acted as secretary and Mr Atkins as treasurer.[64] By 1835, virtually all of the city's music professors had joined, together with a substantial number of amateurs, and a series of monthly concerts were planned for the following spring. In December 1835 a press notice announced the first 'practice meeting' at Mr Hickie's Concert Room.[65] It was at this venue that a series of five public concerts commenced the following March.

Detailed programmes and reviews of two of the concerts appeared in the local press. The programmes showed signs of impeccable design, reflecting a professional and artistic confidence among the city's key musicians. The second concert, held on 1 March, featured established professionals such as William Forde, James Roche and Robert Bowden, and younger musicians. A performance of the slow movement of Haydn's 'Emperor' quartet (Op 76, No. 3 in C) by Robert Bowden and three of his pupils, Masters Keays, Lambkin and Coghlan, was a highlight of the evening. Richard Keays sang one of his own compositions and Walter Travers performed an air and variations for the violin, an arrangement by Forde.[66] The reviewers in two of the local newspapers acknowledged the valuable role that these events played in the city. The reviewer in *The Constitution* opined that 'if followed up in the spirited manner in which it has commenced, it will realise in our City, that which has long been a desideratum – a most delightful and rational source of pleasurable enjoyment'.[67] A similar sentiment was expressed in the *Southern Reporter*, as part of the review of the third concert:

> If the only result of those rational and delightful amusements consisted in the fostering and producing of a spirit of ambitious aspiration calculated to awaken energies which would otherwise lie dormant, we might have to congratulate the admirers of musical excellence upon the discovery of a judicious and unfailing mode of developing neglected or forgotten genius, and of raising an art to which society owes many of its higher and more enduring charms, by cheering on its votaries with a well earned approbation.[68]

William Gilliespie, who had composed an overture for the occasion, was noted in particular:

> Mr Gillespie's production has shewn him to be a Musician of respectable attainments, pure taste, and correct idea of Orchestral harmony; and we feel conscious that his abilities will meet with due appreciation when taste shall reject its antiquated prejudices – talent attain its proper position – and the public be forced to believe at length that such a thing as genius, and that of no ordinary character, may be born and educated under an Irish as well as an Italian sky.[69]

Charles Sullivan, 'a young aspirant to musical fame, received praise in *The Constitution* for his 'beautifully expressive style in slow movement, brilliant touch, and elasticity of finger'.[70] However, the tone of the review in the *Southern Reporter* was reproachful to the city's concert goers:

> 'Count Balthazar', the magnificent production of the Chevalier Newkom, gave Mr Roche an opportunity of displaying to advantage the rich resources of his deep and melodious voice; and he exhibited an ease, flexibility and distinctness in mastering the difficult passages of this piece, such as nothing short of an inimitable knowledge of the difficulties of his profession, and a skilful idea of the means by which they are to be overcome, could have enabled him to attain.[71]

A hint of bitterness is evident in the comments on James Roche's performance, which concluded: 'It would only be necessary, that Mr Roche should adopt a German or an Italian name, to be considered amongst the highest ranks of his art.' The anxiety over Italian and, more recently, German pre-eminence in musical composition and performance that had entered current thinking in London may have prompted such comments,[72] in addition to the series of foreign musicians who had delighted and astonished local audiences since 1830.

The lack of public support for local professional musicians alluded to in this report appears to have persisted. Despite a successful series and supportive press coverage, there is no evidence of further public activity by the Philharmonic, or references to its meetings. Despite its dedication and serious intent, the society had ceased to exist by 1837, when William Harrington presented £26 of its remaining funds to the Fever Hospital and House of Recovery.[73] The fate of this society highlights the status of music in the city at this time, and invites comparison with the relative success of the Society for Promoting the Fine Arts, founded in 1815, with broadly similar aims of fostering established and aspiring local professionals.[74] Though not without its difficulties, the latter society sustained annual exhibitions in the city for two decades. Two other societies, the Literary and Scientific Society, established in 1834, and the Cuvierian (1835) each survived several decades and contributed significantly to the city's cultural and intellectual environment. The Literary and Scientific Society, in particular, provided a broad-based forum for the study of, and discussion and reflection on, cultural issues.

Although the Philharmonic Society concerts featured only male musicians, local women had begun to claim a place as instrumentalists on the concert platform. In 1836, a piano performance by Miss Rogers was a key point of interest in a review of Richard Keays' benefit concert. Her performance of Carl Czerny's variations on 'Le petit tambour' earned the following praise:

> The lady's execution upon the Piano Forte called forth the acclamation of the house, and procured for her the praises of skilful musicians. She possesses an uncommon command of the instrument – a firm style – a *volant* finger – and a capability of overcoming, with little exertion, compositions of the most difficult and elaborate kind.[75]

Miss Rogers was the daughter of a military bandsman and clarinettist then based in the city. Her father's connections facilitated a concert on a lavish scale, engaging the bands of the Light Dragoons and the 52nd Regiment, under the patronage of the Smith Barrys, the Beamishes and several high-ranking military officers.[76] The first act concluded with Bellini's duet 'Il rival salvor tu dei' from *I Puritani* performed by 'double military band', and the second act commenced and concluded with the overtures to *Der Freischütz* and *Fra Diavolo* respectively, also played by military band. The duet 'Amor possente nome' from Rossini's *Otello* was sung by Miss Rogers and Richard Keays, and a trio from *Il barbiere di Siviglia*, 'Ah, quell colpo', was sung by Miss Rogers, Richard Keays and Mr Roche. Eleven-year-old Miss Catherine Rogers, a younger sister, performed 'bravura variations on the favourite Romance in Méhul's *Joseph* by Henri Herz'. Miss Rogers herself performed Herz's Grand Fantasia on Rossini's *Guillaume Tell*.[77]

Harpist Mrs Harrington was listed on Cork concert programmes and theatre notices from 1833 onwards.[78] A former student of Nicholas Bochsa and an exponent of his innovative techniques, Mrs Harrington (née Eudosia Shee) had studied harp at the RAM as a student from 1823 until 1825.[79] Her husband, double-bass player Thomas Harrington, had first appeared in Cork at Isaac Collins's concert in 1831, and was a member of the Cork Theatre Royal orchestra in 1835 (see page 84). The couple, then resident in Dublin, spent several weeks in Cork after the conclusion of the winter social season. Mrs Harrington's benefit concert at the Imperial Hotel in May 1836 was a large-scale 'miscellaneous' concert. Directed by her husband, it featured members of the de Begnis opera company, who were concurrently performing a season of Italian opera at the Theatre Royal. The programme featured three overtures and predominantly Italian vocal repertoire, and Mrs Harrington performed a Bochsa harp fantasia.[80]

Giuseppe de Begnis' operatic company gained attention outside the theatre when several of its members performed in two large-scale sacred music performances. The first of these was held at the South Chapel on 6 June, in aid of St Patrick's Orphan Asylum. A sub-committee formed to oversee the event was chaired by Francis Bernard Beamish (1814–98).[81] Miss Waters, Signora Aldericci, Signor de Begnis, Richard Keays and James Roche were the principal singers. Five vocal pieces by Rossini were performed, two from the oratorio *Mose in Egitto* and three Latin liturgical pieces. Pieces sung in English were Kent's 'Lord hear my prayer' and two Handel arias. Two pieces by Mazzocchi were performed: a sacred piece composed for Signor de Begnis, and an overture 'composed expressly for this occasion'. Members of the Band of the 85th Regiment augmented the orchestra, which was led by Robert Bowden.[82] A second performance of sacred music held at the Theatre Royal in June consisted of selections from *Messiah* and *The Creation* 'on the same splendid scale as that lately performed at the South Chapel, and by the same celebrated Artists with additions'.[83] This event was not linked to charitable support. On 30 June, de Begnis held a 'Grand Dramatic Concert' at the Theatre Royal, combined with scenes from *Il barbiere di Siviglia* and Meyer's *Il fanatico per la musica.*

Military band performances of arrangements of operatic overtures were, by this time, firmly established as part of the musical canon enjoyed by concert audiences. In addition, these bands provided the instrumental forces required to perform larger orchestral works. Such involvement led to the patronage of high-ranking military officers at concerts, adding prestige to an event. For her benefit in July 1836, Miss Waters, a member of De Begnis's company, secured the patronage of General Sir Thomas Arbuthnot (1776–1849), who had 'most kindly promised to attend', and the officers of the garrison.[84] Described as a 'Grand Dramatic Performance and Musical Melange', the programmes consisted of a short concert, followed by a number of scenes from *Il barbiere di Siviglia*, for which the singers were supported by 'an efficient chorus', and an orchestra that was 'complete and numerous in every department'.

The arrival of virtuoso pianist Henri Herz (1803–88) in September 1836 was well publicised in the local press. A puff preview in the *Southern Reporter* announced his 'electric performances' that had been heard in Paris, Vienna, Berlin, London and Dublin.[85] He gave three concerts and advertised instruction on the pianoforte for the duration of his stay. Fantasias on popular melodies were a programme staple item during this decade. Herz's opening evening concert at the Theatre Royal featured a premiere performance of 'A New Manuscript Fantasia [...] on the following Irish Melodies "Peas upon a Trencher", "Moll Roone", "Planxty Connor", "The Soldier's Greeting", "Gentle Sheelagh", "Nora Kista", and Finale'.[86] Two of his concerts included extemporaneous performances on any popular melodies presented to him in written form. Two programmes featured his concerto in C minor, described in *The Constitution* as 'well suited to afford gratification, being short, brilliant and beautiful'.[87] A unique feature of his concert tours was the use of multiple pianos, featured at the conclusion of his final concert, consisting of a 'Double Quartett [*sic*] for Four Pianofortes, and eight performers', for which he engaged local pianists Messrs Stephens, Gillespie senior, Carroll, McCarthy, Coghlan, Gillespie junior, and Charles Sullivan.[88] All three concerts featured the Band of the 35th Regiment, led by Mr Snelling. All of Herz's concerts included elements that would ensure audience satisfaction, including repertoire, audience participation and virtuosity.

In early February of the following year, Jakubowski Sankson (1801–73), a Polish Jew, gave two concerts at the Imperial Hotel on the wood harmonica, a type of xylophone which he described as 'a new instrument of his own invention'.[89] A version of this instrument featured in Polish folk music and Kletzmer music, but had not yet appeared in the European orchestra. Jakubowski, who performed in Jewish orthodox dress, had toured Britain in 1836, and was acclaimed for his virtuosity in the performance of airs and variations.[90] The details of his programmes are undocumented. Norwegian violinist Ole Bull arrived in Cork later in February, appearing at the Theatre Royal for three nights with Watkins Burroughs and his Belfast company, when his performances were interspersed with comic theatrical pieces.[91] Bull had given four performances at Dublin's Theatre Royal and two at the Rotunda prior to his arrival in Cork.[92]

The *Cork Standard and Evening Herald*, as the *Evening Herald* had now been renamed, provided the following comments, which allude to a sense of 'other' in this Nordic musician:

> Mr Ole Bull is a native of Norway, and a very young man. When the irruptions of the northern nations overwhelmed the Empire, and destroyed the arts and civilisation, it was little imagined that the heart of Scandinavia would at a future period send forth artists to delight and improve the world.[93]

A morning concert at the Imperial Hotel in early March provided an opportunity for a full programme, which was published in *The Constitution*.[94] Bull's solo pieces included an *Adagio Religioso*, introducing the 'Lamentation of a mother for the loss of her child', *Polacca Guerriera* (*The Polish Warrior*) (1935) and a 'National Concerto – Homage to the Land of Melody' with 'variations on several Irish Airs including "Rory O'Moore" and "St Patrick's Day"'. His supporting instrumentalists were Smith, violin, Mr Wren, flute, and Richard Keays, cello, who also sang three songs.[95]

Pianist Sigismond Thalberg (1812–71) arrived in Cork in December 1837, giving a concert at the Imperial Hotel and another at the Theatre Royal three days later, supported by singers Mr J. Bennett and Signor Berrettoni. On both occasions Miss Rogers, singer and pianist, and her clarinettist father, also participated. Mr Rogers led the band of the 1st Royal Dragoons in performing the overtures, which opened each half of the concert at the theatre.[96] Thalberg performed three of his compositions at each concert, which for the second concert consisted of fantasias on 'National Russian Airs', 'National Airs "God save the Queen" and "Rule Britannia"', and 'Grand Favourite Themes from Beethoven's Symphonies'.[97] Unlike Paganini, Herz and Bull, he did not incorporate Irish material in his performances. The Collard and Collard piano on which he performed was subsequently offered for sale at Bowden's Musical Warehouse in January 1838.[98]

By the late 1830s, the Imperial Hotel had become the most prestigious of the city's concert venues, favoured by visiting artists for morning concerts (see Table 7.1).[99] The use of this location was a move towards establishing a more elite concert environment than was offered at the theatre. The foremost touring soloists of the decade, with the exception of Paganini, each presented a morning concert at this venue in addition to their evening concerts.

Table 7.1. Morning concerts as advertised at the Imperial Hotel, 1826–40.

YEAR	PERFORMER/S	ADMISSION
1826	George Aspull	5s
1828	Mrs Ashe	5s
1831	Isaac Collins	5s, children 3s
1832	Russian Horn Band (3)	3s 6d, children 2s
1832	Mrs Ashe	5s
1833	Professor Holder	2s 6d
1834	Giulio Regondi	3s (2s 6d)
1836	Herr & Madame Boai (3)	3s, children half price
1836	Henri Herz	5s, gallery 3s, family 1 guinea
1837	Jakobowski Sankson (2)	2s 6d, 1s
1837	Ole Bull	5s, gallery 3s
1837	Francis Robinson	7s, gallery 3s 5d, family £1
1838	Nicholas Bochsa	6s, family 1 guinea
1838	Romer/Balfe	4s, gallery 2s
1839	Nicholas Bochsa	6s
1839	Trinidad Huerta	5s (4s)
1839	Distin family	4s, children half price
1839	Misses Smith	4s
1839	Sigismond Thalberg	6s, gallery 3s
1839	Miss Rossini Collins	4s, gallery 2s, children half price
1840	Franz Liszt	5s

Current theatre prices were 4s, 3s, 2s and 3s, 2s, 1s.

As shown in Table 7.1, the admission prices ranged from 4 to 7 shillings (with concessions for children), which would have been more expensive than those at the Theatre Royal, which, at the three-tiered rates of 4s, 2s and 1s, were more widely affordable.

Immediately following his inaugural theatrical performances at the refurbished Cook Street Theatre, Frank Seymour engaged Nicolas-Charles Bochsa, who arrived in Cork in April 1838 to give five concerts, presented as theatrical interludes.[100] Like many visiting performers, he included material of local and Irish interest. His concert of 19 April included 'a new Caprice, entitled "A Visit to Cork"', featuring several Irish airs.[101] The programme for the last of the theatre concerts consisted of three of his compositions, two of which incorporated Irish melodies.[102]

> PART I
> Introduction and brilliant variations on Mozart's favourite air 'O dolce concento' (The melody given in harmonics to imitate the Musical Glasses), concluding with an Air from *Robert le Diable.*
>
> PART II
> 'The Garland of Shamrocks, or the Homage of a Modern Harper to the Ancient Irish Harp', introducing several Irish melodies.
>
> PART III
> 'Extravaganza, introducing the favourite air 'Jim Crow', and the celebrated Irish Air, 'The Sign of the Fork', concluding with 'The Bard's Legacy'.

The theatre concerts were well received, the writer in the *Southern Reporter* noting that 'the performance of Bochsa on the harp brought forth reiterated peals of applause. Indeed he may well be called the Paganini of the day.'[103] After the conclusion of his theatre concerts, he gave a Farewell Concert at the Imperial Hotel, supported by Richard Keays and Miss Rogers.[104] The obscurity of his performance drew sharp criticism in the *Cork Standard*:

> The room at the Imperial Hotel is more suited for a performance on the Harp than a Theatre, and therefore told better; we would wish that great

> musical men would learn, and adhere by one leading, and most agreeable rule, to adapt their performances to every ear, and strike home to every heart. This is a simple rule, yet it is the grand criterion of everything sublime. We have compared music with poetry before, when registering – not our criticism on, but – our admiration of Bochsa's eminent powers: the great and decisive test of the excellence of poetry laid down by the master-critic of Antiquity is that it please all and at all times. It should be so too with Music; and, as it requires neither learning nor intellect to understand, (that is to feel) good Poetry, the sensibilities being the only tribunal to pronounce on it, so it demands neither science nor judgement to know what exquisite music is. The great drawback on all performances by eminent musicians is the ambition in them to show off in what is most difficult not to excel in what is really enrapturing. Bochsa had that fault too, and imagines the metaphysics of music will please as well as sound: but, Germans must be metaphysicians about every thing: and, if he be not one of that craniological description of people, his music is excessively like all the perplexing productions of their country. But, little matter that, if Bochsa be properly enriched for his monotonous difficulties and sweeping passages; there is little or no metaphysics about that part of the Concert.[105]

Although Bochsa's nationality may have been mistaken, this critique of the performance betrays an antipathy to the abstraction of contemporaneous German music, evidence of a growing xenophobic attitude to German and Italian music and musicians that had appeared in recent British pamphlets and journals.[106] However, later critics have agreed that Bochsa's reputation and career were very much overblown.[107] He returned to Cork in March of the following year for a four-night concert engagement at the Theatre Royal, accompanied on this occasion by Mrs H.R. Bishop (nee Anna Riviere), second wife of Henry Bishop and 'Primo soprano of the Philharmonic and Ancient Concerts, London', and her sister, Miss Riviere, 'pianiste of the Nobility's Concerts, London'. Mrs Bishop had left her husband and three children to tour with Bochsa.[108] The combined act was well received:

> The fame of Bochsa has spread over the world, and renders it unnecessary for us to say a word on the subject. Of Mrs Bishop's singing we have merely room this post to say that a more finished artist has seldom visited the city. The effect she produced on her audience last night was fully

Figure 7.3. Distin family, 1845.

> testified by the loud and hearty cheers with which her efforts were so well greeted. In 'The Dream of Home' and 'Nil [*sic*] cor piu non mi sento', she was loudly and rapturously encored. The Double Fantasia by Mr Bochsa and Miss Riviere was loudly and deservedly applauded.[109]

In mid-March 1839 Frank Seymour engaged the Distin family brass quintet for five nights at the Royal Victoria Theatre, which coincided with Bochsa's final concert at the Theatre Royal. This English family group, who had begun touring in 1837, consisted of John Distin (1798–1863) and his four sons, George, Henry John, William Alfred and Theodore. Mrs Distin, wife of John Distin senior, accompanied on the piano.[110] Their performances at the theatre were framed by minor dramatic pieces. Among their popular repertoire was 'the much-admired "Echo hunting duet" on two French Horns by Messrs H. and N. Distin', and Mr H. Distin's performance of 'Balfe's Celebrated air "The Light of other days" on the new invented instrument, Distin's Patent Walking Stick Cornetto, manufactured expressly for him by Marcus Moses of Westmoreland Street, Dublin'.[111] The group was re-engaged for a further five nights, followed by a farewell benefit night on 8 April. A full 'Grand Morning Concert' at the Imperial Hotel, held on 9 April, followed the theatre engagements, featuring the singing of Miss Hamilton, of Dublin's Theatre Royal, who was currently engaged at the Royal Victoria Theatre.[112] However, Seymour apparently prevailed upon the group to give one further performance at the Royal Victoria, 'previous to their final departure for America', which was to be 'an entire new Grand Concert (in two parts)'.[113] The Distins gave at least fifteen performances during this extended engagement, and undoubtedly contributed to the subsequent popularity of brass instruments in the city.

Another touring musician who appeared in March was the Spanish guitarist Trinidad Huerta (1800–74/5), who had given a number of concerts in Dublin over the previous winter season.[114] Active in London since the 1820s, Huerta's technical virtuosity gained him the title 'the Paganini of the Guitar'. For his first concert at the Imperial Hotel, he was supported by singer Miss Hamilton.[115] Huerta appears to have then left the city to perform elsewhere, returning to give two more concerts at the Imperial Hotel on 30 May and 14 June, for which he had mustered the support of several local musicians. The first of these featured several string players.[116] For the second concert, he was supported by local singers William Wheeler and William Hackett, with William Gillespie at the piano.[117] Two weeks later, Huerta, Wheeler and Hackett gave a morning concert at the Columbine Rooms in Queenstown (now Cobh).[118] He made a final appearance at the Royal Victoria Theatre, in a benefit for Mr Smith, leader of the orchestra, when he performed 'a celebrated Fantasia, composed by himself', and 'a Spanish march, in which he will give imitations of several instruments'.[119]

Thalberg returned to Cork in October and performed three concerts at the Imperial Hotel. Alexander D. Roche, who organised the concerts and supplied two seven-octave pianos from the firms of Érard and Collard and Collard, participated in the concerts, along with Michael Balfe and his wife Lina Roser-Balfe (*c.* 1810–88), who was on her first visit to Cork. The Balfes sang duets by Donizetti, and each contributed a solo ballad in each half of the programmes. Roche performed a ballad by A.P. Herrmann and, at the final concert, Balfe sang Roche's ballad 'O twine me a bower'. Thalberg's performances were highly acclaimed:

> We see one man sitting at a Piano Forte, and we hear Music, chords and accompaniments, that appear to come from the hands of a dozen. He produces tones from a comparatively tiny instrument that imagination might fancy were the vibrations of a stupendous organ. Whether we are musical or not musical, we can only listen to him with wonder, astonishment and delight.[120]

> There was in his playing no labouring for stage effect; but on the contrary, the mild and unassuming manner of the great artist encreased the pleasure that all felt in hearing, what may justly be called the very perfection of piano-playing. His execution was beyond the attempt of criticism, uniting lightness with strength and firmness of touch. He at one moment produced delicious music, exquisite and fairy-like, and at another the very grandest volumes of sound, as if his hands, and the ordinary powers of the splendid instrument on which he played were far more than doubly multiplied. The national air 'God save the Queen' and 'Rule Britannia' were distinctly heard, though involved in a very labyrinth of the most puzzling and intricate variations, that seemed like a wantonness of melody, while they exhibited the very extreme of power and science.[121]

In March 1840, press advertisements appeared for concerts by 'the Sightless son of song – Hannigan, the celebrated performer on the Union pipes'. Thomas O'Hannigan (1806–63) from Cahir, County Tipperary, was a blind piper who moved in both private and public concert circles, performing at theatres in Dublin and London.[122] His three Cork concerts took place in 'the Large Room, over Mr Ronayne's Glass Warehouse' at 121 Patrick Street, performing 'on that National Instrument the Irish Pipes, with many highly admired and popular Airs, Melodies, Scotch Sonnets, etc. the modern "Overtures" and "Duets", "Waltzes by Strauss", and other celebrated composers, and several other Pieces too numerous for the limits of a Handbill.'[123] An advertised list of national, popular and operatic selections and arrangements to be performed at this second concert shows the extent of his flexibility in accommodating urban audience preferences:

> … an entire new selection of song tunes, Strauss Waltzes, Jigs, Reels, National Melodies, including selections from the operas of *Der Freischütz*, *Fra Diavolo*, *La Nozzi* [*sic*] *di Figaro*, etc also, 'The Last Rose of Summer', 'My Native Highland Home', 'Nora Creina', 'The Coolin' (with variations), 'Fill the Bumper Fair' (with variations), 'Rory O'More', 'The Huntsman's Chorus' (with variations), 'Savourneen Dheelish', 'Bonaparte's March' (with its Quick Step), 'Molly Astore', 'The Angel's Whisper', 'O Nanny', etc and a number of other airs too numerous for insertion.[124]

He returned to Cork to give another concert in September.[125]

For the spring season at the Victoria Theatre, Seymour engaged the Alpine singers, whose concerts were incorporated into the theatre programmes. Like previous groups of this type, they appeared in national costume, and sang 'some of their most popular mountain melodies – accompanying themselves on their own instruments, the violin, harp, guitar and flageolet'.[126] Rossini Collins, the prodigy violinist, arrived in the city in May with her father, Isaac Collins, and her sisters Emma and Victoria. After an initial concert at the Imperial Hotel, the group performed at the Royal Victoria Theatre for six nights[127] and concluded their visit with two full concerts at the Imperial Hotel, the second 'under the distinguished patronage of the Military and elite of the City'.[128]

The year concluded with the arrival of Franz Liszt and his party of performers, on a tour of Britain and Ireland, that was to continue through 1841–2.[129] Liszt's manager, Louis Henry Lavenu (1818–59), directed the concerts and presided at the piano. The supporting performers were singers Mary Sarah Steele (1816–81), Louisa Bassano (1818–1908), John Orlando Parry (1810–79), and flautist Joseph Richardson (1814–62). Tickets for the concerts were available at Alexander Roche's Musical Repository, and at the bar of the Imperial Hotel, and Roche supplied 'a splendid Horizontal Grand Pianoforte by Collard and Collard, expressly chosen and imported for the occasion'.[130] The group presented morning concerts on 28 December and 1 January, and an evening concert on 30 December, all at the Imperial Hotel. Liszt performed once in each of the two acts. In the first concert, attended by an audience of some 280 people, he performed the overture to *William Tell*, which, it was reported,

> brought all the performer's powers at once into action; and although this composition is one of the fullest scores that Rossini ever wrote, yet the most complete orchestra never produced a more powerful effect both in spirit and unity of execution.[131]

In the second half of the programme, he performed 'Andante-Finale from *Lucia de Lammermoor* and 'Galop chromatique'.[132] A reviewer in *The Constitution* wrote:

> Viewed as a display of Piano Forte playing, it was nothing short of magic. No system of words can accurately describe the power which he possesses of dividing himself, as it were, into two, or sometimes even three

> performers; the feathery delicacy of his touch at one moment, and its enormous forte at another; and the exquisite neatness of the artifices by means of which he, almost every moment, appears to achieve physical impossibilities – such as unreachable extensions – playing figures of opposing character, widely contrasted power, and running through and intersecting each other with the utmost freedom of motion, an arpeggio bass of large dimension, meanwhile continuing an uninterrupted course; and the whole giving much the effect of what some extremely dexterous organist could accomplish – as regards the involution of the parts, we mean – on two claviers and pedals. In that kind of slight-of-hand [*sic*], which addresses itself to the ear, we think he even transcends Thalberg. He seems to occupy more space on the instrument than even his greatest rival.[133]

At the Wednesday evening concert, which was attended by an audience of 300, Liszt performed his 'Hexameron' variations, and in the second half, accompanied Mary Steele in a performance of Schubert's 'The Wanderer'. The second half of the programme also featured an extemporised performance on 'Rory O'Moore', the March in Norma and 'The Last Rose of Summer'.[134]

The intervening days between concerts allowed for some exploration of the locality, which included an excursion to Cobh, via a ferry at Passage West, and a visit to Collins's theatre in Nelson Place for an evening performance, although Liszt himself declined the latter. The following day, the group's local host Alexander Roche accompanied Liszt and his party on a visit to the Lunatic Asylum, where, in the male ward, John Parry recalls meeting inmate Richard Keays (d. 1842), who had been active as a professional singer and teacher in the city until 1838.[135]

The morning concert on New Year's Day was poorly attended, due to it being a Saint's Day, although the Anglican Bishop attended. The first half of the programme featured sacred music. In addition to vocal items by Handel and Haydn, and Parry's performance of Pergolesi's 'O Lord have mercy upon me', Liszt performed his arrangements of the Overture to *Messiah*, and Schubert's 'Ave Maria'.[136] Shortly after the concert, the group departed for Clonmel.

Concert promotion and organisation in Cork had consolidated during the 1830s. The availability of the Theatre Royal and the Imperial Hotel, together with lively press communication provided in the *Southern Reporter* and *The Constitution*, facilitated the numerous touring musicians that arrived to perform in the city. This survey of concerts from 1830 up to Liszt's visit in December 1840 shows the pervasive influence and popularity of Italian operatic selections and the persistence of the English glee. Canonic repertoire was balanced with improvised virtuosic works, and the creative impulse of the performer was afforded high status.

The dazzling skills of Paganini set a new level of audience engagement with virtuosity, followed by Isaac Collins ('the English Paganini'), Trinidad Huerta ('the Paganini of the guitar'), and Nicholas Bochsa ('the Paganini of the harp'). Herz, Thalberg and Liszt demonstrated the piano's capability of imitating a full orchestra. The fascination with foreign performers stood in contrast to an apparent lack of support for the local Philharmonic Society, whose existence was short-lived, despite promotional efforts. Its failure to survive indicated a loss of opportunity for the artistic advancement of local music and the collaboration and critical milieu in which performance and composition could flourish. While retaining his London residency and connections, William Forde was a central figure in the city's concert development, pioneering orchestral conducting and repertoire, and enriching programme content with orchestral overtures and instrumental solos.

8

'RATIONAL RECREATION': THE SPREAD OF AMATEUR MUSIC-MAKING, 1840-1870

Detail from 'Opening of the Temperance Institute'.
ILLUSTRATED LONDON NEWS

The Cork people were intense lovers of music, and some of us, whose taste inclined rather to literature or to pictorial art, used to grumble now and then because of the supremacy which the majority of our population gave to the craft of the musician.[1]

The taste for music in Cork has of late been developing itself. Choral societies, singing classes, concerts, musical soirées are so abundant that it is impossible to speak in praise of one without having to eulogise a host of others.[2]

In 1841, Cork was still Ireland's second largest centre of population – the census of that year recorded 80,720 inhabitants – but from this time onwards was to be overtaken in economic status by the rapidly expanding industrial city of Belfast. Cork retained its importance as Munster's major trading port, and was at the centre of commercial expansion. Appropriate electoral representation on the city Corporation was an important outcome of the 1840 Municipal Reform Act, and municipal elections thereafter returned around 70 per cent Catholic seats, a closer representation of the Catholic proportion of Cork's population.[3] This legislation finally ended the monopoly of the Friendly Club, and heralded an era of change.

The early 1840s saw a number of cultural developments in the city. Established in 1845, Queen's College undertook much of the educational role initiated several decades earlier by the Royal Cork Institution (RCI), although the latter continued as an influential cultural body. The RCI headquarters on Nelson Place was the venue for meetings and lectures of the Cork Literary and Scientific Society and the Cuvierian Society. From the repeal supporters emerged a group of young political idealists, among them Denny Lane, Isaac and Ralph Varian, and Michael Joseph Barry, sons of merchants, all drawn to the new romantic nationalist ideas then prevalent in the Dublin circle led by Thomas Davis, forming the core of the Young Ireland movement in Cork.[4] Michael Joseph Barry, Isaac Varian, Denny Lane and Mary Ellen Downing ('Mary') contributed to the organisation's song-books, particularly *Spirit of the Nation* (1845). Barry's 'Step Together' and 'The Green Flag' and Lane's 'Kate of Araglen' gained canonic status in the twentieth century by their inclusion in An t-Athair Pádraig Breathnach's *Songs of the Gael.*

Widespread problems in a changing world were recognised by reformers on both sides of the Atlantic, leading to initiatives aimed at self-improvement through education, literacy, numeracy, self-regulation and practical skills. Broadly aimed at preparation for employment, such values were embedded in the philosophy of Edmund Rice's Christian Brothers schools, established in Cork at the North Monastery (1818) and Sullivan's Quay (1828). Outside of public schooling, the RCI and the Mechanics Institute (1825) offered classes in technical skills for working men. The moral and social benefits of 'rational recreation' were recognised, and the activities of reading and engaging in music were encouraged.

Over the previous two decades, habitual drunkenness among the lower classes in Ireland, England, Scotland and North America was a cause for concern among religious leaders. The proliferation of public houses, the low cost of spirits, and the poor example given by the upper classes were cited as causes.[5] The American Temperance Society was established in Boston in 1826. As temperance ideals spread across the Atlantic, societies were established during the 1820s in Dublin and Belfast, and in New Ross in 1829. A number of Protestants and Dissenters actively promoted temperance in Cork, including Rev. Nicholas C. Dunscombe, curate of St Peter's church,[6] William Martin, a Quaker, and Unitarian Richard Dowden. By 1836 there was a network of temperance societies in the city.

To strengthen the cause and embrace the Catholic population, an invitation was extended to the Capuchin friar Father Theobald Mathew to join the movement.[7] Appointed president of the Cork Total Abstinence Society (CTAS) in 1838, he became a driving force in the movement, holding weekly meetings at a schoolhouse, and later at Conway's horse bazaar on Sullivan's Quay, which had a capacity to hold 4,000 people.[8] He inspired thousands to take the 'pledge' of total abstinence from alcohol. In his appeal for sobriety, Mathew was supported financially by both Catholic and Protestant merchants.[9] Although not Mathew's intended outcome, however, the association became a predominantly Catholic one. Mathew viewed music simply as a purposeful recreational activity in the Temperance Room: 'It will keep the members together to have the band in the room, and [...] the boys and girls are so fond of the music, that it would be a pity to disappoint them.'[10] The first Temperance Concert and Tea Party was held at the Monastery Schools in Douglas Street in January 1839, assisted by Edward Moeran at the piano.[11]

In February 1841, liberal politician and writer John Francis Maguire

(1815–72) established the *Cork Total Abstainer*; or the *Irish Temperance Journal*, a weekly publication that ran for several months. Maguire replaced it with the *Cork Examiner*, a thrice-weekly publication, supporting Repeal of the Act of Union and constitutional nationalism.[12] Encouragement of literacy in English was part of Mathew's drive towards self-improvement, and reading rooms were established within temperance societies. Maguire's *Cork Examiner* became a powerful tool of Catholic agency in the city, presenting a liberal, nationalist standpoint akin to that held by the *Cork Mercantile Chronicle* over a decade previously.

The temperance band initiative proved to be an immediate success.[13] On Easter Monday in 1841, twenty-three bands, most of them in uniform, marched through the streets of Cork.[14] On 28 March 1842, a report of a Grand Temperance Procession in Cork, attended by Father Mathew and the Lord Mayor, appeared in the *Freeman's Journal*:

> Nothing could exceed the exciting interest of the scene throughout the early part of the morning, as the different societies, each headed by numerous and well-trained bands of music, playing their most favourite airs, continued to pour in from every road leading to the city. In the city of Cork alone there are no less than nineteen temperance bands, each as large and nearly as efficient as the best regimental bands. They have all been taught at great expense by the most skilled professors, and the proficiency at which they have arrived is creditable alike to themselves and to their instructors.[15]

Thirty-nine Cork temperance society bands were listed in this report, including six 'female societies' (see Appendix 1). Meetings, concerts, processions and festivals were regular features of the city's temperance societies. Over sixty bands were reported to have attended the Annual Temperance Procession of the CTAS the following year.[16] From a strong base in Cork, the Total Abstinence movement, with its associated temperance society bands, rapidly spread countrywide.

The infrastructures for these undertakings were the temperance halls or temperance reading rooms established within Cork's local temperance societies. Concerts were organised to raise funds, which, along with members' subscriptions, contributed to the rent, heating and lighting of the hall, and the payment of a bandmaster.[17] In many instances, local businessmen and employers provided financial support. John Besnard Jr funded the fitting-up of the bandroom of the Church Street Temperance Society and purchased instruments and uniforms for the band.[18] The band of the Brickfields Temperance Society consisted mainly of men and boys apprenticed as ship's carpenters to the yard of Wheeler and Hickson.[19] Festivals, such as the Mayor's Temperance Festival, held in January 1844,[20] were important events. However, sustaining the bands proved to be 'a constant expense' for Mathew,[21] and after 1842 the surge in membership began to abate.[22] One of the most effective advocates for temperance among the poorer classes was Rev. James O'Regan, who continued to administer the 'pledge' over the following decades, addressing his communities in Irish when required.[23] He remained active in the Barrack Street area, which endured as a centre of temperance, and maintained a band.[24]

Accounts of performances, festivals, concerts, and open-air events indicate that the bands performed a range of popular repertoire. Arrangements of classical and operatic favourites are mentioned in some reports. At an Emigrants' Farewell in 1841, the overture to Auber's *Masaniello* was performed.[25] At a similar event held the following April, the 'favourite airs' of 'See the conquering hero comes', 'St Patrick's Day', 'Rule Britannia' and 'God Save the Queen' were performed.[26] A report of a tea festival at the Brickfields Room described the band as 'quite surprising. They have received instruction but for a short period, and now execute the most scientific pieces of Bellini and Straus [*sic*] with taste, precision and facility'.[27] In April 1842, the Church Street Temperance Band published a press notice thanking John O'Callaghan of Knockaderry, County Limerick, for an arrangement of a 'Grand March of His Royal Highness the Prince of Wales'.[28] Thomas Davis endeavoured to promote the use of national melodies by temperance bands with the regular publication of arrangements of airs in the *Dublin Monthly Magazine* throughout 1842 and 1843.[29] Irish airs may have been implied in an account of a tea festival at the Globe Lane room in March 1842, which stated that 'several beautiful airs were then played by the band, and these were diversified by songs, comic and sentimental, sung by the female members of the society'.[30] It is likely that the bands learnt material according to the choice of their instructors, who were mainly military bandsmen, for whom operatic selections had become standard. By 1846, a poor view of the bands was apparent in an article in *The Nation* entitled 'Music Festivals for the People':

> Of the temperance bands established by Father Mathew, many still exist, particularly in the county towns; but their music is of a very questionable

> character, and seldom rises above 'We'll never get drunk again'; and even such wretched tunes they only play at processions, or on Sunday evening, when the weather permits, in the street; but very seldom in their rooms, for which, indeed, the selection of instruments is by no means adapted. We seldom hear them play one of our fine old airs, and as for an overture or piece of sacred music with few exceptions, it is quite out of question.[31]

Band membership provided opportunities for public display of identity. Contemporary accounts suggest that street performances at weekends were often viewed as civic disturbance. German traveller and writer Johann Georg Kohl commented on the caterwauling ['*Katzenmusik*'] sounds produced by a band outside his window in the Commercial Hotel on a Saturday night in 1842.[32] Although letters in *The Constitution* in that year signalled the issue as a matter for public concern, the band members were vehemently defended by the editor of the *Southern Reporter*.[33] On 12 February 1846, *The Constitution* published an anonymous letter to the Mayor of Cork, complaining that

> whilst that peaceable and respectable portion of the community, the Wesleyan Methodists, were at service in their chapel, Patrick street, a Temperance Band passed, and as they approached that place of worship, they commenced the most terrible peals on their musical instruments, thereby interrupting the affecting solemnity of the congregation. The effect was painful and distressing in the extreme.

An editorial comment on a similar occurrence was published in *The Constitution* in May of that year.[34] It is quite likely that, in some cases, deliberate sectarian provocation was part of the motivation to assemble for outdoor performances. A report in the *Cork Examiner* in 1859 reported that some of the Cork temperance bands were 'in the habit of going down to Bandon on Sunday by train, and of playing in the town and its neighbourhood after church service, incurring the wrath of some local Orangemen, who were annoyed by 'the music and the sight of a green flag with a harp, and "No 1. Barrack street" on it'. Members of the group were prosecuted under the illegal processions act.[35]

'SINGING FOR THE MILLION'

It was during the peak of the temperance movement in Cork in 1842 that music pedagogue Joseph Mainzer (1801–51) appeared in the city, on an invitation by William Keleher of the CTAS committee. Mainzer's system of teaching singing to the masses had already spread rapidly in England.[36] He was not an innovator in this regard: Guillaume Wilhem's (1781–1842) system for teaching singing to classes using solfa notation had been adopted for public elementary instruction in Paris in 1833, and was later extended to adult classes.[37] As a former teacher of music at a seminary in Germany, Joseph Mainzer had published *Singschule* (1831), an elementary treatise on the rudiments of music. His political activities forced him to flee Germany, however. Against a backdrop of social reform in Paris during the 1830s, he held free evening singing classes for working men and artisans, using a revised version of *Singschule* entitled *Méthode de chant: pour voix d'hommes* (1836), his charismatic personality gaining public attention.[38] Following his arrival in London in May 1841, his solfa classes based on the fixed-doh system stimulated the interest of educators, aided by his new English manual *Singing for the Million* (1841). Having established four classes in London, he formed a committee of teachers to extend his work in several of the larger English provincial towns, and in 1842 he was invited by the CTAS to introduce singing classes in Cork, his objectives well aligned with those of the temperance movement.[39]

Two months prior to Mainzer's scheduled arrival, William Forde wrote to Richard Dowden, requesting him to forward a letter to William Keleher of the CTAS expressing his interest in becoming involved in the venture, stating that he had studied both Mainzer's and Wilhem's methods in London.[40] To support his case, he published the following notice in the *Cork Examiner* on 8 July:

> SINGING FOR THE MILLION
> From the best authority, we can inform our readers that Mr W. Forde, the well-known Professor of Music, intends to form Singing Classes in this city, which will bring the study and practice of Vocal Music within the means of the humblest of the people. We need not expatiate upon the effects which must result from this project, with regard to the habits and moral character of that portion of the community, to whom a pleasing and improving occupation of spare time has been always, unhappily, of difficult or hopeless attainment. The citizens of Cork will be gratified to

> learn that their late instance of kind feeling towards Mr Forde has enabled him to devote his time to a critical examination of the systems of Wilhem and Mainzer, both now in full operation in London.[41]

On 29 July, in another article entitled 'Popular singing' published in the *Cork Examiner*, Forde's position was clarified:

> We understand that Mr Forde's preference and adoption of the system of Wilhem, is the result of a careful and scrutinizing personal observation of the working of *that* and *another* method of popular vocal instruction. Mr Mainzer is a man of private fortune. He is not a professional musician. But, what may be wanting in profound knowledge of the Art he professes to disseminate, is in some degree compensated by an ardent desire to benefit his fellow-men, by giving them an innocent and improving means of employing unoccupied time. He is a philanthropist; but his method of teaching music cannot (in our humble opinion) for a moment bear comparison with that of Wilhem, who was a man deeply skilled in all branches of the science of music, and gifted with a mind possessing the truest logical and analytic powers.[42]

Wilhem's method had in the meantime inspired an adaptation by English teacher John Hullah (1812–84), whose successes in teaching groups of pupils in London gained him public acclaim and, later, official endorsement within the English school system.

Mainzer's arrival in Cork in August 1842 was heralded in a newspaper notice entitled 'Music and Sobriety'.[43] The *Cork Examiner* reported that 600 tickets had been purchased for Mainzer's first lecture at the Corn Exchange, entitled 'Music for the Million'.[44] According to the *Cork Examiner*, it was attended by 'respectable tradespeople, principally members of the Temperance Society'.[45] Accompanying Mainzer was James Uglow (*c.* 1814–94).[46] Uglow had served as organist at St James's Cathedral, Cheltenham, and was also a prodigy singer and violinist. For a fee of two shillings for sixteen lessons with Uglow, pupils would be 'enabled to Read and Sing simple Music at sight', the fee payable at six-pence per month.[47] During the first week of September, Forde published several notices in the *Southern Reporter* and the *Cork Examiner* expressing his reservations about Mainzer's approach.[48] The first of the *Examiner* notices was an advertisement to the public for his 'Voice of the People' assembly at the Corn Exchange. A defensive and cautionary tone is apparent in his second notice, addressed to his fellow teachers of music in Cork, warning them that: 'You will have strangers coming amongst you to take your places – unknown men to us [...] they will enter our public and private Schools; and, beginning with Singing, they will end with Instrumental Teaching.' He concluded by inviting his colleagues to a consultation meeting. The third notice advertised a singing class for the cultivation of sacred music. Forde was evidently leaving nothing to chance in defending his profession against what he believed was charlatanism. Otherwise known for his modest character, Forde's reaction to Mainzer's movement was becoming increasingly strong. A few days later, on 12 September, a notice in the *Cork Examiner* listed Mainzer's appointed professors for Cork and its vicinity:

> Mr [James] Uglow, 3, York Street
> Mr [Robert] Orr, member of the Cork Cathedral Choir[49]
> Mr [William] Heazle, organist of Upper Shandon[50]
> Mr J[ohn] Seymour, jnr, organist of St Patrick's[51]
> Mr Tomkins, for Bandon and its vicinity

However, on 16 September, two notices for singing classes appeared in the *Cork Examiner*, Uglow's morning and evening classes, 'Singing for the Million' at the Imperial Hotel, and Forde's singing classes at his premises at 129 Old George's Street. It appears that Forde had sustained his enterprise, alongside Uglow's. A letter to Theobald Mathew by Alexander King, Minister of the Independent Chapel, was published in the *Cork Examiner* on the subject of 'Music and Morals: popular education and social improvement'. While praising Mathew's achievements in the temperance movement and his encouragement of recent developments in popular singing through 'The Voice of the People' and 'Singing for the Million', he argued:

> It must be obvious, that *neither music nor temperance can impart information, or implant those truths which are the necessary basis of moral sentiment.* The one fits the mind for receiving instructions, and the other greatly aids the improvement of a moral taste; but directly to *communicate* either, they both are powerless.[52]

Citing Plato, he stated that musical instruction alone is inadequate, and that, in fact, it could lead to emasculation, and even insurrection. He proposed that the teaching of music should be allied with Christian teachings.[53] His letters, addressed to Fr Mathew, Dr Murphy and Daniel O'Connell, published in subsequent editions of the *Cork Examiner*, continued to develop his argument, and were subsequently published as a collection in London.[54]

To meet the needs of temperance associations, William Young's *Catholic Choralist*, published in Dublin in 1842, contained a section dedicated to 'Temperance Hymns' consisting of temperance-inspired verses set to 'airs' from Haydn, Mozart, Pleyel, Webb, Beethoven', etc., and the book included a lengthy commentary on the spiritual, moral and physical benefits of frequent singing.[55] The extent of its success is not easy to assess. However, a collection compiled the following year by Clare poet William MacNamara Downes, entitled *Temperance Melodies for the Teetotalers of Ireland*, was evidently successful, as three editions appeared in that year.[56] Having consulted Father Mathew on the matter, he decided on a national musical basis as a setting for his verses, and twelve of Moore's *Irish Melodies* were chosen.[57] Another proposal received by Mathew from a Mr Cavanagh, 'Gaelic Temperance Bard', was the 'Erin go bragh' songbook.[58]

In January 1843, Uglow announced a 'Singing for the Million' festival, billed as the first Mainzerian festival in Cork, consisting of an evening programme on 3 January and a morning programme on 5 January at the Imperial Clarence Rooms. Each concert featured class singing interspersed by solos on violin, piano and voice by James Uglow.[59] Uglow was also employed at the North Monastery School for boys, run by the Christian Brothers, where the first juvenile Total Abstinence Society in Ireland was newly established.[60] In April 1843, Uglow directed a performance of sacred music by a class of 150 pupils, wearing temperance medals, at a charity sermon in aid of the Christian Brothers schools.[61] Uglow also established his own private teaching practice in Cork, and performed in several local concerts, having established good professional relationships with the local professionals. After eighteen months in Cork, however, he returned to Cheltenham, where he was re-appointed as organist at St James's Cathedral.[62]

No further publicity notices for the 'Singing for the Million' project appeared after this time. The waning of interest in Mainzer's system has been attributed to the narrow scope of his pedagogical approach, based on the French fixed doh system. As sharps and flats were introduced in progressively difficult melodies, pitch relationships were not so easily represented with solfa syllables. Once a basic standard had been achieved, there was little or no progression, a plausible explanation for Mainzer's constant moving to new locations with his classes.[63] The teaching of singing at the Christian Brothers schools begun by Uglow was effectively sustained, however. An article in *The Nation* in 1846 drew attention to the limited success of the movement:

> Some attempts were made to introduce the continental mode of teaching vocal music, on the plan adopted by Hullah and Mainzer, but unfortunately it was ill supported, and is all but given up at present; yet, any person who has had the pleasure of hearing the boys of the Christian Brothers Schools at Cork sing at the charity sermons preached in aid of those excellent establishments, must be convinced of the value of the system, and must feel regret that it is not universally carried out.[64]

Charity sermons held in 1849 and 1850 included choruses performed by the singing classes of these schools.[65] Fundraising for the Temperance Halls continued to generate musical events which included both vocal and band performances (see Figure 8.1).

Figure 8.1. Notice of dress ball and concert in aid of the Mary Street Temperance Hall, 1844.
CORK CITY AND COUNTY ARCHIVES

The strong middle-class involvement in the temperance movement is evident from press accounts of the activities of the Temperance Institute for Literature and Science at 10 Academy Street, from 1845 to 1847. Its establishment in 1845 was reported in the *Illustrated London News* together with a line drawing of this fashionable venue[66] (see Figure 8.2). Among the institute's leading members were brothers Isaac S. (1812–68) and Amos Varian (1823–1904) and their cousin Ralph Varian (*c.* 1820–*c.* 1886).[67] All Unitarians of an established family of manufacturers, they were vehement advocates for social reform. In April 1846, four hundred attendees at a soirée were entertained by Kearney's string band and by two Irish harpers, who sang national airs to their own accompaniment.[68] A soirée held in 1847 to commemorate the anniversary of the birth of Father Mathew at the institute was again reported as an evening of 'literature, eloquence and music', on which occasion William Gillespie performed on a 'full-toned' piano, and the institute's Glee Club performed several pieces. A quadrille band occupied the orchestral gallery.[69] Among those who frequented the Temperance Institute was Justin McCarthy (1830–1912), a young man of strong literary leanings, who worked as a reporter with the *Cork Examiner*.[70] In his autobiographical work, *The Story of an Irishman*, he describes the institute as having 'a large hall, a library and rooms for reading and writing [...] used as a place of evening resort for those of the movement', and that its membership consisted of Catholics, Protestants and Dissenters.[71] By the time this establishment flourished, the temperance movement had already lost much of its initial momentum, and by the spring of 1849 a local auctioneer occupied the premises.[72]

ST MARY'S CHORAL SOCIETY

Though still a small minority, the city's middle classes had become increasingly active in cultural pursuits by the early 1840s. An article published in the *Cork Examiner* in October 1842 considered their musical needs and announced a new venture:

> Whilst we hail with pleasure the impetus given to the more general cultivation of the delightful science of Music, and while we rejoice at the prospect of its wider diffusion among the humbler classes of society which 'Singing for the Million' promises, before long, to realize, still we cannot but regret that the noblest works of the great masters are as yet

Figure 8.2. Opening of the Temperance Institute, Academy Street, 1845.
ILLUSTRATED LONDON NEWS, COURTESY OF CORK CITY LIBRARY

> a closed volume to those whose position in society, whose refinement and whose musical education render them most calculated to receive the purest enjoyment from their beauty and grandeur. Without Choral Societies being established in our city, the effective performance of those magnificent works cannot be realized; and without witnessing the full and perfect embodiment of the sublime conceptions of the great master-minds of the Art, the student can form no accurate idea of music in its most exalted sense. To fill up this blank, and afford this rare intellectual treat, a 'Choral Society' has been projected by some few spirited individuals, Professional and Amateur [...][73]

During the early nineteenth century, choral societies were a feature of many English cities and towns, organised for the performance of oratorio and other large-scale works.[74] The idea of forming such a society in Cork was mooted a few months previously, when a *Cork Examiner* editorial preview of an oratorio held to celebrate the installation of the new organ at St Mary's Church posed the question: 'May we hope that this is but the first of a series of Oratorios? that an occasion so favourable may be seized and a Sacred Choral Society formed?'[75] (see page 208). Based on the recent successes of Gillespie's choir at St Mary's, the new society, under his leadership, was established in 1842 'for the cultivation of Sacred Music'. The Cork Choral Society, also referred to as St Mary's Choral Society, aspired to perform three oratorios annually in support of a number of local charities, namely, the Fever Hospital, the Lying-in Hospital, the North Infirmary, the South Infirmary and the Cork Dispensary. An evenly balanced committee of Catholic and Protestant doctors, businessmen and clergy included Dr Denis Bullen, Rev. John Quarry, John Besnard, Denny Lane, Dr Denis O'Connor, Mr H. Hewitt, Dr Richard Fowler and Mr Joseph Shee (distiller), with William Harrington Jr as treasurer and William Gillespie as secretary.[76]

An audience of about 400 attended the society's inaugural performance on 8 December 1842. The seventy-strong mixed-voice choir presented selections from the works of Handel, Haydn, Mozart, Beethoven, Rossini, Pergolesi, Mendelssohn, Zingarelli and Callcott. The soloists were James Roche, James Uglow, Robert Orr, and 'a lady', with conductor William Forde, chorus master Edward Sweeny, and W.F. Gillespie accompanied on the organ.[77] The concert provided audiences with an opportunity to hear Uglow's 'fine, rich, full, deep-toned and manly voice', as described in the *Cork Examiner*, and that 'his low notes are peculiarly fine, and we have seldom heard any vocalist descend *so low* and yet retain the music of the note so perfectly'.[78] Forde, Gillespie and Sweeney led the society's second oratorio performance on 23 February 1843, consisting of vocal selections from Spohr, Guglielmi, Mendelssohn, Handel and Haydn, with choruses by Handel, Beethoven and Spohr. The principal singers were Fanny Russell (Mrs Wookey), Mr Seymour, James Uglow and James Roche.[79] Mrs Wookey first appeared in Cork in 1843. Formerly active as a professional singer in London, she was resident for some years in Cork, and sang at concerts, charity sermons and oratorios, particularly those connected to Catholic charities.[80]A third performance in May consisted of selections from Handel's *Messiah* and *Jeptha*, Rossini's *Mose in Egitto*, Mozart's (wrongly attributed) 12th Mass, and Haydn's *The Creation*, featuring brothers James and Alexander D. Roche.[81] In 1850, the Choral Society performed an oratorio in support of the completion of the Dominican Priory, attached to St Mary's on Pope's Quay.[82]

ANTIENT CONCERTS SOCIETY

Established in 1846 for 'the cultivation of Classical vocal music, particularly by the choral composers of the ancient masters',[83] the Cork Antient Concerts Society was modelled on the Dublin society of the same name, founded by Joseph Robinson in 1834.[84] The London *Morning Post* announced the establishment of the new society 'for the purpose of introducing to the citizens of Cork the music of the great masters, on the principle adopted in London, Dublin, etc.'[85] The new Cork society aspired to present two or three annual concerts, featuring mainly large-scale vocal works, including oratorio excerpts. A society of some forty performing members and eighty non-performing members was envisaged.[86] Like its Dublin counterpart, it was the preserve of the city's social elite: its patron was The Right Hon the Earl of Bandon, the president was Sir William Abraham Chatterton, and vice presidents were Colonel Chatterton, KH, MP, The Rev. Archdeacon of Cork, The O'Donovan and Cooper Penrose, Esq. The honorary secretary in 1847 was George Tottenham, and from 1848 George Chatterton undertook the role for over a decade. The conductor was John McCarthy, stipendiary of St Fin Barre's choir.

Unlike the Dublin Antient Concerts Society's minimal use of newspapers,[87] the *Cork Examiner* and *The Constitution* published profuse notices of the Cork society's concert previews, programmes and reviews. The Protestant basis of the Dublin society appears to have been replicated to a large degree in the Cork organisation. The *Cork Examiner* provided a critical response to its activities from the outset. The first concert, held at the Imperial Hotel on 23 March 1847, consisted of selections from Handel's *Messiah* and a performance of Mozart's 12th Mass, 'absurdly styled "Service" in the printed programme', according to the *Cork Examiner* reviewer.[88] This matter also provoked a letter to the editor:

> Sir – May I beg the favour of a space in your journal to ask the Committee of this infant Society, upon what authority they have misnamed Mozart's Mass, and why they have put in their programme Mozart's *Service* – was it to show the great professors of the Continent and of London that *they* must no longer retain the frightful word *Mass* in their musical nomenclature? Or was it that they feared to offend a little bigoted section of their audience, by the introduction into their bill of fare, of this little harmless, simple word of four letters – *Mass*? Was it that, Christian-like, their narrow-mindedness got the better of the good resolution made at the opening of their society, viz. to know no political or religious distinctions? Yes, Sir, they may have been influenced by one or all of these motives, but at least in their *debut*, they might have avoided the *semblance* of a slight to their very *few* Catholic members, and the *fewer* auditors of this persuasion who attended the Concert. 'Tis pitiable to see this petty religious bigotry displaying itself so early in a public musical society, where harmony in every sense of the word should exist. So much for the *first performance* of the Antient Concerts: What will be the next? Your obedient servant, Basso.[89]

Nonetheless, an overflowing audience was reported, and the gallery of the concert room was arranged to accommodate some 100 persons. The society's strong affinity with Dublin was evident in the choice of vocal soloists, Miss Searle and Mr Richard Smith (son of Dr Smith), both of Dublin. Local singers Robert Orr, A.D. Roche, James Keays and R. Wheeler, all of whom were singers in St Fin Barre's choir, also performed lesser solo roles, and the boys of the North Monastery featured in the choruses with the adult singers. James Brealsford Stephens presided at the pianoforte and John McCarthy conducted the orchestra, which was led by Robert Coghlan and John Smith. A second concert was given a week later, the proceeds intended for the Relief of the Destitute of the City, as the effects of the Famine were evident by this time. The accounts for this concert, published in the *Cork Examiner*, show that, after the performers' fees and expenses were paid, a sum of £21 19s 8d was available for the relief fund. Of the performers, only trumpeter Oakden, bassoonist Kent (both of the Royal Dragoons), and Mr Sippi had performed gratis for the event.[90] Another concert in support of famine relief was given the following week at the Imperial Hotel, directed by Robert Bowden.[91] Apart from these two events, there is little evidence that the Famine impacted on Cork's public music life. A comment on conditions of the starving poor in the city appears in an account written some fifty years later:

> It was quite wonderful that anyone had the heart to go to concerts or anything else in the way of amusements at that time, for the ghastly presence of a great famine brought almost everything to a hideous standstill. Sad sights were to be seen in the city every day when the poor famine-stricken people used to creep in from the outlying districts to look for a morsel of food. They were found dead or dying in the doorways of the city every day.[92]

It is interesting to note that the Society of British Musicians also held a Grand Orchestral Concert at the Hanover Square Rooms during this week, conducted by William Sterndale Bennett (1816–75), for which the proceeds were intended for the relief of the 'distressed Irish'.[93] There is no evidence that other musical societies organised fundraising events specifically for famine relief, or had any association with any of the voluntary relief groups that had been established in the city.[94] The apparent indifference of the choral societies to the Famine, which was rife in County Cork, highlights the narrow aspirations and agendas of this and St Mary's Choral Society. Like their eighteenth-century counterparts, these societies were a means of social display and sociability, and their level of charitable support rarely extended to causes other than their stated ones. The clearly defined channels of the local charitable societies that already existed prevailed.

The Constitution and the *Cork Examiner* reported audiences of between 600 and 800 at the Antient Concerts Society's performances at the Imperial Hotel over the next two years. The criticism of the use of the term 'Service' instead of 'Mass' in the programmes was reiterated by the writer in the *Cork Examiner*, who also took issue with the engagement of so many Dublin soloists over local singers. Like its metropolitan counterpart, the society's concert repertoire consisted mainly of sacred works by Handel, Haydn and Mendelssohn.[95] A review of the society's first concert in 1849 in *The Constitution* provided some reflections on its progress. Besides its expansion from 20 to 170 members in three years, it had 'reconciled the hostile professors of both parties, and promoted good fellowship amongst those who had long been separated'. The review concluded with an assertion of the heightened aesthetic surrounding 'antient' music:

> [...] in an antient concert, where musical taste is properly educated, it is not the power or character of a singer's voice which will be estimated, but the expression and judgement with which he performs the part allotted to him.[96]

The conflict between sacred and secular taste, and the benefits of a mixed programme were recurring themes in press reviews. A performance in April 1850 consisted of a selection from Haydn's *The Seasons* followed by a mixed programme. The *Cork Examiner* writer approved of the inclusion of lighter items on the programme:

> The fact of its being more mundane in its character, and less spiritual and elevated, was considerably in its favour; for though a well-executed oratorio is a very good thing in its way, and affords a high degree of intellectual pleasure when rarely enjoyed, still grandeur and majesty become tiresome in a short time, and ordinary mortals cannot endure the idea of being perpetually lifted above the ordinary level of human emotions, and long to return to those objects, whether in art or literature, which appeal to the feelings of the heart, and are more consonant with the habits and associations of every-day life.[97]

Works by Mendelssohn featured in the society's programmes. Joseph and Frank Robinson featured in a performance of Mendelssohn's *Elijah* in May 1849 at the Imperial Hotel. The Dublin Antients had given the Irish premiere of this work in December 1847.[98] A review in *The Constitution* commented on the lack of an organ (the part was played by James Stephens on piano), and on the need for a proper concert hall in the city.[99] The first concert of the 1850–51 season in December featured Louisa Pine in a performance of selections from *Elijah* and *The Creation*. Miss Victoire Balfe (1837–71) and Dublin amateur bass baritone John Stanford (father of Charles Villiers Stanford)[100] also drew praise in a review.[101] A concert held at the Corn Exchange in June 1851 consisted of selections from *Samson*, *Messiah*, and a solo from Mendelssohn's oratorio *St Paul*, and the second part was miscellaneous, consisting of a vocal quartet dated 1545, 'Alla Trinita Beata', among other items. Mendelssohn's operetta *Son and Stranger* formed the first part of a concert given by the society at the Imperial Hotel in January 1852 and a miscellaneous second half included a madrigal by Cooke.[102]

NATIONAL EXHIBITION 1852

Following the success of the 1851 Great Exhibition at London's Crystal Palace, a National Exhibition to promote Irish industry was organised in Cork from June to September 1852. The extensive cruciform Exhibition Buildings, adjoining the Corn Exchange on Albert Quay, were erected as temporary structures to accommodate the exhibits. The Fine Arts Hall, designed by Sir John Benson, housed an organ supplied by William Telford (1809–85) of Dublin, fronted by orchestral seating. The opening was an auspicious occasion, attended by the Lord Lieutenant and his entourage, its national importance reflected in the employment of a large contingent of Dublin musicians. Conducted by Joseph Robinson, the performance featured an Inauguration Ode, 'In Praise of Industry', composed by Dublin organist and conductor Robert Prescott Stewart (1825–94) to a text by John Francis Waller. The 200-strong performing forces included members of Dublin's University Choral Society and the Antient Concerts Societies of Dublin and Cork, and an orchestra led by Richard Levey, also of Dublin. Handel's 'Hallelujah' chorus and an arrangement of his Grand Coronation Anthem, with new words by Waller, were also performed.[103]

The exhibition, which ran from June to September, provided a major boost to Irish manufacturers and craftsmen. A detailed account was published in John Francis Maguire's booklet *The Industrial Movement in Ireland as Illustrated by the National Exhibition 1852*.[104] The collection of musical instruments at the exhibition, Maguire admitted, was 'by no means large', explaining that 'we are content, in most cases, to purchase them from the London makers, whose capital and reputation render competition in the more costly articles altogether hopeless'. Among the few locally made instruments exhibited was a church organ made by J. Seymour Murphy of Cork, and a double-bass and two cellos by John Murphy, and violins and cellos by William Whitehead. Maguire noted the excellence of Denis Harrington, uilleann pipe maker of Hanover Street,[105] whose pipes 'are as justly celebrated as the pianos of Broadwood or Collard'. He concluded his comments on the music section with a lengthy description of the excellent workmanship of Patrick Connell

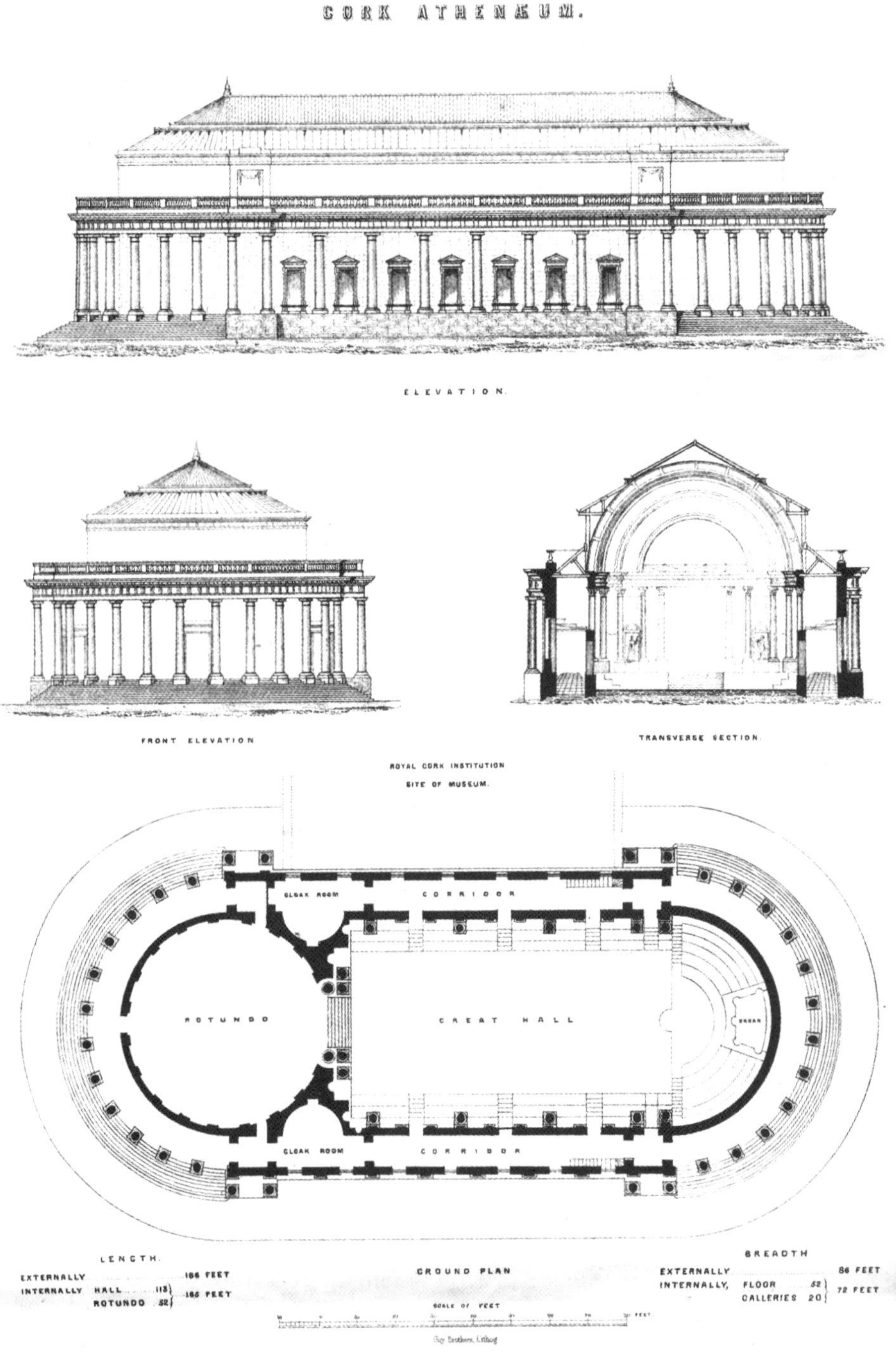

Figure 8.3. Cork Athenaeum, architectural drawings, 1854.
CORK CITY AND COUNTY ARCHIVES

of 11 Hanover Street, who made strings for violins and harps for over thirty-five years, described as 'fully equal to the Italian, and superior to the English'.

THE ATHENAEUM

The committee of the Antient Concerts Society had discussed the need for a music hall for Cork as early as 1849. Members of the Royal Cork Institution moved to achieve this goal. After the conclusion of the Exhibition, the Executive Committee and the RCI made a proposal to the corporation to retain and reconstruct the Fine Arts Hall on the Institution's grounds.[106] Overseen by Sir John Benson and William Brash, the new building was described as 'a modification of the Great Hall [...] but so altered and so improved as to leave but a faint outline of the original design'. Finally completed in 1853, the Athenaeum, as the new building was named, occupied a vacant site belonging to the Royal Cork Institution on Nelson Place (now Emmet Place).[107] It was managed by 'a committee of 21 gentlemen elected annually; two-thirds by the shareholders, and one third by the managers of the Royal Cork Institution'.[108] The *Cork Examiner* noted in July 1854:

> Almost unperceived one of the most beautiful structures of which our city can boast, has sprung into existence, and under the above title, is destined, we trust, to be a long seat of intellectual recreation and improvement.[109]

At a meeting in July 1854 it was resolved to secure £2,000 in shares to complete the project:

> We have a noble hall for public purposes, whether for concert, either of our local musical societies, such as our ancient concerts, or for the performance of Italian and English operas; and again, for all purposes of public lectures on scientific or literary subjects: for cheap popular lectures for the working classes, and as a place of assembly for public meetings in our city.[110]

To equip the building as a concert room, an organ was purchased from the London firm of Bevington, at a cost of £750.[111] It was installed in the recess of the western end of the building, which was fitted with seating for an orchestra of some 200 performers. A rotondo measuring 52 feet in diameter was separated from the great hall by a row of Corinthian columns (see Figure 8.3). This area could either be screened off or converted into a single extension of the hall. The auditorium, including the galleries, had the capacity for 2,000 people.[112] An inauguration of the Athenaeum planned for 28 November 1854 was postponed, and the event was finally held on 22 May 1855.[113]

In 1853, the Antient Concerts and St Mary's Choral Societies amalgamated, presenting the first joint concert in January 1854 at the ballroom of the Imperial Hotel. The concert represented a new departure in repertoire, featuring William Bexfield's (1824–53) oratorio *Israel Restored* (1851).[114] First performed at the Norwich Festival of 1852, it was an early example of English nineteenth-century oratorios adhering to the Handelian model.[115] Before his untimely death, the composer himself dispatched the musical score with the request that the society would undertake its performance.[116]

This concert featured Cork-born bass singer John Valentine Blake (d. 1867).[117] From a prominent Catholic family, Blake had recently completed three years of vocal study at the London Royal Academy of Music (RAM). He was a son of Jeremiah Blake, a bootmaker with premises at 59 George's Street, who was acquainted with John Stanislaus Joyce (father of James Joyce) during his early years in Cork.[118] His brothers Jeremiah C. Blake and Alfred Blake (b. 1849) were prominent attorneys in the city.[119] He gave a series of concerts in Cork in December 1853 with Tralee-born pianist Arthur O'Leary (1834–1919), a fellow student of the RAM.[120] The Antient Concerts Society presented no concerts over the next five years. In 1859 and 1860, the society was revived under George Chatterton,[121] and further brief revivals were attempted in 1863 under A.D. Roche, and in 1868 under Edward O'Mahony.[122]

CORK AMATEUR HARMONIC SOCIETY

Since the establishment of Queen's College, the RCI's role as an educational body was considerably diminished, and it now assumed the role of fostering cultural organisations within the city, particularly at the new Athenaeum. It was the driving force behind the establishment of the Cork Harmonic Society in 1855. Its president, Sir Thomas Tobin (1807–81), was vice-president of the RCI and president of the Athenaeum. The vice presidents of the new society were the mayor, The O'Donovan, John Francis Maguire MP and Thomas Hewitt.[123] Penrose Beale acted as founding honorary secretary, subsequently taken over by Jeremiah C. Blake. John W. McCarthy was the society's conductor. It was a mixed-denomination society committed to charitable support, favouring local soloists for its performances. An early announcement of the new society appeared in the *Cork Examiner* in November 1855, enumerating the contributions of its now foundering predecessor:

> It is now some two or three years since the Antient Concert Society ceased its functions, and since then there has been no performance in this city, by local talent, or, we might even say, by the strangers who pay us a passing visit, of music of a really high class. While that body was in existence the citizens had an opportunity at least two or three times a year of hearing some of the great works which form the classics of music, and its silence is a loss to the public that it is most desirable to see supplied. Accordingly a new society has been formed upon principles somewhat similar, and with the same object, that of rendering in public performances some of the masterpieces of harmony.
>
> [...] it brings together for a common pursuit, persons of different classes and creeds, and spreads amongst them that friendliness and cordiality which the act of co-operation always engenders, and on the public, in giving them a true intellectual and refined enjoyment, and in awakening a taste for the highest class of art.
>
> The new body, too, will have the additional advantages of being able to render its performances more popular, as there is now available a building peculiarly adapted for concerts, and which can accommodate immense numbers. With the old society it was a matter of necessity that admission be dear, and consequently confined to a comparative few; while on the other hand the immense size of the Athenaeum, the building, we presume, that will be used on these occasions, will enable the new body to popularize their performances.[124]

The annual subscription for performing members (vocal or instrumental) was five shillings. Non-performing members paid an annual subscription of one guinea, which entitled them to attend concerts and rehearsals. At the society's second concert at the Athenaeum in April 1856, T.J. Sullivan displayed the powers of the Bevington organ, and singers Miss McCarthy, John V. Blake and Mrs Russell performed in a mixed programme of 'madrigals, selections from operas, and the entire of Locke's music of Macbeth'.[125] By 1860, the society was known as the Cork Amateur Harmonic Society. In May of that year, violinist John Jones led the orchestra and performed solos at a concert that raised £25 for the South Infirmary.[126]

Controversy and division entered this society's activities in 1861, when some of its members opted to avail, gratis, of the newly opened Protestant Assembly Rooms for a concert in May in aid of the North Infirmary. Some of the society's Catholic members refused to perform, resulting in a significant fall-off of public support, and the event only yielded £17 0s 3d, a third of the expected sum.[127] According to the *Cork Examiner*, the society

> was composed of Protestants and Catholics, who played and sang together without a thought of sectarian difference. The ophecleide did not growl one particle more melodiously for being blown by a Papist; a Protestant bow could not B flat squeak a whit more shrilly on a fiddle. But this state of things was too pleasant to last.[128]

Contentious issues had surrounded the Protestant Hall from its inception. In 1858, a dispute arose over the refusal of permission by the Athenaeum committee for a lecture by Italian preacher Fr Alessandro Gavazzi (1809–89), hosted by the Cork Protestant Association. Gavazzi was an ex-priest, whose

Figure 8.4. Opening of the Protestant Hall, South Mall, 1861.
ILLUSTRATED LONDON NEWS, COURTESY OF CORK CITY LIBRARY

attacks on the Roman Catholic religion generated outrage in other cities. Plans were made for a new hall, the County and City of Cork Assembly Rooms at 22 South Mall, known locally as the Protestant Hall. At a ceremony on 12 April 1861, the Earl of Bandon declared it formally open 'for all classes and creeds of the city of Cork'. This impressive building, designed by Richard Bolt Brash (1817–76), was of generous dimensions, measuring 100 feet by 45 feet and 36 feet high, with a platform and tiered seating at the southern end, suitable for either an orchestra or for audiences during lectures. The seventy-voice choir that sang at the opening consisted of adult and child members of St Luke's Tonic Solfa Association, trained by William H. Smith, and the Cork Artillery Band, under the direction of Robert Howard, also performed.[129] The venue was used thereafter mainly by Protestant societies, and became the headquarters of the Church of Ireland Young Men's Association.

CORK CITY AND COUNTY CHORAL SOCIETY

During the last years of the Antient Concerts Society, yet another choral society emerged, prompted by the arrival in 1860 of a new organist at St Fin Barre's, the young James Christopher Marks (1835–1903). A native of Armagh, Marks had been a cathedral chorister at Armagh cathedral, where he studied organ with Robert Turle (1804–77). He held the post of assistant organist there from 1852 until his move to Cork, succeeding James Brealsford Stephens, whose long tenure had ended with his death earlier that year. Marks immersed himself in local musical life, advertising tuition in piano, singing, harmony and thoroughbass at his residence, 49 South Mall.[130] In November, he directed the Cork Amateur Harmonic Society for the first concert of its third season at the Imperial Hotel, followed by a second concert in January 1861.[131] Marks evidently had more ambitious plans, however, and in June 1861, together with Thomas Nagle, organist at St Vincent's (Catholic) Church in Sunday's Well, he established the Cork City and County Choral Society 'for the production and performance of Oratorios and other great Choral Works, both Sacred and secular, upon a scale of magnitude and completeness not hitherto attempted in this City'. Branches of the society were to be established in various towns in the county, and it was envisaged that the orchestra and chorus combined would number 500.[132] The inaugural performances were to take the form of a three-day festival, on the Birmingham model. Nagle acted as secretary to the society, and the treasurer was local merchant Victor Beare Fitzgibbon. Its strong regional emphasis reflected similar festivals in England and Germany.

The society achieved remarkable progress in its initial five months. An Elementary Class met on Friday evenings at the Athenaeum, at which, for a fee of five shillings per season, members were taught 'to read music at sight, and count their time, according to Hullah's system'.[133] Choral rehearsals were held on Monday and Wednesday nights at the Athenaeum.[134] Having observed one of these rehearsals, a writer for the *Cork Examiner* expressed surprise at 'the degree of proficiency [...] in performers so inexperienced', and advocated public support for the venture.[135] Like the Antient Concerts Society, however, the activities of the society quickly became a focus for sectarian bickering. A letter written by secretary Thomas Nagle to the editor of the *Cork Examiner* on 11 January 1862 denied a rumour that the profits of the festival and choral concerts were to be devoted to sectarian purposes, stating that they were 'to be divided equally among the most important charities of this city and county'.[136]

The festival performances at the Athenaeum on 28, 29 and 30 January 1862 featured a choir and orchestra of around 300 performers. A mixed choir of 220 voices included singers from Bandon (20) under Paul Atkinson, Youghal (20) under Charles Sippi, Limerick (30), Armagh and Belfast (15), and Dublin (20). Handel Rogers of St Mary's Cathedral, Limerick, presided at the organ.[137] A number of soloists prominent at the English provincial festivals were engaged, including Hermine Rudersdorff (1822–82), Julia Elton and English bass Willoughby Weiss (1820–67). William Topham (d. 1871), tenor, and John Dunne, counter-tenor, both of Christ Church, Dublin, also sang,[138] with J.F. Horton, tenor, of Cork cathedral and Mr Wood, bass.[139] Amongst the instrumentalists were violinist Richard Levey and cellist Wilhelm Elsner (*c.* 1822–84), both from Dublin.[140] Special late trains to Mallow, Youghal, Bandon and Passage operated on each evening of the festival.

The festival opened on 28 January with Handel's *Judas Maccabeus*, its first full Cork performance. On the following evening, excerpts from *Der Freischütz* were performed, with a Grand Miscellaneous Selection in the second half.[141] A *Cork Examiner* report described it as 'an absolute triumph'. The entire hall was a reserved 'dress' area, which was extended into a large balcony erected over the rotundo, which held another 300 people. The unreserved seats extended into the rotundo area, and the side galleries were also crammed, with the result that 'No room whatsoever was left for the shilling occupants of the rotunda, and that class was erased from the list altogether.' Choral performances of 'The Huntsmans' Chorus' and 'The Bridesmaids' Chorus' from *Der Freischütz* were praised, the latter featuring three amateur soloists.[142] Handel's *Messiah* was performed on 30 January.

The following May, the Cork City and County Choral and Festival Society, as it was now named, presented two concerts at the Athenaeum on consecutive nights, the first with a full performance of Haydn's *The Creation*. Although commenting favourably on the performance, the writer in the *Cork Examiner* was not impressed with the choice of work, being of the opinion that '*The Creation* stands to the *Messiah* as the highest effort of art does to a work of nature'.[143] The second evening featured Rossini's *Stabat Mater* (1841) and a selection from Mendelssohn's *Athalie* (1845). The organist on both evenings was George William Torrance (1835–1907), of Dublin,[144] and the orchestral leader was Richard Levey. The concerts featured visiting singers Scottish soprano Euphrosyne Parepa (1836–74), English tenor George Perren (1827–1909) and Portuguese pianist Arthur Napoleon, on his third visit to the city.[145] Julia Cruise travelled from Dublin to perform. In December, Marks directed two Grand Charity Concerts at the Athenaeum in aid of the 'Distressed Lancashire Operatives and Local Coal Fund'.[146] After this event, the new society, having lasted only a year and a half, made no further appearances, for reasons that are not entirely clear. Marks may have been disillusioned with the demise of the society, as he made few public appearances as conductor over the next few years. He was awarded a BMus Oxon. in 1863, and in 1868 gained a doctorate from Magdalen College, Oxford, for his oratorio *Gideon*.[147] In November 1868, he directed two concerts at the Athenaeum in aid of the funds for the building of the new cathedral, consisting of a performance of *Messiah*, the proceeds devoted specifically to the carvings of the interior.[148]

The foundation stone of a new Church of Ireland cathedral to replace the building of 1735 was laid in 1862, keenly observed by antiquarian Richard Caulfield (1823–87), then president of the RCI, who delivered a lecture on the history of the cathedral and its bishops in January 1864.[149] Under Marks' direction, a full daily choral service was reinstated at St Fin Barre's from May 1864,[150] and thereafter the cathedral fulfilled its potential as a musical institution, and *The Constitution* regularly published details of the music to accompany forthcoming services. The new edifice was completed in 1870 and, at the consecration ceremony on 30 November, St Andrew's Day, Marks performed on a new organ built by the London firm of William

Hill (1789–1870), at a cost of £1,500.[151] Morning Prayer and Litany was accompanied by appropriate psalms and responses. After an evening sermon, the 'Hallelujah' chorus was sung 'with overpowering effect by a choir drawn from all parts of Ireland.'[152] Ironically, a few months later, on 1 January 1871, the Irish Church Act marked the disestablishment of the Anglican Church in Ireland.

As choral activity continued to proliferate during the 1860s, pedagogies for reading musical notation remained an issue. Over the previous decade, London clergyman and pedagogue John Curwen's (1816–80) adaptation of Sarah Ann Glover's (1785–1867) pedagogical model for the use of 'sol fa with a movable doh' had become widely known in England within Anglican Church circles, and was adopted by Sunday school teachers who had begun to realise the limitations of Hullah's system.[153] By 1860, a Tonic Solfa Association was active in Cork. At an event in 1860 entitled 'Annual Tea Festival and Soirée Musicale', a choir of over 130 voices, directed by Rev. B. Stoney, performed Handel's 'Halleluia Chorus' and 'gems from Mendelssohn [...] according to the tonic sol fa system [...], thoroughly trained and effective'.[154] William H. Smith advertised tonic sol fa classes for both children and adults in March 1861,[155] and a letter to the editor of *The Constitution* by 'Verbum Sat' called for 'harmony and a body of singers in our churches', stating that 'the simple *Sol fa* system, which on more than one occasion was brought under the notice of the Cork public and proved to be effective, should be more extensively patronized'. In March 1862, the Tonic Solfa Association hosted two lectures by John Curwen at the Protestant Hall, illustrated by 'a choir of 100 solfaists' under the guidance of Mr W.H. Smith', performing selections of 'social, classical and congregational' music.[156]

The Christ Church Choral Union was founded in 1865, a choir of nearly a hundred amateurs, conducted by John W. McCarthy, organist at Christ Church.[157] This musical society presented mixed programmes for its *Soirées Musicales* at the South Mall Assembly Room. Tenor Henry Baker, a stipendiary of St Fin Barre's Cathedral, sang regularly at these events. Among the amateur singers associated with this group was William Ringrose Atkins. In December 1869, the main programme attraction of a *Soirée Musicale* consisted of selections from an oratorio. *The Prodigal Son*, recently composed by Arthur Sullivan.[158] Amateur instrumentalists who featured in its programmes were violinist John Gilbert and young pianist Bella McCarthy, daughter of the society's conductor. The continued aversion by some of the Catholic community to the Protestant Hall is evident from a notice in the *Cork*

Examiner of a forthcoming concert by this society at this venue in February 1868, which offered support for the event, emphasising that 'the concert, in itself, has nothing of a sectarian or offensive nature'.[159]

Apart from the activities of the large choral societies, the choral conducting activities of Mrs James Halloran during the 1850s and 1860s were reported in the local press. She appears to have been Cork's first female choral conductor, and was active in several charity performances. An advertisement appeared in the *Cork Examiner* in 1853 for her 'Cork Musical Academy, at 72 Grand Parade, offering tuition in the organ, pianoforte and harmonium'.[160] She was referred to in 1853 in an acknowledgement by the Society of St Vincent de Paul (established in Cork since 1846) of the 'kind services of Mrs James Halloran, organist, and the ladies and gentlemen of the choir'.[161] At a charity sermon in aid of the Ladies' Clothing Society in April 1853, she directed a choir in a performance of Handel's 'Worthy is the Lamb' which 'evinced the admirable taste and practical knowledge of the conductor'.[162] Later that year, she directed two concerts by the Cork Amateur Society at the Imperial Hotel, featuring a 'chorus of 18 voices, including, for the first time in this city, 8 Soprani voices'. Mrs Halloran performed an *Andante* by Thalberg and a fantasia by Rossellen on the piano.[163] She held another series of concerts at the Athenaeum in the spring of 1855.[164] For the first of these, in February, she was 'assisted by the first professional talent in this city, and by distinguished amateurs of the counties and cities of Cork and Waterford'.[165] This concert provided 'an opportunity of accurately estimating the capabilities of the building for choral and musical purposes'.[166] Over the next seven years, she was the principal organist for events held at the Athenaeum.

Vocal performances by the inmates of the City and County of Cork Blind Asylum (founded in 1840) were frequently reported in the local newspapers from the 1840s onwards.[167] The first concert at the Athenaeum was given in January 1855, in aid of the Blind Asylum.[168] Promenade concerts in aid of this charity continued as an annual event at the venue, usually held in May. The concerts and promenades featured music composed by former and current teachers employed at the asylum, who included A.P. Herrmann and Mr McCarthy. From 1862, music teachers at the Asylum were singer John V. Blake, and Robert Howard of the Royal Cork Artillery, who directed a band there. [169]

Choral music featured among the activities of several new community and religious organisations that emerged from 1850 onwards. The Cork Church of Ireland Young Men's Association was established in 1850 under the patronage of the Lord Bishop of Cork, with premises at the Diocesan Council House at 52 South Mall. Taking on many of the functions previously associated with the Temperance Institute, the association provided a library, reading rooms, lectures, concerts and other entertainments.[170] In May 1861 Rev. Joseph R. Cotter delivered a lecture on music with vocal and instrumental illustrations by Professor O'Donoghue of Limerick. Master Howard of the Royal Cork Artillery Band performed selections on the cornopean.[171]

Earliest reports of the Catholic Young Men's Society (CYMS), founded in 1852, indicate that musical instruction and performance featured among its activities. With premises at Castle Street, formerly the People's Hall, it provided a library, reading rooms, evening classes and lectures, for an annual fee of eight shillings.[172] In its first year, John Fleming, organist at the North Cathedral, held classes in Gregorian chant.[173] A press report of a lecture in 1854 noted the performance of glees by the singing class before the commencement, under Fleming's direction.[174] A soirée held on the society's third anniversary featured singing by Edwin Sims Reeves, John V. Blake, Maxwell Sullivan and John Fleming.[175] In 1859, the society presented two illustrated lectures at the Athenaeum on 'Moore's Irish Melodies' by John William Glover (1815–99), organist at Dublin's Pro-Cathedral since 1848.[176] Members were admitted free, and admission to the public was at the rates of 1 shilling and 6d. During the early 1860s, Mrs O'Halloran directed concerts by the society's Harmonic Guild, which consisted of both instrumental and vocal ensembles.[177] From 1866, the society's music professor was Thomas Nagle, who attempted to establish a Choral Union based within the society, modelled on the Christ Church Choral union, founded the previous year.[178] The programme of the First Grand Concert of the union held at the Athenaeum shows that it aimed to combine Catholic and Protestant musical forces, featuring soprano Miss McKenna, soloist at the North Cathedral, and tenor Henry Baker of St Fin Barre cathedral choir. The programme was unusual for the time, consisting of a first half featuring several movements of a Mozart Mass, with Rossini's 'Inflammatus' (*Stabat Mater*), and an organ sonata by Mendelssohn,[179] performed by R. Sutton Swaby, former organist at St Vincent's Church (see page 215). The second half of the concert featured operatic selections by the vocalists, and concluded with two choral pieces – 'Let Erin Remember' and 'God Save the Queen'.[180] The venture was a further example of Nagle's persistence in attempting to create musical platforms that integrated Catholic and Protestant tastes and interests. The CYMS continued to be an important provider of music tuition, presenting annual concerts and soirées and guest lectures on a range of musical topics.[181] A report presented at the 37th Annual Meeting of the society in 1889 referred to lectures presented on musical topics in the previous year, including 'Old songs of our native lands' by Cornelius Cremen, a society member. John Gilbert lectured on 'Song' and 'History of Minstrels and Minstrelsy', bringing a number of musicians to illustrate his lecture. The annual report also referred to two promenade concerts.[182] Music was only one of many areas of study in this society, which was arguably the most significant organisation that facilitated education for Catholic young men of the city's middle classes.

A new initiative in charity choral concerts was launched at the Athenaeum in January 1865. A Grand Amateur Concert in aid of the Fever Hospital was organised, consisting entirely of amateurs brought together especially for the occasion.[183]The eighty-strong chorus, drawn from 'the most respectable families in and about Cork', was trained and conducted by James Roche, and the solo performers, both vocal and instrumental, were also members of the families of the local gentry.[184] In a festooned auditorium, this gala performance drew a capacity audience, and the reviewer of the *Cork Examiner* noted the display of fashionable attire worn by both performers and audience. Another concert based on this model was presented in 1868 in aid of the Nile Street hospital, directed by J.C. Marks. The reviewer referred to the strong visual effect created by 'graceful festoons of laurel and hothouse plants', superintended by Mr J.F. Mahony of the School of Art. A Haydn string trio was performed by Mrs Leahy, Captain Pigott Beamish and Alexander Jack, in which Beamish 'proved himself a highly accomplished violinist, playing with brilliancy and judgement'.[185] Excerpts from Marks' oratorio *Gideon*, his doctoral piece, were performed at another 'Grand Amateur Concert' at the Athenaeum in January 1869.[186]

AMATEUR BAND REVIVAL

In 1860, in line with other developments aimed at improving civic recreations, Robert Howard proposed setting up a Cork citizens' band for public occasions. He stated that he could, 'at any time, procure 30 excellent musicians, inhabitants of Cork, who, with a little training, will be sufficiently perfect', to 'perform during the evenings at the Mardyke, New Wall, and other public places, where a promenade could be formed, and where the citizens could enjoy a pleasant stroll and a musical treat, simultaneously'.[187] Howard, who was English, came to Cork as a trumpet major with the City of Cork Artillery

Band, and was employed for many years as teacher and bandmaster at the Blind Asylum. An article in the *Cork Examiner* the following year questioned the recent appearance of this band, that in contrast to the customary role played by military bands at public events, 'there is novelty in their being summoned to give a running accompaniment to onslaughts on the Church of Rome'.[188] This comment probably relates to the band's performance at the recent opening of the Protestant Hall (see pages 190–191). There were no further references to Howard's proposed citizens' band project in any of the city newspapers.

Press notices during the mid-1860s indicate that several of the features of the earlier temperance movement – halls, readings rooms, festivals and bands – had been recently revived in many locations across the city.[189] The unveiling of a memorial bronze statue of Father Mathew on Patrick Street in October 1864, a few years after his death in 1856, led to a rekindling of interest in Mathew's legacy. Known by locals since that time simply as 'the statue', it became an iconic feature of Cork's main street, a fitting tribute to the city's greatest popular leader. The procession on that day featured performances by several local temperance bands. In 1866, the following notice appeared in the *Cork Examiner*:

> Temperance Bands in Cork
> The idea that used to be formerly associated with the name of a 'Temperance band' would give a very inadequate notion of the orchestra that has been formed in connection with the temperance movement, fostered by the Rev John McNamara. A dozen instruments, each playing an independent tune, was the general type of music of the temperance bands of long ago. That which has been formed by Rev Mr McNamara is one that will eventually be regarded as a credit to the city, and a source of great enjoyment to the citizens at large.[190]

The band was part of a confraternity based in the parish of St Mary and St Anne. Mr J. Gready, bandmaster of the 2nd Queen's Regiment, was its first instructor, a role subsequently undertaken by Thomas J. Nagle, and by George Brady from 1867. The band consisted of almost fifty men and boys. The instruments, supplied by Besson of London, had cost £265.[191] In December 1868, the *Cork Examiner* published an appeal to the citizens of Cork for more subscribers, describing St Mary's as a band 'which does more to vindicate and uphold the reputation of their city, for musical taste and talent, than any local organization that now exists'.[192] The writer, who had attended a band practice, identified pieces rehearsed as quadrilles from Louise Jullien's opera *Pietro il grande* (1852), and excerpts from Verdi's *Il trovatore* (1853). A promenade performance by the band at the Navigation Wall (now the Marina) in June consisted of the following programme, typical of military band repertoire:[193]

Grand March (Faust)	Gounod
Valse 'Soldaten Lieder'	Gung'l
Selection from *Linda di Chamonix*	Donizetti
Quadrille 'Gipsy Girl'	Clarke
Polonaise	Peter, Prince of Oldenburg
Galop 'Flick and Flock'	Hertel

The band established a reputation for the quality of its performances both at religious ceremonies at the cathedral and at public events in the city. George Brady again directed the band during the summer of 1869, at a number of outdoor evening promenades at the Navigation Wall,[194] and appeared again at the Athenaeum the following year as part of John Fleming's concert.[195] When Fr McNamara left the cathedral to take up a new post in 1875, the band continued, but an article published in the *Cork Examiner* indicates that it had reached a critical financial state.[196]

The Barrack Street Temperance Society appears to have had an unbroken existence since the 1840s, largely through the activities of Rev. Mr O'Regan.[197] By December 1866, a report of a festival held by the members of this society described the performance by a new band, seven months in training, playing on new Besson instruments.[198] A list of subscribers published in the *Cork Examiner* in September 1869 indicates that this band enjoyed wide public support.[199] By 1871, the St Francis Band had been established, under the auspices of the Franciscans, and directed by Cornelius Sullivan.[200]

Bands became firmly embedded in a range of local communities, temperance societies and workplaces, taking roles at civic and religious functions previously assigned to military bands. Radical activity by bands was occasionally reported in the press. On an invitation to perform at the Irish Exhibition at the Olympia in London in 1888, the members of the Barrack Street Band refused to play 'God Save the Queen' to conclude their performance. The incident was widely reported in English provincial newspapers.[201] The bandmaster, George Brady, defended the action, stating that the band was entirely Catholic, and that he was the only Protestant connected with it. He informed the press that the band had not rehearsed it, and he would not allow the band to play it unrehearsed. He was also reported to have stated that he considered the exhibition as a purely non-political affair and that he wished to have nothing to do with politics, but only to look at the matter from a musician's point of view.[202] Apart from the temperance and trade bands, neighbouring community fife and drum bands were associated with violent inter-factional confrontations in what was reported as 'the Band nuisance' between 1879 and 1882.[203]

From the early 1840s, the unprecedented emergence of new dynamic musical institutions, founded without reference to past musical structures, changed the landscape for amateur music making. The founding of five major choral societies within two decades was indicative of a widespread gravitation towards choral singing. Although each of these eventually lapsed, choral singing as a cultural practice endured in various forms across a range of associations, institutions and communities. The band movement, with its own repertoire and performance traditions, was equally significant. The large membership of these organisations accommodated many levels of musical competence, and proficient amateurs emerged across most economic and social groupings.

Although the Famine was undeniably a watershed for many aspects of Irish cultural history, Cork city's social and musical life took a different path, stimulated by two other pivotal historical developments, Catholic Emancipation (1829) and the Municipal Reform Act (1841), removing the barriers to full civic participation. Performances in a range of settings, indoor and outdoor, by amateur bands and choirs, provided citizens with opportunities for musical expression and civic display. The contributions of William Gillespie and Thomas Nagle provided the necessary expertise and unwavering commitment in asserting the Catholic musical presence, while seeking a fair and non-sectarian basis for large-scale choral events.

9

CATHOLICISM AND MUSIC, 1800–1900

The Consecration of the Roman Catholic Church of St Mary's, Pope's Quay, Cork *c.* 1842, by James Mahony.

COURTESY OF IRELAND'S GREAT HUNGER MUSEUM, QUINNIPIAC UNIVERSITY, HAMDEN, CT

In common with the rest of Ireland, Cork has of late years made great effort to assimilate in some degree the externals of Catholic worship with the dignity its essence possesses in the eyes of our people. Though not a remarkably wealthy community, nor progressing with extraordinary rapidity in the path of prosperity, our achievements are such as we need not be ashamed of. Within twenty years our City has seen spring up several new and splendid churches, and at least three convental structures; while other great architectural works are still in progress.[1]

The resurgence of the Catholic Church during the nineteenth century was a defining feature in Irish social history, and an important aspect of Irish national identity.[2] The universality of the Latin liturgy enabled the ready adoption of the sizable corpus of solemn Mass settings of the Viennese Classical tradition to supplement the standard plainchant usage. In post-Emancipation Ireland, the expansion of music, together with the building of new churches and the consolidation of institutionalised religious practice, were key developments in the formation of the modern Catholic Church.[3]

Among William Brady's records is an early reference to the Catholic parish of St Fin Barre's in Cork, dated 1700:

> Colman Sarsfield is Popish Priest of this and the united parishes. He has a mass-house near Red Abby [*sic*]. He was bred at Bordeaux, in France, in the Irish seminary. […] Sarsfield, the Priest of this parish, saies mass twice every Sunday morning, and the rest of the Priests in Ireland, by order of the Pope, have the privilege of saying two masses in one day, by reason of the great extent of most parishes or unions.[4]

The mass house was described in an early account as 'a long cabin, that will contain about 400 persons'.[5] According to Walsh, Colman Sarsfield (d. 1752) enjoyed a level of toleration in his pastoral duties at St Fin Barre's, known popularly as the South Chapel.[6] In 1727, during the episcopacy of Bishop McCarthy Rabach (1727–47), the thatched church near Douglas Street was destroyed by fire and replaced the following year by a slated building.[7]

In 1728, a slated church was also built at Shandon on the northern suburbs of the city, in the parish of St Mary and St Anne, known locally as the North Chapel. The Penal Laws were still nominally in force in 1766, when the South Parish Chapel was built in Dunbar Street under the leadership of Fr Daniel O'Brien (1701–81), financially supported by influential local Catholic middle-class families the Gallweys, Stacpooles, Drinans, Callanans, Goulds and Aikenheads.[8] The new church consisted of an aisle and north transept, which was further extended in the late eighteenth century.[9] Seating in Catholic churches was normally confined to the galleries, with or without rough benches in the main body of the church. However, the South Parish Chapel was fitted with pews inscribed with the names of those who had contributed to its building, giving this church a degree of affluence and comfort for its congregation.[10] Following the Catholic Relief Bill of 1778, a new phase of building and reconstruction was initiated throughout Ireland, as the remaining mass houses were replaced with stone buildings. Cork's chapel of SS Peter and Paul, Carey's Lane, known locally as the 'Middle Parish', was built in 1786.[11]

The standard liturgies of the Mass and the Office were sung since medieval times in plainchant on special religious occasions, and otherwise recited. According to a report by Bishop Moylan in 1802, Mass was celebrated on Sundays and holy days in the city's three parish churches, with sung Vespers and Benediction in the late afternoon, followed by a sermon at six o'clock.[12] Vespers consisted of hymns and psalms, traditionally sung in plainchant. Charles Étienne Coquebert de Montbret, a French visitor to Cork in 1790, attended High Mass at the North Chapel and found it curious that the congregation did not join with the choir in the singing of hymns.[13] The tendency of Catholic Mass-goers to use the occasion for private devotions was not a specifically Irish phenomenon. Similar observations occur in English sources, where it was associated with recusant liturgical practice.[14] Congregational responses were typically sung or recited by the altar servers or the choir, a practice that also carried over into the singing of hymns. This musical disconnection between choir and congregation persisted in Irish Catholic churches into the twentieth century.

In 1793, the *Hibernian Chronicle* published two reports of music performed at commemorative Masses relating to contemporary events in France.[15] In February, Solemn Office and High Mass were held at St Peter and Paul's Chapel (Carey's Lane) for the deceased king of France, which included vocal and instrumental music, the earliest liturgical musical performance in Cork reported in the press. It was clearly an important public event, attended by 'a very numerous and respectable congregation of most religious persuasions'.[16] In November of that year, Office and High Mass were celebrated at the North Chapel for 'the repose of the soul of Marie Antoinette, late Queen of France'. The *Hibernian Chronicle* reported that: 'The Chapel was hung in black, the ceremony grand and awful, the vocal and instrumental performers were excellent, and the funeral sermon was the best we ever remember.'[17] These occasions reflected the Franco-Hibernian culture that prevailed in Cork around the turn of the nineteenth century, when many well-off Catholic families sent their children to France to be educated. The earliest press reference to a musical performance at the South Chapel dates from November 1799, as part of a Mass to mark the death of Pope Pius VI, when the band of the Loyal Cork Legion performed and Rev. Dr McCarthy delivered a sermon.[18]

Fr Florence McCarthy supervised further structural developments to the South Chapel from 1799. In 1807 proposals were invited for the addition of a second wing, in order to provide accommodation for the increased population of the parish,[19] and in 1809 the south transept was added.[20] According to MacSweeney, a new two-manual organ by Hugh Russell of London was inaugurated on 6 March 1808.[21] Robert Bowden, one of the city's leading musicians, and a Protestant, served as organist and directed musical performances at this chapel from 1814.[22] In 1809, a new two-manual organ by Russell was installed in Carey's Lane Church.[23]

In 1799, Moylan initiated a project to rebuild the North Chapel in his own mensal parish, replacing a building that dated from the late 1720s.[24] In 1802, he issued an appeal for financial assistance, which yielded substantial donations 'not only from Catholic, but from very many non-Catholic citizens'.[25] The consecration of the Cathedral of St Mary and St Anne, Cork's first Roman Catholic cathedral, on 22 August 1808 was an auspicious occasion, featuring vocal and instrumental music, including a fifty-strong children's choir. The *Cork Mercantile Chronicle* reported that:

> On Monday last, the beautiful Chapel of the Blessed Virgin Mary, called the *North Chapel*, having at length attained its destined perfection, was dedicated to the service of God with a solemnity unexampled in these islands [...] The service itself consisted of the *Veni Creator Spiritus*, the *Ave Maris Stella*, the Litany and the usual hymns, psalms and prayers for the Benediction of a Church; to which succeeded High Mass and a part of the *Te Deum*.

> The Verger, in a surplice, led the way, followed by the Processional cross-bearer between two Acolythes [*sic*] with candles; next fifty children of the choir in surplices, two and two together.[26]

The procession of dignitaries was 'followed by a full band of musicians and singers'. In 1810, a notice in the *Cork Mercantile Chronicle* announced the appointment of H. de Monti as 'Organist and Master of Music' at the new cathedral.[27] Hurka de Monti (*c*. 1753–1823) was an Austro/Hungarian military officer who moved to Glasgow around 1788.[28] Apart from an advertisement in the *Cork Mercantile Chronicle* offering instruction in singing, piano and harp in 1810,[29] there is no record of his musical activities in Cork. A connection with the Cork Ursuline Convent is evident from the subsequent publication in 1861 by Novello of '*A Selection of Sacred Music, adapted to the religious ceremonies of "Reception and Profession," composed expressly for the use of the Ursuline Community, Blackrock, Cork*, by H. de Monti.'[30] However, de Monti appears to have left his post at St Mary's by 1813, when Edward Moeran, a former member of St Fin Barre's cathedral choir, took over the post as organist at the Catholic cathedral, retaining it until 1858.

The churches of the regular orders, the Dominicans, Franciscans, Capuchins and Augustinians, maintained local congregations despite suppression in previous centuries. Established in Cork since medieval times, the Franciscan community occupied a house on North Mall and, sometime before 1759, the community opened a chapel and house in Broad Lane. [31] Extant records of the new Broad Lane friary and chapel indicate the presence of choirboys from 1821.[32] A chapel built by the Augustinian order in Brunswick Street in 1780 was equipped with an organ built by Robert Woffington of Dublin.[33]After lying idle for a number of years, it was restored in 1808 by Marsden Haddock, who gave a performance on the refurbished instrument.[34]

Paraliturgical devotion was a key aspect of Irish Catholicism prior to the Famine. Hymns in Irish circulated orally, and local printers and publishers were important agents in the supply of popular devotional literature and hymns.[35] In Munster, the phenomenal success of Tadhg Gaelach Ó Súilleabháin's (1715–95) collection of twenty-five religious songs in Irish, *Pious Miscellany*, indicated the continuity of this tradition. First published posthumously in Clonmel in 1802, these songs were widely known in Munster during the poet's lifetime. The work then underwent a series of Cork editions, beginning with two imprints of a 'sixth' edition in 1817 by John Connor and Jeremiah Geary respectively.[36] Subsequent Cork editions by Connor (1821, 1829), Fergusson

(1821), Dillon (1822, 1823, 1828, 1831, 1833, 1841), and Thomas Geary (1827, 1837) indicate a strong pre-Famine market for this popular devotional work. With English titles and editorial material, the texts are in Irish in roman type. Ó Súilleabháin's intense religious poetry is set to various tunes, such as 'Carolan's Devotion', 'Sean Ó Duibhir an Ghleanna', 'Úr Mhic na Croinne', 'The Flowers of Edinburgh' and 'Éamonn an Chnoic'.[37] The tunes, which would have been widely familiar, are not notated.

Dillon's 1841 edition, published with corrections and annotations by Cappoquin poet Pádraig Denn (1756–1828), 'with additional pious Compositions, in English and Irish', includes the following note in the preface:

> During the long nights of winter, a hymn or song out of this little book may be sung in every Roman Catholic family. It would better do so, than suffer the vile compositions that have been daily sung through the public streets, to be introduced therein [...]

It also highlights the continuing use of Irish within the city's Catholic community. Although Moylan, in correspondence with the papal secretary, had stated that Fr Florence McCarthy's lack of knowledge of Irish was inconsequential for the carrying out of his duties, Moylan's successor from 1815, Dr John Murphy, learnt Irish in order to communicate with his people.[38]

Nonetheless, English had begun to dominate many Catholic church occasions by the early nineteenth century, and new styles of church music were coming into use. An advertisement notice published in the *Cork Mercantile Chronicle* in 1816 points to the existence of a growing choral tradition in the Catholic churches:

> Roman Catholic Church Music
> J. McKenna continues, as usual, to write and arrange Church music, adapted for large and small Choirs, and for the annual festivals – consisting of treble, tenor, counter-tenor, bass and instrumental parts. From the very recent encouragement these selections of Sacred Music have met with, as also the unbounded gratification they have afforded in the country chapel choirs, where established, as well as the request of several respectable country gentlemen, he is induced to renew this notice to the public. He likewise instructs, in the Gregorian and Modern systems of singing, church and other music. NB All kinds of concert music transcribed and transposed on moderate terms.[39]

James McKenna was listed as Professor of Music, at 62 Douglas Street, in *Slater's Directory* of 1846. There is little documentation relating to annual church festivals in Cork. However, a letter written in 1822 by a County Wexford schoolmaster who directed two local church choirs refers to a range of events that may have been representative of general practice:

> We do have great work here on festivals. On Corpus Christi we have a procession of the Blessed Sacrament, on Palm Sunday a procession of palm, on 15th August, our patron day, a grand solemn Mass and procession of candles. Every Sunday in Lent we sing round the stations, and on other festivals we have a benediction of the Blessed Sacrament, all which serve very much to excite devotion in the people.[40]

Following Catholic Emancipation in 1829, a new phase of Catholic church building commenced. The opening of St Mary's Dominican church at Pope's Quay in Cork in 1839 was viewed as a significant moment in the history of Irish Catholic liturgy by a correspondent for the *Freeman's Journal*, who reported the consecration ceremony:

> The music of the sacred service was beautifully executed, and the surpassing splendor, solemnity and magnificence of the whole scene was such that the heart thrilled with emotion, tears of joy sparkled in the eye, and one could not avoid exclaiming 'we have lived to see all the glories of the ancient religion of Ireland restored!'[41]

After the clergy sang some Latin psalms, a 'powerful, sweet and well-trained' choir sang High Mass, with William Gillespie performing on a 'sweet-toned' organ.[42] Located on a prominent site overlooking the River Lee's north channel, the new church was an imposing edifice, designed gratuitously by Cork architect Kearns Deane, younger brother of Thomas Deane. The prior had solicited widely for donations for the building fund in Cork, Limerick, England, and from a number of private sources, and by a 'weekly penny collection from the industrious and poorer classes'.[43] The judicious management of funding by the prior had proved highly effective, and the project was emblematic for the entire Catholic community, and a catalyst for change in the public profile of Catholicism in the city.

William F. Gillespie's appointment as organist was an inspired move. A Protestant from a large and respected family of musicians, organ technicians and music shop owners, he had distinguished himself in his early years as a pianist. His father, John Gillespie, ran a music shop on the Grand Parade and advertised as a piano tuner and repairer. His uncle, William Gillespie, held the post of organist at Christ Church since 1804. As organist and choirmaster at St Mary's, Gillespie's outward-looking, energetic and skilled approach to his duties produced a remarkable series of musical events over the first two years of its existence.

A choir of a dozen singers was formally established at St Mary's Pope's Quay in 1841, consisting of four sopranos, two altos, four tenors and two basses. In October, the Festival (Feast) of the Rosary was celebrated with High Mass. A sung Mass by Mozart was performed by the choir, with guest singers Scottish tenor John Wilson (1800–49) and English bass Adam Leffler (1808–57), who were at that time engaged at the Victoria Theatre. The *Cork Examiner* reported that 'a vast number of Protestants and Dissenters, with difficulty found room in the over-crowded building'.[44] Despite the performative aspect, the writer noted that 'the music was in accordance of the sacred mystery of the Mass'.

In May 1842, a Grand Oratorio performance marked the inauguration of a new Gray and Davison organ at the church, conducted by William Forde, and featuring local singers Alex D. Roche, John McCarthy, James Keays, Mr E. Sweeny, Mr (William) Shea and James Roche, with several amateurs and a fifty-strong voluntary chorus.[45] The inclusion of several Protestant musicians as performers provoked a letter in *The Constitution* criticising the profanity of the music:

> To this, Sir, I answer – be the music never so splendid – yet God's praises alone are not sung. Be the chapel never so richly decorated – yet, within its walls the glory due to God is 'given to another, and His praise to graven images'. But Sir, is the ear always to be indulged? Is the eye always to be gratified?

The 'idolatrous practices' of the participating Protestant musicians were decried.[46] The programme featured selections from Handel, Mozart, Haydn and Rossini. Among those invited to attend was William Coppinger of Patrick's Hill, one of the city's Catholic gentry[47] (see Figure 9.1). In August 1842, the Festival of St Dominic was celebrated with a solemn High Mass, sung by the choir and assisted by singer, composer and Anglican minister Joseph Phillip Knight (1812–87) and a Mr Hudson.[48] Composer of several

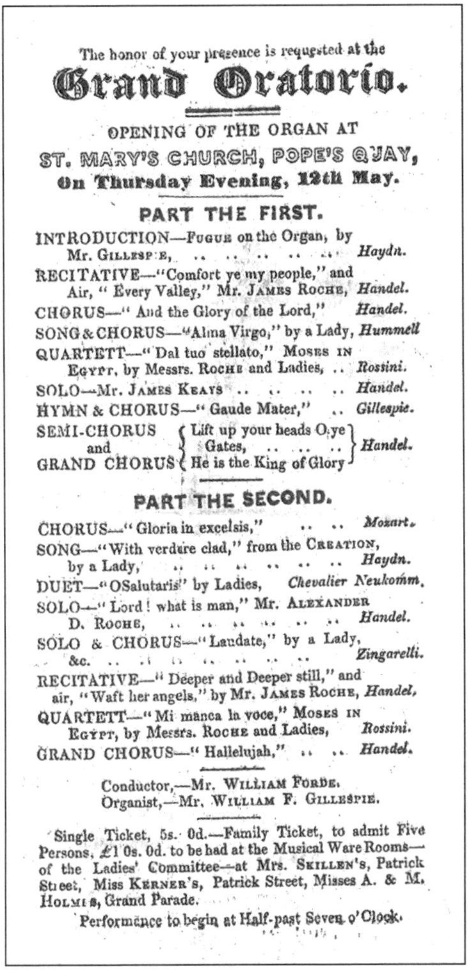

The honor of your presence is requested at the

Grand Oratorio.

OPENING OF THE ORGAN AT

ST. MARY'S CHURCH, POPE'S QUAY,

On Thursday Evening, 12th May.

PART THE FIRST.

INTRODUCTION—FUGUE on the Organ, by Mr. GILLESPIE, ... *Haydn.*
RECITATIVE—"Comfort ye my people," and Air, "Every Valley," Mr. JAMES ROCHE, *Handel.*
CHORUS—"And the Glory of the Lord," *Handel.*
SONG & CHORUS—"Alma Virgo," by a Lady, *Hummell*
QUARTETT—"Dal tuo stellato," MOSES IN EGYPT, by Messrs. ROCHE and Ladies, .. *Rossini.*
SOLO—Mr. JAMES KEAYS .. .. *Handel.*
HYMN & CHORUS—"Gaude Mater," .. *Gillespie.*
SEMI-CHORUS and GRAND CHORUS { Lift up your heads O ye Gates, ... He is the King of Glory } *Handel.*

PART THE SECOND.

CHORUS—"Gloria in excelsis," .. .. *Mozart.*
SONG—"With verdure clad," from the CREATION, by a Lady, ... *Haydn.*
DUET—"O Salutaris" by Ladies, *Chevalier Neukomm.*
SOLO—"Lord! what is man," Mr. ALEXANDER D. ROCHE, ... *Handel.*
SOLO & CHORUS—"Laudate," by a Lady, &c. .. .. *Zingarelli.*
RECITATIVE—"Deeper and Deeper still," and air, "Waft her angels," by Mr. JAMES ROCHE, *Handel.*
QUARTETT—"Mi manca la voce," MOSES IN EGYPT, by Messrs. ROCHE and Ladies, *Rossini.*
GRAND CHORUS—"Hallelujah," .. .. *Handel.*

Conductor,—Mr. WILLIAM FORDE.
Organist,—Mr. WILLIAM F. GILLESPIE.

Single Ticket, 5s. 0d.—Family Ticket, to admit Five Persons, £1 0s. 0d. to be had at the Musical Ware Rooms—of the Ladies' Committee—at Mrs. SKILLEN's, Patrick Street, Miss KERNER's, Patrick Street, Misses A. & M. HOLMES, Grand Parade.

Performance to begin at Half-past Seven o'Clock.

Figure 9.1. Grand Oratorio, 1842: invitation to William Coppinger.
CORK CITY AND COUNTY ARCHIVES

popular songs, Knight was on a visit to Cork as a member of a group accompanying a guitarist, Monsieur Bradi.

While Gillespie was at the centre of progressive musical developments at St Mary's, it appears that he acted as a local correspondent for *The Musical World*, a London music journal. In 1845 a report in this journal featured a short article entitled 'Music in Cork', in which his achievements at St Mary's were commended, stating that 'nothing could surpass the abominable rubbish performed in the Catholic churches, in the way of music, before this choir was formed'.[49] In that year, Edwin Sims Reeves, who was in Cork with a company of singers led by Dublin organist Alban Croft, sang at this church in Mozart's 12th Mass.[50] Edwin Reeves (d. 1882), brother of English tenor John Sims Reeves (1821–1900), had been employed as professor of music at the

Viceregal Lodge in Dublin before moving to Cork.[51] He established himself as a performer and teacher, performing solo roles in large-scale works.

By 1857, when T.J. Sullivan succeeded Gillespie as organist at St Mary's, Catholic liturgical music in the city had consolidated. In May of that year, Sullivan placed an advertisement in the *Musical Times and Singing Class Circular* for a 'female soprano [...] thoroughly conversant with the Catholic Church music'.[52] The choral structure adopted in Catholic churches consisted of a few salaried singers, who acted both as soloists and choir leaders, and a voluntary mixed choir. The account book of St Francis Church includes records of stipends paid to a leading soprano singer, and either a tenor or bass.[53]

John Fleming (*c.* 1820–77) succeeded Edward Moeran as organist at St Mary's Cathedral in 1858. A Catholic from Old Chapel Lane on the north side of the city, where his father was a cooper, he had studied organ with William Gillespie, piano with John McCarthy and singing with James Roche.[54] According to an account by Cornelius Cremen, he had attended the Christian Brothers school in Peacock Lane (North Monastery), where his talent as a singer was noted at music class. Prior to his cathedral appointment, he had served as organist at St Augustine's Church from 1855 to 1858.

A number of women held posts as organists during the 1850s and early 1860s, as female instrumentalists entered the public sphere. Mrs James Halloran was organist and choir director at the South Parish Church for some time up to 1855.[55] In May of that year, the *Cork Examiner* published the following notice:

> Mrs Halloran
> We are happy to learn that the talents of Mrs Halloran, late organist of the South Parish Chapel, has attracted attention outside this city, and that she has been engaged to manage the organ and choir of the Church of SS Peter and Paul, Clonmel. During the period of her employment in the South Chapel, her performance as a musician, and her taste in selections for festivals, sermons, etc, were matters of very general admiration. This lady was also indefatigable in her exertions to develop local talent, in which her success was evidenced both by the choral performances of the choir, and the approbation which the concerted pieces sung at her late concert elicited.[56]

However, she appears not to have settled in the new post. She returned to Cork and served as organist of St Francis Church, from April 1856 until

February 1858.[57] In December 1857, American soprano Lucy Escott (*c.* 1828–95), English basses Charles Durand, aka Charles Bingley (1827–1904), and Aynsley Cooke (1834–94), who were also performing with the National English Opera Company at the Theatre Royal, sang in Haydn's 3rd ('Imperial') Mass, accompanied on the organ by Mrs O'Halloran (now with the 'O' prefix).[58] The woman with the longest tenure was Norah Britton (neé O'Callaghan), organist and choir director at St Francis Church from 1865 until 1884.[59] In April 1865, Edward Mahony conducted a performance of Mozart's Mass No. 1 at this church, featuring Miss M. Sylvanie, stipendiary soprano, with Miss O'Callaghan, organist, and led by violinist Bartholomew Britton.[60]

Although the foundation stone for Fr Mathew's new Church of the Holy Trinity on Charlotte Quay was laid in October 1832, the building project suffered many delays and setbacks, and the church was finally consecrated on 10 October 1850. The ceremony on this occasion featured a performance of Haydn's 4th Mass, directed by William Gillespie, who played piano. In addition to a choir and solo voices, an instrumental ensemble consisted of John Smith, first violin, Dominick Smith and Mr Boullemier, second violins, James Smith, cello, and John Murphy, double bass.[61] Mrs Halloran was appointed as organist, and Mr and Mrs Patten were engaged as soloists for the choir.[62] In 1854, an organ built locally by John Seymour Murphy, which had been displayed at the Cork International Exhibition of 1852, was purchased for the church at a cost of £310.[63] The instrument was inaugurated on 6 November with a performance by Mrs Halloran of 'Chorus of the Priests' and March from Mendelssohn's *Athalie*. She was commended in the *Cork Examiner* for 'the taste and judgement with which she developed the varied resources of the instrument, – the full organ, pedals, flute, oboe, trumpets, one and all were shown off to the very best advantage'.[64]

As Archbishop of Armagh and Primate of Ireland, Cardinal Paul Cullen (1803–78) was a key figure in the development of Catholic structures and infrastructures at both diocesan and parochial levels during the mid-nineteenth century. Having spent his early career years in Rome, he sought to reform Irish Catholic religious observance and align it with Roman practice.[65] The Synod of Thurles, convened by Cullen in 1850 on instruction from Rome, issued two decrees on church music, stipulating the use of music that was 'solemn and Ecclesiastical', and that only settings of Latin texts should be sung at Mass. It also advised the rectors of seminaries to ensure that students were versed in plainchant.

Catholic assertiveness was on the rise throughout Ireland during the 1860s. Between 1850 and 1875 there was an unprecedented increase in church attendance, with closely regulated religious observance, under firm episcopal control, unifying urban and rural, rich and poor in what has been termed a 'devotional revolution'.[66] A daily publication from 1861, the *Cork Examiner* provided reports and announcements relating to liturgical musical performances on the major Catholic feast days, highlighting these occasions in the public sphere. Among Cullen's ultramontanist strategies in Ireland was the introduction of the elaborate Catholic devotion of *Quarant' Ore* ('Forty Hours' devotion'). A revival of a sixteenth-century Italian practice, it consisted of a two-day public adoration of the Blessed Sacrament, beginning and concluding with High Mass, and including a procession, followed by Benediction and Vespers.[67] It was inaugurated in Cork by Bishop William Delaney in June 1855, held successively in each of the principal city churches over the course of a week.[68] This ceremony of *Quarant' Ore* was celebrated annually at the North Cathedral during the 1860s as part of the Corpus Christi liturgical celebrations, expanding the capacity for elaborate liturgical music. For these occasions, John V. Blake conducted the choir and John Fleming officiated at the organ. The masses which were featured at Corpus Christi were either Mozart's 12th or Haydn's 'Imperial', both standard repertoire by this time, accompanied by full orchestra, augmented by regimental bands. Members of the choir listed in 1864 were:

Choir at St Mary's Cathedral (Corpus Christi celebrations 1864)

Miss McKenna (soprano), Miss Fitzpatrick (contralto)

Miss Dalton, Miss Haly, Miss O'Connor

Tenors: Mr W. Rice, Mr M. Millerick, Mr T. Sexton, Mr D. Nunan

Basses: Mr E. Mahony, Mr E. Hackett, Mr J. Sullivan,
Mr M. O'Mahony, Mr J. O'Mahony, Mr S. Russell

The Corpus Christi celebrations of 1869 included a performance of Johann Hummel's (1778–1837) *Alma virgo* at the Offertory of the Mass, opening with a showy operatic soprano solo. In 1865 and 1866, Christmas liturgical services at the North Cathedral featured Beethoven's Mass in C, 'with full orchestra accompaniment', including members of the band of the 2nd regiment, directed by Mr J. Gready.[69]

Newly composed masses were occasionally performed on religious feasts. A mass by John Fleming was performed on the Feast of the Epiphany at the cathedral in 1862, in which he himself sang the alto solos, with Miss McKenna, soprano, Mr Millerick, tenor, and Edward Mahony, bass. A writer in the *Cork Examiner* commented on the particular excellence of the fugal section of the Gloria, 'almost all of the Kyrie Eleison, and the Incarnatus, and the conclusion of the Credo'.[70] On Ascension Thursday in 1865, John Fleming directed a new mass by Irish songwriter Wellington Guernsey (1817–85) at the cathedral. According to a writer in the *Southern Reporter*, this was the first performance of Guernsey's sacred music in Cork, and was 'of a very high order, and in many parts called to mind some of the greatest composers of Church music'.[71]

Having succeeded Gillespie at St Mary's Church from the mid-1850s, T.J. Sullivan continued to develop the choir and expand its repertoire. In April 1869, he directed a performance of Rossini's *Petite messe solennelle*, 'a novel and beautiful work, [performed] for the first time in Ireland' at the opening and again at the closing of the *Quarant' Ore* ceremonies.[72] Composed in 1863 for twelve solo voices, four soloists and a choir of eight, the composer rewrote the work for four soloists, choir and orchestra in 1867, and this version received much attention after the composer's death in November 1868. This piece, of two hours' duration, was challenging for the choir. A review in the *Cork Examiner* found the work 'wanting in unity and in grasp, and in the religious element. It is too much broken up, there is too much framework and peculiar setting – one might even say it "moves without progression"'. The writer also described 'wearing repetition in some of the solos, which moreover, are protracted to an unusual length'. The writer continued with a discussion of the 'religious element' in music:

> Let a selection from the sacred music of Palestrina, or of Mozart, or Schubert, or Beethoven, be executed side by side with the present work, and the wrapt feeling and the sweet constraint put upon truant thoughts and the delicious and mighty yearning of the whole soul will give a sufficient interpretation of what we mean by the religious in music. With the exceptions given above what are the associations which the music of this mass calls up? Sacred! Does it ever really command the soul? For our part we have to plead guilty to frequently catching ourselves in the attitude of one whose ears are busily engaged with harmonies and whose thoughts

> are no less busily intent upon watching the varied play of the universally acknowledged art of the Maestro, with very calm soul the while. We leave to the learned to determine whose is the sin.[73]

The work was performed again the following year, at a Mass celebrated to mark the opening of the church's new chancel.[74]

The elaborate repertoire performed on these occasions may seem to the modern observer to have been at variance with the policy of discipline and control that was applied in the interests of promoting institutional Catholicism. The Synod of Thurles directive for 'solemn and ecclesiastical' music did not exclude the highly operatic idiom of Mozart, Beethoven, Hummel and Rossini. From the official viewpoint, these works were settings of Latin liturgical texts, and the idiom appears not to have come under scrutiny. Along with candles, incense and vestments, this music appealed to the senses, and possessed the power to 'instil veneration by an appreciation of their ritual beauty and instrinsic mystery'.[75] The organists and choir directors thus far enjoyed freedom in the choice of choral material, limited only by the musical and technical capacity of their singers.

Among the participants in liturgical musical performances on major religious festivals at the North cathedral from the late 1860s was St Mary's band. It was established some years previously by Rev. John McNamara, curate of St Mary's from 1848 until 1875, as part of the Society of the Immaculate Heart, a confraternity set up by Bishop Moylan around the turn of the nineteenth century, and revived at the cathedral some years previously.[76] Cleric-led confraternities such as this sprang up all over Ireland during the years of Cullen's devotional reforms.[77] The band performed at a charity sermon at the cathedral in aid of the Christian Brothers in March 1869, in a programme that included selections from Rossini's *Stabat Mater* (1842) and the 'Gloria' from Mozart's 12th Mass, in addition to the Pope's Hymn.[78] The band featured at the Corpus Christi celebrations at the North cathedral in 1869, concluding Vespers with a performance of the 'Inflammatus', a soprano aria from Rossini's *Stabat Mater* 'in a very creditable manner' and 'Cujus animam', a tenor solo from the same work. Both pieces, with slow harmonic rhythm, would have been effective as adaptations for band. 'Cujus animam' was performed at the Vespers ceremony again the following year, and an arrangement of Rossini's *Tantum ergo* (1847).[79]

A new church designed by Sir John Benson was built on a prominent site at Sunday's Well for the Vincentian community, and consecrated in 1856. Following a fundraising draw, a new Telford organ was installed in June 1859.

The inauguration featured 'a choir of well-known amateurs' directed by Joseph Roeckel, a French immigrant, with Mr Caulfield of Dublin presiding at the organ.[80]

The church's musical traditions commenced with the appointment of Thomas Nagle as organist and choir director in February 1860.[81] A former student of T.J. Sullivan, Nagle was outward-looking in his new role. In August of that year, his choir was joined for the conclusion of the *Quarant' Ore* ceremonies by members of the London Operatic Company, who were currently on a visit to the city. Their director, William Meyer Lutz (1822–1903), was organist of St George's Cathedral, London.[82] On a return to Cork in April 1861, Lutz and his company participated in a performance of Mozart's 12th Mass, to raise funds for the completion of the great eastern stained-glass window for the church.[83] In August 1861, Nagle directed the first Cork performance of Henry Farmer's (1819–91) Mass in B flat (1847) at the opening ceremony of *Quarant' Ore*.[84]

In August 1863, Nagle resigned from his post at St Vincent's and was replaced by R. Sutton Swaby, formerly organist at St Malachy's Church in Belfast.[85] A solo organ recital given by Swaby in November was perhaps the first such event in Cork. The recital featured arrangements of overtures to Balfe's *Geraldine* (1843), Auber's *Haydée* (1847) and Mendelssohn's *Athalie*.[86] He also performed a Bach pedal fugue in E minor, which may have been BWV 533, or the more virtuosic BWV 548 ('the Wedge'). He performed at a range of local events, such as a bazaar at the Athenaeum in aid of the Society of St Vincent de Paul.[87] Another recital by Swaby in April 1864 featured works not previously featured on Cork programmes.[88]

Offertory No 4	Lefébure-Wély
Slow movement	Haydn
Prelude and Fugue	J.S. Bach
Overture *Stradella*	Flotow
Overture *Maritana*	Wallace
Song 'Maid of Judah'	Kucken
Larghetto	Spohr
Military March	Borodin

He also performed some of these works at the Dublin International Exhibition in 1865.[89] Such performing ambitions may not have aligned with the ethos of

St Vincent's, as Swaby remained in the post for only a year. By this time, he had advertised seeking a new appointment and was engaged at the Church of the Immaculate Conception in Wexford.[90] By 1868, William Sergeant had been appointed as organist at St Vincent's, and retained the post until at least 1871.[91]

Efforts to rebuild the North cathedral during the 1860s met with continuing difficulties. Following an unsuccessful attempt to add another tower, elaborate plans were drawn up in 1868 under the direction of Sir John Benson, but these were eventually scaled down, due to inadequate funding.[92] Provision was made for a new organ, however. An article entitled 'Organ building in Ireland', published in the *Cork Examiner* on 7 September 1870, reported on the progress of a new organ at St Mary's Cathedral by Charles Spackman Barker (1804–79), an English organ builder who had spent several years in Paris, and whose recent arrival in Ireland was prompted by the destruction of his workshop as a result of the Franco-Prussian war.[93] Barker had patented a pneumatic lever in England in 1832, which was claimed to have been the earliest such device, but it was not until he commenced work in Paris in 1841, on the invitation of the French builder Aristide Cavaillé-Coll (1811–99), that the Barker Lever achieved wide acclaim at the Abbey of St Denis.[94] An editorial note published in the *Irish Builder* of January 1871 expressed regret, however, that

> a very expensive organ to be placed in the Catholic Cathedral, Cork, has been entrusted to a French firm. We must question the propriety of such doings, the pounds and pence collected from the people should, when possible, be spent in this country.[95]

While the organ was under construction, Barker moved to Cork with the intention of residing permanently there. In May, he completed the repair and rebuilding of the organ of the Ursuline Convent chapel in Blackrock, adding two pedal stops, a sub-bass of 16 feet, a *violoncelle* of 8 feet, and a *voix céleste* was added to the swell organ.[96] In May 1871, he published a circular in several editions of the *Cork Examiner* seeking work in 'the Building, Improvement and Repair of Organs on the latest and most improved principles', and placed an advertisement in *Wilkie's Cork City Directory*.[97] By June 1873, he had been commissioned to build an organ for St Patrick's Church in Monkstown, County Dublin, and had remodelled the organ in Marlborough Street cathedral, Dublin, which however was not successful.[98]

On the completion of a phase of building work at the Cork cathedral in July 1871 came a press notice announcing a Monsieur Chevraux as the new organist, with a summary of his credentials.[99] There are no further local documentary references to this organist, however, and records indicate that, by 1873, the Belgian musician Léopold de Prins was appointed, retaining the position until 1895.[100]

The Cecilian movement sought reform and regulation of Catholic liturgical music by adherence to the compositional techniques of sixteenth- and early seventeenth-century sacred *a capella* polyphony, and by greater attention to the singing of plainchant.[101] The movement had emerged over the previous two decades in the Bavarian cathedral city of Regensburg, where Francis Xavier Haberl (1840–1910) directed the choir from 1871, and in 1874 established a church music school. He undertook the completion of the entire Palestrina works, begun by Breitkopf and Härtel in 1862, and he established the Palestrina Society in 1879.[102] His *Magister Choralis* was an influential manual of Gregorian chant. The movement spread in France, Spain and Belgium.

Belgian brothers Léopold and Francis Prosper de Prins (1829–84) were among the earliest advocates of Cecilian principles in Ireland. From 1876, they edited a quarterly journal, *St Cecilia*, and became active members of the Dublin-based Irish Society of St Cecilia, founded by Rev. Nicholas Donnelly (1837–1920) in 1878.[103] Donnelly's English translation of Haberl's *Magister Choralis* (1877) provided a valuable manual on chant and liturgy for English-speaking readers and practitioners. In seeking reform of Irish Catholic church music, the society advocated the use of music that was purely liturgical in character, as exemplified in Gregorian chant and polyphonic music in the style of Palestrina, ideals that were promoted in the society's journal *Lyra Ecclesiastica*, established by Donnelly in 1878. The society's list of approved liturgical repertoire included newly composed works by contemporary Cecilian composers, the majority of whom were German, but Irish organists were gradually added to the list. Improvement of the quality of congregational singing was another major concern of the society.[104]

Léopold de Prins first appeared in Cork in 1864, advertising piano tuition and singing classes, introducing himself as a graduate of the Royal Conservatorium, Brussels.[105] He immersed himself in local professional musical life. A report of a concert in Youghal in 1864 described him as 'one of the true continental musicians, the ease and elegance of his melodies and songs without words, the brilliant execution of his passages being really thrilling'.[106] De Prins had by this time published a Mass in F for 3 voices (soprano, tenor, bass) with organ accompaniment.[107] His brother, Francis Prosper de Prins, took up the post of organist and choirmaster at the Redemptorist church, Mount St Alphonsus, in Limerick in 1862, an appointment likely to have been made through the Redemptorists' Belgian connections.[108] By 1867 Léopold de Prins had moved to Limerick, where he served as organist at the Catholic St John's Cathedral, and became a central figure in the city's concert life.[109]

By 1872, Léopold de Prins had returned to Cork as the newly appointed cathedral organist, succeeding John Fleming, who died in 1877.[107] Christmas Day High Mass at the cathedral in 1876 featured the Kyrie and Gloria from Gounod's *Missa angeli custodes* (1873), a work austere in style with organ accompaniment, and 'Sanctus and Agnus Dei' by Ziegler, with 'Adeste fideles', referred to as an anthem, at the Offertory.[111] Further reports of de Prins's activities appeared in *Lyra Ecclesiastica* in 1879:

> On St Patrick's Day, we had a great solemnity at the cathedral, the Mayor and corporation present. Music of the mass was Zangl's of the Cecilian Catalogue. I had seventy voices in the chorus. The effect was fine, all said they had never heard anything more effective and religious at the same time.[112]

Movements by Stehle, Bernabei and de Prins himself were performed at High Mass at the cathedral in 1883.[113]

The last of the city's Catholic churches to be built was SS Peter and Paul's, to replace the older Carey's Lane chapel. Designed by French architect Edward W. Pugin (1834–75), the new Gothic-style building surpassed all of the existing city churches in scale and grandeur. At a ceremony marking its dedication for worship in 1866 an amateur choir directed by T.J. Sullivan performed Beethoven's Mass in C.[114] In 1870, High Mass on Christmas Day consisted of 'seven or eight voices' accompanied by harmonium, the lack of a proper organ highlighted in a press report.[115] The church was consecrated in 1874, and a new organ by Bryceson of London was inaugurated on 5 June 1876, at a ceremony featuring Léopold de Prins and a choir of 100 voices.[116] Theodore Gmür (1860–1929), a young Swiss organist, arrived in 1878 to take up the position of organist and choirmaster, an appointment procured through private recommendation.[117]

One of Léopold de Prins' pupils in Cork was Joseph Seymour (*c.* 1853–1922). According to Brown and Stratton's *British Musical Biography*, Seymour was appointed to SS Peter and Paul's in 1878 to succeed his father.[118] This would have been a temporary or short appointment, as Gmür was appointed to this post in December 1878. In 1880, Seymour left Cork to study with Belgian organist Jaak Nikolaas Lemmens (1823–81) in Mechelen (Malines), and subsequently to Regensburg, where he studied for six months with Haberl. On his return to Ireland in 1881, he was appointed as organist at St Andrew's Church, Westland Row, Dublin, replacing Alois Volkmer. In 1883, he took over the editorship of *Lyra Ecclesiastica*.[119] His church music compositions were a significant contribution to Catholic liturgical repertoire in Ireland and England.

The church of the Vincentian community at Sunday's Well also became a centre for Cecilian reform during the 1870s, initially through the activities of a young priest, Fr Edward Gaynor (1850–1936). A native of Moate, County Westmeath, Gaynor taught science at St Vincent's school, Castleknock, Dublin, and travelled widely during the early years of his career. He was influenced by continental developments in Catholic church music and, following his transfer to Cork, established a Palestrina Choir at St Vincent's during the 1870s.[120] Herr Thinnes was appointed as organist during the early 1870s, and he introduced new choral repertoire by German Cecilian composers, Michael Haller (1840–1915) and Obersteiner, reported in *Lyra Ecclesiastica*:

> In Herr Thinnes, we have found a real church musician, a man who knows as if by instinct, what is suitable and what is not suitable for the House of God [...] He has been indefatigable in his work of training the choir, and is now crowned with success. We had Haller's *Missa Tertina* [*sic Tertia*] on Christmas Day, *Introit*, *Gradual* and *Communion* were Gregorian, and the offertory was a piece by Obersteiner. We have learned several Cecilian motets, and we do two of the Psalms of Compline every Sunday in Falso Bordone.[121]

In 1879, a young German musician, Hans Conrad Swertz (1857–1927), was appointed as assistant to Thinnes, and succeeded him when Thinnes resigned due to ill health later that year and returned to Germany.[122] His credentials as a graduate of the Munich Conservatory and of the Regensburg church music college would have ensured his suitability for the post. As the fourth continental organist to be appointed in Cork during the 1870s, Swertz represented a new generation of church musicians in Ireland, entrusted with artistic leadership whilst adhering to Cecilian principles of church music reform. From an economic perspective, Ireland's expanding church infrastructures provided professional opportunities for emerging continental organists, who faced increased competition in their native countries.

During the 1880s, renewed efforts to promote Cecilian principles were made at St Mary's, Pope's Quay. Founded by Fr Coleman, St Mary's Choral Society, the second society of this name, was established to promote congregational singing, and to propagate a taste for the study of 'real church music'. Advisory to Fr Coleman was Fr Rooke. At the society's annual meeting in 1885, the choir demonstrated the contrasts between the *Tantum ergo* by Rossini and a setting by Benedictine composer Utto Kornmüller (1824–1907), and between a setting of *Salve mundi domina*, which Coleman described as being 'more of the drawing room', and the Gregorian *Salve Regina*. A solo 'O Salutaris' was sung, as an example of an inappropriate mode of church performance, and contrasted with Haller's *Laetentur coeli*.[123]

By the last decade of the century, the Cecilian influence on Cork's Catholic churches was evident on most occasions, but concerted music continued to feature, as several press reports serve to illustrate. In 1892, the *Cork Examiner* contained a preview of two forthcoming sung Masses at St Vincent's, for the *Quarant' Ore* and the Feast of St Vincent, respectively, which were described as 'a complete contrast'. Gounod's 'Sacré coeur' mass (1877) was described as 'essentially an orchestral Mass in his best style, full of melody and modulation'. In contrast, Liszt's *Missa choralis* (1865) was described as 'full of rich and grand choruses, mostly worked out of some theme of a Gregorian chant in four to eight parts. Its harmonies show a master's hand, always rich, and impregnated with Liszt's individuality.' Written while Liszt was in Rome, it exemplifies his adherence to 'purely vocal and liturgical music'. The forty-strong choir at St Vincent's had recently given its first Irish performance.[124]

In 1895 Swertz was appointed as organist and choirmaster at St Mary's Cathedral, and in the tradition of that cathedral directed large-scale works for mixed choir with orchestral accompaniment.[125] In July 1896, the *Cork Examiner* published a description of *Quarant' Ore* ceremonies at St Vincent's, featuring Swertz's successor, Sidney Sykes, at the organ. The mass celebrated on this occasion featured a Kyrie and Gloria by Czech composer Jan Kalivoda (1801–66), and a Credo from Gounod's *Messe solennelle*.[126] Elsewhere in the city, concerted sacred works were also performed on major liturgical feasts. On 28 December 1896, the *Cork Examiner* published a summary of the music performed at High Mass in each of the city's churches at noon on Christmas Day[127] (see Table 9.1).

Table 9.1. Music at Christmas Day High Masses in Cork churches, 1896.

CHURCH	MUSIC PERFORMED	PERFORMING FORCES
Cathedral	Dvorak Mass	Sixty voiced choir (cond Swertz)
	Liszt, Kyrie from *Missa choralis*	
	Stehle 'Domine Deus' motet in seven parts	
St Mary's	Beethoven Mass in C	Thirty voiced choir
	Gradual: 'Adeste'	
	Offertory: Mozart 'Ave verum'	
SS Peter & Paul's	Concone Mass in E flat	Choir (cond Gmür)
	Gradual: 'Adeste'	
	Offertory: Motet 'Tui sunt coeli' (Gmür)	
	Benedictus (Gmür)	Sop solo with cello obbligato
	Close: Gounod 'Pontifical March'	Orchestra
St Vincent's	Kyrie: Fr Turner	Choir (cond Sykes)
	Gloria and Credo (Schmidt's Mass in E flat)	
	Novello's 'Adeste'	
	Pater Noster: Niedermeyer	
	Agnus Dei: Kalliwoda [Kalivoda]	
St Augustine's	Kammerlander's Mass Op 48	Choir, soloists, orchestra

This list shows that in addition to works by Cecilian composers, Viennese classical works remained as stable repertoire, and new or recent works by a range of composers were performed in all churches. Though not associated with the German Cecilian movement, Gounod and Liszt composed in an austere style influenced by Rome. Dvorak's Mass in D, the 'Luzany Mass', was published as an organ version in 1887. At a liturgical celebration in 1897 on the occasion of the transference of the relics of Blessed Thaddeus McCarthy (*c.* 1455–92), former Bishop of Cork, to the cathedral, a choir of over sixty voices performed Charles Villiers Stanford's Mass in G (Op 46) and Swertz's *Ecce sacerdos magnus*, composed for the occasion, concluding the ceremony with Andreas Romberg's (1767–1821) *Te Deum*.[128] By the turn of the twentieth century, Gmür's choir at SS Peter and Paul's Church had performed masses by Beethoven (in D and C), Haydn (nos 1, 2, 3, 5, 12, 14), Mozart (nos 1, 12, 16), Schubert (in B♭), Cherubini (in E♭), Concone (*Missa solennelle*) and Mercadante (in B♭), in addition to three masses by Gmür himself.[129]

On Easter Sunday 1899, this choir gave the first performance in the then British Isles of *Missa Pontificalis* by the young Italian priest-composer Lorenzo Perosi (1872–1956).[130] These reports suggest that, despite the vehemence of the Cecilian movement, performances of more elaborate concerted works, both older and more recent, were not precluded. It also highlights the severity of Pope Pius X's *Motu proprio*, issued in 1903, which prescribed a strict adherence to plainchant and Renaissance polyphony, favouring male voices in cathedral choirs, a policy which challenged and undermined the traditions built up over the previous half century.

The emergent musical traditions in Cork's Catholic churches during the latter half of the nineteenth century are a little-explored aspect of the cultural heritage of the devotional revolution in the history of Irish Catholicism. Emmet Larkin has suggested that, for the Irish, the symbolic language and cultural heritage of the new Catholic devotion generated a new, Catholic, identity.[131] As part of the enactment of new liturgical practices and rituals in Cork's churches, a new musical canon emerged as a defining feature of Catholic worship. The collective participation of local soloists, choir and band members, and the power of the music itself, generated authentic musical settings in which congregations identified with and attuned to the structured, sensuous works of the European tradition.

10

'A GLORIOUS FUTURE'

Detail from Gmür's song 'To God and Ireland True'.

During the late nineteenth century, the relationships between audiences, auditoria and repertoire became a matter for closer consideration by concert organisers. Attracting full houses and providing appropriate music presented new challenges. The demand for 'high class' music by elite or discerning audiences was regarded as an essential element in a sophisticated, prosperous city. A new generation of merchants and professionals supported initiatives that were specifically aimed at a broader social spectrum, in which inclusivity and affordability were key issues. Since the opening of the Athenaeum, the provision of concerts that catered for the 'shilling' audiences was considered to be both socially responsible and commercially expedient.

The promenade concert originated in Paris during the late 1830s, where musicians such as Philippe Musard began to turn their attention to provision of music accessible to the working classes.[1] Promenade concerts on the Musard model were adopted in London in 1838 and became a feature of Dublin musical life from 1840 onwards, both at the Rotunda and at James Barton's New Music Hall in Abbey Street.[2] French composer of light music Louis Jullien (1812–60) established himself in London as a conductor at balls and concerts, presenting his signature quadrilles and galops. A flamboyant and charismatic personality, with conducting flair and entrepreneurial skills, he went on to present his own highly successful promenade concerts, his orchestra augmented by leading soloists, performing annually in Dublin during the 1840s.

For over a decade after the burning of the Theatre Royal in 1840, Cork lacked a large capacity concert venue. Although Seymour's theatre in Cook Street served adequately as a theatre, it was rarely used for concerts. As the city's promoter of concerts by visiting performers, A.D. Roche secured the use of the Corn Exchange for three concerts by Jullien and his band in July 1849. Italian soprano Fanny Tacchinardi Persiani (1812–67) was the principal guest performer and Italian double bassist Giovanni Bottesini (1821–89) performed in the orchestra. The first programme featured 'The Allegro and Storm' from Beethoven's 'Pastoral' Symphony, and the final concert programme featured a movement from Mendelssohn's Symphony in A Minor ('Scottish'), and a Fantasia from Meyerbeer's *Le prophète*. The admission prices were limited to 3s 6d and 2 shillings, and a great attendance by the 'elite of the city and county' was reported; the shilling audience was not catered for.[3]

Figure 10.1. Theatre Royal, Cork, 1867.
ILLUSTRATED LONDON NEWS, COURTESY OF CORK CITY LIBRARY

The site of the old George's Street Theatre was redeveloped by English circus proprietor Pablo Fanque (1796–1871) as a performing space known as the Circus Royal, completed in 1850.[4] This venue was modified to accommodate Jullien and his orchestra on their next visit in January 1851, again hosted by Roche.[5] For the three performances on this occasion, the price range extended down to shilling gallery tickets, in addition to 3s and 2s 6d, facilitated by the building's tiered architecture. The guest soloist was German mezzo-soprano Henrietta ('Jetty') Treffz (1818–78), and performances by a troupe of French drummers provided additional musical spectacle.

On 8 June 1853, the George's Street Theatre was reopened, following major reconstruction, now in the ownership of Richard C. Burke.[6] In October, the premier performance of William F. Gillespie's ballad opera *Celestina, or the Alcalde of Gardara* was staged there, conducted by John McCarthy and featuring Miss Lanza from the Theatre Royal, Dublin. Mrs Halloran, who trained the choruses, presided at the piano.[7] The reviewer in the *Southern Reporter* lauded Gillespie as 'a composer of originality, imagination and scientific knowledge of his glorious art'.[8] The new theatre also resumed its role as a major concert venue.

Touring celebrities planning concerts in Cork could now choose between the Theatre Royal, the Imperial Hotel and the Athenaeum. Many opted for the new Athenaeum. A number of events presented at this venue during its first fifteen years provide a snapshot of mid-century concert life and its variegated audiences. On 1 and 2 March 1855, Louis Jullien's orchestra gave two concerts, featuring as guest performers French pianist and composer

Marie Pleyel (1811–75) and English soprano Charlotte Dolby (1821–85). On this visit, a shilling ticket admitted members of the public to the 'Promenade in the Rotunda'.[9] On a return visit by Jullien and his orchestra in 1858, the writer in the *Cork Examiner* bluntly identified a conflict of interests in Jullien's programme:

> There were, of course, items of music of an inferior class, whose redeeming qualities were their performance by artists such as he has grouped together, and his own arrangements, which are so well calculated to display the powers of his famous orchestra, but we were pleased to find that none of the pieces were absolute specimens of the clap-trap which has been associated with his name, but for which he is probably less to blame than the audiences who must be tempted by such stuff to listen to the master pieces that he is entitled to credit for popularizing amongst them.[10]

The writer also expressed dismay that the opening piece, Beethoven's *Leonora* overture, was 'unfortunately lost to most of those in the lower part of the hall', owing to the bustle created by latecomers.

In November 1856, the Athenaeum Committee presented a series of 'Saturday Evening Musical Promenades' featuring local musicians, including Mrs Halloran and the Misses Hickie. A report of the first of these in the *Southern Reporter* noted that, despite a good attendance, it was 'sadly deficient in that element which we would wish to see predominant on such occasions – the working people', despite a reduction of the admission cost to 3 pence.[11] The following November, an initiative to provide a series of three 'Concerts for the People' was advertised, featuring 'cheap and good music, sustained by sterling talent'. The programmes featured singer Miss Maria Simpson in 'Selections from Operas, Melodies, Ballads and Concerted Music'. T.J. Sullivan presided at the organ. Admission was at the rate of 1 shilling for reserved seats, promenade 6d and gallery 3d.[12] The sixth anniversary of the Catholic Young Men's Society in 1858 was marked by a promenade concert, and this concert model became a feature of this society's public events for the remainder of the century. Shilling gallery tickets were also available for Sigismond Thalberg's three piano recitals at the Athenaeum in November 1862.[13]

Visiting singers of international repute commanded the highest admission fees, regardless of venue. In November 1849, the eagerly awaited concerts by Limerick-born soprano Catherine Hayes (1818–1907) were held at the

Imperial Hotel, for which Roche advised early application for reserved seats at 6 shillings (unreserved 5 shillings, gallery 3 shillings).[14] In August 1852, Roche, in an opportunistic move, organised two operatic concerts at the Exhibition Buildings, following the conclusion of the Exhibition.[15] Singers Giulia Grisi (1811–69), tenor Giovanni Mario (1810–83), Madlle Bertrandi, Signor Galvani, Susini, Federico Lablache (1815–87) and Mr F. Mori featured in two grand concerts.[16] Concerts featuring Swedish soprano Jenny Lind (1820–97) and Hungarian violinist Joseph Joachim (1831–1907) at the Athenaeum in 1859 attracted capacity audiences.[17] The 'startling' range of admission prices was noted in the *Cork Examiner*: single reserved and numbered seats 15s, unreserved seats 7s 6d, and gallery 5s.[18] More moderate rates prevailed for three concerts by Catherine Hayes at this venue in 1861, ranging from four shillings down to one shilling. One of her supporting singers, Signor Burdini, sang A.D. Roche's ballad 'I watch for thee in starless night'.[19]

Concerts based on Italian operatic excerpts continued to have enduring popular appeal. Despite this, a concert by local singers featuring mainly Italian operatic pieces provoked sharp-toned comments in relation to the music of Verdi in the *Cork Examiner*.[20] Miss Fletcher's solo piece, 'Ernani involami' from *Ernani* (1844), was described as 'one of Verdi's characteristic pieces, showy and difficult, but without further merit'. Signor Piberi's performance of 'Dagli immortali vertici' from *Attila* (1846) was described as 'an air with a good deal of spirit, and with a beauty of melody not usually found in Verdi's compositions'.[21] This particular negative view of Verdi was reiterated in a review in the *Cork Examiner*, in September of the same year, of a concert of operatic repertoire presented by singers from the Royal Italian Opera, Covent Garden, headed by French mezzo-soprano Pauline Viardot Garcia (1821–1910).[22] The selection was pronounced as 'neither popular nor good, being chiefly from the works of that most vicious of modern composers, Verdi; nevertheless, so excellent was the singing that this defect was almost entirely forgotten'.[23] The venom shown towards Verdi in these reviews may have concurred with the views expressed in *The Athenaeum* journal by Henry Chorley in 1846, which ranked 'Verdi-mania' low in the taste spectrum of London concert-goers.[24] However, the stance of the proprietor of the *Cork Examiner*, John Francis Maguire, was more likely to have been related to Verdi's association with the Italian nationalist movement, and in particular his sympathy for the 1848 revolution in Rome, which had forced Pope Pius IX into temporary exile.[25] Maguire had a particular interest in this topic: the first edition of his book *Rome and its Ruler*, based on letters he had written while in Rome, published in 1857, sold out, and was re-published in 1859 as *Rome: its ruler and its institutions*.[26] Such comments were among the rare examples of religio-political consensus clashing with concert repertoire.

By 1859, it was widely acknowledged that the Athenaeum suffered serious acoustical problems, with the added discomfort of draughts during the colder months.[27] During the 1860s, its suitability as a venue for music of a more popular type was increasingly exploited. The popular Christy's Minstrels, a blackface group from Wilson and Montague's theatre in Liverpool, performed four concerts at the Athenaeum in January 1860, with prices scaled 'to meet the resources of all classes', ranging from 2s 6d for reserved and numbered seats, 1s 6d for unnumbered seats, and gallery 1s, with further reductions for children under ten years of age. Second prices applied to all but the galleries.[28] This troupe returned to Cork on several occasions during the 1860s, performing at both the Athenaeum and the Theatre Royal.[29] By 1867, a local group of young gentlemen formed The Minstrel Boys, in imitation of the Christy's Minstrels, and from 1867 to 1870, their 'full dress amateur concerts' at the Athenaeum in aid of local charities achieved great support from the elite of the city. A report of their first concert in December 1867 opened with the words 'Charity and burnt cork go capitally together' and the programmes included 'Christy's music', Orpheus glees and burlesque acts.[30]

In 1867, a commercial venture by the Refreshment Rooms Company to provide popular promenade concerts at the Athenaeum at an affordable cost met with considerable success.[31] The first concert was held on 9 December, consisting of vocal and instrumental music, directed by William Alcock, organist of Cloyne cathedral, and featured performances by the Band of the 81st Regiment, who performed the overture from Rossini's *Semiramide* with 'a dash, brilliancy and precision that made it seem the product of only one huge instrument'. The bandmaster, Herr Fischer, also performed some violin solos, which were commended in the review. The pricing of 1s for the galleries and 6d for the great hall ensured wide affordability. The *Cork Examiner* reported that

> It was evident, looking at the great bulk of the very large audience, that these concerts have hit the taste, and suit the circumstances of a large and most respectable class of the community – including the better class tradesman, the small shopkeeper, the clerks, and the decent artisan, with their families, for whom there has not, within the memory of living menu, been good and cheap amusement of this class provided in this city.[32]

Nicholas D. Murphy was among the city magistrates and gentlemen who attended the event.

Over the next two years, Thomas Nagle presented 'First Class Concerts at moderate charges' or 'Popular concerts', using a similar structure, but without the 6d price.[33] The four vocal soloists were Miss Bessie Herbert and Miss Fennell, of the Philharmonic and University Choral Societies of Dublin, Henry Baker of St Fin Barre's Cathedral, and Grattan Kelly of St Patrick's and Christ Church cathedrals in Dublin, and J.C Marks conducted. In June 1868, William Wheeler, organist at Christ Church, presented a concert at the Athenaeum entitled 'Ireland, its Scenery, Music and Antiquities', featuring the Band of the 62nd Regiment, directed by Mr Carey, and a number of local singers in a programme of 'new songs, dances, sketches and instrumental selections'. In addition to arrangements of works by Rossini and Verdi, the band performed the 'Kate Kearney Valse' by Charles Coote (1807–79). The admission price range of 2s/1s/6d was retained.[34] Nagle responded with a 'Popular Concert of Irish Music' at the Athenaeum in August 1868, directed by J.C. Marks, again featuring Herbert, Fennell, Baker and Kelly. Opening with a quartet setting by Robinson of 'Let Erin Remember', the concert consisted of vocal solos, duets and quartets, based mainly on arrangements of Moore's songs. The concerts were subsequently performed in several Munster towns.[35] William Alcock again directed a series of promenade concerts in September 1869, to coincide with the Cork Park Races. St Mary's band featured in these, performing selections from Donizetti's *Lucia di Lammermoor* (1839) and *Linda di Chamonix* (1842), in addition to 'some pleasant dance music'.[36] Such concerts proved an overall success, and developed a tradition of popular concerts that was viable and attractive to a wide audience.

MUSICAL SOCIETIES

The Cork Musical Society was established in January 1869 for 'the study and practice of music of a high class'.[37] Established by Presbyterian businessman and philanthropist Sir John Arnott (1814–98) with Robert Walker Jr,[38] the society, which was 'composed of persons of various creeds and opinions, properly excluded from its motives all national or party predilections, [who] based their exertions upon the broad ground of Christian charity'.[39] The address of the society was Nelson's Place, and weekly meetings were held and recitals were given at the 'Rotondo' of the Athenaeum and at the Imperial Hotel. The society's repertoire included a Haydn symphony and an *allegretto* and *andante* by Beethoven, in addition to overtures.[40] J.C. Marks was its director and conductor.[41] Having enlisted 200 subscribing members by the end of its first year, the society was no longer financially dependent on Arnott. The entire performing forces of the society numbered 150, which included eighty-five female singers, twenty tenors, twenty basses and twenty-five instrumentalists.

This society's membership included a new generation of active city professionals, some of whom were noted musical connoisseurs. The founding secretary, Robert Walker Jr, was a civil engineer and architect,[42] who worked on the building of both St Fin Barre's Cathedral and Queenstown cathedral.[43] The honorary secretary in 1871 was architect Arthur Hill (1846–1921).[44] In addition to being an accomplished pianist, he was proficient on the oboe, an unusual accomplishment for an amateur at this time. The vice president, Captain Richard Pigott Beamish (1832–99), an amateur violinist, was a member of an influential family that had patronised Cork's musical societies since the beginning of the nineteenth century.[45] The society held a concert in aid of the funds of the Lying-in Hospital, Nile Street, at the Athenaeum in January 1870,[46] and another concert at this venue in November 'in aid of the sick and wounded in the Franco-German War'. An orchestra featured Herr Diedrich and Robert Coghlan, violins, and George Brady, cello, with William Marks at the organ, and members of St Mary's Band were the principal wind players. The programme featured songs in French and German, which were 'well executed and very warmly received'. Amateur singers who performed were Robert Walker and Mrs Empson, in a concert that was 'well and fashionably attended'.[47]

The society continued to use this venue and, by November 1780, some efforts had been made to improve its physical condition: 'The rotunda has been solidly divided off, and by means of screens the doors are to be prevented from sending Arctic winds through the reserved seats, while the whole building will be thoroughly warmed.'[48] It had become widely acknowledged that the Athenaeum was an unsatisfactory performance venue, and had not reached its projected potential as a centre of cultural activity. In 1883, the Musical Society used the Protestant Hall for a concert that featured choral and orchestral forces totalling 130, in a performance of Rossini's *Stabat Mater*.[49] Major concerted works performed over its first fourteen years included several new choral works, among them Michael Costa's oratorio *Naaman* (1865), Frederick H. Cowen's cantata *The Rose Maiden* (1872), Niels Gade's cantata *The Crusaders* (1866), Stainer's sacred cantata *The Daughter of Jairus* (1878), and Arthur Sullivan's oratorio *The Martyr of Antioch* (1880). Older standard oratorio repertoire, Handel's *Messiah*, *Samson*, *Judas Maccabeus*, Mendelssohn's *Elijah* and *St Paul*, and Haydn's *The Creation*, also featured on its programmes.

The Cork Orchestral Union, established in 1876 'for the study and performance of high-class orchestral works', represented a new departure in amateur musical activity.[50] It was directed and conducted by William Ringrose Atkins (1848–1905), a member of the Christ Church Choral Union. From a wealthy County Cork family, Atkins was an accountant with a keen interest in music and the visual arts.[51] In his earlier years, he regularly attended the leading English and continental music festivals and was a member of the Royal Institute of Music, Florence, and a Fellow of the London Philharmonic Society.[52] The society consisted of subscribing and performing members, with Michael Cagney as secretary. The all-male orchestra, which by 1879 consisted of over forty players, presented concerts of mainly orchestral music at the South Mall ('Protestant') Assembly Rooms over the ensuing years, led by Robert D. Howard (son of bandmaster, Robert Howard) and conducted by Atkins. The concerts were aimed at an elite audience. Full dress was required, and a half guinea admission to each of the concerts entitled the subscriber to five tickets. Although the orchestra consisted mainly of amateurs, it included professional musicians Theodore Gmür, Charles A. Pridmore, violins, and George Brady, cello. Skilled amateurs included violinist Bartholomew Britton, and cellists William Harrington and Alexander Jack (d. 1908), Professor of Engineering at Queen's College (1855–1906) and Registrar of Queen's College (1876–1906)[53] (see Appendix 2).

The society aimed to perform the 'choicest classical orchestral work of the great composers, never before played in Cork, together with pieces better known to the general public, including overtures, Symphonies, &c., &c., by Beethoven, Mozart, Weber, Schubert, &c.'; and it also intended to give specimens of chamber music, for both string and wind instruments.[54] A concert in February 1880 featured a programme of Irish music and works by Irish composers: overtures by Balfe and Rooke, songs by Balfe, Wallace and A.D. Roche, arrangements of Irish melodies by Joseph Robinson and Beethoven, a quintet arrangement by Robert Prescott Stewart, concluding with a 'Festal March', composed expressly for the orchestra by Thomas R. Jozé of Dublin.[55] A substantial item on the programme was Arthur Hill's performance of John Field's Piano Concerto No. 6 in C major.[56] At a concert in 1883, the orchestra gave the first Irish performance of a quartet by the Italian composer Luigi Ferdinando Casamorata (1807–81).[57] In 1881, the orchestra was described in *The Musical Times and Singing Class Circular* as 'the largest and most important in Ireland'.[58] In 1882, a leatherbound watercolour, painted by local artist John Gilbert, was presented to Atkins by members of the society in acknowledgment of his 'services to the cause of music in Cork'.[59] The society lapsed after 1883, however, the year in which Atkins commenced his own professional accountancy practice.

The establishment in 1876 of the Orchestral Club of the CYMS aimed to fulfil a perceived need for 'a thoroughly capable orchestra for the production of music of a high class on special occasions, such as important religious and other public ceremonies'.[60] It was led by Bartholomew Britton and conducted by John W. McCarthy, and included some of the 'best elements of St Mary's band', which was by this time in demise. Its first concert, held at the society's rooms in Castle Street, highlighted the inadequate capacity and suitability of this venue.

THE MUNSTER HALL AND CORK OPERA HOUSE

By 1873, Robert Walker Jr had supervised major refurbishments to the interior of the Athenaeum to rectify acoustic problems and draughts. The rotundo was converted into a vestibule and sealed off from the main hall.[61] The building was reopened as the Munster Hall, 'a more sensible and satisfactory, though less pretentious designation' according to a writer in the *Irish Builder*.[62] Further modifications supervised by London theatre architecture specialist Charles John Phipps (1835–97) rendered it suitable for theatrical presentations. The Munster Hall, under new proprietors James Scanlan (1833–1909), a local estate agent, and John George McCarthy (1829–92), solicitor, became a new theatre venue.[63] In 1877, a new limited company was formed under Scanlan's management.[64] The name was changed to Cork Theatre Royal and Opera House, later shortened to Cork Opera House.[65] Scanlan's effectiveness in attracting new companies to Cork was noted in *The Era* in 1882, which stated that the new theatre had provided 'an almost uninterrupted succession of popular entertainment, nearly all good, and some of them of rare excellence, and many thousands of Cork citizens of all ranks and classes have participated in these innocent and refining enjoyments'.[66] This wide reach of the theatre's audience base was again referred to in 1885:

> [...] instead of being obliged to take whatever offered, [the directors] are now in a position to select and discriminate, and Cork, instead of being

> excluded from the circuits of the best companies, is now regularly visited by them, and all classes of citizens from the highest to the humblest are afforded the advantage of seeing good artists and hearing fine musicians.[67]

In 1888, the company that governed the Opera House declared insolvency, Scanlan resigned, and a new company was formed.[68] Among the operatic companies who performed at the Cork Opera House during the last two decades of the century were the Carl Rosa Company, the D'Oyly Carte Company and the Moody-Manners Company. Among the soloists who performed there were Irish tenors Barton McGuckin (1852–1913) and Joseph O'Mara (1864–1927), the latter in a production by the London Opera Comique company of Charles Villiers Stanford's *Shamus O'Brien* in 1896, conducted by Granville Bantock (1868–1946).[69]

CORK MUNICIPAL SCHOOL OF MUSIC

Two prominent members of the Cork Musical Society, Arthur Hill and Nicholas D. Murphy, envisaged a major plan for music education in Cork, to be achieved by seeking equivalent status with art and science education, both of which had been fostered in the city since the early decades of the century. Nicholas D. Murphy (1811–90) was a liberal MP for the city of Cork from 1865 until 1880. The proposal may have been inspired by reports of the opening of the National Training School of Music in South Kensington, which were published in the *Cork Constitution* in May 1876.[70] This privately endowed institution was an important precedent in the provision of systematic professional training for musicians. In 1876, a meeting was held at the Royal Cork Institution to establish schools of science and music, and to expand the School of Art. Hill later described the process:

> Owing to a defect in the Irish Libraries and Museums Act of 1855, under which the Cork School of Art existed, it was found necessary to get a short Amendment Act passed, which after taking the necessary powers for art, Mr Murphy availed of for the purposes of music, by introducing a clause to the effect 'that the terms Science and Art in the principal Act shall be deemed to include the Science and Art of Music'.[71]

The passing of an Amendment Act in 1877 enabled the Cork Borough Council to allocate a portion of its rates for musical instruction, which was fixed at £350. A general committee of some fifty citizens 'of all shades of political and religious views' was appointed to manage the School of Art and the proposed School of Music.[72] The honorary secretaries of the committee were James Brenan, head of the School of Art, and Arthur Hill. Murphy and Hill had taken the unprecedented move of seeking government support for a public music school, a landmark achievement for the city.

In December 1878, Cork Municipal School of Music was opened in temporary premises at 51 Grand Parade, a former dispensary house. A detailed account of the occasion was published in the *Cork Examiner* on 3 December 1878 entitled 'A glorious future for music in Cork'.[73] Léopold de Prins performed on a Kirkman piano, presented as a gift to the school, and Messrs Broadwood provided a piano at a nominal cost. Among the school's minutes was a draft entitled the 'Organisation of the school', which commenced with a statement of its purpose:

1. The Cork School of Music is designed to provide a sound and systematic course of musical training for all classes and to elevate the general character of musical taste in Cork.

2. Teaching should not be entirely confined to those who are gifted with special talent, but by preserving a system of classification, pupils of ordinary ability as well should be enabled to enlarge their knowledge of the art and develop technical skills as far as their prowess will admit.[74]

Further points detailed the division of study into junior, senior and advanced levels. Admission to junior level was to be unrestricted, but progression to further levels was subject to assessment, conducted by external examiners. The conducting of annual examination of students was thus a key objective within the school. The aspiration to 'elevate the general character of musical taste in Cork' shows a broad alignment with the aim of fostering 'high-class' music, and implies the creation of wider audiences for such music. A later committee report expressed the school's objective as 'the diffusion of an accurate and intelligent idea of the principles and practice of Music, *as an Art*, rather than as a mere pastime, or frivolous Amusement'.[75]

Five staff members initially provided day and evening tuition in piano, violin, voice, harmony, solfeggio and choral class. The curriculum provided three years of mandatory classes in solfeggio and harmony, with optional classes in piano for violin students. The fee for the solfeggio classes was £3 per year. A term of fifteen weekly lessons in instrumental tuition was

Table 10.1. Categories of students enrolled at Cork School of Music, 1878–84.

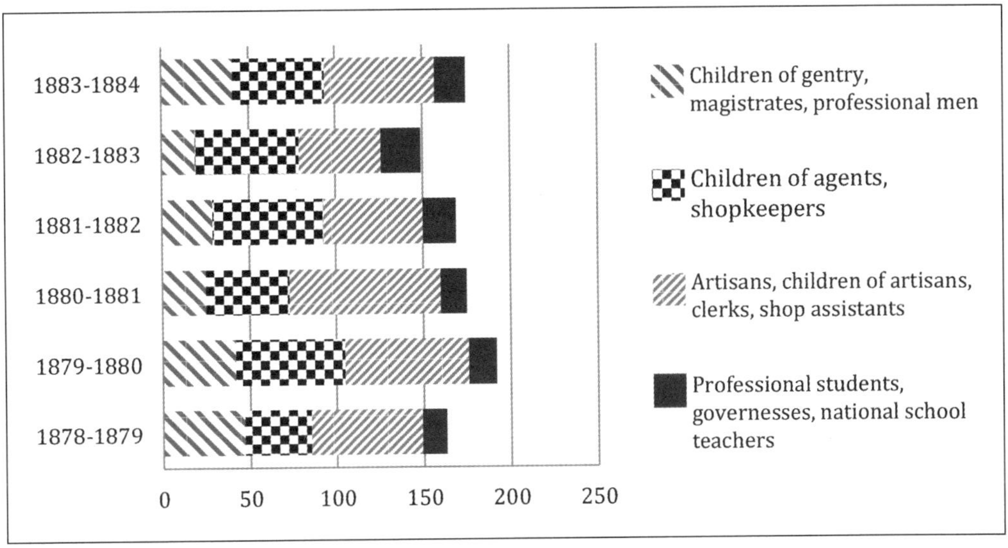

charged at the rate of £3, or £4 10 for twice-weekly lessons. For instrumental tuition, three pupils attended an hour lesson. This arrangement, referred to as *enseignement collectif*, 'universally adopted in similar institutions abroad', was considered 'more instructive to a pupil than a solitary lesson of any length'.[76]

The initial enrolment was 163 students, from a range of socio-economic backgrounds. Over the first ten years, the average annual enrolment was 175 students. Annual reports from the early years of the school provide a statistical breakdown of students by father's employment status (see Table 10.1). An adult class consisted mainly of young teachers from a number of local schools. Thirty-three scholarships were dispersed through various religious denominations to offer free tuition to poor children who showed musical talent. A number of young people were enrolled on reduced fees on the basis of 'entering upon the study of music as a means of earning their bread as governesses, national school teachers, etc.'[77] John Arnott provided two annual scholarships in piano and voice production.

The city's music professors formed the core of the teaching staff: T.J. Sullivan (voice cultivation, solfeggio, choral class), Robert Coghlan (violin and viola), Léopold de Prins (pianoforte), J.C. Marks and A.J. Smith (harmony) provided tuition in the first year.[78] The hourly payment rate for instrumental teaching was 5s 6d and the payment for orchestral class (one hour per week) was 7 shillings. In 1882, Hans Conrad Swertz joined the staff, teaching Advanced Harmony, and Composition the following year. Although cello tuition had been offered during the first five years of the school's existence, no students had enrolled for this instrument and the committee proposed removing it from the prospectus. Also in 1882, Arthur Hill proposed a special solfeggio class for boys from seven to fifteen years old, at a nominal fee of £1 per annum. The scheme met with 'some success, but not such as might be expected if parents exhibited the same interest in the musical education of their sons that they do in that of their daughters'.[79] His comment is borne out in the gender balance of the school's students – a list of examination results issued in 1891, examined by Francis Davenport, shows an overwhelming majority of female candidates.[80]

Annual examinations were conducted in association with London's Royal Academy of Music. W.A. Barrett, Examiner to the Education Commissioners at Whitehall, visited twice for inspection, acting as deputy for John Hullah.[81] Examiners during the following two decades were Henry R. Eyres of London's Royal Academy of Music (1880 to 1884), Dr Joseph Smith of the Royal University of Ireland (1885 to 1888), and Francis William Davenport of the Royal Academy of Music (1889 to 1900). Among those in the Advanced Harmony Class who passed with honours in 1883 was Frederick St John Lacy (1862–1935), who was to become the first lecturer in Music at Queen's College in 1906.[82] Diplomas were awarded in the same session to Helen Bayley, Mary Bergin, Amy Whitford, Richard Bransfield and Cornelius Paul.

The devising of a structure for publicly funded music education was progressive for its time, and its benefits to the citizens of Cork were widely acknowledged. On a visit to Cork in August 1878, the Lord Lieutenant, the Duke of Marlborough, had, in his final address to the mayor, lauded

> those who have the interests of the city at heart, and most eminently my friend, Mr Murphy, [who] have contributed to a school of music, which, I have no doubt, will draw forth a good deal of talent, and will be one of the most humanizing, one of the most civilizing influences, that could be brought to bear on a community.[83]

In October 1891, the school was relocated to 8 Morrison's Island. Developments during the 1890s included the acquisition of an organ (for the organ class and orchestral work) through the recommendation of Swertz, who purchased a Liszt cabinet organ at a cost of £150 and hired it out to the school for £15 a year.[84] The Corporation grant proved inadequate over the years following the school's establishment, and appeals were frequently made to secure government aid for the school. Correspondence with the Department of Science and Art, South Kensington, London, was ongoing for several years, and in 1895 instrumental and vocal music was sanctioned as a subject of instruction under Section 8 of the Technical Instruction Act 1889, providing an annual grant of £250.[85]

Within the limited available resources, efforts were made to extend access to the school's educational resources. In 1893, the committee minutes record a proposal that members of the Catholic Young Men's Society and similar societies of other denominations be enrolled for tuition in pianoforte, violin, and voice production, at a 25 per cent fee reduction, subject to the stipulation that the professors concerned consent to bearing the fee reduction from their salaries.[86] This gave rise to the first professional dissent among the teaching staff, and was eventually discontinued. By 1899, a band sub-committee was formed to organise band promenade concerts, chaired by William Ringrose Atkins, resulting in thirty performances given during the summer, featuring the Blackpool National Band, the Butter Exchange Band and the Workingman's Prize Band.[87]

The voluntary committee of the Cork School of Music (CSM) involved a number of individuals with strong support for music education. Foremost of these was Arthur Hill, who served on the committee for several years. In addition to being a keen amateur musician, he was a member of the Royal Musical Association (RMA). In 1877 he presented a paper to this association entitled 'On a suggested improvement in staff notation', which proposed a system of simple stave signs to denote relative pitch, to assist singers when sight-reading. Ten years after the school had been opened, Hill presented another paper to the RMA entitled 'Rate-aided schools of music', outlining his strategies in Cork, proposing that the Irish Amendment Act be extended to Britain to enable similar developments in publicly funded music education there.[88] Like Hill, Captain Richard Pigott Beamish was a member of the Musical Society. He chaired the CSM committee for a number of years, continuing the support of local music that had been associated with the Beamish family since the early nineteenth century. Fr Edward Gaynor, who served on the committee for several years during the final decade of the century, was a strong advocate for the use of tonic solfa in Irish primary schools. To this end, he established an Association for the Advancement of Music in Primary Schools in Cork, and in December 1892 organised the first schools choral competition in Ireland at the Cork School of Art.[89]

His *St Patrick's Hymn Book*, published in 1892, was endorsed by the Dublin Diocesan Commission on Ecclesiastical Music and included the *nihil obstat* of Maynooth College and the *imprimatur* of the Archbishop of Dublin. The publication included sets of hymn cards for the use of 'schools and sodalities, etc.', each card in the set of twenty-five consisting of the words and tonic solfa of an entire hymn.[90] He presented lectures on the topic of tonic solfa to the CYMS and the Cork Literary and Scientific Society.[91]

Despite many financial challenges, the Cork Municipal School of Music was well supported locally, and incorporated the educational interests of key institutions within the city: the Catholic Young Men's Society, the amateur bands and the city's churches. The school's all-embracing policy welcomed a wide spectrum of citizens, and sustained an educational institution that effectively transcended sectoral and denominational interests.

INDUSTRIAL EXHIBITION 1883

An indication of the transformation of public music in Cork city was its expanded role at the Industrial Exhibition of 1883. A sub-committee for music at the exhibition included Thomas Crosbie, editor of the *Cork Examiner*, Richard Pigott Beamish, Colonel Shuldham and Mr R. Penrose-Fitzgerald, with co-opted members Wiliam Ringrose Atkins and Arthur Hill.[92] A series of concerts was held over the duration of the exhibition from July to late September, embracing events to appeal to a range of musical tastes. The city's principal musical institutions were featured: Cork Musical Society, directed by J.C. Marks, the Cork Orchestral Union, directed by William Ringrose Atkins, students of the Cork School of Music, directed by T.J. O'Sullivan, and the Butter Exchange Band. A resident orchestra for the exhibition, directed by Robert D. Howard, gave four afternoon promenade concerts each week during the months of July and August.

Located in buildings specially constructed at the Corn Exchange, the exhibition commenced with a procession of trades from Wellington Bridge to the Exhibition Buildings, featuring the Butter Exchange Band. The opening evening concert was on a model similar to that of the 1852 Exhibition, featuring an orchestra, choir and soloists conducted by Joseph Robinson, by then regarded as Ireland's foremost conductor, performing selections from Mendelssohn's *Hymn of Praise* and Haydn's *The Creation*, featuring members of the Cork School of Music Choir and instrumentalists of

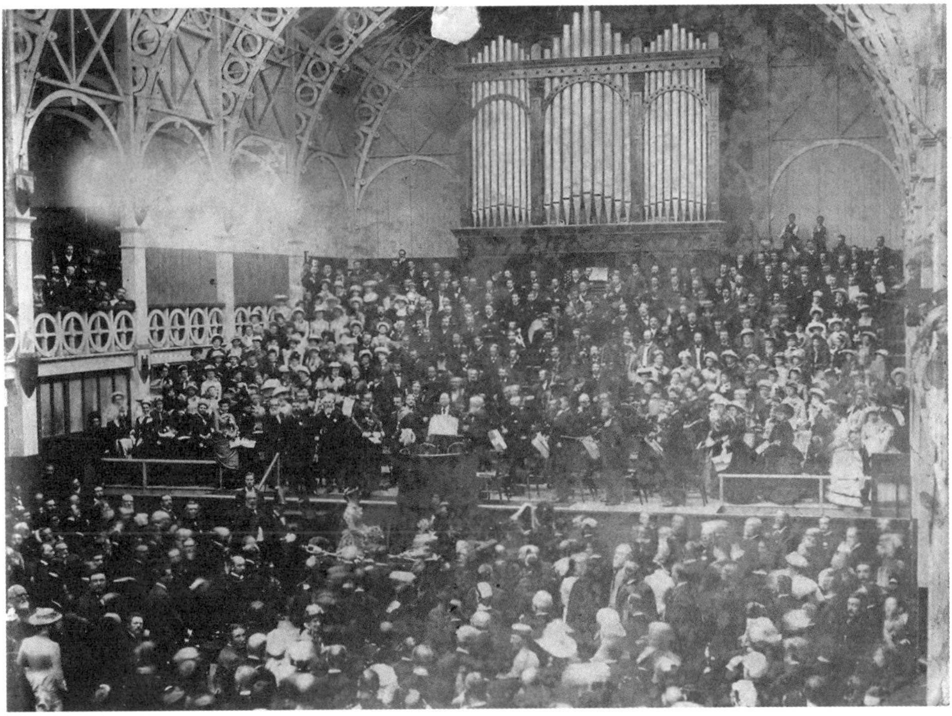

Figure 10.2. Cork Exhibition, 1883. CORK CITY AND COUNTY ARCHIVES

the Cork Orchestral Union. A review in the *Cork Constitution* referred to Robinson's mastery of the medium, noting the 'wonderful effects of light and shade which throughout appeared to be produced so easily'.[93] A report on the musical instrument exhibits deplored the decline of smaller local industries in favour of centralised factories. In this class were featured mainly imported pianos from local dealers Cox & Atkins of Patrick Street, and Gunn & Ferguson of Winthrop Street. William Bennett of Anglesea Place, Cork, exhibited a hand-made violin, and William Cope of Cecil Street, Limerick, exhibited a piano.[94] The organ in the great hall was supplied by Cork organ-builder Thomas Magahy. With the exception of the metal piping, procured from London, all parts of this instrument were locally made. A series of recitals were given by local and visiting organists: Messrs Daly, Nunan, Smith, Sullivan and Swertz (Cork), Dr Smith, Signor Cellini and Mr Hamilton Croft (Dublin), Miss F.D. O'Callaghan (Kinsale), Mr G.F. Moran (Carlow), Mr J.F. Murray (Limerick), Mr J.A. Rooks (Bradford) and Mr Stocks Hammond (Huddersfield).

A concert given by the Cork Musical Society, numbering 350 between choir and orchestra, performed Mendelssohn's *Elijah* in September conducted by Marks, with an orchestra led by Robert D. Howard. A review by a correspondent in the *Freeman's Journal* noted that 'the dramatic element of the great master's music was wholly ignored, and the work was therefore deprived of much of its interest for the audience'.[95] The Cork Orchestral Union performed a programme of new music that included movements from Ebenezer Prout's Concerto in E Minor for organ and orchestra, a concert overture (from manuscript) by Karl Zoeller (1840–89), an orchestral fantasia, *Souvenir d'Irlande*, by Signor Bonicoli, bandmaster of the 9th East Norfolk Regiment, and a grand march composed by William Ringrose Atkins. The performance of two movements of Prout's organ concerto by H.C. Swerz on the Magahy organ was deemed 'effectual' in a review in the *Cork Constitution*, but the piece was regarded as 'too lengthy'.[96]

One of the leading features of the exhibition, according to the organising committee, was the 'Grand Military and Civilian Band Contest', held in the great hall on 21 and 22 September. Military band contests had been popular in Britain since the 1860s and a few had been held in Dublin[97] but were a novelty in Cork. Seven British military bands competed in the military section. The adjudicators were Dr Joseph Smith (Royal University of Ireland), J.P. Clark (Scots Guards) and Mr van Maanen (Royal Irish Constabulary). In contrast to the opening concert, music of a decidedly popular character was presented on the final day of the exhibition, including a spectacular performance by the combined bands of the Royal Scots' Grays, the King's Regiment, the King's Own Borderers, and the Duke of Cornwall's Light Infantry. The highlight of the programme was Louis Jullien's celebrated 'British Army Quadrille', played by massed bands marching through the building, joined by Scottish pipers, drummers, fifers and trumpeters.[98] In its massed effects, this military-style spectacle epitomised the spirit of the industrial era.

AMATEUR OPERATIC SOCIETIES

As a 'fringe' event of the exhibition, the Cork Amateur Operatic and Dramatic Society presented Gilbert and Sullivan's *The Pirates of Penzance* at the Theatre Royal on 18, 19 and 20 July, directed by Theodore Gmür. Admission prices for the performances ranged from 4s for dress circle and orchestral stalls, 2s 6d for upper circle, pit 1s and gallery 6d.[99] In February 1881, Robert D. Howard directed an orchestra and chorus of eighty performers in a performance of Paul McSwiney's (1856–89) opera *Amergen*, described in *The Era* as 'a new and original opera', set in Ireland during the time of the Viking invasions.[100] A critic in *The Constitution* was less than enthusiastic, however, in stating 'we fear that Mr McSwiney will yet find that he cannot reach the top of the ladder without commencing at the bottom', and that 'his work often appear[s] more like a number of melodious phrases following each other at hazard, rather than as one continuous whole'.[101] Dublin soprano Bessie Craig, who sang the lead part of Adela, was the only professional member of the cast. The following year, Gmür directed the Cork Amateur Operatic and Dramatic Society in Gilbert and Sullivan's *Patience*, and thereafter produced both full productions and operatic recitals, with financial support from Sir John Arnott.[102] In 1886, a recital of *Il trovatore* was presented, featuring Lucy Ashton Hackett, Mrs Jerome Murphy, George Waters, J. O'Sullivan and Joseph O'Mara, who travelled from Limerick for the event.[103] In 1887 and again in 1890 he directed operatic recitals of William Vincent Wallace's *Maritana*, featuring Lucy Ashton Hackett, Edith Adams and Joseph O'Mara.[104] In 1890, the society presented *Edelweiss*, an opera by Gmür, based on a libretto by F.W. Broughton of London, which had several revivals in ensuing years. A review in the *Freeman's Journal* of a performance of this work by a set of local amateurs in 1893 was critical of the quality of the libretto.[105]

Amateur opera reached new heights under the direction of Arthur Tuer (1854–96), who arrived in Cork in the late 1880s. Born near Bradford, Tuer worked as chorus master at London's Savoy Theatre, and was choirmaster at the Church of St Mary of the Angels, Bayswater.[106] He was appointed as Professor of Solfeggio and Voice Culture at the Cork School of Music in 1887 to replace T.J. Sullivan.[107] Under his direction, the Cork Amateur Opera Company flourished.[108] In 1890, he directed amateur performances of Alfred Cellier's *The Sultan of Mocha* (1874) and Gilbert and Sullivan's *Princess Ida* (1884).[109] The society's production of Robert Planquette's operetta *Rip Van Winkle* ran for six nights at the Cork Opera House in 1891. In 1894 he directed an amateur production of Planquette's comic opera *Les Cloches de Corneville* (1877) in a week of performances at the Cork Opera House, which merited a positive review in the *Freeman's Journal*.[110] His career was cut short in 1896 when, at the age of forty-one, he died of pneumonia.[111] Founded in 1886, the Cork Amateur Orchestral Society, directed by Robert D. Howard, flourished during the last decade of the century, providing orchestral support for productions by the Amateur Operatic Society.[112] A list of performing members at a concert in 1896 shows that over a third of the string section was female, and Miss Scanlan was the pianist (see Appendix 3).

THE MUSIC PROFESSION

At the opening of the School of Music in 1878, Léopold de Prins had thanked the committee for 'the boon it had conferred on the music profession by placing it on a level with Science and Art'.[113] The profession had indeed gained in status through the establishment of the school, and the expansion of Catholic churches continued to provide professional opportunities. The combined prospects attracted musicians from abroad. Arthur Tuer succeeded Sullivan at St Mary's, Pope's Quay, in the 1880s, and was engaged at the School of Music. Another new appointee was William H. Hannaford, Mus Bac. Cantab, who arrived in 1891 to take up the post of organist at Christ Church, and was employed at the School of Music as teacher of piano and solfeggio.[114]

As church organist, conductor, teacher and community musical leader, Gmür exemplified the status of the professional musician in the late nineteenth century. He contributed to a number of flourishing Catholic educational organisations. Under his leadership, the Catholic Young Men's Society continued to expand its musical activities. Committee minutes for the years 1888–9 include references to a lecture on 'Minstrelsy' by John Gilbert, singing classes and promenade concerts.[115] By 1891, the society held evening classes in tonic solfa and harmony, orchestral music, piano and voice production.[116] Gmür also taught at the Cork School of Music and at St Angela's, a city-centre Catholic school for girls. He was involved in a diverse range of other cultural groups. In 1890 he established the Cork Musical Club, a male-voice choir.[117] He conducted the choruses at the first Annual Grand Concert of the Medical Students' Association of Queen's College.[118]

Not all of the city's musicians prospered, however. James Roche, veteran singer and teacher, was declared a bankrupt in 1871, spared in the local newspapers, but reported in the *Freeman's Journal*.[119] J.C. Marks appeared on a bankrupt list in the *Glasgow Herald* in 1888.[120] The personal circumstances of these musicians are not known, but increased professional competition during the last quarter of the nineteenth century may have been a contributory factor. Roche had signalled his reduced state when he advertised a benefit concert in 1866, stating that it was 'the first time in over 30 years that he asked fellow citizens to patronize his concerts'.[121] To protect professional interests, the Munster Society of Professional Musicians had been established for a short time when, at a meeting in September 1893, a proposal to affiliate with the Incorporated Society of Musicians was unanimously passed. A meeting held in that year was attended by twenty-two musicians, which included five women.[122]

THE GAELIC REVIVAL

The defeat of the second Home Rule Bill in 1893 had left a major political issue unresolved, leading to much political tension and conflict. In the same year the Gaelic League was established with the aim of reviving the Irish language, music and traditions. Within months a Cork branch was established, with C. O'Kelly and Cornelius Cremen as honorary secretaries.

The recovery of Irish national music prompted the idea of an Irish music festival, the Feis Ceoil, which had been mooted in Dublin musical circles since 1894 under the guidance of Lurgan-born organist, lecturer and writer on music Annie Patterson (1868–1934). The original plan was that the Feis would circulate between the centres of Dublin, Belfast and Cork. In December 1896, a number of Cork musicians and cultural leaders convened a public meeting to discuss this issue. Among those present were Fr Gaynor, Theodore Gmür and J.C. Marks, in addition to the Mayor, the honorary Secretary of the Cork Literary and Scientific Society, and representatives of the Dublin Feis Ceoil committee. From a report in the *Cork Examiner*, it is evident that those present envisaged the Feis as a means of retrieving 'before it is too late, the fragments of [the] ancient music, which was fast fading from the minds [...] and the hearts of the present generation'. Following an impassioned discussion on the issue of Ireland's native music, it was proposed that a subscription list be opened, and a Guarantee Fund started. The first Feis Ceoil was successfully held in Dublin the following year, and twice thereafter it was held in Belfast. It subsequently became an annual Dublin event, amid much dispute and lack of consensus amongst its organisers as to its ultimate purpose.[123] Gmür and Marks remained active on one of its sub-committees, and Gmür acted as adjudicator in subsequent years.[124] Gaynor contributed to the wider debate on cultural nationalism. In May 1900, he gave a lecture to the National Literary Society in Dublin on 'The Characteristics of Irish Airs' illustrated with vocal examples, accompanied by Brendan Rogers,[125] and in 1905 his article on 'Irish Music' was published in the *New Ireland Review*.[126]

The Gaelic League's annual St Patrick's Day concerts, held in Cork from 1895 onwards, brought traditional Irish music to the fore. The third annual concert, held at the Assembly Rooms, featured a performance on the Irish pipes by Robert Thompson, harp solos and several vocal performances of Irish traditional airs. Some of the programme items were to be performed at the forthcoming Feis Ceoil in Dublin. Under the direction of Fr Gaynor, a choir of children from SS Peter and Paul's schools sang 'The Shan Van Vocht' and 'My Native Land'. Another intending Feis competitor was Miss Lizzy

Figure 10.3. Gmür's song 'To God and Ireland True'.
CIT CORK SCHOOL OF MUSIC

Barry, who performed solo Irish airs on the violin.[127] Robert Thompson won first prize in the piping competition at the Feis Ceoil in 1897 and 1898.[128]

Gmür's sympathies with Irish nationalist thinking were reflected in a series of songs composed during the last two decades of the century, settings of poems by Timothy Daniel Sullivan (1827–1914), nationalist, journalist and politician, and editor of *The Nation*. Of these, 'There is no land like Ireland' was performed in 1885 at the National League in London.[129] In 1886, Gmür presented a set of 'Irish Patriotic Songs' to William Gladstone,[130] leader of the British Liberal Party, who became Prime Minister in February 1886, pledging to achieve Home Rule for Ireland.[131] Two songs by Gmür on texts by Sullivan that appeared later that year were 'The Green Flag' and 'Westward Ho', published as a set. A short review of the songs in *The Nation* stated that:

> The melody of 'Westward Ho' is exceedingly pretty and plaintive: it is somewhat in the style of an old Irish air, with a tenderness running through it, which suits the words well. The music of 'The Green Flag' is vigorous and stirring.[132]

Gmür also set a poem by Fenian poet Ellen O'Leary (1831–89), 'To God and Ireland True' (Figure 10.2).

On an intensely debated aspect of Irish cultural nationalism, Annie Patterson wrote in 1901:

> The field is still open for the formation of a purely 'Irish school' of native composition, a school as distinctive and national as that which, the domain of opera, finds its highest exponent in Wagner, or which lends peculiar and individual charm to the works of Dvorak and Grieg [...] If anyone has the capabilities of giving encouragement to the rise of this 'Irish school', I cannot help thinking it is Herr Gmür, who having come among us from a land (Switzerland) thoroughly in sympathy with the Irish race, and having married an Irish wife and made Ireland his home and the centre of his life interests, has become – in the words of the old chroniclers – 'More Irish than the Irish themselves'.[133]

Patterson's vision of an 'Irish School' was based on a continental musical model, emanating from a core in Germany, Austria, Italy and France, where, as Martin Dowling puts it, 'the deep and sustained investments in the human and physical capital required of symphonic music and opera had created a resilient and magnetic field', following from which elites in peripheral countries concerned themselves with 'catching up or leaping forward in the competitive international field of state-sponsored classical music'.[134] All of this stood in stark contrast to Ireland, and particularly to the provincial environment in which Gmür and his musical contemporaries lived and worked. Their compositional outputs were largely functional. Masses and other sacred pieces were composed over the previous decades by many of the church organists, notably Fleming, de Prins, Gmür and Swertz. Songs and piano music constitute the other main category, generally light in nature, marketable, and often written to commemorate local events, or dedicated to local persons or institutions. Gmür's collaborative song compositions with Sullivan nonetheless were modest achievements in a nationalist vein. Seven of the eight published compositions by Swertz were songs, published in London and Liverpool during the 1890s.[135] Daniel Nunan, organist at St Augustine's Church, was a prolific composer of short pieces, many of them commemorating local events such as the 'Mathew Centennial March', 'The Cork Exhibition Waltzes', 'The Presentation Mazurka', the latter dedicated to the staff and students of Presentation College, Cork.[136] The *Mistletoe Waltzes* by Harriet Horgan were published by Duff & Hodgson, London, in 1848. In the field of opera, Gillespie's *Celestina*, Gmür's *Edelweiss* and McSwiney's *Amergen* were rare achievements, composed for local amateur production. J.C. Marks' oratorio *Gideon* was a doctoral piece. The dearth of interest in composition that did not rely on a text, whether sacred or secular, or on popular dance forms, to inspire or structure musical content is the most striking aspect of the output of these composers. Also, with the exception of Marks' *Gideon*, their works were largely aimed at amateur performance.

Instrumental compositions by William Ringrose Atkins were performed at concerts by the short-lived Cork Orchestral Union. It is perhaps ironic, but hardly surprising, that the concerts featuring new or recent orchestral works, both Irish and continental, were directed by a relatively wealthy amateur musician with time and financial resources to support these artistic endeavours. Widely travelled, outward-looking, actively interested in artistic ventures, Atkins possessed many of the attributes and privileges that would enable him to sponsor, perform or undertake the composition and performance of substantial new musical works. This type of artistic undertaking was one of many that attempted to fill what Martin Dowling refers to as the 'musical vacuum at the top of Irish society', an inability or unwillingness among the landed classes or their urban counterparts to sponsor the type of cultural institutions that were part of most European cities, and moreover, to support a national musical culture.[137]

A characteristic feature of Cork's musical life throughout the period of this study was the lack of a forum dedicated to musical creativity, musical theory or knowledge exchange, providing composers with opportunities for critical discussion and reflection. All of the societies that engaged the energies of professional musicians existed for the benefit of amateurs, effective and laudable though many of these were. Cork did not have a concert society until the twentieth century, unlike Belfast, where societies forged links with Manchester's Hallé Orchestra. Furthermore, the *modus operandi* of Cork's amateur societies was to restrict their activities to very specific ends. The crossover that might have resulted in the advocacy of substantial works of a nationalist character simply did not exist. The Literary and Scientific Society, for instance, took a keen interest in issues relating to cultural nationalism, whereas the choral and musical societies were dedicated solely to musical performance of large-scale concerted works.

Amateurs of the late nineteenth century, as practitioners, as audience or as patrons, fared well, however, shaping the city's musical infrastructures in significant and enduring ways. A number of formidable amateurs were catalysts for change, notably religious non-conformists such as Arthur Hill and Sir John Arnott, who were motivated by recognition of the social value of music. By the beginning of the twentieth century, Cork's variegated musical scene flourished under strong professional leadership, sponsored by the churches and charitable and educational institutions. Although many musical organisations remained rooted in distinct communities of religion and social class, a number of musical bodies transcended the city's traditional social and political divisions. Such aims had underpinned organisations such as the Cork Musical Society and the Cork School of Music.

The question of popular taste also needs to be considered. Atkins was the only musician to present concerts that did not feature brass bands, ballads, glees, or operatic selections. For all others, these genres were essential to audience retention. Programmes from the mid-nineteenth century onwards consistently provide evidence of efforts to balance elite and popular taste, or, in some cases, Protestant and Catholic musical preferences. Musical societies in general were short-lived; the majority survived for less than ten years, but through the activities of successive societies, performance traditions were sustained, and newer choral music was explored alongside canonic and popular works. Although a new era in popular entertainment began with the first screening of films at the South Mall Assembly Rooms in April 1896, and the opening of the Palace Theatre of Varieties in April 1897,[138] amateur musical societies remained the life-blood of the city's music into the twentieth century. The Cork Orchestral Union was revived in 1903 under the direction of Ferrucio Grossi, and Heinrich Tils founded the Cork Choral Union in 1901, continuing the traditions of amateur musical performance across a range of settings that were to remain firmly embedded in the city's cultural life.

Appendices

APPENDIX 1
CORK TEMPERANCE SOCIETY BANDS IN 1842

FEMALE SOCIETIES

Coal Quay Room No. 2
Pump Lane Room
Bandon Road Room
Coal Quay Room No. 2
Barrack Street Room
Henry Street Room

MALE SOCIETIES

Ballinamoght and Mayfield
South Main Street, Middle or No 2
Blarney Lane
Coach Street
Mallow Lane No 2
Clarence Street or St Simon's
Church Street
Fair Lane No 2
York Row
Mallow Lane No 1 or St Patrick's
Great-Britain St Lower, or No. 3
Globe Lane
Barrack Town
Fair Lane No. 1
Austen's Lane
Barrack Street
Denmark Street
Leitrim Street
George's Street
Capwell or Franciscans
Clarence Street No. 2
Dunbar Street
Cove Street, Upper or No. 1
Brown Street
Douglas
Clarence Street No. 1
Douglas Street
Blackpool
Coal Quay
Evergreen
Brickfields
Maypole Road
Hanover Street

Source: *Freeman's Journal*, 30 March 1842

APPENDIX 2
CORK ORCHESTRAL UNION MEMBERS 1880

Violin I
R.D. Howard, principal
B. Britton
T. Doherty
J. Gilbert
G. Murphy
C.A. Pridmore
D. Tidmarsh

Violin II
D. Seymour, principal
R. Doherty
T. Gmür
S. Harrington
H. Jack
C.H. Sawyer
R. Twomey

Violas
A. May, principal
T. Bradley
J. Brightwell
D. Leahy
W. Leahy
E.F. McGragh

Violoncellos
W. Harrington, principal
G. Brady
G. Ferguson
A. Jack
V. Sullivan

Contrabasses
E. Dunne, principal, T. Anderson, W. George, S. Smith

Flutes:	M.V. Cagney, J.M. Galgey
Piccolo:	R. Hansen
Oboes:	R. Yeabsley, W. Brien
Clarinets:	Enrico Bernini, J. Wynne
Bassoons:	G. Oliver, C. Lawrence
Cornets:	John Reidy, H. Dahl, J. Welstead
Horns:	A. McCelland, W. Creedon
Trombones:	S. Heywood, J. Slatter
Euphonium:	W. Murray
Bombardon:	P. Doolan
Timpani:	R. Twomey, Jr
Side drum & triangle:	J. Brightwell
Bass drum & cymbals:	I. Keely
Accompanists:	A. Hill, C.A. Pridmore, T. Waters
Librarian:	R. Lonergan
Conductor:	W. Ringrose Atkins

Source: Concert Programme Collection, Cork City Library

APPENDIX 3
CORK AMATEUR ORCHESTRAL SOCIETY – ORCHESTRA MEMBERS 1896

Conductor R.D. Howard

Violin I
P.F. Scanlan, principal
Miss Barke
Miss Humphreys
Miss J. O'Connor
Miss A. O'Donoghue
Miss E. Reynolds
Miss Sparling
J.S. Daly
J. Gilbert
J. Gleeson
T. Jordan

Violin II
S. Spiro, principal
Miss E. O'Connor
Miss Hennessy
Miss Jordan
J. Duff
D. Keating
J. Lawton
W.T. Kingsworth
H.E. Smith

Violas
Miss Fielding
Dr D.C. O'Connor
R. Twomey
W. Johnston

Violoncello
D.V. O'Sullivan
V. Sullivan
Miss E. O'Connor
P. Fielding
C.A. O'Neill

Basses:	D. Leahy, T. Noble
Flutes:	S. Byford, W. Jordan
Piccolo:	W. Trenwith
Oboe:	P. Morrison
Clarinets:	J. Wynne, R. Cross
Bassoons:	H.R. Bourke, C. Giles
Cornets:	A. Fowler, R. Sisk
Euphonium:	Fred Lenten
Horns:	R.H. O'Sullivan, R. Jenkins
Trombones:	William Sims, W. Barrett
Timpani:	H. Lee
Cymbals:	P. McCarthy
Pianoforte:	Miss Scanlan

Source: *Cork Examiner*, 30 November 1896

Endnotes

CHAPTER 1

1. Joseph Boruwlaski, *The Memoirs of Count Boruwlaski* (Durham: Humble, 1820), p. 242.

2. Mark McCarthy, 'The Forging of an Atlantic Port City: socio-economic and physical transformations in Cork, 1660–1700', *Urban History*, vol. 28, no. 1, 2001, pp. 25–45.

3. Ibid., p. 25.

4. John B. O'Brien, 'Population, Politics and Society in Cork, 1780–1900', in Patrick O'Flanagan and Cornelius G. Buttimer (eds), *Cork: history and society* (Dublin: Geography Publications, 1993), pp. 702–3. A detailed account of the economic development of Cork city is given in David Dickson, *Old World Colony: Cork and south Munster, 1630–1830* (Cork: Cork University Press, 2005).

5. Dickson, 'Huguenots in the urban economy of eighteenth-century Dublin and Cork', in C.E.J. Caldicott, H. Gough and J.P. Pittion (eds), *The Huguenots and Ireland: Anatomy of an Emigration* (Dublin: Glendale Press, 1987), p. 321.

6. *Walker's Hibernian Magazine*, January 1786, p. 597.

7. Thomas Campbell, *A Philosophical Survey of the South of Ireland in a series of letters to John Watkinson M.D.* (London: W.S. Strahan and T. Cadwell, 1777), p. 220.

8. Mark McCarthy, 'Turning a World Upside Down: the metamorphosis of property, settlement and society in the city of Cork during the 1640s and 1650s', *Irish Geography*, vol. 33, no. 1, 2000, pp. 37–55; T.C. Barnard, 'The Political, Material and Mental Culture of the Cork Settlers, *c.* 1650–1700', in O'Flanagan and Buttimer (eds), *Cork: history and society*.

9. W.J. Smyth, 'Territorial, Social and Settlement Hierarchies in Seventeenth-Century Kilkenny', in W. Nolan and K. Whelan (eds), *Kilkenny: history and society* (Dublin: Geography Publications, 1990, pp. 150–1).

10. Richard Caulfield (ed.), *The Council Book of the Corporation of the City of Cork from 1609 to 1643, and from 1690 to 1800* (Guildford: J. Billing, 1876), p. 311.

11. Maureen Wall, 'The Rise of a Catholic Middle Class in Eighteenth-Century Ireland', *Irish Historical Studies*, vol. 11, no. 42, 1958, pp. 96–8; Dickson, *Old World Colony*, pp. 166–9.

12. Mrs [Anne] Mathews, *Memoirs of Charles Mathews, Comedian*, 4 vols (London: Bentley, 1839), vol. 1, p. 109. See, for example, Cornelius G. Buttimer, 'A Paul Street Poem, *c.* 1760', *JCHAS*, vol. 93, 1988. pp. 126–37, which examines a Gaelic poem in praise of a Paul Street tailor who crafted a new bag for the poet's pipes.

13. Ian d'Alton, *Protestant Society and Politics in Cork, 1812–1844* (Cork: Cork University Press, 1980), pp. 90–1; Maura Murphy, 'Municipal Reform and the Repeal Movement in Cork, 1833–1844', *JCHAS*, vol. 81, 1976, pp. 1–18; Neil Cronin, *The Medical Profession and the Exercise of Power in Nineteenth-Century Cork* (Dublin: Four Courts Press, 2014), pp. 50–2; Peter J. Jupp and Stephen A. Royle, 'The Social Geography of Cork City Elections, 1801–30', *Irish Historical Studies*, vol. 29, no. 113, 1994, p. 15.

14. John B. O'Brien, 'Population, Politics and Society in Cork, 1780–1900', p. 710.

15. Dickson, *Old World Colony*, p. 413.

16. Peter Borsay, *The English Urban Renaissance: culture and society in the provincial town, 1660–1770* (Oxford: Clarendon, 1991), p. 131.

17. *Munster Journal*, 15 May 1749.

18. Ibid., 18 March 1750/1.

19. James O'Toole, rev. Sara Smyth, *NEWSPLAN – Report of the Newsplan Project in Ireland* (London: British Library and Dublin: National Library of Ireland, 1998); Máire Kennedy, 'William Flyn (1740–1811) and the Readers of Munster in the Second Half of the Eighteenth Century', in John Hinks, Catherine Armstrong and Matthew Day (eds), *Periodicals and Publishers: the newspaper and journal trade, 1750–1914* (London: Oak Knoll Press and the British Library, 2009).

20. David A. Fleming, 'Diversions of the People: sociability among the orders of early eighteenth-century Ireland', *Eighteenth Century Ireland/Iris an Dá Chultúr*, vol. 17, 2002, pp. 99–111.

21. J.H. Plumb, *The Commercialisation of Leisure in Eighteenth-Century England* (Reading: University of Reading, 1973) provides a seminal discussion on this topic. The concepts put forward here are further developed in Borsay, *The English Urban Renaissance*.

22. Hugh Cunningham, *Leisure in the Industrial Revolution, c. 1780–c. 1880* (London: Croom Helm, 1980), p. 16.

23. Dickson, *Old World Colony*, p. 421.

24. Thomas Crofton Croker, *Researches in the South of Ireland, 1812–1822* (1824) (Dublin: Irish Academic Press, 1981).

25. James Kelly and Martyn Powell (eds), 'Introduction', in *Clubs and Societies in Eighteenth-Century Ireland* (Dublin: Four Courts Press, 2010).

26. Petri Mirala, 'Masonic Sociability and Its Limitations: the case of Ireland', in Kelly and Powell (eds), *Clubs and Societies in Eighteenth-Century Ireland*, p. 316.

27. 'Provincial Grand Lodge of Munster/Hibernian Lodge, No 95, Cork' http://www.munsterfreemason.com/craft-lodges/hibernian-lodge-no-95-cork/ accessed 16 October 2016.

28. Mirala, 'Masonic Sociability', p. 321.

29. Ibid., p. 325.

30. A masonic festival dinner held at the Imperial Hotel in August 1843 featured the singing of glees, duets and trios by Brothers Moeran, Roche, Keays and McCarthy. *CE*, 23 August 1843. An account of a ceremony for the Masonic Installation of Colonel Chatterton K.H. as Provincial Grand Master of Munster, held in Cork in 1849, identifies William Gillespie as Provincial Grand Organist, and refers to music performed by Brothers A.D. Roche, Wheeler and McCarthy. *CE*, 29 June 1849.

31. David A. Fleming, 'Clubs and Societies in Eighteenth-Century Munster', in Kelly and Powell (eds), *Clubs and Societies in Eighteenth-Century Ireland*, pp. 436–7; Jacqueline Hill, 'National Festivals, the State, and "Protestant Ascendancy" in Ireland, 1790–1829', *Irish Historical Studies*, vol. 24, no. 93, 1984, p. 32.

32. Dickson, *Old World Colony*, p. 424.

33. Notices in *CEP*, cited in Audrey Robinson, 'Anglo-Irish Music in Cork, 1750–1800', MA thesis (St Patrick's College, Maynooth, 1996), pp. 71–3.

34. *HC*, 14–17 August 1775.

35. Trevor Herbert and Helen Barlow, *Music and the British Military in the Long Nineteenth Century* (New York: Oxford University Press, 2013), pp. 44–5.

36. Ibid., p. 52.

37. *HC*, 14 July 1792.

38. Anthony Marmion, *The Ancient and Modern History of the Maritime Ports of Ireland*, 3rd edition (London: Cox, 1858), p. 542; Samuel Lewis, *Lewis' Cork: A Topographical Dictionary of the Parishes, Towns and Villages of Cork City and County*. Introduction by Tim Cadogan (1837, reprinted Cork: Collins, 1998), p. 156; Francis H. Tuckey, *County and City of Cork Remembrancer* (Cork: Osborne Savage, 1837), p. 222.

39. Dickson, *Old World Colony*, p. 425.

40. Herbert and Barlow, *Music and the British Military*, p. 249.

41. Thomas Bartlett, *Ireland: a history* (Cambridge University Press, 2010), pp. 179–81; C.B. Gibson, *A History of the City and County of Cork*, 2 vols (London: Newby, 1861), vol. 2, pp. 219–30; Tuckey, *Remembrancer*, p. 180; John Fitzgerald, *The Cork Remembrancer* (Cork: J. Sullivan, 1783), pp. 203–4, p. 234.

42. Fitzgerald, *The Cork Remembrancer*, p. 237.

43. Thomas Bartlett, *Ireland*, pp. 179–81, 188–90; Dickson, *Old World Colony*, p. 445; James Kelly, 'Volunteers', in W.J. McCormack (ed.), *The Blackwell Companion to Modern Irish Culture* (Oxford: Blackwell, 1999), pp. 595–6.

44. Barra Boydell, 'The United Irishmen, Music, Harps, and National Identity', *Eighteenth-Century Ireland*, vol. 13, 1998, p. 48.

45. Síle Ní Chinnéide, 'A New View of Cork in 1790', *JCHAS*, vol. 78, 1973, p. 5.

46. 'Townshend's Comment on Musgrave's Memoirs', *The Critical Review, or Annals of Literature*, vol. 36, October 1802 (London: S. Hamilton, 1802), pp. 184–6.

47. *CS*, 16 March 1840.

48. *CEP*, 12 January 1758, 4 November 1762.

49. Ibid., 30 December 1762. This is an early reference to Dublin guitar and keyboard instrument maker William Gibson, listed in *Wilson's Dublin Directory* in 1770.

50. Ibid., 18 August 1768.

51. Ibid.,13 June 1768.

52. Borsay, *The English Urban Renaissance*, p. 138; J.H. Plumb, 'The New World of Children in Eighteenth-Century England', *Past and Present*, vol. 67, no. 1, 1975, pp. 64–95; P.J Miller, 'Women's Education, "Self-Improvement" and Social Mobility: a late eighteenth-century debate', *British Journal of Educational Studies*, vol. 20, no. 3, 1972, pp. 302–14.

53. *CJ*, 25–28 January 1754.

54. Tuckey, *Remembrancer*, pp. civ–cv.

55. *CJ*, 12 January 1756.

56. *CMC*, 1 June 1810.

57. Ibid., 17 June 1816.

58. Robert Day, 'Eighteenth Century Trade Circulars and Invoices of Cork Traders', *JCHAS*, vol. 7, 1901, pp. 166–71. *CG*, 6 April 1793.

59. *CJ*, 24 April 1769.

60. *HC*, 21 December 1769.

61. Virginia Pleasants, 'The Early Piano in Britain (*c.* 1760–1800)', *Early Music*, vol. 13, no. 1, 1985, p. 40.

62. *HC*, 27–30 December 1779.

63. Ibid., 11 September 1783.

64. Ibid., 16 January 1792.

65. *CG*, 4 July 1795.

66. *HC*, 4 June 1795; *NCEP*, 29 March 1796, 26 May 1796.

67. *The Rover*, no. 25, 5 March 1796, p. 100.

68. *HC*, 24 February 1791.

69. *CG*, 8 June 1793.

70. John Nixon's *The New Cork Directory for the Year 1795* (Cork: Haly, 1795).

71. Boydell, 'The United Irishmen, pp. 44–51.

72. Mary Louise O'Donnell, 'A Driving Image of Revolution: the Irish harp and its utopian space in the eighteenth century', *Utopian Studies*, vol. 21, no. 2, 2010, p. 254; Clare O'Halloran, 'Harping on the Past: translating antiquarian learning into popular culture in early nineteenth-century Ireland', in Melissa Calaresu, Filippo de Vivo and Joan-Pau Rubiés (eds), *Exploring Cultural History: essays in honour of Peter Burke* (Farnham: Ashgate, 2010).

73. Jean Louis de Lolme, *The British Empire in Europe: part the first, containing an account of the connection between the kingdoms of England and Ireland* (London, 1787), p. 131, quoted in Mary Louise O'Donnell, *Ireland's Harp*: *The shaping of Irish identity c.* 1770–1800 (Dublin: UCD Press, 2014), p.17.

CHAPTER 2

1. Charles Smith, *The Ancient and Present State of the County and City of Cork*, 2 vols (Dublin: Wilson 1774), vol. 2, p. 399.

2. *The Present State of the Charitable Infirmary of Corke for the Year 1750* (Cork: G. Harrison, 1750), pp. 3–4; Laurence M. Geary, *Medicine and Charity in Ireland, 1718–1851* (Dublin: University College Dublin Press, 2004), pp. 22–3; John Nixon, *The New Cork Directory for the Year 1795*: … to which is Added, A Correct List of the Freemen at Large (Cork: Haly, 1795).

3. James Kelly, 'Charitable Societies: their genesis and development, 1720–1800', in James Kelly and Martyn J. Powell (eds), *Clubs and Societies in Eighteenth-Century Ireland*, pp. 92–3. See also Denis Arnold, 'Charity Music in Eighteenth-Century Dublin', *Galpin Society Journal*, vol. 21, 1968, pp. 162–74.

4. Tim Carter, 'The Sound of Silence: models for an urban musicology', *Urban History*, vol. 29, no. 1, 2002, p. 14. Detailed accounts of Dublin's musical life during the eighteenth century are given in Brian Boydell, *A Dublin Musical Calendar, 1700–1760* (Dublin: Irish Academic Press, 1988), and *Rotunda Music in Eighteenth-Century Dublin* (Dublin: Irish Academic Press, 1992). Musical culture in eighteenth-century London is explored in Simon McVeigh's *Concert Life in London from Mozart to Haydn* (Cambridge: Cambridge University Press, 1993) and Ian Taylor's *Music in London and the Myth of Decline: from Haydn to the philharmonic* (Cambridge: Cambridge University Press, 2010).

5. B.L. Add MS 47026, cited in Brian Boydell, 'Music, 1700–1850', in T.W. Moody and W.E. Vaughan (eds), *New History of Ireland IV: eighteenth century Ireland, 1691–1800* (Oxford: Clarendon, 1986), p. 614. Sir John Perceval, 1st Earl of Egmont (1683–1748), was elected to the Irish House of Commons for County Cork in 1703.

6. The earliest accounts of concert activity in provincial British cities and towns were associated with amateur musical societies. See Michael Tilmouth, 'The Beginnings of Provincial Concert Life in England', in Christopher Hogwood and Richard Luckett (eds), *Music in England: essays in memory of Charles Cudworth* (Cambridge: Cambridge University Press, 1983), pp. 1–17. See also Elizabeth Chevill, 'Clergy, Music Societies and the Development of a Musical Tradition: a study of music societies in Hereford, 1690–1760', in Susan Wollenberg and Simon McVeigh (eds), *Concert Life in Eighteenth-Century Britain* (Aldershot: Ashgate, 2004), p. 35. See also Peter Borsay, *The English Urban Renaissance: culture and society in the provincial town, 1660–1770* (Oxford: Clarendon, 1991), pp. 332–5. Brian Boydell lists eighteen musical societies that were active in Dublin during the years 1700–60. See Boydell, *A Dublin Musical Calendar*, pp. 267–9.

7. W.H. Grattan Flood, 'Notes and Queries: Cork musical societies in 1733', *JCHAS*, vol. 22, 1916, p. 193. The tradition of holding concerts on St Cecilia's Day dates back to at least 1683 in London, and, by the early eighteenth century, musical societies in other English cities had adopted the tradition. Annual concerts on St Cecilia's Day were held by a musical society in Dublin from the 1720s. William Henry Husk, *An Account of the Musical Celebrations on St Cecilia's Day in the Sixteenth, Seventeenth and Eighteenth Centuries, to which is Appended a Collection of Odes on St Cecilia's Day* (London: Bell & Daldy, 1857), pp. 106–9.

8. W.H. Grattan Flood, 'Notes and Queries: early Cork musical societies', *JCHAS*, vol. 26, 1920, p. 40.

9. William Rufus Chetwood, *A Tour through Ireland, in several Entertaining Letters, wherein the Present State of that Kingdom is consider'd and the most Noted Cities, Towns, Seats, Rivers, Buildings, &c. are Described ... to Which is Prefix'd a Description of the Road from London to Holy-Head. By Two English Gentlemen*. 2nd edn (Dublin, 1748), p. 90

10. W.H. Grattan Flood, 'Notes and Queries: Handel's "Messiah" in Cork', *JCHAS*, vol. 26, 1920, p. 40.

11. William Smith was listed as one of the trustees of the North Charitable Infirmary in 1755. *CJ*, 10 March 1755.

12. *Faulkner's Dublin Journal*, 22–26 November 1744. Brian Boydell, 'Music, 1700–1850', in Moody and Vaughan (eds), *A New History of Ireland*, p. 615.

13. Taylor, *Music in London and the Myth of Decline*, pp. 23–5.

14. Cyril Ehrlich, *The Music Profession in Britain since the Eighteenth Century: a social history* (Oxford: Clarendon, 1985), p. 3

15. See Boydell, *A Dublin Musical Calendar*, and *Rotunda Concerts in Eighteenth-Century Dublin*, and T.J. Walsh, *Opera in Dublin, 1705–97: the social scene* (Dublin: Allen Figgis, 1973).

16. Boydell, *A Dublin Musical Calendar* pp. 18–19.

17. Seán Donnelly, 'The Famousest Man in the World for the Irish Harp', *Dublin Historical Record*, vol. 57, no. 1, 2004, pp. 38–49.

18. The author has compiled a comprehensive list of public concerts performed in Cork from 1754 to 1840. See Susan O'Regan, 'Public Concerts in the Musical Life of Cork, 1754–1840', 2 vols. Unpublished PhD dissertation (Cork Institute of Technology, 2008).

19. Richard Caulfield (ed.), *The Council Book of the Corporation of the City of Cork from 1609 to 1643, and from 1690 to 1800* (Guildford: J. Billing, 1876), p. 392.

20. Some examples are *CJ*, 26 September 1857, *CEP*, 4 February 1760, *CEP*, 21 September 1767.

21. *Munster Journal*, 18 February 1750/1.

22. See Barra Boydell,'"Whatever has a foreign tone/We like much better than our own": Irish music and Anglo-Irish identity in the eighteenth century', in Mark Fitzgerald and John O'Flynn (eds), *Music and Identity in Ireland and Beyond* (Farnham: Ashgate, 2014), pp. 25–8.

23. Frank Llewelyn Harrison, 'Music, Poetry and Polity in the Age of Swift', *Eighteenth Century Ireland/Iris an Dá Chultúr*, vol. 1, 1986, pp. 38–9.

24. A letter written in 1750 by Mrs Mary Delany referred to Kenmare's horn players. See Angélique Day (ed.), *Letters from Georgian Ireland: the correspondence of Mary Delany, 1731–1768* (Belfast: The Friar's Bush Press, 1991), p. 46.

25. *CJ*, 16 December 1754. Palma may be identified as the singer Signor Bernardo Palma, who directed the Gentleman's Morning Concert in Fishamble Street, Dublin in 1757. See Boydell, *A Dublin Musical Calendar*, p. 317. Another singer, Felippe Palma, performed in the Smock Alley Theatre in 1758–9. See Philip H. Highfill, Kalman A. Burnim and Edward A. Langhans (eds), *A Biographical Dictionary of Actors, Actresses, Musicians, Dancers, Managers and Other Stage Personnel in London, 1660–1800*, 16 vols (Carbondale and Edwardsville: Southern Illinois University Press, 1973–93), vol. 2, p. 155.

26. By April 1755, Russwurm had not returned to his employment in Killarney and a notice appeared in the *Corke Journal* announcing Lord Kenmare's intention to sue him for breach of contract. *CJ*, 3 April 1755.

27. A theatre performance of Richard Steele's *The Conscious Lovers* by a touring Dublin company in 1754 had featured a solo on the German flute by Mr Murphy. *CJ*, 22 August 1754. In 1759, Murphy 'died at his lodgings near South Gate, Cork [...] an eminent performer on the German Flute', *Faulkner's Dublin Journal*, 10 July 1759, cited in Boydell, *Calendar*, p. 285.

28. *CJ*, 3 February 1755, 7 April 1755.

29. *CJ*, 7 April 1755. Francis Woder was listed as fourth state musician in 1740. See list transcribed by W.J. Lawrence from the Dublin Public Records Office, quoted in John C. Greene and Gladys L.H. Clark, *The Dublin Stage 1720–1745: a calendar of plays, entertainments, and afterpieces* (Bethlehem, London and Toronto: Lehigh University Press, 1993), p. 12.

30. *CEP*, 24 March 1760. A similarly worded announcement for Mahony's concert appeared in *Faulkner's Dublin Journal* in 1758. Boydell, *Calendar*, p. 236.

31. *CJ*, 24 March 1760.

32. T.J. Walsh, *Opera in Dublin 1705–1797*, p. 290.

33. *CJ*, 13 May, 27 May 1762.

34. Thomas Lawrence, *The History of the Guitar in Ireland, 1760–1866*, 2 vols. Unpublished PhD dissertation (University College Dublin, 1999), vol. 1, p. 13.

35. David J. Rhodes, 'Passerini Family', *EMIR*, vol. 2, p. 823.

36. *CJ*, 1 July 1762.

37. They had attempted a similar venture in Bath in 1758. See Jenny Burchell, *Polite or Commercial Concerts? Concert management and orchestral repertoire in Edinburgh, Bath, Oxford, Manchester, and Newcastle, 1730–1799* (New York: Garland, 1996), p. 149.

38. *CJ*, 7 October 1762.

39. *CEP*, 3 October 1763.

40. *CJ*, 26 September 1757.

41. Boydell, *Calendar*, p. 271; Boydell, *Rotunda Music*, p. 37.

42. *CEP*, 22 April 1773.

43. Highfill et al., *A Biographical Dictionary*, vol. 2, p. 235. The vox humana was a type of tenor oboe. See Boydell, *Rotunda Music*, p. 98.

44. *The Present State of the Charitable Infirmary of Corke for the Year 1750* (Cork: G. Harrison, 1750), pp. 3–4.

45. Ibid., p. 6.

46. William Thomas Parke, *Musical Memoirs; comprising an Account of the General State of Music in England, from the First Commemoration of Handel, in the Year 1784, to the Year 1830*, 2 vols (London: Colburn & Bentley, 1830), vol. 1, p. 234.

47. A detailed account of Tenducci's marriage and subsequent trial is the subject of Helen Berry's *The Castrato and His Wife* (Oxford: Oxford University Press, 2011).

48. *CEP*, 28 May 1767.

49. Dorothea's account of the events was published in Dorothea Tenducci, *A True and Genuine Narrative of Mr and Mrs Tenducci. In a Letter to a Friend at Bath. Giving a Full Account. From Their Marriage to the Present Time* (London: Pridden, 1768).

50. Berry, *The Castrato and His Wife*, pp. 126–7.

51. *CEP*, 28 May 1767.

52. Todd Gilman, *The Theatre Career of Thomas Arne* (Lanham: Rowman & Littlefield, 2013), p. 416

53. *CEP*, 28 May 1767.

54. Ibid., 11 June 1767.

55. *CJ*, 24–27 August 1767.

56. *CEP*, 7 September 1767.

57. Ibid., 21 September 1767. A ridotto was a type of entertainment fashionable during the eighteenth century, consisting of music and dancing, often in masquerade, held in Dublin since the 1730s. Greene and Clark, *The Dublin Stage*, p. 70.

58. *CEP*, 9 July 1770, 29 April 1771, 31 May 1773.

59. John Windele, *Historical and Descriptive Notices of the City of Cork and Its Vicinity* (Cork: Bolster, 1846), p. 125. See, for example, *CEP*, 2 June 1768.

60. *CEP*, 2 November 1769.

61. Francis H. Tuckey, *The County and City of Cork Remembrancer or Annals of the County and City of Cork* (Cork: Osborne Savage, 1837), p. ci.

62. Rev. C.B. Gibson, *The History of the County and City of Cork*, 2 vols (London, 1861; reprinted, Cork: Fencor, 1974), vol. 2, p. 215.

63. Máire Kennedy, 'William Flyn (1740–1811) and the Readers of Munster in the Second Half of the Eighteenth Century', pp. 83–4.

64. *HC*, 29 November 1769.

65. Kennedy, 'William Flyn', pp. 84–5.

66. Gibson, *The History of the County and City of Cork*, p. 250; F.H. Tuckey, *Remembrancer of the County and City of Cork*, p. 167.

67. Kennedy, 'William Flyn', p. 83.

68. *HC*, 5–8 June 1775.

69. Ibid., 10–14 August 1780; Evelyn Bolster, *A History of the Diocese of Cork from the Penal Era to the Famine* (Cork: Tower, 1989), p. 144.

70. *CEP*, 19 September, 10 November, 29 November, 12 December 1768.

71. Sean Donnelly, 'A German Dulcimer Player in Eighteenth-Century Dublin', *Dublin Historical Record*, vol. 53, no. 1, 2000, p. 77.

72. *CEP*, 1 July 1773.

73. Ibid., 9 July 1770.

74. Ibid., 4 June 1770.

75. William Hart, 'Rachael Baptist', in James Maguire and James Quinn (eds), *Dictionary of Irish Biography: from the earliest times to the year 2002*, 9 vols (Cambridge: Cambridge University Press, 2002), vol. 1, pp. 462–3.

76. *CEP*, 8 May 1777.

77. See McVeigh, *Concert Life in London from Mozart to Haydn*, p. 91.

78. *CJ*, 22–24 December 1770; Borghese's opera *The Fair Venetian* was produced in Dublin in 1776. See Kenneth Langevin, 'Antonio Borghese', *NGrove2,* vol. 3, p. 898. Borghese was listed as a composer of a song performed at the Pantheon concerts in London in 1790. See Simon McVeigh, 'The Professional Concert and Rival Subscription Series in London, 1783–1793', *RMA Research Chronicle*, vol. 22, 1989, p. 126.

79. Virginia Pleasants, 'The Early Piano in Britain (*c.*1760–1800)', *Early Music*, vol. 13, no. 1, 1985, p. 40.

80. *CJ*, 23–25 March 1771.

81. David J. Rhodes, 'Arne Family', *EMIR*, vol. 1, pp. 31–3; McVeigh, *Concert Life in London from Mozart to Haydn*, p. 110.

82. *HC*, 1 October 1770; W.H. Grattan Flood, 'Michael Arne in Cork in 1770', *Musical Times and Singing Class Circular*, vol. 44, no. 723, 1903, p. 320.

83. *HC*, 11–15 September 1777. The musical establishment at Cloyne was actively revitalised by Bishop Charles Agar during the 1770s. See Triona O'Hanlon, 'Cloyne Cathedral', *EMIR*, vol. 1, p. 210.

84. Harrison, 'Music, Poetry and Polity in the Age of Swift', p. 39.

85. *HC*, 22–26 August 1776.

86. *HC*, 15–18 November 1779.

87. *CEP*, 4 November 1782.

88. *HC*, 26 December 1791; *CEP*, 2 January 1792.

89. 3 vols (Cork: William Flyn, 1782). Vol. 1 is held at the Royal Irish Academy. *The Vocal Magazine of Compleat British Songster Consisting of such English, Scotch and Irish Songs, Catches, Glees, Cantatas, Airs, Ballads, as are Deemed Most Worthy of Being Transmitted to Posterity* (London: Harrison, 1781).

90. *HC*, 24–27 March 1777.

91. Ibid., 6–9 July 1778.

92. Published by Bremner, Preston and Kerpen from 1762 onwards.

93. Ibid., 19 August 1765. *CEP*, 4 September 1768. She had given six performances at the Rotunda, Dublin, in 1777. Boydell, *Rotunda Music*, p. 55; Jennifer O'Connor, 'Anne Catley', *EMIR*, vol. 1, p. 178.

94. William Weber, 'Mass Culture and European Musical Taste, 1770–1870', *International Review of the Aesthetics and Sociology of Music*, vol. 25, nos 1–2, 1994, pp. 178–9.

95. *HC*, 14–18 October 1779.

96. Ibid., 8, 11, 18 November 1773.

97. Samuel Briggs, *The Book of the Varian Family, with Some Speculation as to their Origin, etc.* (Cleveland, OH: Printed by T.C. Schenk, 1881), p. 16.

98. *HC*, 3 May 1790.

99. *NCEP*, 27 May 1793.

100. John Nixon, *The New Cork Directory for the Year 1795; Holden's Triennial Directory*, fourth edition for 1805, 1806, 1807, second volume (London: W. Glendinning, 1805). John Buckley, musician, is listed as having married Catherine Browne at St Fin Barre's Cathedral on 21 July 1790.

101. *HC*, 8 February 1787, 5 March 1781.

102. Deborah Rohr, *The Careers of British Musicians 1750–1850: a profession of artisans* (Cambridge: Cambridge University Press, 2001), p. 131.

103. *HC*, 8–11 May 1780.

104. Ibid., 30 March 1786.

105. Ibid., 7 November 1782.

106. *CEP*, 17 June 1784.

107. *HC*, 11 September 1783.

108. John C. Greene, *Theatre in Belfast* 1736–1800, (Bethlehem: Lehigh University Press, 2000), p. 200; Highfill et al., vol. 8, pp. 134–5; Boydell, *Rotunda Music*, p. 218; *HC*, 22 September 1783.

109. *HC*, 22 September 1783.

110. Ibid., 12 August, 7 October 1782. German bandmaster Herr Rakeman had performed on the clarinet at Smock Alley Theatre in 1775. See John C. Green, *Theatre in Dublin, 1745–1820: a calendar of performances. Searchable index – Musicians/Instruments/Performnce Dates/Venues, http://digital.lib.lehigh.edu/lupress/dublintheatre/MusicianInstrumentSDATVenue.pdf*, accessed 22 August 2016.

111. *HC*, 22 September 1783.

112. Boydell, *Rotunda Music*, p. 218.

113. *HC*, 23 September 1784.

114. *CEP*, 24 January 1785.

115. *HC*, 18 April 1785.

116. Ibid., 5 May 1785.

117. *CEP*, 19 October 1786; Rachel Talbot, 'Charles Weichsel', *EMIR*, vol. 2, pp. 1048–9.

118. Boydell, *Rotunda Music*, p. 133. Simon McVeigh states that it had been available as a published score in London from January 1784: McVeigh, *Concert Life*, p. 96.

119. *HC*, 29 March, 14 May 1787; Boydell, *Rotunda Music*, p. 140.

120. Obituary: 'Mr Andrew Ashe', in *The Gentleman's Magazine*, vol. 10, August 1838, pp. 216–18; Peter Downey, 'Andrew Ashe', *EMIR*, vol. 1, p. 38.

121. *HC*, 11 August 1788; Boydell, *Rotunda Music*, p. 116.

122. *HC*, 18 September 1788, 22 November 1790.

123. *CEP*, 17 July 1780; Richard Woodward, *Cathedral Music* (London: Welcker, 1771), included settings of *Te Deum*, *Jubilate*, and music for a complete service. See Barra Boydell, 'Richard Woodward [the Younger]', *EMIR*, vol. 2, p. 1073.

124. A.P.W. Malcolmson, *Archbishop Charles Agar: churchmanship and politics in Ireland, 1760–1810* (Dublin: Four Courts Press, 2002), pp. 319–20, quoted in Barra Boydell, 'Manuscript Sources from Irish Cathedrals: the Cashel cathedral choir-books, a preliminary report', *Brio*, vol. 39, no. 2, 2002, p. 24.

125. *HC*, 16 December 1784. Oratorio was revived in Dublin in 1786 with a performance modelled on the London Handel 'Commemoration' concerts, engaging the choirs of the Dublin cathedrals, and was continued and expanded over the following three years. Derek Collins, 'Concert Life in Dublin in the Age of Revolution', unpublished PhD dissertation (Queen's University Belfast, 2001), p. 180.

126. *HC*, 17 January 1788.

127. Ibid., 10 March 1788.

128. *CEP*, 27 March 1788.

129. *HC*, 5 May 1788.

130. Ibid., 24 April 1788.

131. Ibid., 5 May 1788.

132. *CEP*, 7 July 1788, reprinted in the *Dublin Chronicle* 17 July 1788.

133. *CEP*, 12 February 1789; *HC*, *2* April 1789.

134. *CEP*, 9 April 1789.

135. Ibid., 9 August 1790.

136. Ibid., 8 July 1790.

137. This topic is discussed in detail in William Weber's *The Rise of Musical Classics in Eighteenth-Century England: a study in canon, ritual and ideology* (Oxford: Clarendon, 1996).

138. Boydell, *Rotunda Music*, p. 144. Gautherot had performed a concerto by Viotti at the Professional Concert series in London in February 1789, which was billed as 'her first appearance in England'. See Simon McVeigh, 'The Professional Concert and Rival Subscription Series in London, 1783–1793', *RMA Research Chronicle*, vol. 22, 1989, pp. 75, 97.

139. *CG*, 28 September 1791.

140. Ibid., 1 October 1791.

141. Roger Cotte writes of Louis Vogel that 'Legend has it that he was the son of the Count of Poligny, a nobleman in the service of Louis XVI', and that he was flautist in the orchestra of the Theatre des Variétés until 1798. Roger Cotte, 'Louis Vogel', *NGrove2*, vol. 26, p. 860.

142. *CG*, 8 June 1793.

143. *CEP*, 24 June 1793.

144. *CG*, 8 June 1793.

145. A concert by violinist Louisa Gautherot in 1791 was also to include James Roche performing a piano concerto. However, the concert was postponed and the alternative programme that was eventually presented featured Roche performing a harpsichord lesson by Clementi. *CG*, 28 September 1791.

146. *CG*, 23 November 1793.

147. Simon Fleming, *A Century of Music Production in Durham City, 1711–1811: a documentary study* (PhD Dissertation, University of Durham), pp. 103–4. http://etheses.dur.ac.uk/49, accessed 30 August 2016.

148. Joseph Boruwlaski, *The Memoirs of Count Boruwlaski* (Durham: Humble, 1820), pp. 242–7.

149. Ibid., p. 246.

150. Ibid., p. 247.

151. Petri Mirala, 'Masonic Sociability and Its Limitations', p. 321, n. 36.

152. A similar pattern was evident in Belfast, where no concerts were recorded in 1794, although four concerts took place in 1795. See Roy Johnston, *Bunting's Messiah* (Belfast: The Belfast Natural History and Philosophical Society, 2003), p. 51.

153. *HC*, 29 August 1796.

154. Ibid., 12 September 1796.

155. Parke, *Musical Memoirs*, vol. 1, p. 234.

156. Derek Collins, 'Concert Life in Dublin', p. 144.

157. *HC*, 3 October 1796, 19 September 1796.

158. She was identified in some sources as Maria Poole. An 'aria for Miss Poole', dated 1791–95, now lost or unidentified, is listed among Haydn's works in James Webster and George Feder (eds), *The New Grove Haydn* (London: Macmillan, 2002), p. 87. Miss Poole had sung at Salomon's concert in 1792, and the Professional Concert Series at Hanover Square in 1793.

159. *CEP*, 20 October 1796.

160. *HC*, 14 September 1797. Collins, *Chronology* lists no Dublin concerts after May of that year.

161. Clark, 143 refers to a general decline in theatre attendance in Ireland in 1798–9.

162. *CA*, 28 March 1799.

163. William Weber, *Music and the Middle Class: the social structure of concert life in London, Paris and Vienna between 1830 and 1848*, 2nd edition (Aldershot: Ashgate, 2004), p. 3.

164. Rohr, *The Careers of British Musicians*, p. 101.

CHAPTER 3

1. Thomas Crofton Croker, MS 'Recollections of Cork' (1833) IRL-Dtc MS 1206, p. 36

2. Standard works on the subject are Abe Acheson, *A History of the Church of Ireland, 1691–2001*, 2nd edition (Dublin: Columba, 2002); Toby Bernard, 'Church of Ireland, 1660–1760', in W.J. McCormack (ed.), *The Blackwell Companion to Modern Irish Culture* (Oxford: Blackwell 1999), pp. 112–13. Music in the Church of Ireland is the subject of W.H. Grindle's *Irish Cathedral Music: a history of music at the cathedrals of the Church of Ireland* (Belfast: The Institute of Irish Studies, Queen's University Belfast, 1989), and Michael Thompson, 'Church of Ireland', *EMIR*, vol. 1, pp. 195–7.

3. Transcribed sources are William Maziere Brady, *Clerical and Parochial Records of Cork, Cloyne, and Ross*, 3 vols (Dublin: Thom 1863), and Richard Caulfield, *Annals of St Fin Barre's Cathedral, Cork* (Cork: Purcell, 1871). Henry J. Keogh, 'Musical Perspectives at St Fin Barre's', *JCHAS*, vol. 81, 1966, pp. 129–37.

4. Brady, *Clerical and Parochial Records*, vol. 1, pp. 252–75, provides details of appointees from 1591 until 1842, the year in which appointments were suspended.

5. Henry Cotton, *Fasti Ecclesiae Hibernicae*, 6 vols (Dublin: Hodges & Smith, 1848–78), vol. 1, pp. 280–1.

6. Caulfield, *Annals of St Fin Barre's*, p. 22.

7. Ibid., pp. 22–3.

8. Brady, *Clerical and Parochial Records*, vol. 1, pp. 257–8; Caulfield, *Annals of St Fin Barre's*, p. 41.

9. Caulfield, *Annals of St Fin Barre's*, p. 42. Contrary to general Anglican practice, the term 'chorister' was used in St Fin Barre's records for the gentlemen of the choir rather than the choirboys.

10. Cited in Brady, *Clerical and Parochial Records*, vol. 1, pp. 256–7.

11. Cited in ibid., pp. 264–5.

12. Caulfield, *Annals of St Fin Barre's*, p. 52.

13. Ibid., p. 54.

14. Acheson, *A History of the Church of Ireland*, p. 39. *The Whole Book of Psalms collected into Englishe Metre* (1584) was gradually replaced by Nicholas Brady and Nahum Tate's *A New Version of the Psalms of David Fitted to the Tunes Used in Churches* (1696).

15. Acheson, *A History of the Church of Ireland*, pp. 36–7.

16. Caulfield, *Annals of St Fin Barre's*, p. 55. Probably French born and trained, John Baptiste Cuvillie (d. Dublin 1728) was Ireland's leading organ builder in the early eighteenth century. Paul McKeever, 'John Baptiste Cuvillie', *EMIR*, vol. 1, p. 274. Cuvillie was an employee of London organ builder Renatus Harris, to whom the Cork organ has also been attributed. See Stephen Bicknell, *The History of the English Organ* (Cambridge: Cambridge University Press, 1996), pp. 138–9.

17. Caulfield, *Annals of St Fin Barre's*, p. 55.

18. Ibid., p. 62.

19. Acheson, *A History of the Church of Ireland*, p. 37; Smith, *The Ancient and Present State of the County and City of Cork*, vol. 1, p. 379.

20. Caulfield, *Annals of St Fin Barre's*, p. 68.

21. Ibid., p. 69.

22. *Faulkner's Dublin Journal*, 22–26 December 1744; Brian Boydell, *A Dublin Musical Calendar 1700–1760* (Dublin: Irish Academic Press, 1988), p. 101; W.H. Grattan Flood, 'Notes and Queries: Handel's "Messiah" in Cork', *JCHAS*, vol. 26, 1920, p. 40.

23. Smith was listed as one of the directors of the Charitable Musical Society responsible for the creation of six new beds at the North Charitable Infirmary in 1755. *CJ*, 10 March 1755.

24. Smith, *The Ancient and Present State*, vol. 1, p. 379. Note the local usage of the term 'chorister' for the men singers.

25. Brady, *Clerical and Parochial Records*, vol. 1, p. 269.

26. Tuckey, *Remembrancer*, p. 134.

27. Caulfield, *Annals of St Fin Barre's*, p. 76.

28. A native of Saxony, Ferdinand Weber arrived in Dublin in the 1740s and established a successful practice as maker, tuner and repairer of organs and harpsichords. Barra Boydell, 'Ferdinand Webber', *EMIR*, vol. 2, p. 1048.

29. Lewis Gibson, *A Letter to the Revd. the Dean and Chapter of the Cathedral Church of St. Fin-Barry, Cork* (Cork: Printed by R. Dobbyn, 1782). Gibson had been a chorister at St Patrick's, Dublin, and an unsuccessful candidate for the post of organist there in 1777. See also Grindle, *Irish Cathedral Music*, p. 53.

30. *HC*, 2 May 1782.

31. Grindle, *Irish Cathedral Music*, p. 220.

32. d'Alton, *Protestant Society and Politics in Cork*, pp. 56, 65.

33. Triona O'Hanlon, 'Cloyne Cathedral', *EMIR*, vol. 1, p. 210; Samuel Lewis, *Lewis's Cork*, p. 125.

34. Nigel Yates, *The Religious Condition of Ireland, 1770–1850* (Oxford: Oxford University Press, 2006), pp. 73–84; Tríona O'Hanlon, 'Lewis Gibson and "Miss Mathews": two eighteenth and early nineteenth century provincial Irish cathedral composers and the editing of their work', *Proceedings of the 1st Annual Conference of the Society for Musicology in Ireland* (Maynooth, 2003), p. 42.

35. An address in Tuckey Street was given for Delamain in *HC*, 16 September 1782 and in Nixon, *Directory*, 1795.

36. *HC*, 12 January 1797.

37. Tríona O'Hanlon, 'Henry Delamain', *EMIR*, vol. 1, p. 292.

38. Thomas Crofton Croker, *Researches in the South of Ireland Illustrative of the Scenery, Architectural Remains and Superstitions of the Peasantry with an Appendix Containing a Private Narrative of the Rebellion of 1798* (Dublin: Irish Academic Press, 1981) (London, 1824).

39. Caulfield, *Annals of St Fin Barre's*, p. 89.

40. Ibid., p. 90.

41. *CMC*, 14 September 1808.

42. Keogh, 'Musical Perspectives of St Fin Barre's', p. 136, quoting Caulfield, *Annals of St Fin Barre's*, pp. 91–3; *CMC*, 30 July 1817.

43. *CA*, 20 August 1816.

44. Caulfield, Richard, MS Transcriptions, Boole Library, UCC IRL–C, U83.

45. Grindle, *Irish Cathedral Music*, p. 220.

46. Caulfield, *Annals of St Fin Barre's*, p. 92.

47. David Weyman, *Melodia Sacra or the Psalms of David*, vol. 1 (Dublin: George Allen, 1812). O'Hanlon, 'Henry Delamain'.

48. John Pentland Mahaffy, 'About Irish Church Music', *Irish Church Quarterly*, vol. 1, no. 2, 1908, pp. 93–8.

49. Barra Boydell, 'Richard Woodward [the younger]', *EMIR*, vol. 2, p. 1073.

50. James Kent, *Twelve Anthems* (London: Preston, nd. [*c*. 1790]).

51. Caulfield, *Annals of St Fin Barre's*, p. 91.

52. St Fin Barre's Cathedral: Oeconomist's accounts, 1806–33. RCB Library, IRL-Dcb C.20.4.1.

53. Caulfield, *Annals of St Fin Barre's*, pp. 92–3.

54. Acts of the Dean and Chapter of Cork, 1817–66, RCB Library, IRL-Drcb C.20.1.5.

55. Caulfield, *Annals of St Fin Barre's*, p. 94.

56. St Fin Barre's Cathedral: Chapter accounts, 1832–42, RCB Library, IRL-Drcb C.20.4.3.

57. Caulfield, *Annals of St Fin Barre's*, p. 98.

58. Ibid., p. 99.

59. Ibid.

60. *Finny's Royal Almanac for the year of our Lord 1843* (Cork: George Purcell, 1842), p. 59; *The County and City of Cork Almanac* (Cork: Jackson, 1844), p. 101

61. W.G., 'Music in Cork', *The Musical World*, vol. 20, 1845, p. 98, reprinted in *CE*, 7 March 1845.

62. John J. O'Shea, 'Churches of the Church of Ireland in Cork City', *JCHAS*, vol. 48, 1943, pp. 30–5; Cultural Heritage Ireland website, http://www.culturalheritageireland.ie/index.php/heritage-sites-and-centres/152-heritage-sites-christ-church-cork-city, accessed 28 September 2016.

63. Smith, *The Ancient and Present State*, vol. 1, p. 395.

64. 'A Tour through the South of Ireland', *Walker's Hibernian Magazine*, January 1786, p. 596.

65. Philip Luckcombe, *A Tour through Ireland in 1779* (London: J. & R. Byrne, 1780), p. 120.

66. *CMC*, 17 August 1814.

67. Caulfield, *Council Book*, p. 732.

68. Robert Day, 'Notes and Queries: recollections of the Church of the Holy Trinity, Cork', *JCHAS*, vol. 4, no. 38, 1898, pp. 140–4.

69. W.H. Grattan Flood, 'Dublin Harpsichord and Pianoforte Makers of the Eighteenth Century', *Journal of the Royal Society of Antiquaries of Ireland*, vol. 39, no. 2, 1909, p. 141.

70. Caulfield, *Council Book*, p. 752.

71. Ibid., p. 792.

72. Luckcombe, *A Tour through Ireland*, p. 20.

73. Richard Caulfied, MSS Transcriptions – Annals of Christ Church, UCC Boole Library U/83/3.

74. James Kelly, 'Charitable Societies: their genesis and development, 1720–1800', p. 89.

75. Ibid., pp. 89–90.

76. Holy Trinity Vestry Book, RCB Library P.527.5.3.

77. Holy Trinity Minute Book, 1820–91. RCB Library, IRL-RCB, P. 257.5.3

78. Richard Caulfield, Annals of the Cathedral of St Colman Cloyne (1882) record a payment to 'James Roach late organist' of one quarter salary made at Cloyne cathedral in September 1782.

79. Caulfield, *Council Book*, p. 981.

80. Boydell, 'St Michan's Church, Dublin: the installation of the organ in 1725 and the duties of the organist', *Dublin Historical Record*, vol. 46, no. 3, 1993, p. 105.

81. Richard Caulfield, 'Annals of Christ Church', Boole Library, UCC, IRL-C, U83/3.

82. Holy Trinity Parish Book, 1782–1801; Caulfield MS, Annals of Christ Church.

83. William Stawell Gillespie (1776–*c*. 1855) was a member of a family that included at least two generations of organists, organ tuners and music sellers in Cork during the nineteenth century. William Gillespie (1818–89) was an architect. From Banbridge, County Down, Gillespie first came to Cork as government inspector of linen yarns. I am grateful to Mrs Wynne Parker, Auckland, New Zealand, a descendant of this family, for this information.

84. *The Freeholder*, 1 March 1813.

85. Holy Trinity Minute Book, 1820–91, RCB P.527.5.4.

86. Holy Trinity Vestry Book, 15 May 1815.

87. Holy Trinity Minute Book, 1820–91.

88. Nixon, *The New Cork Directory for the Year 1795*; Samuel Lewis, *Lewis' Cork*, p. 186. A brief history of the institution is given in C.B. Gibson, *A History of the County and City of Cork*, 2 vols (London: Newby, 1861), vol. 2, pp. 336–7.

89. Michael V. Conlon, 'Register of the Boys of St Stephen's Hospital, Cork', *JCHAS*, vol. p. 62, 1957, p. 47, 53.

90. *The Freeholder*, 12 April 1824.

91. Holy Trinity Minute Book, 1820–91.

92. *The Freeholder*, 12 April 1825.

93. Holy Trinity Minute Book, 1820–91.

94. Robert Day, 'Notes and Queries: recollections of the Church of the Holy Trinity'.

95. Holy Trinity Minute Book, 1820–91, entry for 18 March 1824. This advertisement duly appeared on 26 March. *CN*, 26 March 1824.

96. *CMC*, 10 April 1833; Slater's *Directory* of 1846 lists William Gillespie as clerk and organist at Christ Church.

97. The Historical Records of the County and City of Cork, Ireland, http://www.corkrecords.com/StPetersIndex.htm, accessed 22 August 2016.

98. Acheson, *A History of the Church of Ireland*, p. 87; *HC*, 24 October 1782.

99. *CEP*, 17 May 1787.

100. *HC*, 26 July 1787.

101. Caulfield, *Council Book*, 11 September 1788, p. 1030.

102. *HC*, 28 October 1790. Marsden Haddock was one of the unsuccessful applicants. He published a notice in the *Hibernian Chronicle* informing his friends that, although unsuccessful on this occasion, 'he is already appointed an organist in this city'. *HC*, 1 November 1790.

103. *HC*, 28 October 1790.

104. Ibid., 11 December 1788.

105. *CEP*, 18 April 1791.

106. Ibid.

107. St Peter's Vestry Book, IRL-Drcb P.324.5.

108. Ibid.

109. McCarthy, 'Turning a World Upside Down', p. 46.

110. J.C., 'Dr Caulfield's Annals of the Parish Church of St Maria de Shandon, now St Ann's Shandon, Cork', in *JCHAS*, vol. 10, 1904, p. 273.

111. *CEP*, 22 October 1789.

112. *CN*, 9 July 1840.

CHAPTER 4

1. John O'Keeffe, *Recollections of the Life of John O'Keeffe*, 2 vols (London: H. Coburn, 1826), vol. 1, p. 225.

2. A detailed survey of theatre in the Irish provincial towns and cities is presented in William Smith Clark's *The Early Irish Stage: the beginnings to 1720* (Oxford: Clarendon, 1955) and *The Irish Stage in the County Towns, 1720 to 1800* (Oxford: Clarendon, 1965. A more recent comprehensive study is John C. Greene, *Theatre in Dublin, 1745–1820: a history*, 2 vols (Bethlehem: Lehigh University Press, 2011), supplemented by a six-volume *Calendar of Performances*. Key studies of English theatre include Allardyce Nicoll, *A History of English Drama, 1660–1900*, 3 vols (Cambridge: Cambridge University Press, 1952–9), and his *British Drama*, 5th edition (New York: Barnes & Noble, 1962), Jane Girdham, *English Opera in Late Eighteenth-Century London: Stephen Storace at Drury Lane* (Oxford: Clarendon, 1997), Roger Fiske, *English Theatre Music in the Eighteenth Century* (London: Oxford University Press, 1973), Michael R. Booth, *The Theatre in the Victorian Age* (Cambridge: Cambridge University Press, 1991). T.J Walsh's *Opera in Dublin, 1705–1797: the social scene* (Dublin: Allen Figgis, 1973), *Opera in Dublin, 1798–1820: Frederick Jones and the Crow Street Theatre* (Oxford: Oxford University Press, 1993) and *Opera in Old Dublin, 1819–1838* (Wexford: The Wexford Festival, 1952) present detailed descriptions of operatic productions on the Dublin stage.

3. Clark, *The Irish Stage in the County Towns*, p. 77.

4. Nicoll, *A History of English Drama, 1660–1900*, vol. 3, Late Eighteenth Century Drama, pp. 22–5.

5. Robert Hitchcock, *An Historical View of the Irish Stage*, 2 vols (Dublin: Marchbank, 1788–94), vol. 2, p. 110.

6. John C. Greene, 'The Repertory of the Dublin Theatres, 1720–1745', *Eighteenth-Century Ireland/Iris an Dá Chultúr*, vol. 2, 1987, pp. 133–48.

7. Jane Girdham, *English Opera in Late Eighteenth-Century London*, pp. 128–31; Clark, *The Irish Stage in the County Towns*, p. 292.

8. Todd Gilman, *The Theatre Career of Thomas Arne* (Lanham: Rowman & Littlefield, 2013), pp. 387, 389.

9. *CJ*, 21 May 1767.

10. *HC*, 20 November 1769.

11. Ibid., 6 December 1770. Frances Ashmore (later Mrs Sparks) was introduced to Dublin theatre audiences by Tenducci in 1760, and remained active there as a singer for a further twenty-five years. See Walsh, *Opera in Dublin*, p. 43.

12. Clark, *The Early Irish Stage*, pp. 137–9; La Tourette Stockwell, *Dublin Theatres and Theatre Customs 1637–1820* (Kingsport, Tennessee: Kingsport Press, 1938), p. 358. According to Windele, Dingle Lane was located off the North Main Street. See John Windele, *Historical and Descriptive Notices* (Cork: Bolster, 1846), p. 124.

13. Stockwell, *Dublin Theatres and Theatre Customs*, p. 358.

14. Windele, *Historical and Descriptive Notices*, p. 124; Hitchcock, *An Historical View*, vol. 1, p. 83.

15. Clark, *The Irish Stage*, pp. 70–1; Hitchcock, *An Historical View*, vol. 2, pp. 39–40.

16. Booth, *The Theatre in the Victorian Age*, p. 16.

17. Clark, *The Irish Stage*, p. 99.

18. Ibid., pp. 3–4; St Vincent Troubridge, *The Benefit System in the British Theatre* (London: The Society for Theatre Research, 1967), p. 19.

19. Clark, *The Irish Stage*, p. 71.

20. Ibid., p. 80. The Theatre Royal patent had been transferred from Smock Alley Theatre to Crow Street Theatre in 1759.

21. Christopher Morash, *A History of Irish Theatre 1601–2000* (Cambridge: Cambridge University Press, 2002), p. 45

22. 'Memoirs of Spranger Barry, Esq.', *Walker's Hibernian Magazine*, vol. 5, 1775, pp. 321–3.

23. Esther K. Sheldon, *Thomas Sheridan of Smock Alley* (Princeton: Princeton University Press, 1967), p. 240.

24. Clark, *The Irish Stage*, p. 81.

25. Robert M. Sillard, *Barry Sullivan and his Contemporaries: a histrionic record,* 2 vols (London and Manchester: Slater, 1846), vol. 1, p. 23.

26. Christopher Morash, A *History of Irish Theatre*, p. 80.

27. Theodore Fenner, *Opera in London: views of the press, 1785–1830* (Carbondale and Edwardsville: Southern Illinois University Press, 1994), p. 70.

28. Hitchcock, *An Historical View*, vol. 1, p. 39.

29. See, for example, Helen M. Burke, *Riotous Performances: the struggle for hegemony in the Irish theatre, 1712–1784* (South Bend, Indiana: University of Notre Dame Press, 2003), and Helen M. Burke, 'The Revolutionary Prelude: the Dublin stage in the late 1770s and early 1780s', *Eighteenth-Century Life*, vol. 22, no. 3, 1998, pp. 7–18.

30. Christopher Morash, *A History of Irish Theatre*, p. 72.

31. *HC*, 6 September 1773.

32. See Helen Burke, 'Eighteenth-Century Touring and Irish Popular Culture', in Nicholas Grene and Chris Morash (eds), *Irish Theatre on Tour* (Dublin: Carysfort Press, 2005).

33. *HC*, 9 September 1773; Walter G. Strickland, *A Dictionary of Irish Artists*, 2 vols (Dublin: Maunsell, 1913), vol. 2, pp. 477–8.

34. *HC*, 21–24 August 1780.

35. O'Keeffe, *Recollections*, vol. 1, p. 247; *HC*, 26 July 1774.

36. Clark, *The Irish Stage*, pp. 325–6; Heinz Kosok, '"George my belov'd King, and Ireland my honour'd Country": John O'Keeffe and Ireland', *Irish University Review*, vol. 22, no. 1, 1992), p. 49

37. Clark, *The Irish Stage*, p. 105.

38. Robert Owenson's daughter Sydney Owenson, later Lady Morgan, was an important literary and cultural figure in the early nineteenth century. E. Byrne-Costigan, 'Sydney Lady Morgan (1776–1859)', *Dublin Historical Record*, vol. 38, no. 2, 1985, p. 61.

39. *HC*, 2–5 October 1780.

40. Ibid., 21–29 August 1780.

41. Ibid., 8 October 1781.

42. Lady Morgan [Sydney Owenson], *Memoirs, Autobiography, Diaries and Correspondence* (London: Dixon, 1862), p. 65.

43. *FJ*, 28 May 1812. Quoted in Burke 'The Revolutionary Prelude, pp. 7–18.

44. Helen Burke, 'Eighteenth-Century Theatrical Touring and Irish Popular Culture', in Grene and Morash (eds), *Irish Theatre on Tour*, p. 120.

45. Clark, *The Irish Stage*, p. 89; see also *HC*, 19 August 1765; Catley returned to Cork for the 1768 season, *CEP*, 4 April 1768.

46. *CEP*, 31 July 1766; *CJ*, 31 July 1766.

47. Nicoll, *A History of English Drama*, vol. 3, p. 23. See also Hugh Cunningham, *Leisure in the Industrial Revolution c.1780–c.1880* (London: Croom Helm, 1980), p. 28. Cunningham argues here that this development was associated with a lowering of the status of the audiences, but also with wider availability of theatre for popular entertainment.

48. *HC*, 17–21 August 1786.

49. Fenner, *Opera in London*, p. 662.

50. *HC*, 28 August 1783.

51. Ibid., 18 September 1783.

52. Ibid., 22 September 1783.

53. Ibid., 8 August 1791.

54. *CG*, 20 August 1791.

55. Ibid. Joseph Reinagle was a member of the Band of the Holywell Music Room in Oxford during the 1790s. See Susan Wollenberg, *Music at Oxford in the Eighteenth and Nineteenth Centuries* (Oxford: Oxford University Press, 2001), p. 55.

56. *CG*, 24 August 1791.

57. Ibid.

58. Walsh, *Opera in Dublin, 1798–1820: Frederick Jones and the Crow Street Theatre*, pp. 72–80, provides a detailed account of the Dublin performances.

59. *CMC*, 19 September 1808.

60. Walsh, *Opera in Dublin*, p. 41; Fenner, *Opera in London*, pp. 166–7.

61. Ita Beausang, 'Cooke Family', *EMIR*, vol. 1, pp. 237–40.

62. *CMC*, 28 September 1808.

63. Ibid., 30 September 1808.

64. Ibid., 3 October 1808.

65. Michael Kelly and Theodore Edward Hook, *Reminiscences of Michael Kelly: of the King's Theatre, and the Theatre Royal Drury Lane, including a period of nearly a half century, with original anecdotes of many distinguished persons, political, literary, and musical*, 2 vols (London: Colburn, 1826), vol. 2, p. 242.

66. *HC*, 24 September 1772.

67. Ibid., 11–14 September 1775.

68. Ibid., 3 October 1791.

69. *HC*, 28 September 1797.

70. Ibid., 22–26 August 1776. In the earliest sources, the air 'Loghaber' was variously described as Irish or Scottish. See John Glen, *Early Scottish Melodies* (Glen: Edinburgh, 1900), pp. 87, 261.

71. Brian Boydell, *Rotunda Music in Eighteenth-Century Dublin*, p. 226.

72. *HC*, 21 August 1777.

73. Ibid., 3 September 1795.

74. Clark, *The Irish Stage*, p. 127.

75. *HC*, 22 October 1792. Probably Smollett Holden (*c*. 1755–1813), Dublin composer and music publisher, who specialised in composition of military music. Barra Boydell and Pat O'Connell, 'Smollet[t] Holden', *EMIR*, vol. 1, p. 493.

76. *CMC*, 18 September 1797.

77. *HC*, 9 September 1793.

78. Barry S. Brook et al., 'Francois-Joseph Gossec', *NGrove 2*, vol. 10, pp. 186–90.

79. *HC*, 28 July 1796, 8 September 1800.

80. *CMC*, 5 September 1804.

81. Francis Attwood, brother of composer Thomas Attwood (1735–1838), arrived in Cork with the Crow Street Theatre Company in 1800. Formerly active in musical circles in Oxford, he settled in Cork in early 1801 and established a music academy and a fencing academy. He left the city the following year. *CA*, 19 May 1801.

82. Cooke led the Crow Street Theatre band from the age of fifteen. He was son of Bartlett Cooke, an oboist at the Smock Alley Theatre. Beausang, 'Cooke Family'.

83. Christopher Morash, *A History of Irish Theatre*, p. 6; Claire Connolly, 'Irish Romanticism, 1800–1830', in Margaret Kelleher and Philip O'Leary (eds), *The Cambridge History of Irish Literature*, vol. 1 (Cambridge: Cambridge University Press, 2006), p. 429.

84. Thomas Wilson Croker, *Familiar Epistles to Frederick E. Jones, Esq. on the Present State of the Irish Stage*, 5th edition (Dublin: Graiseberry & Campbell, 1805), pp. 47–8.

85. *CMC*, 5 September 1804.

86. John C. Greene, *Theatre in Dublin, 1745–1820: a calendar of performances*, 6 vols (Bethlehem: Lehigh University Press, 2011), vol. 6, pp. 3366, 3454, 3505.

87. Robert Bowden married Eliza Coghlan at Christ Church in December 1808. Holy Trinity Register of Marriages.

88. *CMC*, 9 September 1808.

89. *HC*, 3 February 1783.

90. 'Obituary, Mr Connor', *The Gentleman's Magazine*, vol. 140, 1826, p. 566; Windele, *Historical and Descriptive Notices*, p. 138; *CN*, 7 October 1805; Edward A. Scott, wine merchant with a premises at 9 George's Street, advertised in *CMC*, 11 October 1805.

91. *SR*, 22 May 1855, 10 December 1864. 'Cork Worthies of the Last Century', *JCHAS*, vol. 22, 1916, p. 84.

92. *SR*, 10 December 1864, 'Testimonial to Miss Webb'.

93. *CMC*, 9 December 1805, 26 February 1808, 2 May 1810; see also Thomas Crofton Croker, 'Recollections of Cork' (1833), p. 330, IRL-Dtc MS 1206.

94. *CMC*, 7, 18 October 1805.

95. *Boyle's Magazine*, 8 December 1806, 5 January 1807.

96. Ibid., 16 February 1807.

97. Windele, *Historical and Descriptive Notices*, p. 124; Francis H. Tuckey, *The County and City of Cork Remembrancer* (Cork: Osborne Savage, 1837), p. 218. Mr Davis' Equestrian company performed at this venue in March 1801. *HC*, 2 March, 5 March, 9 March 1801.

98. *CMC*, 17 November 1806, 17 December 1806.

99. Ibid., 20 March 1807, 3 April 1807. Possibly a Mr Clarke who managed and owned theatres in Tralee and at Kirwan's Lane in Galway. R.J. Kelly, 'The Old Galway Theatres', *Journal of the Royal Society of Antiquaries of Ireland*, vol. 4, no. 4, 1914, p. 360.

100. *CMC*, 8 May 1807.

101. Ibid., 27 April 1810.

102. Ibid., 23 May 1810.

103. Ibid., 26 December 1810. An account of Miss Macauley's career is given in William Evans Burton, 'Mad Actors', *Burton's American Gentlemen's Magazine and Review*, vol. 3, 1838, pp. 181–5.

104. *CMC*, 25 September 1814. *The Freeholder*, 5 February 1813, refers to a revival in 1813, which is contradicted in the *CMC*.

105. Tickets for a performance on 9 January 1815 were supplied by Mr Ingram, Mr Garde, Mr Besnard and Felix Daly. *The Freeholder*, 9 January 1815.

106. *CMC*, 28 December 1814.

107. Ibid., 26 April 1815.

108. *CMI*, 13 April 1815.

109. *CA*, 18 April 1815.

110. *CMC*, 24 July 1812.

111. Ibid., 19 June 1815.

112. Ibid., 13 December 1815.

113. Ibid., 27 November 1815.

114. *The Freeholder*, 3 December 1815.

115. *CMC, 10* January 1816.

116. Robert Bowden, '"Soldier" rest' the favourite minstrel song in the popular melo-drama of the Lady of the Lake, sung with much applause' (Cork: T. Sheppard, [nd]), NLI Add Mus 12, 949.

117. *SR*, 20 March 1817.

118. *The Freeholder*, 21 March 1818.

119. Ibid., 9 February 1822.

120. Ibid., 8 September 1834.

121. The set of casts of works in the Vatican collection were supervised by Italian sculptor Antonio Canova (1757–1822) at the request of Pope Pius VII, intended as a gift for the Prince Regent, later King George IV. The casts had arrived in Cork through the intervention of Viscount Ennismore, a friend of the Prince Regent. See Peter Murray, 'Art Institutions in Nineteenth-Century Cork', in Patrick O'Flanagan and Cornelius G. Buttimer (eds), *Cork History and Society* (Dublin: Geography Publications, 1993), pp. 825–6.

122. Sillard, *Barry Sullivan*, vol. 1, p. 23.

123. *A respectful appeal to the intelligent and generous among his fellow citizens by Francis Seymour.* Cork, 1849, Cork City and County Archive, U140/J/8/5.

124. *CMC*, 10 March 1817.

125. 'Biographical memoir of Miss Byrne', *Theatrical Inquisitor [and Monthly Mirror]*, vol. 12, January 1818, pp. 2–5; Daniel Byrne-Rothwell, *The Byrnes and the O'Byrnes: a social history of the clan*, 4 vols, vol. 2 (Isle of Colonsay, Argyll: House of Lochar, 2010), pp. 211–12.

126. *The Freeholder*, 6 April 1817. James Chalmers worked as a scene painter at Crow Street and then at the Cork Theatre Royal. He was appointed as drawing master at the Royal Cork Institution in 1819. 'Marianne' was likely to have been Marinari, an Italian scene painter who also worked at Crow Street Theatre in the second decade of the nineteenth century. Both artists are listed in Walter G. Strickland's *A Dictionary of Irish Artists*, 2 vols (Dublin: Maunsell, 1913), vol. 1, p. 165, vol. 2, p. 102.

127. According to Sillard, Seymour was a native of Cork, having run a hardware business on Patrick Street. Sillard, *Barry Sullivan*, vol. 1, p. 26.

128. Greene, *Theatre in Dublin, 1745–1820: A Calendar of Performances*, vol. 6, p. 4300.

129. Ibid., p. 4329.

130. *CMC*, 13 April 1818. See Gillian Nash, 'Frank Seymour and the Cork Theatre, 1832–1850', unpublished MA thesis (University College Cork, 1977), p. 10.

131. *CMI*, 17 May 1821.

132. Roy Johnston with Declan Plummer, *The Musical Life of Nineteenth Century Belfast* (Farnham: Ashgate, 2015), p. 115.

133. Dublin's Hawkins Street Theatre was opened in January 1821.

134. *CMI*, 11 October 1821. This adaptation of Mozart's opera was first produced at Covent Garden in 1819. See Fenner, *Opera in London*, pp. 484–6. The original version of *Le Nozze di Figaro* had received its first production in Dublin in October 1819. See Walsh, *Opera in Dublin*, p. 248.

135. *The Freeholder*, 15 October 1821.

136. He took a benefit at the Cork Theatre Royal on 4 November 1822. *CN*, 4 November 1822.

137. Nash, p. 11.

138. Sillard, *Barry Sullivan*, vol. 1, p. 28.

139. *The Freeholder*, 30 November 1821.

140. Rohr, *The Careers of British Musicians*, p. 106.

141. Fenner, *Opera in London*, p. 139.

142. Leanne Langley, '"Our Thing Called Opera": some Covent Garden productions of the 1820s through contemporary eyes', *The Musical Times*, vol. 123, no. 1678, 1982, pp. 836–8.

143. *SR*, 26 July 1825.

144. Ibid., 2 August 1825. First performed in Berlin in 1821, the first London production was in 1824.

145. *CN*, 4 August 1825.

146. Christopher Morash, *A History of Irish Theatre*, pp. 81–82; See also J.W. Flynn, *The Random Recollections of an Old Playgoer: a sketch of some old Cork theatres* (Cork: Guy, 1890), pp. 25–6.

147. *SR*, 24 April 1827.

148. Ibid., 18 April 1829.

149. Ibid., 28 April 1829.

150. *CN*, 9 May 1829.

151. Johnston with Plummer, *The Musical Life*, pp. 112–15.

152. *CN*, 15 November 1832. The full programme was printed in *The Constitution*.

153. Berndt Lindfors, *Ira Aldridge: the vagabond years, 1833–1852* (New York: University of Rochford Press, 2011), pp. 27–42.

154. *CS*, 28 August 1837.

155. *The Freeholder*, 3 November 1834.

156. *CEH*, 10 November 1834.

157. James D. Brown, *Biographical Dictionary of Musicians, with a Bibliography of English Writings on Music* (Paisley and London: Gardner, 1886), p. 73.

158. *CMC*, 18 September 1835.

159. *CN*, 26 September 1835.

160. Walsh, *Opera in Old Dublin*, p. 72.

161. *CN*, 1 October 1835.

162. *CEH*, 11 September 1833.

163. *SR*, 25 August 1838.

164. Sillard, *Barry Sullivan*, vol. 1, p. 42.

165. Ibid., pp. 42–3.

166. Ibid., pp. 51–3; *CE*, 29 October 1841: John Collins, 'Minor theatre' was listed in Aldwell's *Post Office General Directory 1844–5*.

167. *CE*, 10 January 1844.

168. Ibid., 30 August 1847.

169. *CN*, 17 March 1838; Sillard, *Barry Sullivan*, vol. 1, p. 55. The Diorama had been established at 26 Cook Street in 1826. From September to November 1834, it had been fitted up for a number of theatrical productions, including a brief revival of the Apollo Society. *CMC*, 3 November 1834.

170. *SR*, 17 April 1838.

171. Ibid., 9 June 1838.

172. *CS*, 14 June 1839.

173. *CN*, 14 August 1838.

174. *CS*, 8 August 1838.

175. *CN*, 30 August 1838.

176. *SR*, 30 August 1838.

177. *CN*, 17 August, 20 August 1839. Richard Levey was leader of the band at Hawkins Street Theatre from 1834 to 1880.

CHAPTER 5

1. David Dickson, *Old World Colony*, p. 369.

2. Ian d'Alton, *Protestant Society and Politics in Cork, 1812–1844* (Cork: Cork University Press, 1980), p. 71.

3. Ibid., pp. 137–8.

4. Dickson, *Old World Colony*, pp. 494–5; Fergal Gaynor, 'The Laocoön in Cork: the classical tradition in the city of Mahony and Maginn', *Classics Ireland*, vol. 15, 2008, pp. 34–51.

5. Francis H. Tuckey, *The County and City of Cork Remembrancer* (Cork: Osborne Savage, 1837), p. 218.

6. David Dickson, 'Second City Syndrome: reflections on three Irish cases', in S.J. Connolly (ed.), *Kingdoms United? Great Britain and Ireland since 1500: integration and diversity* (Dublin: Four Courts Press, 1998), p. 103.

7. 'Progress of the Cork Society', *The First Number of the Reports of the Society in Dublin for Promoting the Comforts of the Poor*, vol. 1 (London: W. Bulmer, 1800), pp. 1–10.

8. Laurence M. Geary, 'John Milner Barry and Public Health in Early Nineteenth-Century Cork', *JCHAS*, vol. 106, 2001, p. 134.

9. Ibid., p.135.

10. *HC*, 14 May 1801.

11. *CA*, 13 August 1801

12. Colman O'Mahony, *In the Shadows: life in Cork, 1750–1930* (Cork: Tower Books, 1997), p. 46. The House of Industry is referred to in the travel writing of Rev. James Hall, who was in Cork around 1807. Courtenay Moore, 'A Forgotten Tour in Ireland', *JCHAS*, vol. 7, no. 51, 1901, pp. 174–5.

13. Collins, 'Concert Life in Dublin in the Age of Revolution', unpublished PhD dissertation (Queen's University Belfast, 2001), p. 191.

14. *HC*, 13 August 1801.

15. Ibid.

16. *CA*, 13 August 1801.

17. Ibid., see Collins, 'Concert Life', p. 48.

18. *HC*, 13 August 1801.

19. *CMC*, 23 August 1802.

20. Ibid., 8 September 1802.

21. Ibid., 31 January 1803.

22. Ibid., 7 October 1804.

23. Dáire Keogh, *Edmund Rice and the First Christian Brothers* (Dublin: Four Courts Press, 2008), pp. 142–4.

24. Peadar McCann, 'Charity Schooling in Cork in the Late Eighteenth and Early Nineteenth Century', Part 1, *JCHAS*, vol. 86, 1981, p. 30.

25. Evelyn Bolster, *A History of the Diocese of Cork: from the penal era to the famine* (Cork: Tower Books, 1989), p. 143.

26. Keogh, *Edmund Rice*, p. 143.

27. Timothy P. O'Neill, 'The Catholic Church and Relief of the Poor, 1815–1845', *Archivium Hibernicum*, vol. 31, 1973, pp. 132–45; C.S. Begadon, *Laity and Clergy in the Catholic Renewal of Dublin c. 1750–1830*, PhD dissertation (NUI Maynooth, 2009), http://eprints.maynoothuniversity.ie/2412/ accessed 18 October 2016.

28. *CMC*, 22 October 1810.

29. Ibid., 6 December 1811.

30. Ibid., 14 December 1814.

31. Dickson, *Old World Colony*, p. 479.

32. *CMC*, 27 December 1816; *SR*, 8 February 1817, *CA*, 24 November 1818.

33. *CN*, 18 December 1822.

34. *CMC*, 31 December 1823.

35. *The County and City of Cork Almanac, calculated and adapted by C. Thompson* (Cork: F. Jackson, 1843), p. 81.

36. *CMC*, 25 May 1807.

37. Ibid., 24 August 1807, *CMC* 5 November 1807.

38. Ibid., 18 January 1808.

39. Ibid., 22 February 1808.

40. Ibid., 27 March 1808.

41. Ibid., 10 August 1808. A new Wesleyan chapel was opened for worship on Patrick Street in 1805.

42. *CMC*, 26 April 1809.

43. Ibid., 27 April 1810.

44. Ibid., 24 July 1811. The Bath Rooms, Blackrock, were opened in 1808. *CMC*, 18 April 1808.

45. *Holden's Triennial Directory*, fourth edition, for 1805, 1806, 1807, second volume (London: W. Glendinning, 1805); William West, *A Directory and Picture of Cork and its Environs* (Cork: West, 1810); *Connor's Cork Directory for the Year 1817* (Cork: Connor, 1817).

46. *CEP*, 4 September 1783.

47. *CMC*, 3 October 1806; *CA*, 21 October 1806.

48. *CA*, 6 May 1800.

49. *CMI*, 17 August 1816.

50. *SR*, 14 October 1817.

51. *CA*, 26 October 1816.

52. *CMC*, 21 July 1817.

53. Derek Collins lists Logierian academies in Dublin run by Jonathan Blewitt, William Walsh, John Spray and Mr Smith jointly, Browne, William S. Conran and E.C. Allen. See Derek Collins, 'Music in Dublin', in Richard Pine and Charles Acton (eds), *To Talent Alone: the Royal Irish Academy of Music, 1848–1998* (Dublin: Gill & Macmillan, 1998), p. 26.

54. Adèle Commins, 'Johann Bernhard Logier', *EMIR*, vol. 2, pp. 597–9.

55. *CA*, 26 December 1818; Ita Beausang, 'Jonathan Blewitt', *EMIR*, vol. 1, pp. 101–2.

56. *CA*, 5 January 1819.

57. Samuel Lewis, *Lewis' Cork*, pp. 52–3.

58. William M. Thackeray, *The Irish Sketchbook 1842, with numerous engravings on wood drawn by the author* (London: Sutton, 1990), p. 70.

59. Asenath Nicholson, *Ireland's Welcome to the Stranger: or, an excursion through Ireland in 1844* (New York: Baker & Scribner, 1847), p. 252.

60. *CE*, 28 July 1852, 3 August 1857.

61. *HC*, 26 December 1791; *NCEP*, 2 January 1792.

62. *CMC*, 8 May 1807. Windele's report of the establishment of a Harmonic Society in the 1790s may have referred to the Catch and Glee Club.

63. *CMC*, 23 April 1810. See John Windele, *Historical and Descriptive Notices of the City of Cork and its Vicinity* (Cork: Bolster, 1846), p. 125. In the 1820s, the Harmonic Society held its dinner meetings at the Imperial Hotel.

64. Síle Ní Chinnéide, 'A New View of Cork in 1790', *JCHAS*, vol. 78, 1973, p. 4.

65. *CMI*, 27 February 1821.

66. *CMC*, 16 May 1810.

67. Ibid., 18 May 1810.

68. *CN*, 4 November 1822.

69. *CMC*, 14 March 1834.

70. Ibid., 14 March 1834.

71. *CS*, 7 December 1838.

72. W.G., 'Music in Cork', *The Musical World*, vol. 20, 1845, pp. 98–9.

73. A newly opened military academy, at which Ware claimed to have taught.

74. *CMC*, 30 October 1811, 31 January 1814.

75. Ibid., 20 October 1813.

76. Ibid., 25 October 1813.

77. *The Freeholder*, 17 February 1824.

78. *CA*, 29 November 1803.

79. *CMC*, 28 November, 2 December 1803; *CA*, 29 November 1803.

80. *CMI*, 23 May 1812.

81. *CA*, 24 May 1806.

82. *CMC*, 8 June 1807.

83. *The Freeholder*, 13 May 1822.

84. Ibid., 27 May 1823.

85. Simon McVeigh, 'The Professional Concert and Rival Subscription Series in London, 1783–1793', *RMA Research Chronicle*, vol. 22, 1989, p. 2.

86. *CMC*, 29 October 1806.

87. Ibid., 17 April 1810.

88. Ibid., 3 April 1809.

89. Ibid., 7 April 1809.

90. These singers had given eight private concerts with Mr Spray, pianoforte, at 7 Westmoreland Street, commencing in December 1813. Collins, 'Concert Life in Dublin', p. 259.

91. *CMC*, 10 May 1815.

92. Ibid., 17 May 1815.

93. James D. Brown and Stephen S. Stratton, *British Musical Biography: a dictionary of musical artists, authors and composers born in britain and its colonies* (Birmingham: Stratton, 1897), p. 15.

94. Pucitta composed twenty-three operas, and provided music for Angelica Catalani.

95. Fenner, *Opera in London*, pp. 127–8; Walsh, *Opera in Dublin*, p. 175.

96. *CA*, 2 October 1813. A similar programme was performed at the Theatre Royal, Crow Street, Dublin, on 26 October. Collins, *Concert Life in Dublin – 'Chronology of Concerts'*.

97. *CMC*, 31 July 1815.

98. Ibid., 9 August 1815.

99. Simon McVeigh, *Concert Life in London from Mozart to Haydn*, p. 94.

100. *CMC*, 4 July 1803; John C. Greene, *Theatre in Dublin, 1745–1820: a calendar of performances*, p. 3355.

101. *CMC*, 12 September 1804.

102. Ibid., 23 August 1805.

103. Rosemond Mountain (née Wilkinson). See Highfill et al., *A Biographical Dictionary*, vol. 10, pp. 346–52. Walsh identifies her as Sara Mountain.

104. Highfill et al., *A Biograpical Dictionary*, vol. 10, pp. 345–6.

105. Michael Kassler, *A.F.C. Kollmann's Quarterly Musical Register (1812): an annotated edition with an introduction to his life and works* (Aldershot: Ashgate, 2008), pp. 74, 77.

106. *CMC*, 4 August 1815.

107. Ibid., 1 February 1811. John Spray had held the post of vicar choral at St Patrick's and Christ Church cathedrals in Dublin since 1795. See Barra Boydell, *A History of Music at Christ Church Cathedral, Dublin* (Woodbridge: Boydell, 2004), pp. 104, 124.

108. Dickson, *Old World Colony*, p. 479.

109. *CMC*, 15, 22 February 1811.

110. Ibid., 29 March 1811.

111. *SR*, 12 January 1826.

112. *CMC*, 16 January 1826.

113. *CN*, 17 January 1826.

114. *CMC*, 18 January 1826.

115. Captain Francis O'Neill, *Irish Minstrels and Musicians: the story of Irish music* (Chicago: Regan Printing House, 1913; reprinted Cork: Mercier Press, 1987), pp. 200–1.

116. *CMC*, 9 January1809, 4 April 1810.

117. O'Donnell, *Ireland's Harp*, pp. 68–75.

118. *CMC*, 18 December 1812. Following the success of the Belfast Harp Festival of 1792, the Belfast Harp Society was founded in 1808 by a number of individuals. Mary Louise O'Donnell, 'Belfast Harp Society', *EMIR*, vol. 1, p. 81.

119. Aiken McClelland, 'The Irish Harp Society', *Ulster Folklife*, vol. 2, 1975, p. 17.

120. *CMC*, 9, 16, 18 February 1814; O'Donnell, 'Belfast Harp Society'.

121. *CMC*, 16 February 1814. Patrick Kelly had advertised tuition on 'single and double flageolet, flute and clarionet' in 1813.

122. *CMC*, 8 October 1813.

123. Ibid., 28 September 1827.

124. Ignaz Moscheles, *Recollections of Ireland*, Op 69 (London: Cramer, Addison & Beale, 1827).

125. *Morning Post*, 10 April 1826, 16 June 1827.

126. Joep Leerssen, *Remembrance and Imagination: patterns in the historical and literary representation of Ireland in the nineteenth century* (Cork: Cork University Press, 1996), p. 81.

127. Fintan Lane, *In Search of Thomas Sheahan: radical politics in Cork, 1824–1836* (Dublin: Irish Academic Press, 2001), p. 13.

128. Collins, 'Concert Life', p. 275.

129. *Faulkner's Dublin Journal*, 16 August 1813.

130. *CMC*, 17 January 1814.

131. *CA*, 10 February 1814; *The Freeholder*, 12 February 1814.

132. *The Freeholder*, 12 February 1814.

133. Brian W. Pritchard, 'The Provincial Festivals of the Ashley Family', *The Galpin Society Journal*, vol. 22, 1969, pp. 58–77; Pippa Drummond, *The Provincial Music Festival in England, 1784–1914* (Farnham: Ashgate, 2011), p. 11. A four-day festival held in Belfast in October 1813, on the other hand, was locally organised by Edward Bunting, featuring Dublin musicians, in support of a local charitable society with a lengthy list of patrons. See Roy Johnston, *Bunting's Messiah* (Belfast: The Belfast Natural History and Philosophical Society, 2003).

134. Collins, 'Concert Life', pp. 284–5.

135. *The Freeholder*, 9 August 1814.

136. Walsh, *Opera in Dublin 1798–1829*, p. 134.

137. See ibid., pp. 135–8.

138. Fenner, *Opera in London*, p. 333.

139. Programmes for the concerts on 23 and 24 August are held at the Bodleian Library, Oxford, http://www.concertprogrammes.org.uk/html/search/verb/GetRecord/4219 accessed 22 August 2016.

140. *CMC*, 17 August 1814.

141. Ibid., 24 August 1814.

142. *CA*, 23 August 1814.

143. Ibid., 25 August 1814.

144. Ibid., 25 August 1814.

145. Ibid., 27 August 1814.

146. *The General Advertiser, or Limerick Gazette*, 30 August 1814.

147. *CMC*, 27 March 1818.

148. *SR*, 28 March 1818.

149. *Literary and Political Examiner* (Cork: John Bolster, March 1818).

150. *CMC*, 27 March 1818.

151. *SR*, 28 March 1818.

152. *CMC*, 10 April 1818; Tuckey, *Remembrancer*, p. 259.

153. *CMC*, 27 March 1818.

154. Ibid., 10 April 1818.

155. Ibid., 1 April 1818.

CHAPTER 6

1. *CN*, 27 July 1826.

2. Fergal Gaynor, 'The Laocoön in Cork: the classical tradition in the city of Mahony and Maginn', *Classics Ireland*, vol. 15, 2008, p. 35.

3. See Terry Eagleton chapter 'Cork and the Carnivalesque' in *Crazy John and the Bishop and Other Essays on Irish Culture* (Cork: Cork University Press, 1998).

4. Leith Davis, 'Irish Bards and English Consumers: Thomas Moore's "Irish Melodies" and the colonized nation', *ARIEL: a review of international English literature*, vol. 24, no. 2, 1993, p. 23.

5. Joep Leerssen, *Remembrance and Imagination: patterns in the historical and literary representation of Ireland in the nineteenth century* (Cork: Cork University Press, 1996), p. 81.

6. Leanne Langley, 'The Musical Press in Nineteenth-Century England', *Notes: quarterly journal of the Music Library Association*, vol. 46, no. 3, 1990, p. 588.

7. *CMC*, 23 August 1802.

8. Ibid., 8 September 1802.

9. 'Obituary' of Terence Magrath, *Dublin Evening Mail*, 29 March 1865, reprinted in *CE*, 31 March 1865.

10. *Bath Chronicle and Weekly Gazette*, 8 November 1804.

11. Paul F. Rice, *Venanzio Rauzzini in Britain: castrato, composer, and cultural leader* (Rochester: University of Rochester Press, 2015), pp. 333–53.

12. Douglas J. Reid, 'Some Festival Programmes of the Eighteenth and Nineteenth Centuries. 1. Salisbury and Winchester', *RMA Research Chronicle*, vol. 5, 1965, p. 77; *Trewman's Exeter Flying Post*, 19 August 1813; *Salisbury and Winchester Journal*, 2 June 1814.

13. *Salisbury and Winchester Journal*, 20 December 1813.

14. *Morning Chronicle*, 7, 11 July 1814.

15. Ibid,. 22 May 1815.

16. *Jackson's Oxford Chronicle*, 16 March 1816.

17. *Morning Chronicle*, 14 May 1816.

18. *Caledonian Mercury*, 2 April 1818.

19. Quoted in Windele, *Historical and Descriptive Notices*, p. 159.

20. Obituary in *Dublin Evening Mail*, 29 March 1865, reprinted in *CE*, 31 March 1865.

21. Listed as a Professor of Singing with an address at 59 Lower Mount Street in *Pigot and Co's Provincial Directory of Ireland 1824*, p. 82.

22. Cotton, *Fasti Ecclesiae Hibernicae*, vol. 2, p. 88.

23. Ibid,. p. 212.

24. Rohr, *The Careers of British Musicians*, pp. 94–5.

25. Brian Boydell, *A History of Music at Christ Church Cathedral, Dublin* (Woodbridge: Boydell, 2004), pp. 40–1.

26. *FJ*, 9 February 1825.

27. Ibid., 10 May 1825. A series of four 'Subscription Vocal Concerts' had taken place on consecutive Wednesdays at the Rotunda, Dublin, beginning on 9 March 1825. *FJ*, 3 March 1825.

28. *CN*, 17 May 1825.

29. *Dublin Almanac and General Register of Ireland* (Dublin: Pettigrew & Oulton, 1840), p. 187.

30. *Evening Packet*, 26 November, 3 December 1840.

31. *The Dublin Almanac*, 1839, p. 176; 1840, p. 181; 1841, p. 183; 1843, p. 177.

32. *FJ*, 6 October 1853.

33. *Evening Packet*, 30 April 1842, 21 March 1843; *FJ*, 26 April 1852.

34. *CE*, 31 March 1865.

35. Anon, 'Memoir of Samuel Forde – a Cork Artist', *Dublin University Magazine*, vol. 25, no, 147, 1845, pp. 338–57: 338.

36. NLI Add Mus 1872.

37. Michael Kassler, *A.F.C. Kollmann's Quarterly Musical Register (1812): an annotated edition with an introduction to his life and works* (Aldershot: Ashgate, 2008), p. 124; Adèle Commins, 'Johann Bernhard Logier', *EMIR*, vol. 2, pp. 597–9.

38. *CMI*, 16 August 1821.

39. Fenner, *Opera in London*, pp. 361–2.

40. Philip Bate and Fiona Clampin, 'Louis Drouet', *NGrove2*, vol. 17, p. 599.

41. For example, *The Social Concert: a series of popular compositions of the first class, in various styles/ arranged as trios for flute, pianoforte and violincello by William Forde* (London: R. Cocks & Co., c. 1825); *Rossini's favourite operas, arranged for the flute by William Forde* (London: Cocks & Co., nd [before 1830]).

42. Rohr, *The Careers of British Musicians*, pp. 151–2.

43. *SR*, 19 March 1825.

44. *Alphabetical List of Freemen at Large of the Borough of Cork* (1844), IE CCCA U/140/J/02/02/04. The records do not indicate that he was either an eldest son of a freeman or had completed servitude to a freeman, therefore his admission may have been on the occasion of his marriage to an eldest daughter of a freeman or he may have been admitted on the strength of his professional contributions to the city.

45. *The Freeholder*, 23 January 1823.

46. *CMC*, 8 January 1823.

47. Ibid., 29 January 1823.

48. Ibid., 19 September 1823. The Royal Academy's Committee Minutes of 20 March 1828 record that Oury was then a teacher of the violin there. He was a student of Christoph Gottfried Kiesewetter, and taught Mendelssohn in London.

49. Carlo Rovedino, bass singer of the King's Theatre, performed with Madame Catalani's company at Cork's Theatre Royal in 1808 and in Dublin in September 1807.

50. *CMC*, 19 September 1823.

51. Frederick Mathews was organist at Cashel cathedral from 1820 to 1844.

52. Henry Robinson Allen studied singing at the Royal Academy of Music in London from 1830 to 1832, and afterwards had a successful career as a singer and composer in London. Alexis Chitty and George Biddlecombe, 'Henry Robinson Allen', *NGrove2*, vol. 1, pp. 398–9.

53. The building was offered for sale or to let the following June. *CN*, 7 June 1824.

54. *SR*, 25 October 1823.

55. Ibid., 18 October 1823.

56. *CA*, 20 October 1823.

57. Susan O'Regan, 'A Vast Speculation: the Cork grand musical meeting of 1826', *Journal of the Society for Musicology in Ireland*, vol. 5, 2009–2010, pp. 3–19, http://www.musicologyireland.com/jsmi/index.php/journal/article/view/34/59, accessed 9 January 2017.

58. *CN*, 25 July 1826.

59. Ibid., 3 August 1826.

60. Brian Pritchard, 'Some Festival Programmes of the Eighteenth and Nineteenth Centuries. 3. Liverpool and Manchester', in *RMA Research Chronicle*, vol. 7, 1969, p. 1.

61. *SR*, 13 July 1826.

62. A detailed discussion of the organisation, programmes and reception of this event is given in Susan O'Regan's '"A Vast Speculation": the Cork grand musical meeting of 1826'.

63. *CN*, 8 July 1826.

64. *CMC*, 24 March 1826; *CN*, 22 March 1826.

65. *CN*, 25 July 1826.

66. *SR*, 22 June 1826.

67. Ibid., 29 July 1826.

68. Ehrlich, *The Music Profession in Britain*, p. 81. Forde's connection with the RAM appeared in subsequent press notices during the 1830s, for example, *Dublin Evening Mail*, 18 November 1831, *CN*, 20 January 1838.

69. RAM Committee Minutes, 1822–8, 1 June 1826; RAM, Concert Book: May 1824–December 1879, 10 April 1826.

70. John S. Sainsbury, *A Dictionary of Musicians from the Earliest Times*, 2 vols (New York: Da Capo Press, 1966; reprint of 1825), vol. 2, p. 11.

71. Royal Academy of Music, *A List of Pupils Received into the Academy since its Foundation in 1822–3* (London: Royal Academy of Music, 1838), p. 25.

72. RAM, Committee Minutes, vol. 1, 1822–1828; entry of 20 July 1826.

73. RAM, Concert Book, 10 April 1826.

74. *SR*, 13 July 1826.

75. Sainsbury, *Dictionary*, vol. 2, p. 414–15.

76. Ibid., vol. 1, p. 332.

77. Douglas J. Reid, 'Some Festival Programmes of the Eighteenth and Nineteenth Centuries. I: Salisbury and Winchester', *RMA Research Chronicle*, vol. 5, 1965, p. 66.

78. *CN*, 29 July 1826. Érard's 'double escapement' action had been patented in 1821, enabling rapid repetition of notes. See Cyril Ehrlich, *The Piano: a history* (London: Dent, 1976), p. 22.

79. *CMC*, 24 July 1826.

80. *CN*, 1, 3, 5 August 1826.

81. Ibid., 5 August 1826.

82. Ibid., 1 August 1826.

83. *SR*, 12 August 1826

84. Leanne Langley, 'Sainsbury's *Dictionary*, the Royal Academy, and the Rhetoric of Patriotism', in Christina Bashford and Leanne Langley (eds), *Music in British Culture, 1785–1914: essays in honour of Cyril Ehrlich* (Oxford: Oxford University Press, 2000), pp. 74–5.

85. The following year, Cork woman Miss O'Hea enrolled as a student of the Academy, and by 1831 two more students from Cork had enrolled there. Royal Academy of Music, *A List of Pupils Received into the Academy since Its Foundation in 1822–3* (London, 1838), p. 11.

86. *SR*, 1 August 1826.

87. The three Travers brothers were sons of Captain John Travers of South Terrace. *Pigot's City of Dublin and Hibernian Provincial Directory* (London and Manchester: Pigot, 1824).

88. *CN*, 20 September 1828.

89. *The First Dublin Grand Musical Festival 1831* [programmes of the concerts] (Dublin: Underwood, 1831), NLI Ir 780941 d 1.

90. *SR*, 21 May 1833.

91. *CN*, 30 September 1828.

92. *The Freeholder*, 17 October 1828.

93. *CN*, 14 October 1828.

94. Ibid., 21 October 1828.

95. Ibid., 3 October 1829.

96. Ibid., 10 October 1829.

97. *SR*, 17 October 1829.

98. *CN*, 22, 24 October 1829. Against a series of attacks and disturbances around Doneraile by a secret society known as the Whiteboys, a group of local men were charged with conspiracy to assassinate two magistrates and a landlord. The trial was heard by a Special Commission in Cork on 22 October 1829, attended by a large turnout of aristocracy and gentry in a display of solidarity. See Dickson, *Old World Colony*, p. 493.

99. *CN*, 22 October 1829.

100. *SR*, 24 October 1829.

101. *CE*, 24 July, 9 August 1844.

102. Ita Beausang, 'William Forde', *EMIR*, vol. 1, pp. 404–6; Jimmy O'Brien Moran, 'John Edward Pigot', *EMIR*, vol. 2, pp. 839–40.

103. Windele, *Historical and Descriptive Notices*, p. 155.

104. Brown and Stratton, *British Musical Biography*, p. 149.

105. David's brother, Alexander, was the father of Thomas Deane, who by 1811 had designed the Commercial Buildings on South Mall.

106. *SR*, 28 March 1818.

107. John Gilbert, 'A Record of Authors, Artists, and Musical Composers Born in the County Cork', *JCHAS*, vol. 19, 1913, p. 179.

108. *SR*, 11 September 1827. This piece was performed by his sister Miss Roche at her benefit concert in Cork in that year.

109. Zack R. Bowen, *Musical Allusions in the works of James Joyce: early poetry through Ulysses* (Albany: State University of New York Press, 1974), p. 36.

110. *Metropolitan Magazine*, vol. 16, 1836, p. 86.

111. *CN*, 15 October 1829.

112. Ibid., 2 August 1825, 11 August 1827.

113. 'Sketch of the State of Music in London', *The Quarterly Musical Magazine and Review*, vol. 8, 1826, p. 143.

114. *Edinburgh Literary Journal or Weekly Register of Criticism and Belles Lettres*, vol. 5, 26 March 1831, p. 298.

115. *CMC*, 2 August 1833.

116. *Northampton Mercury*, 7 September 1833; *The National Standard of Literature, Science, Music, Theatricals, and the Fine Arts*, no. 57, 1833, p. 185; *FJ*, 28 September 1833.

117. *The National Standard of Literature, Science, Music, Theatricals and the Fine Arts*, no. 57, 1833, p. 185.

118. *The Court Journal: court circular and fashionable gazette*, vol. 5, 1833, p. 442.

119. Ibid., vol. 7, 1835, p. 104.

120. Mrs S.C. Hall, *Lights and Shadows of Irish Life*, 3 vols (London: H. Colborn, 1838), vol. 1, p. vi.

121. *Morning Post*, 18 April, 23 April 1838. See Bernard Webster (ed.), *The Acting National Drama, Comprising every New play, Farce, Melo-drama, Opera, Burletta, etc.*, vol. 4 (London: Chapman & Hall, 1838)

122. *SR*, 9 June 1838.

123. *Evening Packet*, 7 July 1842.

124. *The Musical World*, vol. 20, 1845, p. 272.

125. *Evening Packet*, 7 July 1842; *Yorkshire Gazette*, 6 August 1842; *The Era*, 14 August 1842; *Morning Post*, 29 September 1842.

126. A popular figure in literary circles, English poet Felicia Hemans lived in Dublin from 1831 until her death in 1835.

127. *The Court Journal*, vol. 7, 1835, p. 540.

128. *CS*, 4 July 1838; *CN*, 5, 14 July 1838.

CHAPTER 7

1. Weber, *Music and the Middle Class*, p. 19.

2. Samuel Lewis, *Lewis' Cork: A Topographical Dictionary*, p. 167.

3. Holland MSS, Cork Archives Institute, U 136, I, 408.

4. Conway's Hotel on George's Street was used occasionally as a concert venue from 1823 until 1830. From 1831 it was renamed the King's Arms Hotel, and was the venue for the dinner meetings of the Harmonic Society.

5. *CN*, 6 March 1830.

6. Ignaz Moscheles, *The Tyrolese Melodies*, 3 vols (London, 1827–9); Hans Nathan, 'The Tyrolese Family Rainer, and the Vogue of Singing Mountain-Troupes in Europe and America', *The Musical Quarterly*, vol. 32, no. 1, 1946, p. 67, n. 19; 'The Tyrolese Minstrels', *The Harmonicon*, vol. 5, 1827, p. 149.

7. *CN*, 27 March 1830.

8. Ibid., 4 August 1831.

9. Robert Ricks, 'Russian Horn Bands', *The Musical Quarterly*, vol. 55, no. 3, 1969, pp. 364–71.

10. *CN*, 24 March 1832.

11. Ibid., 15 March 1832.

12. *SR*, 19 July 1832.

13. Tickets for this concert were available from Mr Travers, South Terrace, who may be identified as Captain John Travers. *CN*, 12 June 1830; *SR*, 18 June 1830; *Pigot's City of Dublin and Hibernian Provincial Directory* (London and Manchester: Pigot, 1824).

14. Henry Allen was enrolled as a student at the RAM from January 1830 to June 1832. Royal Academy of Music, *A List of Pupils*, p. 32. In 1844 he performed one of the principal roles in a series of operatic productions at the Princess's Theatre, Oxford Street.

15. *CN*, 12 June 1830.

16. Catherine Ferris, 'Dublin Grand Musical Festival, *1831*', *EMIR*, vol. 1, pp. 324–5.

17. *CN*, 11 November 1830.

18. Rev. J.B. McGovern, 'Boleyne Reeves, Harpist and Poet: a forgotten Cork worthy', *JCHAS*, vol. 15, 1909, pp. 157–63. Kastner referred to Reeves as 'one of the best English players I ever heard': A. Kastner, 'The Harp', *Proceedings of the Musical Association*, 35th session, 1908–9, p. 12.

19. Nicholas Moore Stack was a native of Listowel, County Kerry. He came to Cork at an early age, where he engaged in amateur theatricals. In 1829, he was appointed as Professor of Elocution at the Catholic Colleges of Carlow and Maynooth. 'Items about Irishmen', *The Irish Monthly*, vol. 21, no. 235, 1893, pp. 35–6.

20. *CN*, 11 November 1830.

21. See Boydell, 'Music, 1700–1850', pp. 612–13. The programmes are published in the booklet *The Dublin Musical Festival, 1831*, NLI Ir 7809 d 3; Collins, 'Music in Dublin', p. 16.

22. *SR*, 27 September 1831.

23. *CN*, 29 September 1831.

24. Ibid., 1 October 1831.

25. Ibid., 27 September 1831.

26. Ibid., 1 October 1831.

27. Simon McVeigh, 'An Audience for High-Class Music', in William Weber (ed.), *The Musician as Entrepreneur, 1700–1914: managers, charlatans and idealists* (Bloomington and Indiana: Indiana University Press, 2004), p. 174.

28. *CN*, 27 September 1831.

29. Edward Neill, 'Niccolò Paganini', *NGrove2*, vol. 18, pp. 887–94; Boydell, however, states that it was not performed at the Dublin Festival. See Boydell, 'Music 1700–1850', p. 613.

30. *CN*, 1 October 1831.

31. Ibid., 25 October 1831.

32. *SR*, 15 October 1831.

33. Listed as Mr Harrington in the programme for this and several subsequent concerts, Thomas John Edward Harrington was a student at the RAM from 1824 to 1826 and subsequently settled as a teacher of music in Dublin: Royal Academy of Music, *A List of Pupils*; 'The Royal Academy of Music', *Quarterly Musical Magazine and Review*, vol. 7, no. 16, 1825, p. 145.

34. Kieran Daly, 'Catholic Church/Liturgical Music', *EMIR*, vol. 2, pp. 173–5; Ita Beausang, 'Corri Family', *EMIR*, vol. 1, p. 253.

35. Lisa Parker, 'Samuel J. Pigott', *EMIR*, vol. 2, p. 840.

36. *CN*, 29 October 1831.

37. *Dublin Evening Post*, 18 November 1831.

38. *Belfast Newsletter*, 2 December 1831.

39. *CN*, 5 November 1831.

40. Ibid., 18 September 1832.

41. Hans Joachim Zingel, *Harp Music in the Nineteenth Century* (Indiana University Press, 1992), p. 29.

42. *CN*, 18 October 1832; the *Post Office General Directory* of 1842–3; *CMC*, 12 January 1814; *Pigot's Directory*, 1824.

43. *SR*, 1 August 1833.

44. *CMC*, 2 August 1833.

45. *CN*, 3 August 1833.

46. Ibid., 6 August 1833.

47. Ibid., 3 October 1833.

48. *CMC*, 2 October 1833.

49. *CN*, 10 October 1833.

50. Ibid., 5 October 1833.

51. *CMC*, 22 November 1833; *SR*, 30 November 1833.

52. *SR*, 12 April 1834.

53. A.P. Herrmann may be identified as Anton Popp, formerly of the Herrmann quartet, which had disbanded in 1830. He settled in Cork and was active thereafter as singer, teacher and composer.

54. *CMC*, 14 April 1834.

55. *CEH*, 14 April 1834.

56. He toured as a child prodigy, arriving in London in 1831. Brown, *Biographical Dictionary*, p. 500; Thomas Lawrence 'Giulio Regondi in Ireland', http://www.ucd.ie/pages/99/articles/lawrence.pdf, accessed 22 August 2016.

57. Lawrence, 'Giulio Regondi in Ireland'.

58. *SR*, 29 July 1834.

59. Lawrence, 'Giulio Regondi in Ireland'.

60. *CEH*, 29 September 1834.

61. Lawrence, 'Giulio Regondi in Ireland'.

62. *SR*, 2 August 1834; also appeared in the *Waterford Mirror*, 10 December 1834.

63. *CMC*, 26 September 1834; *CEH*, 29 September 1834.

64. *CN*, 6 December 1831; *SR*, 8 December 1831; J. McCarthy, probably singer John McCarthy, succeeded Sheehy as secretary, and William Harrington, a local druggist/chemist, succeeded Atkins as treasurer.

65. *CN*, 8 December 1835.

66. *CN*, 3 March 1836.

67. Ibid.

68. *SR*, 31 March 1836.

69. Ibid.

70. *CN*, 31 March 1836.

71. *SR*, 31 March 1836.

72. Rohr, *The Careers of British Musicians*, p. 14.

73. *SR*, 13 May 1837.

74. Peter Murray, 'Art Institutions in Nineteenth-Century Cork', in Patrick O'Flanagan and Cornelius G. Buttimer (eds), *Cork: History and Society. Interdisciplinary Essays in the History of an Irish County* (Dublin: Geography Publications, 1993), pp. 819–31.

75. *SR*, 12 April 1836.

76. Ibid., 16 April 1836.

77. Ibid., 21 April 1836.

78. *CN*, Ibid. 10 September, 3 October 1833; *SR*, 7 June 1834.

79. Royal Academy of Music, *A List of Pupils*. A press notice by Mrs Harrington identifies her as 'Professor and member of RAM, London, and pupil of Mr Bochsa': *SR*, 7 June 1834. 'The Royal Academy of Music', *Quarterly Musical Magazine and Review*, vol. 7, no. 16, 1825, pp. 143–69.

80. *SR*, 10 May 1836.

81. Ibid., 26 May 1836. Described as a Protestant liberal, Francis Bernard Beamish was the eighth son of William Beamish, who co-founded a major brewery in the city in 1792. Prominent in many aspects of city life, he openly supported O'Connell, and became Mayor of Cork in 1843. See Ian d'Alton, 'Keeping Faith: an evocation of the Cork Protestant character, 1820–1920', in O'Flanagan and Buttimer (eds), *Cork History and Society*, p. 768.

82. *SR*, 4 June 1836.

83. Ibid., 21 June 1836.

84. Ibid., 16 July 1836.

85. *CEH*, 14 September 1836.

86. *CN*, 17 September 1836.

87. Ibid., 15 September 1836.

88. Ibid., 29 September 1836.

89. *SR*, 31 January 1837; *CS*, 6 February 1837.

90. *Morning Post*, 21 June 1836; David Conway, *Jewry in Music: entry into the profession from the Enlightenment to Richard Wagner* (Cambridge: Cambridge University Press, 2012), p. 108.

91. *SR*, 23 February 1837.

92. Collins, 'Music in Dublin', p. 17.

93. *CS*, 22 February 1837.

94. *CN*, 4 March 1837; *CS*, 3 March 1837.

95. *CN*, 4 March 1837.

96. Ibid., 21 December 1837.

97. Ibid.

98. *SR*, 20 January 1838.

99. In comparison with two recorded morning concerts during the previous decade, twenty-two occurred between 1831 and 1840, sixteen of which took place from 1835 to 1840. Susan O'Regan, 'Public Concerts: the musical life of Cork', vol. 2, 'Calendar of Cork Concerts'.

100. E.J. Lea-Scarlett, 'Bochsa, Robert Nicholas Charles (1789–1856)', *Australian Dictionary of Biography*, National Centre of Biography, Australian National University, http://adb.anu.edu.au/biography/bochsa-robert-nicholas-charles-3019/text4423, published in hardcopy 1969, accessed online 22 August 2016.

101. *CN*, 19 April 1838.

102. Ibid., 21 April 1838.

103. *SR*, 17 April 1838.

104. Ibid., 24 April 1838.

105. *CS*, 30 April 1838.

106. Rohr, *The Careers of British Museums*, p. 14.

107. Lea-Scarlett, 'Bochsa'.

108. Susan Wollenberg, *Music at Oxford in the Eighteenth and Nineteenth Centuries* (Oxford: Oxford University Press, 2001), p. 205.

109. *SR*, 12 March 1839.

110. In advertisements for concerts elsewhere, it was claimed that this instrument was made by the Distins themselves. See Eugenia Mitroulia and Arnold Myers, 'The Distin Family as Instrument Makers and Dealers, 1845–1874', *Scottish Music Review*, vol. 2, no. 1, 2011, pp. 1–2. See also Robert E. Eliason and Lloyd P. Farrar, 'Distin', *NGrove2*, vol. 7, pp. 381–2.

111. *SR*, 30 March 1839.

112. Ibid.

113. Ibid., 18 April 1839.

114. *Dublin Evening Packet*, 10, 26 January 1839.

115. *SR*, 23 March 1839.

116. The supporting musicians were listed as Mr Smith, first violin, Mr Patterson, flute, Mr Walker, violin, Mr J. Smith, second violin, Mr D. Smith, cello, Mr Harrington, double bass: *Southern Reporter*, 23 May 1839.

117. *CN*, 11 June 1839.

118. *SR*, 25 June 1839.

119. Ibid., 15 June 1839.

120. Ibid., 5 October 1839.

121. *CS*, 7 October 1839.

122. Francis O'Neill, *Irish Minstrels and Musicians: the story of Irish music* (Chicage: Regan Printing House, 1913; reprinted Cork: Mercier Press, 1987), p. 203. A poster for a concert given by Hannigan in New Ross is described in Nicholas Carolan, 'A Nineteenth-Century Uilleann Piping Poster', *Ceol na hÉireann*, vol. 2, 1994, pp. 47–52.

123. *CN*, 10 March 1840.

124. *SR*, 21 March 1840.

125. Ibid., 15 September 1840.

126. Ibid., 18 April 1840.

127. Ibid., 2 June 1840.

128. Ibid., 15 August 1840.

129. See Alan Walker, *Franz Liszt. Vol I: The Virtuoso Years* (Ithaca, NY: Cornell University Press, 1987), pp. 359–63, for an account of the section of the tour which included Ireland and the south of England, in which Cork was described as 'the low point of the tour'. See also Seamus Gaffney, 'Liszt in Ireland', *Liszt Society Journal*, vol. 19, 1994, pp. 55–65.

130. *CN*, 29 December 1840.

131. Ibid.

132. Ibid.

133. Ibid., 30 December 1840.

134. David Ian Allsobrook, *Liszt: my travelling circus life* (London: Macmillan, 1991) p. 143.

135. Ibid., pp. 145–6.

136. *CN*, 31 December 1840.

CHAPTER 8

1. Justin McCarthy, *The Story of an Irishman* (London: Chatto & Windus, 1904), p. 44.

2. *Dublin Builder*, 1 May 1866.

3. Maura Murphy, 'Municipal Reform and the Repeal Movement in Cork, 1833–1844', *JCHAS*, vol. 81, 1976, pp. 1–2, 6–7; John B. O'Brien, 'Cork Society in the 1850s', *JCHAS*, vol. 101, 1996, pp. 15–25.

4. See Maura Cronin, 'Young Ireland in Cork, 1840–49', in Tom Dunne and Laurence M. Geary (eds), *History and the Public Sphere: essays in honour of John A. Murphy* (Cork: Cork University Press, 2005), pp. 114–26.

5. John F. Quinn, *Father Mathew's Crusade: temperance in nineteenth-century Ireland and Irish America* (Amherst, MA: University of Massachusetts Press, 2002), pp. 47–8.

6. d'Alton, *Protestant Society and Politics in Cork 1812–1844*, p. 73, n. 86; Colm Kerrigan, *Father Mathew and the Irish Temperance Movement, 1838–1849* (Cork: Cork University Press, 1992), p. 46.

7. Kerrigan, *Fathew Mathew*, pp. 48–9.

8. Quinn, *Father Mathew's Crusade*, p. 60. Father Mathew's house was in Cove Street. Conway's Royal Horse Bazaar was located at Sullivan's Quay. *The County and City of Cork Post Office General Directory, 1842–3* (Cork: Jackson, 1842), p. 18.

9. John B. O'Brien, 'Merchants in Cork before the Famine', in P. Butel and L.M. Cullen (eds), *Cities and Merchants: French and Irish perspectives on urban development, 1500–1900*, Proceedings of the Fourth Franco-Irish Seminar of Social and Economic Historians (Trinity College, Dublin, 1986), pp. 222–3.

10. John Francis Maguire, *Father Mathew: a biography* (London: Longman, Green, Longman, Roberts & Green, 1865), p. 116.

11. *SR*, 26 January 1839.

12. C.P. Hyland, 'The Cork Total Abstainer', *JCHAS*, vol. 100, 1995, pp. 167–71; Marie-Louise Legg, *Newspapers and Nationalism: the Irish provincial press, 1850–1892* (Dublin: Four Courts Press, 1998), pp. 60, 190.

13. See Aiveen Kearney, 'Temperance Bands and Their Significance in Nineteenth Century Ireland', unpublished MA dissertation (University College Cork 1981).

14. Ibid., pp. 58–9.

15. *FJ*, 30 March 1842.

16. Ibid., 20 April 1843.

17. Concert bills at Cork City and County Archives, IE CCCA U140/K/3/75, U140/K/3/58, U/140/K/3/71.

18. *Kerry Examiner and Munster General Observer*, 5 April 1842.

19. *CE*, 27 June 1842. Joseph Wheeler was a prominent figure in Cork shipbuilding, later developing a shipyard at Rushbrooke in the upper Cork harbour.

20. *CE*, 15 January 1844.

21. Maguire, *Father Mathew*, p. 122.

22. Elizabeth Malcolm, 'The Catholic Church and the Irish Temperance Movement, 1838–1901', *Irish Historical Studies*, vol. 89, 1982, p. 5.

23. *CE*, 5 March 1845.

24. Ibid., 4 December 1850.

25. Kearney, 'Temperance Bands' , p. 29.

26. *Kerry Examiner and Munster General Observer*, 5 April 1842.

27. *CE*, 27 June 1842.

28. *SR*, 16 April 1842. John O'Callaghan was master of the Lancastrian School in Knockaderry, County Limerick, in 1818.

29. Kearney, 'Temperance Bands', pp. 23–31.

30. *CE*, 30 March 1842.

31. *The Nation*, 26 December 1846.

32. Johann Georg Kohl, *Ireland, Scotland and England* (London: Chapman & Hall, 1844), p. 95.

33. *SR*, 13 January 1842.

34. *CN*, 12 May 1846.

35. *CE*, 23 March 1859.

36. Percy A. Scholes, *The Mirror of Music, 1844–1944*, 2 vols (London: Novello, 1947), vol. 1, p. 8.

37. William Weber, 'Mass Culture and European Musical Taste, 1770–1870', *International Journal of the Aesthetics and Sociology of Music*, vol. 25, nos 1–2, 1994, p. 184.

38. See Kerry Murphy, 'Joseph Mainzer's "Sacred and Beautiful Mission": an aspect of Parisian musical life of the 1830s', *Music and Letters*, vol. 75, 1994, pp. 33–46; see also Bernarr Rainbow and Gordon Cox, *Music in Educational Thought and Practice: a survey from 800 BC* (Woodbridge: Boydell Press, 2006), pp. 184–6.

39. Rainbow and Cox, *Music*, pp. 200–2; John Hullah, *Wilhem's Method of Teaching Singing Adapted to English Use* (London: J. Parker, 1842).

40. Dowden Collection, IE CCCA/U140/L/035; William Keleher (d. 1849) was Librarian of the Cork Library and a strong advocate for popular learning. J.C., 'Cork Worthies of the Last Century', *JCHAS*, vol. 22, 1916, p. 81.

41. *CE*, 8 July 1842.

42. Ibid., 29 July 1842.

43. See Maria McHale, 'Singing and Sobriety: music and the temperance movement in Ireland, 1838–43', in Michael Murphy and Jan Smaczny (eds), *Music in Nineteenth-Century Ireland* (Dublin: Four Courts Press, 2007), pp. 166–86.

44. *CE*, 29 August 1842.

45. The *Cork Examiner* report listed Fr Mathew, Rev. John Falvey, Rev. P.W. Coffey, Rev. Mr Hort (Unitarian minister), William and Mrs Fagan, N.D. Murphy, Dr McEvers, William Forde, Counsellor Walsh and William Keleher.

46. 'The Career of a Gloucester Chorister Boy', *Cheltenham Chronicle*, 26 April 1864.

47. *SR*, 1 September 1842.

48. Ibid.; *CE*, 7 September 1842.

49. Professor of Music, 1845 *Post Office Directory*.

50. Professor of Singing, 1845 *Post Office Directory*.

51. Professor of Music, 1845 *Post Office Directory*.

52. *CE*, 21 November 1842.

53. McHale, 'Singing and Sobriety', pp. 184–5.

54. Alexander King, *The Might and the Right of the People: letters on popular education, political reform, etc. addressed to Right Rev Dr Murphy, Very Rev T. Matthew and Daniel O'Connell, Esq. M.P.* (London: Ward and Co.; Dublin: J. Robertson; Cork: G. Ridings, 1843)

55. William Young, *The Catholic Choralist* (Dublin: Catholic Choralist Office, 1842). For a more detailed discussion, see McHale, 'Singing and Sobriety', pp. 178–9.

56. William MacNamara Downes, *Temperance Melodies for the Teetotallers of Ireland*, 3rd edition (Cork: S.M. Thompson, 1843).

57. McHale, 'Singing and Sobriety', pp. 180–1.

58. *CE*, 12 September 1842.

59. IE CCCA U140/K/3/55.

60. Dáire Keogh, 'Evangelising the Faithful: Edmund Rice and the reformation of nineteenth-century Irish Catholicism', in Colm Lennon (ed.), *Confraternities and Sodalities in Ireland: charity, devotion and sociability c.1860–c.1960* (Dublin: Columba Press, 2012), p. 67; Marie McCarthy, *Passing It On: the transmission of music in Irish culture* (Cork: Cork University Press, 1999), p. 88, ns 117–18.

61. *CE*, 3 April 1843.

62. 'The Career of a Gloucester Chorister Boy'. *Cheltenham Chronicle*, 26 April 1864.

63. Kerry Murphy, 'Joseph Mainzer's "Sacred and Beautiful Mission": an aspect of Parisian Musical Life of the 1830s', *Music and Letters*, vol. 75, 1994, pp. 44–5.

64. *The Nation*, 26 December 1846.

65. *CN*, 24 March 1849; handbill for charity sermon at North Cathedral, IE CCCA U/140/J/3/3/1.

66. *Illustrated London News*, no. 168, vol. 7, 19 July 1845.

67. Isaac S. and Amos Varian were nephews of Isaac Varian, who was Professor of Flute in the late eighteenth century.

68. *CE*, 24 April 1846.

69. Ibid., 13 October 1847.

70. Born in Dunmanway, County Cork, Justin McCarthy was the son of Michael McCarthy, founder of the *Cork Magazine*. He left Cork in 1852, and followed a successful career in journalism, eventually becoming a member of the Irish Parliamentary Party for County Longford from 1879 to 1900. 'Justin McCarthy', in Rolf Loeber and Magda Loeber with Anne Mullin Burnham (eds), *A Guide to Irish Fiction, 1650–1900* (Dublin: Four Courts Press, 2005), pp, 799–800.

71. McCarthy, *The Story of an Irishman*, pp. 31–40.

72. *CE*, 27 April 1849.

73. Ibid., 12 October 1842.

74. Pippa Drummond, *The Provincial Music Festival in England, 1784–1914*, p. 242.

75. *CE*, 27 April 1842.

76. Ibid., 12 October 1842. This notice included the request that 'Gentlemen wishing to become performing members of the Society will be admitted by ballot, but as this rule has been established only to ensure the respectability and efficiency of the society, the members trust that it will deter none from offering themselves.'

77. Ibid., 9 December 1842.

78. Ibid., December 1842.

79. Ibid., 24 February 1843.

80. Fanny Russell made several appearances in London in 1842: see, for example, *The Musical World*, vol. 17, 1842, pp. 354, 355, 364. She performed 'Savourneen deelish' at a concert in the theatre in Lichfield, ibid., p. 352. Mrs Wookey was listed as Professor of Singing in Cork in *Aldwell's Post Office Directory, 1844*, and advertised in *The Constitution*, 21 September 1844.

81. *CN*, 10 May 1843; CE, 16 May 1843. Published by Novello in 1819 in a set of twelve Masses, Mozart's Twelfth Mass (K. Anh. 232, C1.04) was in fact misattributed, and was probably composed by Wenzel Müller (1767–1835). The work nonetheless enjoyed wide circulation during the nineteenth century.

82. *CE*, 21 October 1850.

83. This stated aim of the society appeared in its first newspaper notice in October 1846, almost identical in wording to that of the Dublin Antient Concerts Society's notice in the *Dublin Almanack and General Register of Ireland* in 1839, quoted in Paul Rodmell, 'The Society of Antient Concerts, Dublin, 1834–64', in Michael Murphy and Jan Smaczny (eds), *Music in Nineteenth-Century Ireland* (Dublin: Four Courts Press, 2007), p. 211.

84. Catherine Ferris, *The Use of Newspapers as a Source for Musicological Research: A case study of Dublin musical life 1840–44* (PhD dissertation, NUI Maynooth, 2011), p. 133, http://eprints.maynoothuniversity.ie/2577/1/Catherine_Ferris_PhD_2011.pdf accessed 16 October 2016.

85. *Morning Post*, 13 October 1846.

86. *CE*, 12 October 1846.

87. Ferris, *The Use of Newspapers*, pp. 137–8.

88. *CE*, 24 March 1847.

89. Ibid., 31 March 1847.

90. Ibid., 9 April 1847; probably Charles Sippi, a member of a family of musicians from Youghal and Lismore who occasionally performed in Cork.

91. *CE*, 29 March 1847. A notice in *CE*, 15 March 1847, includes a list of patrons for the concert.

92. J.W. Flynn, *The Random Recollections of an Old Playgoer: a sketch of some old Cork theatres* (Cork: Guy, 1890), pp. 23–4.

93. *Morning Post*, 5 March 1847.

94. These included the Cork Ladies Relief Society, led by the Countess of Bandon and the Marchioness of Thomond. The Society of Friends (Quakers) formed on organisation for soup kitchens in the city, relying on their own international networks for support. See Christine Kinealy, *Charity and the Great Hunger in Ireland: the kindness of strangers* (London: Bloomsbury, 2013), pp. 64, 150.

95. Rodmell, 'The Society of Antient Concerts', p. 222.

96. *CN*, 8 February 1849.

97. *CE*, 5 April 1850.

98. Rodmell, 'The Society of Antient Concerts, p. 225.

99. *CN*, 8 February 1849.

100. Jeremy Dibble, 'John James Stanford', *EMIR*, vol. 2, pp. 958–9. John Stanford was a soloist in the Dublin Antient Concerts Society performance of Mendelssohn's *Elijah* in 1847. Rodmell, 'The Society of Antient Concerts' p. 225, n. 53.

101. *CE*, 16 December 1850.

102. Programmes for these concerts are held at NLI I 655 1.

103. *Illustrated London News*, vol. 20, 1852, pp. 493–8; *Morning Post*, 3 June 1852; *The Times*, 10 June 1852; *The Morning Chronicle*, 11 June 1852.

104. John Francis Maguire, *The Industrial Movement in Ireland as Illustrated by the National Exhibition, 1852* (Cork: O'Brien, 1853), pp. 109–13; *Official Catalogue of the National Exhibition of the Arts, Manufactures, and Products of Ireland; held in Cork, 1852. With Alphabetical List of the Names of Exhibitors* (Cork: O'Brien, 1852), pp. 22–3.

105. Seán Donnelly, 'Denis Harrington of Cork', *An Píobaire*, vol. 2, no. 30, 1986, p. 2. Denis Harrington was listed as instrument maker with an address at 19 Fort Street in Aldwell's *Post Office Directory* of 1844.

106. *Origin, Constitution and Design of the Cork Athenaeum* (Cork: Guy, nd [1852/3]), IE CCCA U15B/P/A17; *CE*, 10 September 1852 (reprinted from *The Constitution*).

107. C.B. Gibson, *A History of the County and City of Cork*, vol. 2, pp. 317–18; *CE*, 6 October 1854.

108. *CE*, 10 July 1854.

109. Ibid.

110. *SR*, 13 July 1854.

111. *CE*, 6 October 1853.

112. Ibid., 10 July 1854.

113. Ibid., 11 May 1855.

114. *CE*, 18 January 1854.

115. W.B. Squire (Rev. Clive Brown), 'William Richard Bexfield (1824–1853)', in H.C.G. Mullan and Brian Harrison (eds), *Oxford Dictionary of National Biography*, 60 vols (Oxford: Oxford University Press, 2004), vol. 5, pp. 626–7; Howard E. Smither, *A History of the Oratorio: the oratorio in the nineteenth and twentieth centuries* (Chapel Hill, NC: University of North Carolina Press, 2000), p. 291.

116. *CE*, 20 March 1854.

117. The other soloists were John Fleming, Jeremiah Sullivan, both associated with the St Mary's (North) Cathedral, and Thomas Edward Close, tenor, formerly of the Italian Opera, London, and appointed to the choir of St Fin Barre's on the resignation of James Keays in 1850. *CE*, 16 January 1857; Caulfield, *Annals of Saint Fin Barre's*, p. 100.

118. John Wyse Jackson and Peter Costello, *John Stanislaus Joyce: the voluminous life and genius of James Joyce's father* (New York: St Martin's Press, 1998), pp. 30–1; Royal Academy of Music Student Registers, 1837–73.

119. A short biographical entry for Alfred Blake was published in Richard J. Hodges and W.T. Pike, *Cork and County Cork in the Twentieth Century* (Brighton: Pike, 1911), p. 167.

120. *CE*, 12 December 1853. Una Hunt, 'Arthur O'Leary', *EMIR*, vol. 2, pp. 777–8.

121. *CE*, 11 February 1859; *CN*, 17 March 1860.

122. *CE*, 4 February 1863; *CN*, 18 February 1868.

123. Dowden Collection, IE CCCA U140/01/15/05, contains a printed handbill (undated) for one of the society's concerts at the Athenaeum.

124. *CE*, 26 November 1855.

125. *CAG*, 28 March 1856; *The Era*, 13 April 1856.

126. *CE*, 21 May 1860.

127. *CN*, 30 May, 3 June 1861; *CE*, 31 May 1861.

128. *CE*, 31 May 1861.

129. Gibson, *A History*, vol. 2, pp. 322–3; *Illustrated London News*, vol. 37, 1861, p. 400; *SR*, 9 April 1861; *CE*, 17 April 1861.

130. *CN*, 16 October 1860.

131. Ibid., 22 November 1860; *CE*, 25 January 1861; Penrose Beale, Hon Sec.

132. *CE*, 25 June 1861.

133. Ibid.; *SR*, 18, 22 July 1861.

134. *CE*, 25 September 1861.

135. Ibid., 12 September 1861.

136. Ibid., 11 January 1862.

137. Ibid., 6 December 1861.

138. Formerly a singer of Worcester cathedral choir, William J. Topham (d. 1871) was a tenor singer at St Fin Barre's, Cork, for some time up to 1861, when he left to take up the post of first tenor at Christ Church, Dublin. *CN*, 19 April 1861; *CE*, 10 May 1861; *FJ*, 26 September 1871; *Worcestershire Chronicle*, 19 February 1862.

139. A notice published in the *Cork Examiner* on 28 April 1862 announced that Miss Julia Cruise was to take part in the festival concerts.

140. Wilhelm Elsner, a native of Frankfurt, came to Dublin in 1851 to take up the post of Professor of Cello at the Royal Irish Academy of Music. Jennifer O'Connor, 'Wilhelm Elsner', *EMIR*, vol. 1, p. 352. He performed at musical events in Cork on numerous occasions over the following three decades.

141. *CE*, 25 January 1862; *The Musical World*, vol. 40, 1862, p. 23. Taken from *The Cork Herald.*

142. *CE*, 30 January 1862.

143. Ibid., 7, 9 May 1862.

144. Andrew Johnstone, 'George William Torrance', *EMIR*, vol. 2, p. 992.

145. *CE*, 28 April, 9 May 1862.

146. Ibid., 15 December 1862. The 'Distressed Lancashire Operatives' were victims of the so-called 'cotton famine' which occurred in the cotton mills of north-west England. Overproduction in preceding years, and a halt in the supply of raw cotton from America during the Civil War (1861–65), resulted in mass unemployment of workers.

147. Obituary, *Musical Times and Singing Class Circular*, vol. 44, no. 727, 1903, p. 594; Caulfield, *Annals of St Fin Barre's*, p. 109. The event was described in *The Musical World*, vol. 46, 1868, p. 508.

148. *CE*, 13 November 1868.

149. Richard Caulfield, *A Lecture on the History of the Bishops of Cork, and Cathedral of St Fin Barre*, delivered in the lecture room of St Peter's Working Men's Association on Monday 25 January 1864 (Cork: Purcell, 1864), pp. 36–7.

150. Caulfield, *Annals of St Fin Barre's*, p. 102.

151. Ibid., pp. 111–13.

152. *Irish Ecclesiastical Gazette*, 23 December 1870.

153. Rainbow and Cox, *Music in Educational Thought and Practice*, pp. 208–9.

154. *CN*, 29 October 1860.

155. Ibid., 4 March 1861.

156. *SR*, 20, 28 March 1862.

157. *Dublin Builder*, 1 May 1866; *CE*, 13 February 1868, 31 March 1869, 7 December 1869; *CN*, 6 May 1870; *CE*, 9 December 1870.

158. *CE*, 10 December 1869.

159. Ibid., 13 February 1868.

160. Ibid., 7 September 1853.

161. Ibid., 9 November 1853. James Halloran was an attorney with an address at 72 Grand Parade. Mrs Halloran also appended this address to a concert notice in *CE*, 12 February 1855.

162. *CE*, 20 April 1853.

163. *SR*, 23 June 1853; *CE*, 4 July 1853.

164. *CE*, 4 April 1855.

165. Ibid., 12 February 1855.

166. Ibid., 12, 14 February 1855.

167. Ibid., 27 March 1846; *CN*, 3 July 1849.

168. *CE*, 31 January 1855.

169. Gibson, *A History*, vol. 2, p. 329; *CN*, 3 July 1849; *CE*, 20 May 1863.

170. Francis Guy, *City and County Cork Almanac and Directory for 1875–76* (Cork: Guy, 1875).

171. *CN*, 11, 14, 15 May 1861.

172. Francis Guy, *City and County Cork Almanac and Directory for 1891* (Cork: Guy, 1891), p. 98.

173. *CE*, 13 June 1853.

174. Ibid., 20 December 1854.

175. Ibid., 29 October 1855; Maxwell Sullivan (O'Sullivan) was an amateur singer and member of musical societies in Cork and Dublin. Around 1860, he emigrated to America, where he joined the New York Volunteers (the 'Irish Brigade'), and died from injuries sustained in the American Civil War. He was son of Captain John Sullivan (O'Sullivan) (d. 1857), who was also a well-known Cork amateur musician and actor. *CE*, 23 March 1857, 28 April, 2 May 1862.

176. *CE*, 14 November 1859; Paul Collins, 'John William Glover', *EMIR*, vol. 1, p. 435.

177. *CE*, 13 February 1861; *CE*, 20, 30 November 1861; 10 December 1866.

178. Ibid., 17 April 1866.

179. Mendelssohn's *Six Grand Sonatas for the Organ*, Op 65, were published in 1845.

180. *CN*, 18 April 1866.

181. 'Church Music' by Rev. W.H. Anderson; *CE*, 27 January 1858.

182. *The Nation*, 12 January 1889.

183. *CE*, 3 January 1865.

184. Ibid., 7, 11 January 1865.

185. Ibid., 16 January 1868.

186. Ibid., 18 January 1869.

187. Ibid., 18 July 1860.

188. Ibid., 15 April 1861.

189. A letter written by John F. O'Neill appeared in the *Cork Examiner* in February 1863, calling for a revival of 'Total abstinence', and outlining the missionary efforts of the Oblate Fathers in this regard. He described a meeting in Cork on 1 January 1863 of a group of 'Mathewites' attempting to revive the taking of the pledge. *CE*, 6 February 1863.

190. *CE*, 28 November 1866.

191. Established in London in 1858, the firm of Besson developed brass instruments, particularly the cornet.

192. *CE*, 31 December 1868.

193. Ibid., 17 June 1869.

194. Ibid., 2, 16, 17 June, 2 July, 28 August 1869.

195. Ibid., 2 May 1870.

196. Ibid., 16 June 1876.

197. For example, a Temperance Soirée presided over by Richard Dowden was held by this society in March 1851. *CE*, 7 March 1851.

198. *CE*, 29 December 1866.

199. Ibid., 13 September 1869.

200. Ibid., 13 June 1871; *The City of Cork Directory, with which is incorporated the Commercial Directory of Queenstown* (Liverpool: Fulton, 1871), p. 146.

201. *Morning Post*, 22 August 1888; *FJ*, 23 August 1888.

202. *Dundee Courier*, 23 August 1888.

203. Fintan Lane, 'Music and Violence in Working Class Cork: the "Band Nuisance". 1879–1882', *Saothar*, vol. 24, 1999, pp. 17–31; Fintan Lane, 'Musical Bands and Local Identities', in John Crowley, Robert Devoy, Denis Linehan and Patrick O'Flanagan (eds), *Atlas of Cork City* (Cork: Cork University Press, 2005), pp. 209–12.

CHAPTER 9

1. *CE*, 19 December 1861.

2. Key works on the history of Irish Catholicism are Patrick Corish, *The Irish Catholic Experience: a historical survey* (Dublin: Gill & Macmillan, 1985), Desmond Keenan, *The Catholic Church in Nineteenth-Century Ireland: a sociological study* (Dublin: Gill & Macmillan, 1983), Oliver P. Rafferty, *The Catholic Church and the Protestant State: nineteenth century realities* (Dublin: Four Courts Press, 2008).

3. Recent research on Catholic church music in Ireland is presented in Kieran Daly, 'Catholic Church/Liturgical Music', *EMIR*, vol. 1, pp. 173–5, and Frank Lawrence, 'Catholic Popular Devotional Music', *EMIR*, vol. 1, pp. 175–8. The latter half of the nineteenth century has been researched in more detail, for example Kieran Daly's *Catholic Church Music in Ireland, 1878–1903* (Dublin: UCD Press, 2013), Harry White and Nicholas Lawrence's 'Towards a History of the Cecilian Movement in Ireland', in Gerard Gillen and Harry White (eds), *Music and the Church* (Dublin: Irish Academic Press, 1993), and Paul Collins (ed.), *Renewal and Resistance: Catholic church music from the 1850s to Vatican II* (Bern: Peter Lang, 2010).

4. Brady, vol. 1, Clerical and Parochial Records, pp. 265–6.

5. T.A. Lunham, 'Bishop Dive Downes' Visitation of his Diocese, 1699–1702', *JCHAS*, vol. 15, no. 84, 1909, p. 179.

6. Rev. T.J. Walsh, *In the Tradition of St Finbarr* (Cork: Guy, 1951), p. 6.

7. Rev. P. Cahalane, 'The Catholic Parish Churches of Cork', *JCHAS*, vol. 48, 1943, p. 27; Dickson, *Old World Colony*, pp. 257–8.

8. Walsh, *In the Tradition of St Finbarr*, pp. 6–7; Bartlett, *Ireland: a history*, pp. 163–6; Evelyn Bolster, *A History of the Diocese of Cork: the episcopate of William Delaney, 1847–1886* (Cork: Tower Books, 1993), pp. 99–100; Samuel Lewis, *Lewis' Cork: a topographical dictionary of the parishes, towns and villages of Cork city and county* (1837, repr. Cork, 1998), p. 189.

9. Fr Donal Casey, 'St Finbarr's Church, Cork 1766–1966', *The Fold*, vol. 14, no. 3 (September 1966), pp. 11–17.

10. Nigel Yates, *The Religious Condition of Ireland, 1770–1850* (Oxford: Oxford University Press, 2006), p. 227.

11. Lewis, *Lewis' Cork*, p. 189.

12. Sr Mary Pius O'Farrell, 'Bishop Moylan's Report on the Diocese of Cork, 1802', *JCHAS*, vol. 106, 2001, p. 124.

13. Síle Ní Chinnéide, 'A New View of Cork in 1790', *JCHAS*, vol. 78, 1973, pp. 1–13.

14. T.E. Muir, *Roman Catholic Church Music in England, 1791–1914: a handmaid of the liturgy?* (Farnham: Ashgate, 2013), p. 42.

15. An account given in Walsh, *In the Tradition of St Finbarr*, pp. 20–1, states that both masses were held at the South Parish Chapel; the newspaper reports specify other city churches.

16. *HC*, 7 February 1793.

17. Ibid., 14 November 1793. Early reports of music performed at High Mass in Dublin parish churches were published in the *Dublin Evening Post* in 1792. See C.S. Begadon, 'Laity and Clergy in the Catholic Renewal of Dublin', p. 224.

18. *HC*, 4 November 1799.

19. *CMC*, 9 March 1807.

20. Rev. P. Cahalane, 'The Catholic Parish Churches of Cork', *JCHAS*, vol. 48, 1943, p. 27.

21. Pauline MacSweeney, 'The Organ and Harpsichord in Ireland before 1870', MA dissertation (University College, Cork, 1979), p. 109. MacSweeney gives the specification, after Pearce. Charles W. Pearce, *Notes on English Organs of the period 1800–1810, Cathedral, Collegiate, Parochial and Otherwise, taken chiefly from the ms of Henry Leffler* (London, 1911). T.J. Walsh states that the organ was made by Rupert of London and cost 320 guineas: Walsh, *In the Tradition of St Finbarr*, p. 21. To date, this maker has not been traced.

22. *CMC*, 11 May 1814.

23. McSweeney, 'The Organ', p. 109. Specifications after Pierce are also given.

24. Rev. T.J. Walsh, 'St Mary's Pro-Cathedral, Cork', *The Fold*, May 1964, pp. 13–21.

25. O'Farrell, 'Bishop Moylan's Report,' p. 126; Bolster, *The Diocese of Cork*, pp. 186–9; *CMC*, 13 September 1802.

26. *CMC*, 26 August 1808.

27. Ibid., 15 June 1810. H. de Monti subsequently published *Strictures on Logier's System of Musical Education* (Glasgow, 1817).

28. David Baptie, *Musical Scotland, Past and Present* (Paisley: J. & R. Parlane, 1894), p. 42.

29. *CMC*, 15 June 1810.

30. *The Musical Times and Singing Class Circular*, vol. 10, no. 226 (1 December 1861), p. 160. This appears to have been a posthumous publication.

31. William Smith Clark suggests that this chapel may have been established in an existing disused playhouse, indicated on Rocque's survey (1759). See Clark, *The Irish Stage in the County Towns, 1720–1800* (Oxford: Clarendon, 1965), p. 73.

32. Liam Kennedy and Clare Murphy, *Account Books of the Franciscan House, Broad Lane, Cork, 1764–1921* (Dublin: Irish Manuscripts Commission, 2012).

33. Lewis, *Lewis' Cork*, p. 189; Paul McKeever, 'Woffington Family', *EMIR*, vol. 2, p. 1066.

34. *CMC*, 28 September 1808.

35. Frank Lawrence, 'Catholic Popular Devotional Music', *EMIR*, vol.1, pp. 175–8.

36. Richard Sharpe, 'Tadhg Gaelach Ó Súilleabháin's *Pious Miscellany*: editions of the Munster bestseller of the early nineteenth century', *Proceedings of the Royal Irish Academy*, vol. 114C, 2014, pp. 1–59.

37. *Dillon's Genuine Edition of Timothy O'Sullivan's, commonly called Taidhag Gaodhlach's Pious Miscellany. Englarged, improved and corrected, with an appendix of other religious compositions, in English and Irish, by Patrick Denn, Cappoquin* (Cork: Dillon, 1841). For a detailed discussion of this topic see Nóirín Ní Riain's 'The Nature and Classification of Traditional Religious Songs', in Gerard Gillen and Harry White (eds), *Music and the Church*. Irish Musical Studies 2 (Dublin: Irish Academic Press, 1993).

38. Evelyn Bolster, 'The Moylan Correspondence in Bishop's House, Killarney, Part 1', *Collectanea Hibernica*, no. 14, 1971, p. 84.

39. *CMC*, 5 June 1816.

40. Pádraig Ó Súilleabháin, 'Sidelights on the Irish Church, 1811–38', *Collectanea Hibernica*, vol. 9, 1966, p. 75.

41. *FJ*, 23 October 1839.

42. Ibid.

43. Lewis, *Lewis' Cork*, p. 190; Brendan Grimes, 'Funding a Roman Catholic Church in Nineteenth-Century Ireland', *Architectural History*, vol. 52, 2009, pp. 163–4.

44. *CE*, 4 October 1841.

45. *SR*, 7 May 1842; *CE*, 9, 26 May 1842. A description of the organ specifications was given in CE, 20 April 1842, and its inaugural performance at the maker's factory was reported in *The Musical World*, vol. 17, 1842, p. 94. Mr Shea was probably William Shea, who was listed in *Aldwell's Post Office Directory* 1844 as Professor of Music, with an address at 1 Hanover Place.

46. *CN*, 10 May 1842.

47. Grand Oratorio: Invitation sent to William Coppinger, IE CCCA U229/117/19.

48. *CE*, 1 August 1842.

49. W.G. 'Music in Cork', *The Musical World*, vol. 20, 1845, pp. 98–9

50. Flynn, *Random Recollections*, p. 23.

51. Obituary in *The Leeds Times*, 13 May 1882.

52. *Musical Times and Singing Class Circular*, vol. 8, no. 171, 1857, p. 37

53. Kennedy and Murphy, *Account Books of the Franciscan House, Cork.*

54. John Gilbert, 'A Record of Authors, Artists and Musical Composers Born in the County Cork', *JCHAS*, vol. 29, 1913, p. 180; C. Cremen, 'Notes and Queries: John Fleming, musician and composer', *JCHAS*, vol. 39, no. 150, 1934, pp. 102–3.

55. Robert Bowden served as organist at the South Parish Chapel from around 1814. John Seymour was organist there during the 1830s. John V. Blake served as organist at this church from 1857. Thomas Nagle succeeded him in January 1867. *CE*, 14 October 1857; *CAG*, 14 October 1857.

56. *CE*, 7 May 1855.

57. Kennedy and Murphy, *Account Books*, pp. 226–34.

58. *CE*, 28 December 1857.

59. Kennedy and Murphy, *Account Books*; *Guy's Cork Almanac*, 1884.

60. *CE*, 15 April 1865. Bartholomew Britton was a foreman printer at the *Cork Examiner* office. His marriage to Norah, eldest daughter of Mr O'Callaghan of Cork, took place at St Patrick's Church on 27 November 1866. *CE*, 29 November 1866. Britton was proprieter of the *Cork Examiner* from 1877 to 1888. See Legg, *Newspapers and Nationalism*, p. 190. Mrs Britton received payment as organist of St Francis Church from 1868 until 1884, and was listed as organist at St Francis Church in Guy's *City and County Cork Almanac and Directory for 1884*.

61. *CE*, 11 October 1850. A detailed account of the building of this church is given in Patricia Curtin-Kelly, *An Ornament to the City: Holy Trinity church and the Capuchin order* (Dublin: History Press, 2015).

62. *SR*, 19 October 1850.

63. Curtin-Kelly, *An Ornament to the City*, p. 100; *Official Catalogue of the National Exhibition of the Arts, Manufactures, and Products of Ireland; held in Cork, 1852. With Alphabetical List of the Names of Exhibitors* (Cork: O'Brien, 1852), pp. 22–3.

64. *CE*, 6 November 1854.

65. Bartlett, *Ireland*, p. 312; Emmet Larkin, 'The Devotional Revolution in Ireland, 1850–75', *The American Historical Review*, vol. 77, no. 3, June 1972, p. 646.

66. Larkin, 'The Devotional Revolution in Ireland, pp. 625–52.

67. Desmond Bowen, *Paul Cardinal Cullen and the Shaping of Modern Irish Catholicism* (Dublin: Gill & Macmillan, 1983), p. 164.

68. *SR*, 15 June 1855; Bolster, *A History of the Diocese of Cloyne*, p. 226.

69. *CE*, 23 December, 27 December 1865; 24 December 1866.

70. Ibid., 3, 7 January 1862.

71. *SR*, 26 May 1865. Born in Mullingar, County Westmeath, Wellington Guernsey was the son of a military bandsman. In his early years, he had worked in Logier's music shop in Dublin, and Bowden's music shop in Cork. *Belfast Newsletter*, 1 December 1858. A biographical entry in Brown and Stratton's *British Musical Biography* (p. 176) lists a mass in B flat among his compositions. See also Axel Klein, 'Wellington Guernsey', *EMIR*, vol. 1, pp. 449–50. He appeared at the Theatre Royal in Cork in 1853 with a company of singers, performing operatic repertoire and a selection of Guernsey's songs and ballads. *CE*, 16 December 1853.

72. *CE*, 30 April, 4 May 1869.

73. Ibid., 7 May 1869.

74. Ibid., 24 October 1870.

75. Larkin, 'The Devotional Revolution in Ireland', pp. 644–5.

76. O'Farrell, 'Bishop Moylan's Report on the Diocese of Cork, 1802', p. 128; *CE*, 21 June 1867.

77. Bartlett, *Ireland*, p. 304; Colm Lennon and Robin Kavanagh, 'The Flowering of the Confraternities and Sodalities in Ireland, *c.* 1860–*c.* 1960', in Colm Lennon (ed.), *Confraternities and Sodalities in Ireland: charity, devotion and sociability* (Dublin: Columba, 2012).

78. *CE*, 8 March 1869.

79. Ibid., 28 May 1869, 17 June 1870.

80. Ibid., 9 May, 13 June 1859. The specifications of the instrument are given in Gerard Gillen, 'William Telford and the Victorian Organ in Ireland', in Gerard Gillen and Harry White (eds), *Music and the Church* (Dublin: Irish Academic Press, 1993), p. 125.

81. *CE*, 8 February 1860.

82. Ibid., 20 August 1860.

83. Ibid., 12 April 1861, 15 April 1861. The company performed again at St Vincent's in 1868: *CE*, 11 January 1868.

84. Ibid., 19 August 1861. Henry Farmer was an organist and violinist active in Nottingham: *Nottingham Evening Post*, 25 June 1981. His *Mass in B Flat, with Words in Latin and English* was published in 1847, and in Boston and New York in 1859, https://urresearch.rochester.edu/institutionalPublicationPublicView.action?institutionalItemId=24713, accessed 22 August 2016.

85. *Musical Times and Singing Class Circular*, vol. 11, no. 248, October 1863, p. 143.

86. *CE*, 11 November 1863.

87. Ibid., 8 February 1864.

88. Ibid., 13 April 1864.

89. *Evening Freeman*, 18 August 1865.

90. *CE*, 5 March, 15 April 1864. He gave a recital at the Wexford church in November 1867: *CE*, 20 November 1867.

91. Ibid., 5, 10 October 1868, 27 July 1871.

92. Bolster, *A History of the Diocese of Cloyne*, pp. 237–8; *Irish Builder*, 15 July 1869.

93. Guy Oldham and Nicholas Thistlethwaite, 'Charles Spackman Barker', *NGrove 2*, vol. 2, pp. 734–5.

94. Stephen Bicknell, *The History of the English Organ* (Cambridge: Cambridge University Press, 1996), pp. 240–1.

95. *Irish Builder*, vol. 13, 1871, p. 15.

96. *CE*, 10 May 1871. An organ made by J.Walker had been installed at the Ursuline convent in 1842: *The Musical World*, vol. 17, 1842, pp. 86–7. The newly renovated Ursuline chapel organ was inaugurated with a performance by T.J. Sullivan and Monsieur Ferat 'of Mr Barker's Establishment in Paris'.

97. *Wilkie's Cork City Directory 1872* (Cork: Wilkie, 1871), p. 69.

98. *FJ*, 13 June 1873.

99. A notice in *CE*, 26 July 1871, stated that Chevraux had graduated from the Paris Conservatoire with first prize in organ performance and second prize in musical composition, with over ten years' experience as *Maître de Chapelle* and organist at the Abbey of Solesmes and the Church of Notre Dame at Le Havre.

100. Guy's *City and County Cork Almanac and Directory for 1891* and *City and County Cork Almanac and Directory for 1893* list de Prins as teacher at CSM and organist at St Mary's Cathedral, with Swertz as organist at St Vincent's. This conflicts with the reference by Fleischmann to another Belgian, de Paine, who held the post of organist at St Mary's Cathedral during the years 1889–90, after which Swertz was appointed. 'De Paine' may have held an assistant or deputy post, or the name may simply have been a misprint or misreading of De Prins. See James Delany, 'Church Music Reform', in Aloys Fleischmann (ed.) *Music in Ireland: a symposium* (Cork: Cork University Press, 1952), p. 161. See also Joseph P. Cunningham and Ruth Fleischmann, *Aloys Fleischmann (1880–1964): immigrant musician in Ireland* (Cork: Cork University Press, 2010), p. 67, n. 8.

101. Ian Curran, 'Cecilian Movement in Ireland', *EMIR*, vol. 1, pp. 178–80.

102. Jeremy C. Dibble, 'Musical Trends and the Western Church: a collision of the "ancient" and "modern"', in *World Christianities, c. 1815–c. 1914, Cambridge History of Christianity 8* (Cambridge: Cambridge University Press, 2006), pp. 124–6. See also Kieran A. Daly's 'The Irish Society of St Cecilia', *Sacred Music*, vol. 120, no. 2, 1993, pp. 15–25.

103. Paul Collins, 'Strange Voices in the "Land of Song"', in Murphy and Smaczny (eds), *Music in Nineteenth-Century Ireland*, pp. 116–17.

104. Curran, 'Cecilian Movement in Ireland'.

105. *CE*, 24, 27 May, 2 June 1864; *SR*, 4 August 1864. De Prins was listed as a Music Professor in Henry and Coghlan's *Directory for 1867* (Cork: Henry & Coghlan, 1867), p. 254.

106. *CE*, 4 August 1864.

107. London: Novello, *c* .1864, advertised in *Musical Times and Singing Class Circular*, 1 August 1864.

108. Mary Regina Deacy, *Continental Organists and Catholic Church Music in Ireland, 1860–1960,* M.Litt Dissertation (NUI Maynooth, 2005), p. 49 http://eprints.maynoothuniversity.ie/5088/1/Mary_Regina_Deacy_20140623124216.pd, accessed 30 October 2016

109. *Limerick Reporter*, 8 January 1867, 16 August 1870; *Slater's Directory 1870*, p. 141.

110. *CN*, 1 June 1872.

111. *CE*, 27 December 1876.

112. Quoted in Deacy, *Continental Organists*, p. 50, from *Lyra Ecclesiastica*, March 1879, p. 62.

113. Quoted in ibid., p. 52, from *Lyra Ecclesiastica*, February 1883, p. 15.

114. *CE*, 25 June 1866; John Cooke, 'St Peter and Paul's Church, Cork 1866–1966', *The Fold*, vol. 13, no. 12, 1966, p. 15.

115. *CE*, 28 December 1870.

116. Cooke, 'St Peter and Paul's Church', p. 17.

117. Annie Patterson, 'Musicians of the Day: Herr Theodor Gmür', *Weekly Irish Times,* 4 May 1901.

118. James D. Brown and Stephen S. Stratton, *British Musical Biography: a dictionary of musical artists, authors and composers born in Britain and its colonies* (Birmingham: Stratton, 1897), pp. 366–7.

119. 'Obituary of Joseph Seymour', *Musical Times*, vol. 64, no. 959, 1922, p. 7; Curran, 'Cecilian Movement in Ireland'; Paul Collins and David Larkin, 'Joseph Seymour', *EMIR*, vol. 2, pp. 927–8.

120. Deacy, *Continental Organists*, p. 39; Collins, 'Strange Voices', p. 125.

121. Quoted in Deacy, *Continental Organists*, p. 40.

122. Daly, *Catholic Church Music*, p. 51; Collins, 'Strange Voices', pp. 115–17.

123. *CE*, 28 January 1885.

124. Ibid., 16 July 1892.

125. *FJ*, 6 September 1895.

126. *CE*, 20 July 1896.

127. Ibid., 28 December 1896.

128. *FJ*, 13 September 1897.

129. Annie Patterson, 'Musicians of the Day: Herr Theodor Gmür', *Weekly Irish Times*, 27 April 1901; *CE*, 6 July 1896.

130. *The Musical Times and Singing Class Circular*, vol. 40, no. 675, 1 May 1899, pp. 309–10.

131. Larkin, 'The Devotional Revolution in Ireland', p. 649.

CHAPTER 10

1. William Weber, 'Mass Culture and European Musical Taste, 1770–1870', *International Review of the Aesthetics and Sociology of Music*, vol. 25, nos 1–2, 1994, pp. 182–3.

2. Derek Collins, 'Music in Dublin, 1800–1848', in Richard Pine and Charles Acton (eds), *To Talent Alone: the Royal Irish Academy of Music, 1848–1998* (Dublin: Gill & Macmillan, 1998), p. 19; Catherine Ferris, '"Musards all the Go": the fashion of the promenade concert in early 1840s Dublin', Society for Musicology in Ireland Postgraduate Conference, Maynooth, 2009, http://www.catherineferris.com/node/51, accessed 22 August 2016.

3. *CN*, 19 July 1849; *CE*, 9, 27 July, 1 August 1849.

4. *CE*, 4 November 1850; Pablo Fanque (born William Darby) was an English circus proprieter and equestrian performer, who had been an apprentice of William Batty.

5. *SR*, 11 January 1851; *CE*, 20, 24, 27 January 1851.

6. Flynn, *Random Recollections*, p. 39, f.n.

7. *CE*, 3, 12 October 1853. Gillespie's *Celestina* was performed in Dublin the following June as part of Richard Levey's benefit. *CE*, 23 June 1854.

8. *SR*, 4 October 1853.

9. *CE*, 14, 16, 21 February 1855.

10. Richard Caulfield (ed.), *The Council Book of the Corporation of the City of Cork from 1609 to 1643, and from 1690 to 1800* (Guildford: J. Billing, 1876), p. 311.

11. *SR*, 24 November 1856.

12. Ibid., 9 November 1857.

13. *CE*, 15 November 1862.

14. *CN*, 13 November 1849.

15. *CE*, 16 August 1852.

16. Concert programme NLI 6551; Flynn, *Random Recollections*, p. 32.

17. *CE*, 3 October 1959.

18. Ibid., 5, 29 August 1859.

19. Ibid., 1 February 1861; *CN*, 5, 9, 15 February 1861.

20. *CE*, 27 April, 2 May 1855.

21. Ibid., 2 May 1855.

22. Ibid., 12 September 1855.

23. Ibid., 17 September 1855.

24. William Weber, 'Redefining the Status of Opera: London and Leipzig, 1800–1848', *The Journal of Interdisciplinary History*, vol. 36, no. 3, 2006, p. 507.

25. Daniel Snowman, *The Gilded Stage: a social history of opera* (London: Atlantic Books, 2009), pp. 116–19.

26. John Francis Maguire, *Rome: its ruler and its institutions* (London: Longman, Brown, Green, Longmans & Roberts, 1859).

27. Bryan A. Cody, *The River Lee, Cork, and the Corkonians* (1859, reissued Cork: Tower Books, 1974), pp. 88–9; *CE*, 7 November 1859.

28. *CE*, 13 January 1860.

29. Ibid., 15 November 1862, 27 October 1866, 16 November 1868.

30. The honorary secretary of the group was W. Webb Ware. Singers were Mr Pollock, Mr P. Murphy, Mr Harvey, Mr N. Webb Ware, Mr Seymour, Mr Jackson, Mr Fitzmaurice, Mr Wheeler, Mr Minhear, Mr Connor, Mr Tanner. Charities supported included the North and South Infirmaries, the Fever Hospital and the Blind Asylum. Several reports appeared in the *Cork Examiner*, for example, *CE*, 24 December 1867, 12 November 1868, 7 June 1869, 23 April 1870.

31. The Refreshment Rooms Company, run by J.C. Newsom, Timothy Mahony, Francis Lyons, Samuel H. Newsom, operated in premises at George's Quay, Lavitt's Quay and Bachelor's Quay. *Wilkie's Cork City Directory 1872* (Cork: Wilkie, [1872]), p. 293; Guy, *City and County Cork Almanac and Directory for 1875–1876*, p. 529; Guy, *City and County Cork Almanac and Directory for 1891*, p. 93.

32. *CE*, 2, 7, 10 December 1867.

33. Ibid., 23, 28 April 1868, 10 September 1869; *SR*, 11 September 1869.

34. *CE*, 19 June 1868.

35. Ibid., 3, 5 August 1868.

36. Ibid., 1, 3, 4 September 1869.

37. Guy, *City and County Cork Almanac and Directory for 1884*, p. 102.

38. Pauric J. Dempsey and Shaun Boylan, 'Sir John Arnott', in *Dictionary of Irish Biography*, vol. 1, pp. 166–7; Robert Walker Jr was a civil engineer and architect, who in 1873 directed work on the alteration of the Athenaeum prior to its renaming as the Munster Hall. *Irish Builder*, vol. 15, 1873, p. 109.

39. *CE*, 24 November1870.

40. Ibid., 19 March 1869.

41. *Slater's National Commercial Directory of Ireland, 1870*, p. 91; *Slater's Royal National Commercial Directory of Ireland, 1881,* p. 114; Aloys Fleischmann, 'Music and Society, 1850–1921', in W.E. Vaughan (ed.), *A New History of Ireland VI: Ireland under the Union II, 1870–1921* (Oxford: Oxford University Press, 2010), p. 511; *CE*, 19 March 1869.

42. 'Notes from the South', *Irish Builder*, vol. 15, 1873, p. 109.

43. *Belfast Newsletter*, 16 January 1865, reprinted from *The Constitution*.

44. Helen Andrews, 'Arthur Hill', *Dictionary of Irish Biography*, vol. 4, pp. 691–2.

45. Concert Programmes Collection, Cork City Library.

46. *SR*, 1 January 1870.

47. *CE*, 24 November 1870; *The Era*, 27 November 1870.

48. *CE*, 22 November 1870.

49. *CN*, 14 April 1883.

50. Ibid., 5 October 1876; Guy, *City and County Cork Almanac and Directory for 1884*, p. 102.

51. Atkins was a partner in the accountancy firm Atkins Chirnside, of 39 South Mall, later joined by Olden. By the time of Atkins' death in 1905, it had expanded to become the largest such firm in Munster.

52. H.W. Robinson, *A History of Accountants in Ireland* (Dublin: The Institute of Chartered Accountants in Ireland, 1984), pp. 346–7; *CN*, 23 July 1883; *Freeman's Journal*, 8 June 1883.

53. John A. Murphy, *The College: a history of Queen's/University College Cork, 1845–1995* (Cork: Cork University Press, 1995), p. 132; see Appendix 3 for a list of orchestral members in 1880.

54. *CN*, 5 October 1876.

55. Lisa Parker, 'Thomas Richard Gonzalvez Jozé', *EMIR*, vol. 1, pp. 550–1.

56. Programme collection, Cork City Library; *FJ*, 8 February 1881.

57. *FJ*, 8 June 1883.

58. *Musical Times and Singing Class Circular*, vol. 22, no. 457, 1881, p. 146.

59. Names of members appended to the address were: D.V. O'Sullivan, High Sheriff, W.K. Sullivan, President of UCC, Lieut Colonel E.A. Shuldham, Richard Pigott Beamish, JP, R.D. Howard, William Harrington, JP, H. Paul, Alderman, N. Ware Webb, Consul Argt., IE CCCA VEC 6.

60. *CE*, 20 April 1876.

61. *The Era*, 25 May 1873.

62. *Irish Builder*, vol. 15, 1873, p. 109.

63. Scanlan and McCarthy were both prominent members of the CYMS. John George McCarthy was active in its foundation and was president of the society for many years, and James Scanlan was honorary secretary and librarian during the 1860s and 1870s. Guy, *City and County Cork Almanac and Directory for 1875–1876*, p. 570.

64. Among the directors/shareholders were William B. Philpott, J. O'Mullane, Bernard Alcock, John O'Sullivan, Francis Guy, Robert Uniake Fitzgerald Townshend and James Hackett.

65. Richard J. Hodges and W.T. Pike, *Cork and County Cork in the Twentieth Century* (Brighton: Pike, 1911), p. 314.

66. *The Era*, 22 April 1882.

67. Ibid., 30 May 1885.

68. Ibid., 30 June 1888.

69. *CE*, 13 November 1896.

70. *CN*, 22 May 1876; Rainbow with Gordon and Cox, *Music in Educational Thought and Practice*, pp. 224–5.

71. Arthur Hill, 'Rate-Aided Schools of Music', *Proceedings of the Musical Association*, 15th session, 1888–9, pp. 133–49.

72. Ibid., p. 138.

73. The attendees were Nicholas D. Murphy, Thomas Crosbie, M. Scott, Dr W.K. Sullivan, President of Queen's College, Cork, T.J. Sullivan, W. Haughton, William Atkins, William R. Harris, George Brady, W. Ringrose Atkins, William A. Shaw (School of Art) and Rev. Dr O'Brien.

74. Cork School of Music Minute Book, 1878–93, IE CCCA VEC II Bay 1061.

75. *Report of the Committee of the Cork School of Music for the Session 1881–2*, IE CCCA VEC 6.

76. Hill, 'Rate-Aided Schools of Music', p. 139.

77. Ibid., p. 142.

78. Cork School of Music, Professors' Day Book, December 1878 – May 1885, Fleischmann Library, CIT Cork School of Music.

79. Cork School of Music, *Fifth Report, Session 1882/1883* (Cork: Purcell, 1883).

80. *CN*, 15 July 1891.

81. CSM Minute Book, 1878–93, entry for 14 June 1879.

82. *CN*, 14 July 1883.

83. *FJ*, 28 August 1878; *Morning Post*, 29 August 1878.

84. CSM Minute Book, 1894–1904, entry for 8 November 1894.

85. CSM Minute Book, 1878–93, correspondence between G.F. Dunscombe, Department of Science and Art, London SW, and W.H. Corker, Cork School of Music, 2, 14 December 1895, 15 January 1896.

86. CSM Minute Book, 1878–93, 2 November 1893.

87. *Report of the Crawford Municipal Schools of Art and Music for the Year ending July 31st 1900* (Cork: Purcell, 1900), p. 31.

88. Arthur Hill, 'On a Suggested Improvement in Staff Notation', *Proceedings of the Musical Association*, 4th session, 1877–8, pp. 94–101; Hill, 'Rate-Aided Schools of Music'.

89. McCarthy, *Passing It On*, p. 82; Kieran Anthony Daly, *Catholic Church Music in Ireland, 1878–1903: the Cecilian reform movement* (Dublin: Four Courts Press, 1995), p. 142.

90. Fr Edward Gaynor, *St Patrick's Hymn Book* (Dublin: Browne & Nolan, 1892). The publication was reviewed in 'Notes on New Books', *The Irish Monthly*, vol. 20, no. 233, November 1892, pp. 615–16, and in *The Irish Ecclesiastical Record*, vol. 13, 1892, pp. 1052–4.

91. *CE*, 23 November 1892, 21 December 1893, 22 March 1895.

92. *Cork Industrial Exhibition 1883: report of executive committee, award of jurors and statement of accounts* (Cork: Purcell, 1886), p. 10; H.C. Hartnell, *Illustrated Guide to the Cork International Exhibition 1883* (Cork: Guy, 1883), pp. 185–6; *CE*, 4 July 1883; *CN*, 4 July 1883.

93. *CN*, 4 July 1883.

94. *Cork Industrial Exhibition 1883: official catalogue* (Dublin: Leckie, 1883), pp. 135–7.

95. *FJ*, 26 September 1883.

96. *Cork Industrial Exhibition 1883: report of executive committee, awards of jurors and statement of accounts* (Cork: Purcell, 1886), p. 281; reviewed in *CN*, 27 July 1883.

97. A band contest was held as part of the National Exhibition in Dublin the previous year. The adjudicators were R.M. Levey, Thomas Mayne and J.H. Young. *FJ*, 15 November 1882.

98. *Cork Industrial Exhibition 1883: Report of executive committee, awards of jurors and statement of accounts* (Cork: Purcell, 1886), pp. 280–3.

99. *CN*, 18 July 1883.

100. *The Era*, 5 March 1881; Axel Klein, 'Stage Irish, or the National in Irish Opera, 1780–1925', *Opera Quarterly*, vol. 21, no. 1, 2005, pp. 44–6.

101. *CN*, 24 February 1881.

102. Patterson, 'Musicians of the Day'.

103. *CN*, 6 January 1886.

104. Ibid., 7 October 1890.

105. *FJ*, 4 April 1893.

106. Obituary notices in *CN*, 3 February 1896, *The Sheffield Daily Telegraph*, 5 February 1896, *Yorkshire Post and Leeds Intelligencer*, 5 February 1896, *The Era*, 18 February 1896.

107. *CN*, 25 October 1887.

108. Committee members in 1891 were D.J. Daly, H.R. Burke, H.J. Hickie, M.J. O'Sullivan and Francis Lyons, Secretary. Guy's *City and County Cork Almanac and Directory for 1891*, p. 95.

109. *The Era*, 8 February, 1 November 1890; *CE*, 7 February, 7 October 1890.

110. 'Amateur Opera in Cork', *FJ*, 24 November 1894.

111. *The Era*, 8 February 1896.

112. *CE*, 30 November 1896; Guy's *Cork City and County Almanac for 1891*, p. 95; *CE*, 30 November 1896. See Appendix 4 for members who performed in 1896.

113. *CE*, 3 December 1878.

114. Guy's *Cork City and County Almanac for 1891*.

115. Cork Catholic Young Men's Society Minute Book, 1888–94, IE CCCA U341.

116. *CE*, 31 October 1896.

117. Patterson, 'Musicians of the Day.

118. *CN*, 21 January 1897.

119. *FJ*, 18 March 1871.

120. *Glasgow Herald*, 21 July 1888.

121. *CE*, 3 January 1866.

122. Leinster and Ulster branches of the Incorporated Society of Musicians were also established in 1893. See Fleischmann, 'The Organisation of the Profession', *Music in Ireland: a symposium*, p. 77. A report of a Cork meeting in the *Freeman's Journal* of 19 September 1893 lists the following attendees: R. Howard, D. Nunan, T. Gmür, H.C. Swertz, A. Tuer, W.H. Hannaford, J.C. Marks jun., G. Brady, S. Sykes, Mr Walsh, F. Holmes, Queenstown, C. Orr, J.P. Mills, H. Daly, A. Kearney, J. Hurst, H. Brenthall, Miss Corbett, Miss Fitzpatrick, Miss L. Williams, Miss Bergen, Miss Austen.

123. *CE*, 18 December 1896. Karol Mullaney-Dignam and Jimmy O'Brien Moran, 'Feis Ceoil', *EMIR*, vol. 1, pp. 372–3.

124. *FJ*, 28 November 1899.

125. Ibid., 29 May 1900.

126. Edward Gaynor, 'Irish Music', *New Ireland Review*, vol. 24, December 1905, pp. 251–2.

127. *CE*, 22 March 1897.

128. See Martin Dowling, *Traditional Music and Irish Society: historical perspectives* (Farnham: Ashgate, 2014), pp. 160–75.

129. *FJ*, 18 March 1885.

130. *Aberdeen Evening Express*, 25 September 1886.

131. Bartlett, *Ireland: A History*, p. 333.

132. *The Nation*, 27 November 1886.

133. *Weekly Irish Times*, 11 May 1901.

134. Dowling, *Traditional Music*, p. 156.

135. Copies of Swertz's eight published works are held in the Fleischmann papers, UCC archive, and at the British Library. See Séamas de Barra, *Aloys Fleischmann* (Dublin: Field Day, 2006), p. 3, n. 4.

136. Daniel Nunan, *The Cork Exhibition Waltzes, respectfully dedicated to the Right Worshipful the Mayor, D.J. Galvin*, NLI MU-sb-1032.

137. Dowling, *Traditional Music*, p. 156.

138. Denis Condon, '"A Taste in Pictures": the second birth of cinema in Cork', *Alphaville: journal of film and screen media*, no. 6, 2013, p. 5.

Bibliography

Manuscripts

Acts of the Dean and Chapter of Cork 1817–1866 RCB Library, IRL-Drcb C.20.1.5

Alphabetical List of Freemen at Large of the Borough of Cork (1844), IE CCCA U/140/J/02/02/04

Christian Schools Peacock Lane, Sullivan's Quay and Blarney Lane, Annual Sermon, IE CCCA U/140

City of Cork Vocational Education Committee Collection, IE CCCA VEC6

Commonplace Book of the Cork Theatre, Boole Library, UCC, IRL-C, MS 242

Cork Catholic Young Men's Society 1882–1960, IE CCCA U341

Cork School of Music, Minute Book 1878–1897, IE CCCA VEC II, Bay 1061

Cork School of Music, Professors' Day Book December 1878 – May 1885, Fleischmann Library, CIT Cork School of Music

Cork School of Music, Register of Students, 25 November 1878 – 3 October 1895, Fleischmann Library, CIT Cork School of Music

Dowden Collection, IE CCCA, U140

Grand Oratorio: Invitation sent to William Coppinger, IE CCCA, U229/117/19

Holland MSS, IE CCCA U136

Holy Trinity Vestry Book 1782–1819 RCB Library, IRL-Drcb P.527.5.3

Holy Trinity Minute Book 1820–1891 RCB Library, IRL-Drcb P.527.5.4

Minutes of St Peter's Vestry, NLI, IRL- Dn MS 764

Richard Caulfield 'Annals of Christ Church', Boole Library, UCC IRL-C, U83/3

Richard Caulfield MS transcriptions, Boole Library, UCC, IRL-C, U83

Richard Caulfield Notebook, IE CCCA CH3

Royal Academy of Music, Committee Minutes, vol.1 1822–1828

Royal Academy of Music, Concert Book: May 1824 – December 1879

St Fin Barre's Cathedral Chapter Accounts 1749–1808, RCB Library, IRL-Drcb C.20.4.1

St Fin Barre's Cathedral Oeconomist's Accounts 1806–1833, RCB Library, IRL-Drcb C.20.4.2

St Fin Barre's Chapter Accounts 1832–1842, RCB Library, IRL-Drcb C.20.4.3

St Peter's Vestry Book 1752–1846, RCB Library, IRL-Drcb P.324.5.1

Thomas Crofton Croker, 'Recollections of Cork' (1833), Trinity College Library, IRL-Dtc MS 1206

Theatre bills, concert bills and programmes

Concert Programmes, http://www.concertprogrammes.org.uk

Reeves Collection, Royal Irish Academy

Handbill, Victoria Theatre, Cork, IRL-C, MP 902(7)226

Theatre Royal, George's Street, Posters, IE CCCA U313

Theatrical Programmes: nineteenth century Cork [Cork City Library, microfilm 42]

Newspapers

Munster Journal
Corke Journal
Cork Evening Post
New Cork Evening Post
Hibernian Chronicle
Cork Advertiser (1799–1823)
Cork Advertising Gazette
The Constitution (*Cork Constitution*)
Cork Gazette
Cork Mercantile Chronicle
Faulkner's Dublin Journal
Cork Morning Intelligencer
Southern Reporter
Cork Evening Herald (1833–6)
Cork Standard and Evening Herald (1836–41)
Cork Examiner
Evening Freeman (Dublin)
Freeman's Journal (Dublin)
Weekly Irish Times
Morning Post (London)
The Era (London)

Periodicals, Journals

An Píobaire
Archivium Hibernicum
Boyle's Magazine
Brio
Ceol na hÉireann: Irish Music
Collectanea Hibernica
Dublin Builder/Irish Builder
Dublin Historical Record
Early Music
Eighteenth-Century Ireland/Iris an Dá Chultúr
Eighteenth-Century Life
Galpin Society Journal
Illustrated London News
Irish Church Quarterly
Irish Ecclesiastical Record
Irish Geography
Irish Historical Studies
Irish Studies Review
Journal of Social History
Journal of the Society for Musicology in Ireland
Journal of Victorian Culture
Lyra Ecclesiastica
Music and Letters
Musical Quarterly
Musical Times and Singing Class Circular
Musical Times
Past and Present
Proceedings of the Musical Association
Proceedings of the Royal Irish Academy
Quarterly Journal of the Music Library Association
Royal Musical Association Research Chronicle
Social History
Studia Hibernica
Studies
Theatrical Inquisitor [and Monthly Mirror]
The Fold
The Freeholder
The Irish Monthly
The Musical World (London, 1836–91)
The Nation
Urban History
Ulster Folklife
Victorian Studies

Books and other printed sources

A Book of Dates, Operatic, Dramatic, Musical, Compiled for the Strollers (Dublin: Browne & Nolan, 1878)

A Respectful Appeal to the Intelligent and Generous among his Fellow Citizens by Francis Seymour, Cork, 1849, IE CCCA U140/J/8/5

A Short Account of the First Institution of the Charitable Infirmary, St Mary Shandon in the City of Cork (1772)

A State of the Diocese of Cloyne, with Respect to the Several Parishes Thereof (1769)

A Tour through Ireland (London, 1780)

A Tour through Ireland by Two English Gentlemen, 2nd edition (Dublin, 1748)

Acheson, Abe, *A History of the Church of Ireland, 1691–2001*, 2nd edition (Dublin: Columba, 2002)

Aldwell's County and City of Cork Post Office General Directory 1844–5 (Cork: Jackson, 1844)

Allsobrook, David Ian, *Liszt: my travelling circus life* (London: Macmillan, 1991)

Anon., 'Memoir of Samuel Forde, a Cork Artist', *Dublin University Magazine*, vol. 15, March 1845

Archbold, Johanna, 'Book Clubs and Reading Societies in the Late Eighteenth Century', in James Kelly and Martyn J. Powell (eds), *Clubs and Societies in Eighteenth-Century Ireland* (Dublin: Four Courts Press, 2010)

Arnold, Denis, 'Charity Music in Eighteenth-Century Dublin', *Galpin Society Journal*, vol. 21, 1968

Atkinson, Sarah (S.A.), *Mary Aikenhead: her life, her work, and her friends, giving a history of the foundation of the Irish Sisters of Charity* (Dublin: Gill, 1879)

Barnard, T.C., 'The Political, Material and Mental Culture of the Cork Settlers, *c.*1650–1700', in Patrick O'Flanagan and Cornelius G. Buttimer (eds), *Cork: history and society* (Dublin: Geography Publications, 1993)

_____, 'Church of Ireland, 1660–1760', in W.J. McCormack (ed.), *The Blackwell Companion to Modern Irish Culture* (Oxford: Blackwell, 1999)

Bartlett, Thomas, *Ireland: a history* (Cambridge: Cambridge University Press, 2010)

Bashford, Christina, 'Writing (British) Concert History: the blessing and curse of ephemera', *Notes*, vol. 64, no. 3, 2008

_____, and Leanne Langley (eds), *Music and British Culture, 1785–1914: essays in honour of Cyril Ehrlich* (Oxford: Oxford University Press, 2000)

Bate, Philip, and Fiona Clampin, 'Louis Drouet', *NGrove2*, vol. 17, p. 599

Beausang, Ita, 'Cooke Family', *EMIR*, vol. 1, pp. 237–40

_____, 'Corri Family', *EMIR*, vol. 1, p. 253

_____, 'Jonathan Blewitt', *EMIR*, vol. 1, pp. 101–2

_____, 'William Forde', *EMIR*, vol. 1, pp. 404–6

Begadon, C.S., *Laity and Clergy in the Catholic Renewal of Dublin c.1750–1830*, PhD dissertation (NUI Maynooth, 2009), http://eprints.maynoothuniversity.ie/2412/ accessed 18 October 2016

Berry, Helen, *The Castrato and His Wife* (Oxford: Oxford University Press, 2011)

Bicknell, Stephen, *The History of the English Organ* (Cambridge: Cambridge University Press, 1996)

Blake, Donal, 'The Christian Brothers and Education in Nineteenth-Century Ireland', unpublished MA dissertation (University College Cork, 1977)

Bolster, Evelyn, *A History of the Diocese of Cork from the Penal Era to the Famine* (Cork: Tower Books, 1989)

_____, *A History of the Diocese of Cork: the episcopate of William Delaney, 1847–1886* (Cork: Tower Books, 1993)

_____, 'The Moylan Correspondence in Bishop's House, Killarney, Part 1', *Collectanea Hibernica*, no. 14, 1971, pp. 82–142

Booth, Michael R., *Theatre in the Victorian Age* (Cambridge: Cambridge University Press, 1991)

Borsay, Peter, *The English Urban Renaissance: culture and society in the provincial town, 1660–1770* (Oxford: Clarendon, 1991)

_____, 'The English Urban renaissance: the development of provincial urban culture *c.* 1680–*c.* 1760', *Social History*, vol. 2, no. 5, 1977, pp. 581–603

_____, 'Concert Topography and Provincial Towns in Eighteenth-Century England', in Susan Wollenberg and Simon McVeigh (eds), *Concert Life in Eighteenth-Century Britain* (Aldershot: Ashgate, 2004)

Boruwlaski, Joseph, *The Memoirs of Count Boruwlaski* (Durham: Humble, 1820)

Bowen, Desmond, *Paul Cardinal Cullen and the Shaping of Modern Irish Catholicism* (Dublin: Gill & Macmillan, 1983)

Boyce, David George, *Nineteenth Century Ireland: the search for stability*, New Gill History of Ireland, 5 (Dublin: Gill & Macmillan, 2005)

Boydell, Barra, 'Manuscript Sources from Irish Cathedrals: the Cashel cathedral choir-books, a preliminary report', *Brio*, vol. 39, no. 2, 2002, pp. 21–31

_____, *A History of Music at Christ Church Cathedral, Dublin* (Woodbridge: Boydell, 2004)

_____, 'Charles Clagget', *NGrove 2*, vol. 5, p. 888

_____, 'Ferdinand Webber', *EMIR*, vol. 2, p. 1048

_____, 'Richard Woodward [the younger]', *EMIR*, vol. 2, p. 1073

_____, 'The Flourishing of Music, 1660–1800', in Kenneth Milne (ed.), *Christ Church Cathedral: a history* (Dublin: Four Courts Press, 2000)

_____, 'St Michan's Church, Dublin: the installation of the organ in 1725 and the duties of the organist', *Dublin Historical Record*, vol. 46, no. 3, 1993, pp. 101–20

_____, 'The United Irishmen, Music, Harps, and National Identity', *Eighteenth-Century Ireland/Iris an Dá Chultúir*, vol. 13, 1998, pp. 44–51

_____, '"Whatever has a foreign tone/We like much better than our own": Irish music and Anglo-Irish identity in the eighteenth century', in Mark Fitzgerald and John O'Flynn (eds), *Music and Identity in Ireland and Beyond* (Farnham, Surrey: Ashgate, 2014)

_____, and Pat O'Connell, 'Smollet[t] Holden', *EMIR*, vol. 1, p. 493

Boydell, Brian, *A Dublin Musical Calendar, 1700–1760* (Dublin: Irish Academic Press, 1988)

_____, *Rotunda Music in Eighteenth-Century Dublin* (Dublin: Irish Academic Press, 1992)

_____, 'Music, 1700–1850', in T.W. Moody and W.E. Vaughan (eds), *A New History of Ireland IV: Eighteenth Century Ireland, 1691–1800* (Oxford: Clarendon, 1986)

Brady, Maziere William, *Clerical and Parochial Records of Cork, Cloyne and Ross*, 3 vols (Dublin: Thom, 1863)

Briggs, Samuel, *The Book of the Varian Family, with some speculation as to their origin, etc.* (Cleveland, OH, 1881)

Brook, Barry S., David Campbell, Monica H. Cohn and Michael Fend, 'François-Joseph Gossec', *NGrove 2*, vol. 10, pp. 186–90

Brown, James D., *Biographical Dictionary of Musicians, with a Bibliography of English Writings on Music* (Paisley and London: Gardner, 1886)

Brown, James D., and Stephen S. Stratton, *British Musical Biography: a dictionary of musical artists, authors and composers born in Britain and its colonies* (Birmingham: Stratton, 1897)

Burchell, Jenny, *Polite or Commercial Concerts? Concert management and orchestral repertoire in Edinburgh, Bath, Oxford, Manchester, and Newcastle, 1730–1799* (New York: Garland, 1996)

Burke, Helen, 'Eighteenth-Century Theatrical Touring and Irish Popular Culture', in Nicholas Grene and Chris Morash (eds), *Irish Theatre on Tour* (Dublin: Carysfort Press, 2005)

_____, 'The Revolutionary Prelude: the Dublin stage in the late 1770s, and early 1780s', *Eighteenth-Century Life*, vol. 22, no. 3, 1998, pp. 7–18

_____, Riotous Performances: *The Struggle for Hegemony in the Irish Theatre 1712–1784* (South Bend, Indiana: University of Notre Dame Press, 2003)

Butel, P., and L.M. Cullen (eds), *Cities and Merchants: French and Irish perspectives on urban development, 1500–1900*, Proceedings of the Fourth Franco-Irish Seminar of Social and Economic Historians (Trinity College, Dublin, 1986)

Buttimer, Cornelius G., 'Gaelic Literature and Contemporary Life in Cork, 1700–1840', in Patrick O'Flanagan and Cornelius G. Buttimer (eds), *Cork: history and society* (Dublin: Geography Publications, 1993)

Byrne-Costigan, E. 'Sydney Lady Morgan (1776–1859)', *Dublin Historical Record*, vol. 38, no. 2, 1985, pp. 61–73

Byrne-Rothwell, Daniel, *The Byrnes and the O'Byrnes: a social history of the clan*, 4 vols (Isle of Colonsay, Argyll: House of Lochar, 2010)

Cahalane, Rev. P., 'The Catholic Parish Churches of Cork', *JCHAS*, vol. 48, 1943, pp. 26–9

Calaresu, Melissa, Filippo de Vivo and Joan-Pau Rubiés (eds), *Exploring Cultural History: essays in honour of Peter Burke* (Farnham: Ashgate, 2010)

Callender, Michael E., 'The Organs of Cork Cathedral', *The Organ*, vol. 60, 1981, pp. 178–87

Campbell, Thomas, *A Philosophical Survey of the South of Ireland in a Series of Letters to John Watkinson M.D.* (London: W. Strahan and T. Cadell, 1777)

Carolan, Nicholas, 'A Nineteenth-Century Uilleann Piping Poster', *Ceol na hÉireann*, vol. 2, 1994, pp. 47–52

_____, 'Courtney's "Union Pipes" and the Terminology of Irish Bellows-Blown Pipes', p. 54, http://www.itma.ie/images/uploads/unionpipes.pdf, accessed 3 October, 2016

Carr, John, *Analysis of a new work of Travels, lately published in London, The Stranger in Ireland or A Tour in the southern and western parts of that country in the year 1805* (London, 1806)

Carter, Tim, 'The Sound of Silence: models for an urban musicology', *Urban History*, vol. 29, no. 1, May 2002, pp. 8–18

Casey, Fr Donal, 'St Finbarr's Church, Cork, 1766–1966', *The Fold*, vol. 14, no. 3, September 1966

Caulfield, Richard, *Annals of St Fin Barre's Cathedral, Cork* (Cork: Purcell, 1871)

_____ (ed.), *The Council Book of the Corporation of the City of Cork from 1609 to 1643, and from 1690 to 1800* (Guildford, J. Billing, 1876)

_____, *Handbook of St Fin Barre's Cathedral* (Cork, 1881)

_____, *Annals of the Cathedral of St Colman Cloyne* (1882)

_____, 'Notes and Queries: the Cork Theatre in George's Street, 1760–1840', *JCHAS*, vol. 23, 1917, pp. 63–4

_____, *A Lecture on the History of the Bishops of Cork, and Cathedral of St Fin Barre*, delivered in the lecture room of St Peter's Working Men's Association on Monday 25 January 1864 (Cork: Purcell, 1864)

Charlton, David, and Michael Musgrave, 'Johann Bernhard Logier', *NGrove2*, vol. 15, pp. 75–7

Chetwood, William Rufus, *A Tour through Ireland, in several Entertaining Letters, wherein the Present State of that Kingdom is consider'd and the most Noted Cities, Towns, Seats, Rivers, Buildings, &c. are Described … to Which is Prefix'd a Description of the Road from London to Holy-Head. By Two English Gentlemen.* 2nd edn (Dublin, 1748)

Chevill, Elizabeth, 'Clergy, Music Societies and the Development of a Musical Tradition: a study of music societies in Hereford, 1690–1760', in Susan Wollenberg and Simon McVeigh (eds), *Concert Life in Eighteenth-Century Britain* (Aldershot: Ashgate, 2004)

Chitty, Alexis, and George Riddlecombe, 'Henry Robinson Allen', *NGrove2*, vol. 1, pp. 398–9

C. J. 'Cork Worthies of the Last Century', *JCHAS*, vol. 22, 1916, pp. 80–4

Clark, William Smith, *The Early Irish Stage: the beginnings to 1720* (Oxford: Clarendon, 1955)

_____, *The Irish Stage in the County Towns, 1720 to 1800* (Oxford: Clarendon, 1965)

Cody, Bryan A., *The River Lee, Cork, and the Corkonians* (1859, reissued Cork: Tower Books, 1974)

Collins, Derek, 'Concert Life in Dublin in the Age of Revolution', unpublished PhD dissertation (Queen's University Belfast, 2001)

_____, 'Music in Dublin, 1800–1848', in Richard Pine and Charles Acton (eds), *To Talent Alone: the Royal Irish Academy of Music, 1848–1998* (Dublin: Gill & Macmillan, 1998)

Collins, J.T. 'Gleanings from Old Cork Papers', *JCHAS*, vol. 62, 1957, pp. 95–101

Collins, Paul (ed.), *Renewal and Resistance: Catholic church music from the 1850s to Vatican II* (Bern: Peter Lang, 2010)

_____, 'Emissaries to a "Believing and Singing Land": Belgian and German organists in Ireland, 1859–1916', in Paul Collins (ed.), *Renewal and Resistance: Catholic church music from the 1850s to Vatican II* (Bern: Peter Lang, 2010)

_____, 'Strange Voices in the "Land of Song"', in Michael Murphy and Jan Smaczny (eds), *Music in Nineteenth-Century Ireland* (Dublin: Four Courts Press, 2007)

_____, 'John William Glover', *EMIR*, vol. 1, p. 435

_____, and David Larkin, 'Joseph Seymour', *EMIR*, vol. 2, pp. 927–8

Commins, Adèle, 'Johann Bernhard Logier', *EMIR*, vol. 2, pp. 597–9

Condon, Denis, '"A Taste in Pictures": the second birth of cinema in Cork', *Alphaville: journal of film and screen media*, no. 6, Winter 2013, p. 5

Conlon, Michael V., 'Register of the Boys in St Stephen's Hospital, Cork from the 1st Feb, 1780', *JCHAS*, vol. 62, 1957, pp. 46–55

_____, 'Some Old Cork Charities', *JCHAS*, vol. 48, 1943, pp. 86–94

Connolly, Claire, 'Irish Romanticism, 1800–1830', in Margaret Kelleher and Philip O'Leary (eds), *The Cambridge History of Irish Literature*, vol. 1 to 1890 (Cambridge: Cambridge University Press, 2006)

Connolly, Sean, 'Catholics and Catholicism', in W.J. McCormack (ed.), *The Blackwell Companion to Modern Irish Culture* (Oxford: Blackwell, 1999)

Connolly, S.J. (ed.), *Kingdoms United? Great Britain and Ireland since 1500: integration and diversity* (Dublin: Four Courts Press, 1998)

Connor's Cork Directory for the year 1817 (Cork: Connor, 1817)

Conway, David, *Jewry in Music: entry into the profession from the Enlightenment to Richard Wagner* (Cambridge: Cambridge University Press, 2012)

Cooke, John, 'St Peter and Paul's Church, Cork, 1866–1966', *The Fold*, vol. 13, no. 12, June 1966

Corcoran, T., 'John England, 1786–1842: educator, journalist and first bishop of Charleston', *Studies*, vol. 17, March 1928, pp. 18–28

Corish, Patrick, *The Irish Catholic Experience: a historical survey* (Dublin: Gill & Macmillan, 1985)

_____, 'The Catholic Community in the Nineteenth Century', *Archivium Hibernicum*, vol. 38, 1983, pp. 26–33

Cork Industrial Exhibition 1883: official catalogue (Dublin: Leckie, 1883)

Cork Industrial Exhibition 1883: report of executive committee, awards of jurors and statement of accounts (Cork: Purcell, 1886)

Cotte, Roger, 'Louis Vogel', *NGrove2*, vol. 26, p. 860

Cotton, Henry, *Fasti Ecclesiae Hibernicae: the succession of the prelates and members of the cathedral bodies of Ireland*, 6 vols (Dublin: Hodges & Smith, 1848–78), vol. 1, pp. 280–1

Cox, John Edmund, *Musical Recollections of the Last Half-Century*, 2 vols (London, Tinsley bros, 1872)

Cremen, C., 'Notes and Queries: John Fleming, musician and composer', *JCHAS*, vol. 39, no. 150, 1934, pp. 102–3

Croker, John Wilson, *Familiar Epistles to Frederick E. Jones, Esq. on the Present State of the Irish Stage*, 5th edition (Dubln: Graiseberry & Campbell, 1805)

Croker, Thomas Crofton, *Researches in the South of Ireland, 1812–1822* (1824) (London, 1824, repr. Dublin: Irish Academic Press, 1981)

Cronin, Neil, *The Medical Profession and the Exercise of Power in Early Nineteenth-Century Cork* (Dublin: Four Courts Press, 2014)

Crowley, John, Robert Devoy, Denis Linehan and Patrick O'Flanagan (eds), *Atlas of Cork City* (Cork: Cork University Press, 2005)

Cudworth, Charles, Christopher Hogwood and Richard Luckett (eds), *Music in Eighteenth Century England: essays in memory of Charles Cudworth* (Cambridge: Cambridge University Press, 1983)

Cunningham, Hugh, *Leisure in the Industrial Revolution, c. 1780–c. 1880* (London: Croom Helm, 1980)

Cunningham, Joseph P., and Ruth Fleischmann, *Aloys Fleischmann (1880–1964): immigrant musician in Ireland* (Cork: Cork University Press, 2010)

Curran, Ian, 'Cecilian Movement in Ireland', *EMIR*, vol. 1, pp. 178–80

Curtin-Kelly, Patricia, *An Ornament to the City: Holy Trinity Church and the Capuchin Order* (Dublin: History Press, 2015)

d'Alton, Ian, *Protestant Society and Politics in Cork, 1812–1844* (Cork: Cork University Press, 1980)

_____, 'Keeping Faith: an evocation of the Cork Protestant character, 1820–1920', in Patrick O'Flanagan and Cornelius G. Buttimer (eds), *Cork History and Society: interdisciplinary essays on the history of an Irish county* (Dublin: Geography Publications, 1993)

Daly, Kieran, 'Catholic Church/Liturgical Music', *EMIR*, vol. 1, pp. 173–5

_____, *Catholic Church Music in Ireland, 1878–1903: the Cecilian reform movement* (Dubin: Four Courts Press, 1995)

_____, 'The Irish Society of St Cecilia', *Sacred Music*, vol. 120, no. 2, 1993, pp. 15–25

Davis, Leith, 'Irish Bards and English Consumers: Thomas Moore's "Irish Melodies" and the Colonized Nation', *ARIEL: a review of International English literature*, vol. 24, no. 2, 1993

Day, Angélique (ed.), *Letters from Georgian Ireland: the correspondence of Mary Delany, 1731–1768* (Belfast: The Friar's Bush Press, 1991)

Day, Robert, 'Exhibition of Miss Linwood's Pictures in Worsted', *JCHAS*, vol. 11, no. 60, 1903, pp. 262–3

_____, 'Notes and Queries: recollections of the Church of the Holy Trinity, Cork', *JCHAS*, vol. 4, no. 38, 1898, pp. 140–4

Deacy, Mary Regina, *Continental Organists and Catholic Church Music in Ireland, 1860–1960*, M.Litt Dissertation (NUI Maynooth, 2005), http://eprints.maynoothuniversity.ie/5088/1/Mary_Regina_Deacy_20140623124216.pdf, accessed 30 October 2016

Delaney, James, 'Church Music Reform', in Aloys Fleischmann (ed.), *Music in Ireland: a symposium* (Cork: Cork University Press, 1952)

de Barra, Séamas, *Aloys Fleischmann* (Dublin: Field Day, 2006)

de Lolme, Jean Louis, *The British Empire in Europe: Part the First, Containing an account of the Connection between the Kingdoms of England and Ireland, previous to the year 1780* (Dublin: Printed for Mess. Moncrieffe, Gilbert, Colles, etc., 1787)

Dibble, Jeremy C., 'Musical Trends and the Western church: a collision of the "ancient" and "modern"', in *World Christianities, c. 1815–c. 1914, Cambridge History of Christianity 8* (Cambridge: Cambridge University Press, 2006)

_____, 'John James Stanford', *EMIR*, vol. 2, pp. 958–9

_____,and Bennett Zon (eds), *Nineteenth-Century British Music Studies*, vol. 2 (Aldershot: Ashgate, 2002)

Dickson, David, *Old World Colony: Cork and south Munster, 1630–1830* (Cork: Cork University Press, 2005)

_____, Huguenots in the urban economy of eighteenth-century Dublin and Cork', in C.E.J. Caldicott, H. Gough and J.P. Pittion (eds), *The Huguenots and Ireland: anatomy of an emigration* (Dublin: Glendale Press, 1987)

_____, 'Second City Syndrome: reflections on three Irish cases', in S.J. Connolly (ed.), *Kingdoms United? Great Britain and Ireland since 1500: integration and diversity* (Dublin: Four Courts Press, 1998)

_____, and Cormac Ó Gráda, (eds), *Refiguring Ireland: essays in honour of L.M.Cullen* (Dublin: Lilliput, 2003)

Dillon's Genuine Edition of Timothy O'Sullivan's, commonly called Taidhag Gaodhlach's Pious Miscellany. Enlarged, improved and corrected, with an appendix of other religious compositions, in English and Irish, by Patrick Denn, Cappoquin (Cork: Dillon, 1841)

Donnelly, Seán, 'Denis Harrington of Cork', *An Píobaire*, vol. 11, p. 30, May 1986

_____, 'The Famousest Man in the World for the Irish Harp', *Dublin Historical Record*, vol. 57, no. 1, 2004, pp. 38–49

Dowling, Martin, *Traditional Music and Irish Society: historical perspectives* (Farnham: Ashgate, 2014)

Downes, William McNamara, *Temperance Melodies for the Teetotallers of Ireland*, 3rd ed. (Cork: S.M. Thompson, 1843)

Downey, Peter, 'Andrew Ashe', *EMIR*, vol. 1, p. 38

Drummond, Pippa, *The Provincial Music Festival in England, 1784–1914* (Farnham: Ashgate, 2011)

Dublin Almanac and General Register of Ireland (Dublin: Pettigrew & Oulton, 1840)

Dunne, Tom, and Laurence M. Geary (eds), *History and the Public Sphere: essays in honour of John A. Murphy* (Cork: Cork University Press, 2005)

Eager, John, *A Brief Account, with accompanying examples, of what was actually done, at the second examination of Mr Eager's Pupils in Music, educated from Mr Logier's system [...] at Norwich, June 18, 1819* (London: R. Hunter, 1819)

Eagleton, Terry, *Crazy John and the Bishop and Other Essays on Irish Culture* (Cork: Cork University Press, 1998)

Ehrlich, Cyril, *The Piano: a history* (London: Dent, 1976)

_____, *The Music Profession in Britain since the Eighteenth Century: a social history* (Oxford: Clarendon, 1985)

_____, and Dave Russell, 'Victorian Music: a perspective', *Journal of Victorian Culture*, vol. 3, no. 1, 1988, pp. 111–22

Eliason, Robert E., and Lloyd P. Farrar, 'Distin', *NGrove2*, vol. 7, pp. 381–2

Ellsworth, Therese, and Susan Wollenberg (eds), *The Piano in Nineteenth-Century British Culture: instruments, performers and repertoire* (Aldershot: Ashgate, 2007)

Fahy, Angela, 'Residence, Workplace and Patterns of Change: Cork, 1787–1863', in P. Butel and L.M. Cullen (eds), *Cities and Merchants: French and Irish perspectives on urban development, 1500–1900*, Proceedings of the Fourth Franco-Irish Seminar of Social and Economic Historians (Trinity College Dublin, 1986)

Fenner, Theodore, *Opera in London: views of the press 1785–1830* (Carbondale and Edwardsville: Southern Illinois University Press, 1994)

Ferris, Catherine, *The Use of Newspapers as a Source for Musicological Research: a case study of Dublin musical life, 1840–44* (PhD dissertation, NUI Maynooth, 2011), http://eprints.maynoothuniversity.ie/2577/1/Catherine_Ferris_PhD_2011.pdf, accessed 16 October 2016

_____, '"Musards all the Go": the fashion of the promenade concert in early 1840s Dublin', Society for Musicology in Ireland Postgraduate Conference, Maynooth 2009, http://www.catherineferris.com/node/51, accessed 22 August 2016

_____, 'The Music Collections of the Anacreontic Society and the Sons of Handel Society and Music Making in Dublin *c.* 1740–1865', *Brio*, vol. 43, no. 1, 2006

_____, 'Dublin Grand Musical Festival, 1831', *EMIR*, vol. 1, pp. 324–5

Finny's Royal Cork Almanac for 1843 (Cork: George Purcell, 1842)

Fiske, Roger, *English Theatre Music in the Eighteenth Century* (London: Oxford University Press, 1973)

Fitzgerald, Mark, and John O'Flynn (eds), *Music and Identity in Ireland and Beyond* (Farnham: Ashgate, 2014)

Fitzgerald, John, *The Cork Remembrancer* (Cork: J. Sullivan, 1783)

Fleischmann, Aloys (ed.), *Music in Ireland: a symposium* (Cork: Cork University Press, 1952)

_____, 'Music and Society, 1850–1921', in W.E. Vaughan (ed.), *A New History of Ireland VI: Ireland under the Union II, 1870–1921* (Oxford: Clarendon, 1996)

Fleming, David A., 'Diversions of the People: sociability among the orders of early eighteenth-century Ireland', *Eighteenth Century Ireland/Iris an Dá Chultúr*, vol. 17, 2002, pp. 99–111

_____, 'Clubs and Societies in Eighteenth-Century Munster', in James Kelly and Martyn J. Powell (eds), *Clubs and Societies in Eighteenth-Century Ireland* (Dublin: Four Courts Press, 2010)

Fleming, Simon, *A Century of Music Production in Durham City, 1711–1811: a documentary study* (PhD dissertation, Durham University, 2009), http://etheses.dur.ac.uk/49, accessed 30 August 2016

Flood, W.H. Grattan, *A History of Irish Music*, 4th edition (Dublin: Browne & Nolan, 1927)

_____, 'Michael Arne in Cork in 1770', *The Musical Times*, vol. 44, no. 723, 1903, p. 320

_____, 'Organists of St Fin Barre's Cathedral, Cork', *JCHAS*, vol. 24, no. 120, 1918, pp. 171–2

_____, 'Notes and Queries: Cork musical societies in 1733', *JCHAS*, vol. 22, 1916, p. 193

_____, 'Notes and Queries: early Cork musical societies', *JCHAS*, vol. 26, 1920, p. 40

_____, 'Notes and Queries: Handel's "Messiah" in Cork', *JCHAS*, vol. 26, 1920, p. 40

_____, 'Dublin Harpsichord and Piano Makers of the Eighteenth Century', *Journal of the Royal Society of Antiquaries of Ireland*, vol. 39, no. 2, 1909, pp. 137–45

Flynn, J.W., *The Random Recollections of an Old Play-Goer: a sketch of some old Cork theatres* (Cork: Guy, 1890)

Fox, Charlotte Milligan, *Annals of the Irish Harpers* (London: Smith, Elder, 1911)

Foster, Myles Birket, *The History of the Philharmonic Society of London, 1813–1912: a record of a hundred years' work in the cause of music* (London: Lane, 1912)

Gaffney, Seamus, 'Liszt in Ireland', *Liszt Society Journal*, vol. 19, 1994, pp. 55–65

Gaynor, Fergal, 'The Laocoön in Cork: the classical tradition in the city of Mahony and Maginn', *Classics Ireland*, vol. 15, 2008, pp. 34–51

Geary, Laurence M., 'John Milner Barry and Public Health in Early Nineteenth-Century Cork', *JCHAS*, vol. 106, 2001, pp. 131–42

_____, *Medicine and Charity in Ireland, 1718–1851* (Dublin: University College Dublin Press, 2004)

Gibson, C.B., *The History of the County and City of Cork*, 2 vols (London: Newby, 1861)

Gibson, Lewis, *A Letter to the Revd. the Dean and Chapter of the Cathedral Church of St Fin-Barry, Cork* (Cork: Printed by Robert Dobbyn, 1782)

Gilbert, John, 'A Record of Authors, Artists and Musical Composers Born in the County Cork', *JCHAS*, vol. 19, 1913, pp. 168–81

Gillen, Gerard, 'William Telford and the Victorian Organ in Ireland', in Gerard Gillen and Harry White (eds), *Music and the Church*, Irish Musical Studies 2 (Dublin: Irish Academic Press, 1993)

_____, 'Organs and Organ-Building', *EMIR*, vol. 2, pp. 801–3

_____, 'William Telford and the Victorian Organ in Ireland', in Gerard Gillen and Harry White (eds), *Music and the Church*, Irish Musical Studies 2 (Dublin: Irish Academic Press, 1993)

_____, and Harry White, *Music and the Church*, Irish Musical Studies 2 (Dublin: Irish Academic Press, 1993)

Gilman, Todd, *The Theatre Career of Thomas Arne* (Lanham: Rowman & Littlefield, 2013)

Girdham, Jane, *English Opera in Late Eighteenth-Century London: Stephen Storace at Drury Lane* (Oxford: Clarendon, 1997)

Gough, John, *A Tour of Ireland in 1813 and 1814* (Dublin: R. Napper, 1817)

Greene, John C., *Theatre in Dublin, 1745–1820: a history*, 2 vols (Bethlehem: Lehigh University Press, 2011)

_____, *Theatre in Dublin, 1745–1820: a calendar of performances*, 6 vols (Bethlehem: Lehigh University Press, 2011)

_____, *Theatre in Dublin 1745–1820: a calendar of performances. Searchable indexes – Musicians Instruments/Performance Dates/Venues*, http://digital.lib.lehigh.edu/lupress/dublintheatre MusicianInstrumentSDATVenue.pdf, accessed 3 October 2016

_____, *Theatre in Belfast, 1736–1800* (Bethlehem: Lehigh University Press, 2000)

_____, 'The Repertory of the Dublin Theatres, 1720–1745', *Eighteenth-Century Ireland/Iris an Dá Chultúr*, vol. 2, 1987, pp. 133–48

_____, and Gladys L.H. Clark, *The Dublin Stage, 1720–1745: a calendar of plays, entertainments and afterpieces* (Bethlehem: Lehigh University Press, 1993)

Grene, Nicholas, and Chris Morash (eds), *Irish Theatre on Tour*, Irish Theatrical Studies 1 (Dublin: Carysfort Press, 2005)

Griffith, P.J., '"The Irish Musical Fund". Founded 1787; incorporated by Act of Parliament, 1794', *The Journal of the Royal Society of Antiquaries*, sixth series, vol. 4, no. 4, 1914, pp. 365–73

Grimes, Brendan, 'Funding a Roman Catholic Church in Nineteenth-Century Ireland', *Architectural History*, vol. 52, 2009, pp. 147–68

Grindle, W.H., *Irish Cathedral Music: a history of music at the Cathedrals of the Church of Ireland* (Belfast: The Institute of Irish Studies, Queen's University Belfast, 1989)

Guy, Francis, *City and County Cork Almanac and Directory for 1884* (Cork: Guy, 1884)

_____, *City and County Cork Almanac and Directory for 1891* (Cork: Guy, 1891)

_____, *City and County Cork Almanac and Directory for 1875–1876* (Cork: Guy, 1875)

_____, *Directory of Munster, Comprising the Counties of Clare, Cork, Kerry, Limerick, Tipperary and Waterford* (Cork: Guy, 1893)

Hall, Mrs S.C., *Lights and Shadows of Irish Life*, 3 vols, (London: H. Colborn, 1838)

Hall, James, *A Tour through Ireland, particularly the interior and least known parts, 2 vols* (London: R.P. Moore, 1813)

Harrison, Frank Llewelyn, 'Music, Poetry and Polity in the age of Swift', *Eighteenth Century Ireland/Iris an Dá Chultúr*, vol. 1, 1986, pp. 37–60

Hart, William A., 'Africans in Eighteenth-Century Ireland', *Irish Historical Studies*, vol. 33, no. 129, 2002, pp. 31–2

_____, 'Rachael Baptist', in James Maguire and James Quinn (eds), *Dictionary of Irish Biography* (Cambridge: Cambridge University Press, 2002), vol. 1, pp. 462–3

Hartnell, H.C., *Illustrated Guide to the Cork International Exhibition 1883* (Cork: Guy, 1883)

Henry and Coghlan's General Directory of Cork for 1867: for which is incorporated Wynne and Co's business directory of the principal towns in the province of Munster (Cork: Henry & Coghlan, 1867)

Herbert, Trevor, and Helen Barlow, 'The British Military as a Musical Institution, *c.*1780–*c.*1860', *Music and Institutions in Nineteenth-Century Britain* (Farnham: Ashgate, 2012)

_____, *Music and the British Military in the Long Nineteenth Century* (New York: Oxford University Press, 2013)

Highfill, Philip H., Kalman A. Burnim and Edward A. Langhans (eds), *A Biographical Dictionary of Actors, Actresses, Musicians, Dancers, Managers and Other Stage Personnel in London, 1660–1800*, 16 vols (Carbondale and Edwardsville: Southern Illinois University Press, 1973–93)

Hill, Arthur, 'On a Suggested Improvement in Staff Notation' *Proceedings of the Musical Association*, 4th session, 1877–1878, pp. 94–101

_____, 'Rate-Aided Schools of Music', *Proceedings of the Musical Association*, 15th session, 1888–1889, pp. 133–49

Hill, Jacqueline, 'Irish Identities before and after the Act of Union', *Radharc*, vol. 2, 2001, pp. 51–73

_____, 'Loyal Societies in Ireland, 1690–1790', in James Kelly and Martyn J. Powell (eds), *Clubs and Societies in Eighteenth-Century Ireland* (Dublin: Four Courts Press, 2010)

_____, 'National Festivals, the State, and "Protestant Ascendancy" in Ireland, 1790–1829', *Irish Historical Studies*, vol. 24, no. 93, 1984, pp. 30–51

Hinks, John, Catherine Armstrong and Matthew Day, *Periodicals and Publishers: the newspaper and journal trade, 1750–1914* (London: Oak Knoll Press and the British Library, 2009)

Hitchcock, Robert, *An Historical View of the Irish Stage*, 2 vols (Dublin: Marchbank, 1788–94)

Hodges, Richard J., and W.T. Pike, *Cork and County Cork in the Twentieth Century* (Brighton: Pike, 1911)

Hogan, Ita Margaret, *Anglo-Irish Music, 1780–1830* (Cork: Cork University Press, 1966)

Holden's Triennial Directory, 4th edition for 1805, 1806, 1807, second volume (London: W. Glendinning, 1805)

Hullah, John, *Wilhem's Method of Teaching Singing Adapted to English Use* (London: J. Parker 1842)

Hunt, Una, 'Arthur O'Leary', *EMIR*, vol. 2, pp. 777–8

Husk, William Henry, *An Account of the Musical Celebrations on St Cecilia's Day in the Sixteenth, Seventeenth and Eighteenth Centuries, to which is appended a collection of Odes on St Cecilia's Day* (London: Bell & Daldy, 1857)

Hyland, C.P., 'The Cork Total Abstainer', *JCHAS*, vol. 100, 1995, pp. 167–71

Inglis, Brian, *The Freedom of the Press in Ireland, 1784–1841* (London: Faber, 1954)

'Items about Irishmen', *The Irish Monthly*, vol. 21, no. 235, 1893, pp. 33–6

J.C., 'Dr Caulfield's Annals of the Parish Church of St Maria de Shandon, now St Ann's Shandon, Cork', *JCHAS*, vol. 10, 1904, pp. 266–78

Jackson, John Wyse, and Peter Costello, *John Stanislaus Joyce: the voluminous life and genius of James Joyce's father* (New York: St Martin's Press, 1998)

Johnson, Gina, *The Laneways of Medieval Cork* (Cork: Cork City Council, 2002)

Johnston, Roy, 'Concerts in the Musical Life of Belfast to 1874,' unpublished PhD dissertation (Queen's University Belfast, 1996)

_____, *Bunting's Messiah* (Belfast: The Belfast Natural History and Philosophical Society, 2003)

_____, '"That Domestic and Long-Suffering Instrument": the piano boom in nineteenth century Belfast', in Therese Ellsworth and Susan Wollenberg (eds), *The Piano in Nineteenth-Century British Culture: instruments, performers and repertoire* (Aldershot: Ashgate, 2007)

_____, with Declan Plummer, *The Musical Life of Nineteenth-Century Belfast* (Farnham: Ashgate, 2015)

Johnstone, Andrew, 'George William Torrance', *EMIR*, vol. 2, p. 992

Kassler, Michael, *A.F.C. Kollmann's Quarterly Musical Register (1812): an annotated edition with an introduction to his life and works* (Aldershot: Ashgate, 2008)

Kearney, Aiveen, 'Temperance Bands and their Significance in Nineteenth-Century Ireland', unpublished MA dissertation (University College, Cork, 1981)

Keenan, Desmond, *The Catholic Church in Nineteenth-Century Ireland: a sociological study* (Dublin: Gill & Macmillan, 1983)

Kelleher, M., and P. O'Leary (eds), *The Cambridge History of Irish Literature*, vol. 1 to 1890 (Cambridge: Cambridge University Press, 2006)

Kelly, James, 'Volunteers', in W.J. McCormack (ed.), *The Blackwell Companion to Modern Irish Culture* (Oxford: Blackwell, 1999)

_____, 'Charitable Societies: their genesis and development, 1721–1800', in James Kelly and Martyn J. Powell, *Clubs and Societies in Eighteenth-Century Ireland* (Dublin: Four Courts Press, 2010)

_____, and Martyn J. Powell (eds), *Clubs and Societies in Eighteenth-Century Ireland* (Dublin: Four Courts, 2010)

Kelly, Michael, and Theodore Edward Hook, *Reminiscences of Michael Kelly: of the King's Theatre, and the Theatre Royal Drury Lane, including a period of nearly a half century, with original anecdotes of many distinguished persons, political, literary, and musical*, 2 vols (London: Colburn, 1826)

Kelly, R.J., 'The Old Galway Theatres', *Journal of the Royal Society of Antiquaries of Ireland*, vol. 4, no. 4, 1914, pp. 358–64

Kennedy, Liam, 'The Cost of Living in Ireland, 1698–1998', in David Dickson and Cormac Ó Gráda (eds), *Refiguring Ireland: essays in honour of L.M. Cullen* (Dublin: Lilliput, 2003)

Kennedy, Liam and Clare Murphy, *Account Books of the Franciscan House, Broad Lane, Cork, 1764–1921* (Dublin: Irish Manuscripts Commission, 2012)

Kennedy, Máire, 'William Flyn (1740–1811) and the Readers of Munster in the Second Half of the Eighteenth Century', in John Hinks, Catherine Armstrong and Matthew Day (eds), *Periodicals and Publishers: the newspaper and journal trade, 1750–1914* (London: Oak Knoll Press and the British Library, 2009)

_____, 'Eighteenth-Century Newspaper Publishing in Munster and South Leinster', *JCHAS*, vol. 103, 1998, pp. 67–8

Keogh, Dáire, 'Evangelising the Faithful: Edmund Rice and the reformation of nineteenth century Irish Catholicism', in Colm Lennon (ed.), *Confraternities and Sodalities in Ireland: charity, devotion and sociability c.1860–c.1960* (Dublin: Columba Press, 2012)

_____, *Edmund Rice and the First Christian Brothers* (Dublin: Four Courts Press, 2008)

Keogh, Henry J., 'Musical Perspectives at St Fin Barre's', *JCHAS*, vol. 81, 1966, pp. 129–37

Kerrigan, Colm, *Father Mathew and the Irish Temperance Movement, 1838–1849* (Cork: Cork University Press, 1992)

Kinealy, Christine, *Charity and the Great Hunger in Ireland: the kindness of strangers* (London: Bloomsbury, 2013)

King, Alexander, *The might and the right of the people: letters on popular education, political reform, etc. addressed to Right Rev Dr Murphy, Very Rev T. Matthew and Daniel O'Connell, Esq.* M.P.n (London: Ward and Co.; Dublin: J. Robertson; Cork: G. Ridings, 1843)

Kinsella, Stuart, 'David Weyman', *EMIR*, vol. 2, pp. 1051–2

Klein, Axel, 'Stage Irish, or the National in Irish Opera, 1780–1925', *Opera Quarterly*, vol. 21, no. 1, Winter 2005, pp. 27–67

_____, 'Wellington Guernsey', *EMIR*, vol. 1, pp. 449–50

Kosok, Heinz. '"George my belov'd King, and Ireland my honour'd Country": John O'Keeffe and Ireland', *Irish University Review*, vol. 22, no. 1, 1992, pp. 40–54

Lane, Denny, *Then and Now* (Dublin: Gill, 1885)

Lane, Fintan, *In Search of Thomas Sheahan: radical politics in Cork, 1824–1836* (Dublin: Irish Academic Press, 2001)

_____, 'Music and Violence in Working Class Cork: the "Band Nuisance", 1879–82', *Saothar*, vol. 24, 1999, pp. 17–31

_____, 'Musical Bands and Local Identities', in John Crowley, Robert Devoy, Denis Linehan and Patrick O'Flanagan (eds), *Atlas of Cork City* (Cork: Cork University Press, 2005)

Langevin, Kenneth, 'Antonio Borghese', *NGrove2*, vol. 3, p. 898

Langley, Leanne, '"Our Thing Called Opera": some Covent Garden productions of the 1820s through contemporary eyes', *The Musical Times*, vol. 123, no. 1678, 1982, pp. 836–8

_____, 'Sainsbury's *Dictionary*, the Royal Academy, and the Rhetoric of Patriotism', in Christina Bashford and Leanne Langley (eds), *Music in British Culture, 1785–1914: essays in honour of Cyril Ehrlich* (Oxford: Oxford University Press, 2000)

_____, 'The Musical Press in Nineteenth-Century England', *Notes: quarterly journal of the Music Library Association*, vol. 46, no. 3, 1990, pp. 583–92

Larkin, Emmet, 'The Devotional Revolution in Ireland, 1850–75', *The American Historical Review*, vol. 77, no. 3, 1972, pp. 625–2

Lawrence, Frank, 'Catholic Popular Devotional Music', *EMIR*, vol. 1, pp. 175–8

Lawrence, Thomas, 'Giulio Regondi in Ireland', http://www.ucd.ie/pages/99/articles lawrence.pdf, accessed 22 August 2016

Lawrence, W.J., 'Early Irish Ballad Opera and Comic Opera', *Musical Quarterly*, vol. 8, no. 3, 1922, pp. 397–412

_____, 'The Cork Stage in the 18th Century', *Irish Independent*, 24 November 1913

Lea-Scarlett, E.J., 'Bochsa, Robert Nicholas Charles (1789–1856)', *Australian Dictionary of Biography*, National Centre of Biography, Australian National University, http://adb.anuedu.au/biography/bochsa-robert-nicholas-charles-3019/text4423, published in hardcopy 1969, accessed online 22 August 2016

Lee, Grace Lawless, *The Huguenot Settlements in Ireland* (London, 1938, repr. Westminster, MD: Heritage Books, 2008)

Leerssen, Joep, *Remembrance and Imagination: patterns in the historical and literary representation of Ireland in the nineteenth century* (Cork: Cork University Press, 1996)

Legg, Marie-Louise, *Newspapers and Nationalism: the Irish provincial press, 1850–1892* (Dublin: Four Courts Press, 1998)

Lennon, Colm (ed.), *Confraternities and Sodalities in Ireland: charity, devotion and sociability* (Dublin: Columba Press, 2012)

_____, and Robin Kavanagh, 'The Flowering of the Confraternities and Sodalities in Ireland, *c.* 1860–*c.* 1960', in Colm Lennon (ed.), *Confraternities and Sodalities in Ireland: charity, devotion and sociability* (Dublin: Columba, 2012)

Levey, R.M., and J. O'Rorke, *Annals of the Theatre Royal Dublin from its Opening in 1821 to its Destruction by Fire, February 1880, with occasional notes and observations* (Dublin: Dollard, 1880)

Lewis, S., *Lewis' Cork: a topographical dictionary of the parishes, towns and villages of Cork city and county.* Introduction by Tim Cadogan (1837, repr. Cork: Collins, 1998)

Lindfors, Berndt, *Ira Aldridge: the vagabond years, 1833–1852* (New York: University of Rochford Press, 2011)

Loeber, Rolf, and Magda Loeber, with Anne Mullin Burnham (eds), *A Guide to Irish Fiction, 1650–1900* (Dublin: Four Courts Press, 2005)

Loesser, Arthur, *Men, Women and Pianos: a social history* (New York: Simon & Schuster, 1954, repr. New York: Dover, 1990)

Lucas, Richard, 'The Cork Directory for 1787', *JCHAS*, vol. 72, 1967, pp. 135–57

Luckcombe, Philip, *A Tour through Ireland in 1779* (Dublin: J. & R. Byrne, 1780)

Lunham, T.A., 'Bishop Dive Downes' Visitation of His Diocese, 1699–1702', *JCHAS*, vol. 15, no. 84, 1909

MacAuliffe, Margaret M., *The Dominicans in Cork* (Cork: Paramount Printing House, 1939)

MacDonnell, Hercules Henry Graves, *A Book of Dates, Operatic, Dramatic, Musical, compiled for the Strollers* (Dublin: Browne and Nolan, 1878)

Mackerness, E.D., *A Social History of English Music* (London: Routledge & Kegan Paul, 1966)

MacSweeney, Pauline, 'The Organ and Harpsichord in Ireland before 1870', unpublished MA dissertation (University College, Cork, 1979)

Maguire, James, and James Quinn (eds), *Dictionary of Irish Biography: from the earliest times to the year 2002*, 9 vols (Cambridge: Cambridge University Press, 2002)

Maguire, John Francis, *Father Mathew: a biography* (London: Longman, Green, Longman, Roberts & Green, 1865)

_____, *The Industrial Movement in Ireland, as Illustrated by the National Exhibition 1852* (Cork: John O'Brien, 1853)

_____, *Rome: its ruler and its institutions* (London: Longman, Brown, Green, Longmans & Roberts, 1859)

Mahaffy, John Pentland, 'About Irish Church Music', *Irish Church Quarterly*, vol. 1, no. 2, April 1908, pp. 93–8

Marmion, Anthony, *The Ancient and Modern History of the Maritime Ports of Ireland*, 3rd edition (London: Cox, 1858)

Martineau, Russell, 'Jakob Zeugheer', *NGrove2*, vol. 27, p. 796

Mathews, Mrs [Anne], *Memoirs of Charles Mathews, Comedian*, 4 vols (London: Bentley, 1839)

Matthews, Betty, 'The Musical Mahons', *The Musical Times*, vol. 120, no. 1636, 1979, pp. 482–4

McAllister-Harte, Nuala, 'Beavering on the Slopes of Parnassus: the musical life of Derry, 1772–1877', unpublished PhD dissertation (University of Coleraine, 1999)

McCann, Peadar, 'Cork City's Eighteenth-Century Charity Schools: origins and early history', *JCHAS*, vol. 84, 1979, pp. 102–11

McCarthy, C.J.F., 'An Antiquary's Notebook, 7', *JCHAS*, vol. 90, 1985, pp. 198–9

McCarthy, Justin, *The Story of an Irishman* (London: Chatto & Windus, 1904)

McCarthy, Kieran, *Royal Cork Institution: pioneer of education* (Cork: Cork Institute of Technology, 2010)

McCarthy, Marie, *Passing It On: the transmission of music in Irish culture* (Cork: Cork University Press, 1999)

_____, 'The Transmission of Song in National Schools of Mid-Nineteenth-Century Ireland: social, religious and political values in canon', in Michael Murphy and Jan Smaczny (eds), *Music in Nineteenth-Century Ireland* (Dublin: Four Courts Press, 2007)

McCarthy, Mark, 'Turning a World Upside Down: the metamorphosis of property, settlement and society in the city of Cork during the 1640s and 1650s', *Irish Geography*, vol. 33, no. 1, 2000, pp. 37–55

_____, 'The Forging of an Atlantic Port City: socio-economic and physical transformations in Cork, 1660–1700', *Urban History*, vol. 28, no. 1, 2001, pp. 25–45.

McClelland, Aiken, 'The Irish Harp Society', *Ulster Folklife*, vol. 21, 1975, pp. 15–24

McCormack, W.J. (ed.), *The Blackwell Companion to Modern Irish Culture* (Oxford: Blackwell, 1999)

McGovern, Rev. J.B., 'Boleyne Reeves, Harpist and Poet: a forgotten Cork worthy', *JCHAS*, vol. 15, 1909, pp. 157–63

McHale, Maria, 'Singing and Sobriety: music and the Temperance Movement in Ireland, 1838–43', in Michael Murphy and Jan Smaczny (eds), *Music in Nineteenth-Century Ireland* (Dublin: Four Courts Press, 2007)

McKeever, Paul, 'John Baptiste Cuvillie', *EMIR*, vol. 1, p. 274

McVeigh, Simon, '"An Audience for High-Class Music": concert promotors and entrepreneurs in late-nineteenth-century London', in William Weber (ed.), *The Musician as Enterpreneur, 1700–1914: managers, charlatans, and idealists* (Bloomington: Indiana University Press, 2004)

_____, *Concert Life in London from Mozart to Haydn* (Cambridge: Cambridge University Press, 1993)

_____, 'The Benefit Concert in Nineteenth-Century London: from "tax on the nobility" to "monstrous nuisance"', in Bennet Zon (ed.), *Nineteenth-Century British Music Studies*, vol. 1 (Aldershot: Ashgate, 1999)

_____, 'The Professional Concert and Rival Subscription Series in London, 1783–1793', *RMA Research Chronicle*, vol. 22, 1989, pp. 1–135

Miller, P.J., 'Women's Education, "self-improvement" and social mobility: a late eighteenth century debate', *British Journal of Educational Studies*, vol. 20, no. 3, 1972, pp. 304–14

Milne, Kenneth (ed.), *Christ Church Cathedral: a history* (Dublin: Four Courts Press, 2000)

Mirala, Petri, 'Masonic Sociability and Its Limitations: the case of Ireland', in James Kelly and Martyn J. Powell (eds), *Clubs and Societies in Eighteenth-Century Ireland* (Dublin: Four Courts Press, 2010)

Mitroulia, Eugenia, and Arnold Myers, 'The Distin Family as Instrument Makers and Dealers, 1845–1874', *Scottish Music Review*, vol. 2, no. 1, 2011

Moody, T.W., and W.E. Vaughan (eds), *A New History of Ireland IV: eighteenth century Ireland, 1691–1800* (Oxford: Clarendon, 1986)

Moore, Courtenay, 'A Forgotten Tour in Ireland', *JCHAS*, vol. 7, 1901, pp. 172–6

Moore, Thomas, *Irish Melodies with Miscellaneous Poems, with a Melologue upon National Music* (Dublin: John Cumming, 1833)

Morash, Christopher, *A History of Irish Theatre, 1601–2000* (Cambridge: Cambridge University Press, 2002)

Muir, T.E., *Roman Catholic Church Music in England, 1791–1914: a handmaid of the liturgy?* (Farnham: Ashgate, 2013)

Mullan, H.C.G., and Brian Harrison (eds), *Oxford Dictionary of National Biography*, 60 vols (Oxford: Oxford University Press, 2004)

Mullaney-Dignam, Karol, and Jimmy O'Brien Moran, 'Feis Ceoil', *EMIR*, vol. 1, pp. 372–33

Munter, Robert, *The History of Irish Newspapers, 1685–1760* (Cambridge: Cambridge University Press, 1967)

Murphy, John A., *The College: a history of Queen's/University College Cork, 1845–1995* (Cork: Cork University Press, 1995)

Murphy, Kerry, 'Joseph Mainzer's "Sacred and Beautiful Mission": an aspect of Parisian musical life of the 1830s', *Music and Letters*, vol. 75, 1994, pp. 33–46

Murphy, Maura, 'Municipal Reform and the Repeal Movement in Cork, 1833–1844', *JCHAS*, vol. 81, 1976, pp. 1–18

Murphy, Michael, 'The Musical Press in Nineteenth-Century Ireland', in Michael Murphy and Jan Smaczny (eds), *Music in Nineteenth-Century Ireland* (Dublin: Four Courts Press, 2007)

_____, and Jan Smaczny (eds), *Music in Nineteenth-Century Ireland*, Irish Musical Studies 9 (Dublin: Four Courts Press, 2007)

Murray, Peter, 'Art Institutions in Nineteenth-Century Cork', in Patrick O'Flanagan and Cornelius G. Buttimer (eds), *Cork History and Society: interdisciplinary essays on the history of an Irish county* (Dublin: Geography Publications, 1993)

'Music in Cork', *The Musical Times and Singing Class Circular*, vol. 40, no. 674, 1899, p. 257

Myerly, Scott Hughes, '"The eye must entrap the mind": army spectacle and paradigm in nineteenth-century Britain', *Journal of Social History*, vol. 26, no. 1, 1992, pp. 105–31

Nash, Gillian, 'Frank Seymour and the Cork Theatre, 1832–1850', unpublished MA thesis (University College, Cork, 1977)

Nathan, Hans, 'The Tyrolese Family Rainer, and the Vogue of Singing Mountain Troupes in Europe and America', *The Musical Quarterly*, vol. 32, no. 1, 1946, pp. 63–79

Neill, Edward, 'Niccolò Paganini', *NGrove2*, vol. 18, pp. 887–94

Nicholson, Asenath, *Ireland's Welcome to the Stranger: or, an excursion through Ireland in 1844* (New York: Baker & Scribner, 1847)

Nicoll, Allardyce, *A History of English Drama, 1660–1900*, 3 vols (Cambridge: Cambridge University Press, 1952–59)

_____, *British Drama*, 5th edition (New York: Barnes & Noble, 1962)

Nixon, John, *The New Cork Directory for the Year 1795* (Cork: Haly, 1795)

Ní Chinnéide, Síle, 'A New View of Cork in 1790', *JCHAS*, vol. 78, 1973, pp. 1–13

Ní Riain, Nóirín, 'The Nature and Classification of Traditional Religious Songs', in Gerard Gillen and Harry White (eds), *Music and the Church*, Irish Musical Studies 2 (Dublin: Irish Academic Press, 1993)

O'Brien, John B., *The Catholic Middle Classes in Pre-Famine Cork*, lecture delivered at University College Cork, 29 March 1979 (Cork: National University of Ireland, 1979)

_____, 'Agricultural Prices and Living Costs in Pre-Famine Cork', *JCHAS*, vol. 82, 1977, pp. 1–10

_____, 'Cork Society in the 1850s', *JCHAS*, vol. 101, 1996, pp. 15–25

_____, 'Merchants in Cork before the Famine', in P. Butel and L.M.Cullen (eds), *Cities and Merchants: French and Irish perspectives on urban development, 1500–1900*, Proceedings of the Fourth Franco-Irish Seminar of Social and Economic Historians (Trinity College Dublin, 1986)

_____, 'Population, Politics and Society in Cork, 1780–1900', in Patrick O'Flanagan and Cornelius G. Buttimer (eds), *Cork History and Society: interdisciplinary essays on the history of an Irish county* (Dublin: Geography Publications, 1993)

O'Brien Moran, Jimmy, 'John Edward Pigot', *EMIR*, vol. 2, pp. 839–40

Ó Coindealbháin, Seán, 'Schools and Schooling in Cork City, 1700–1831', *JCHAS*, vol. 48, 1943, pp. 44–57

O'Connor, Jennifer, 'Anne Catley', *EMIR*, vol. 1, p. 178

_____, 'Wilhelm Elsner', *EMIR*, vol. 1, p. 352

O'Donnell, Mary Louise, *Ireland's Harp: the shaping of Irish identity c.1770–1880* (Dublin: UCD Press, 2014)

_____, 'Belfast Harp Society', *EMIR*, vol. 1, p. 81

_____, 'A Driving Image of Revolution: the Irish harp and its utopian space in the eighteenth century', *Utopian Studies*, vol. 21, no. 2, 2010, pp. 252–73

O'Farrell, St Mary Pius, 'Bishop Moylan's Report on the Diocese of Cork, 1802', *JCHAS*, vol. 106, 2001, pp. 121–30

Official Catalogue of the National Exhibition of the Arts, Manufactures, and Products of Ireland; held in Cork, 1852. With Alphabetical List of the Names of Exhibitors (Cork: O'Brien, 1852)

O'Flanagan, Patrick, and Cornelius G. Buttimer (eds), *Cork History and Society: interdisciplinary essays on the history of an Irish county* (Dublin: Geography Publications, 1993)

O'Halloran, Clare, 'Harping on the Past: translating antiquarian learning into popular culture in early nineteenth-century Ireland', in Melissa Calaresu, Filippo de Vivo and Joan-Pau Rubiés (eds), *Exploring Cultural History: essays in honour of Peter Burke* (Farnham: Ashgate, 2010)

O'Hanlon, Tríona, 'Lewis Gibson and "Miss Mathews": two eighteenth and early nineteenth century provincial Irish cathedral composers and the editing of their work', *Proceedings of the 1st Annual Conference of the Society for Musicology in Ireland*, Maynooth, 2003

_____, 'Cloyne Cathedral', *EMIR*, vol. 1, p. 210

_____, 'Henry Delamain', *EMIR*, vol. 1, p. 292

O'Keeffe, John, *Recollections of the Life of John O'Keeffe*, 2 vols (London: H. Coburn, 1826)

Oldham, Guy, and Nicholas Thistlethwaite, 'Charles Spackman Barker', *NGrove2*, vol. 2, pp. 734–5

O'Mahony, Colman, *In the Shadows: life in Cork, 1750–1930* (Cork: Tower Books, 1997)

O'Neill, Francis, *Irish Minstrels and Musicians: the story of Irish music* (Chicago: Regan Printing House, 1913, reprinted Cork: Mercier, 1987)

O'Neill, Timothy P., 'The Catholic Church and Relief of the Poor, 1815–45', *Archivium Hibernicum*, vol. 31, 1973, pp. 132–45

O'Regan, Susan, 'A Vast Speculation: The Cork Grand Musical Meeting of 1826', *Journal of the Society for Musicology in Ireland*, vol. 5, 2009–2010, pp. 3–19, http://www.musicologyireland.com/jsmi/index.php/journal/article/view/34/59, accessed 9 January 2017

_____, 'Concert Performers in Cork from 1710 to 1840', *JCHAS*, vol. 114, 2009, pp. 39–50

_____, 'Public Concerts in the Musical Life of Cork 1754–1840', 2 vols, unpublished PhD dissertation (Cork Institute of Technology, 2008)

Origin, Constitution and Design of the Cork Athenaeum (Cork: Guy, nd [1852/3], IE CCCA U15B/P/A17

O'Shea, John J., 'Churches of the Church of Ireland in Cork City', *JCHAS*, vol. 48, 1943, pp. 30–5

_____, 'The Non-Conformist Communities of Cork City', *JCHAS*, vol. 48, 1943, pp. 35–43

Ó Súilleabháin, Pádraig, 'Sidelights on the Irish Church, 1811–38', *Collectanea Hibernica*, vol. 9, 1966, pp. 71–8

O'Sullivan, William, 'Civic Institutions in Cork', *JCHAS*, vol. 48, 1943, pp. 82–5

O'Toole, James, (rev. Sara Smyth), *NEWSPLAN – report of the Newsplan Project in Ireland* (London: British Library and Dublin: National Library of Ireland, 1998)

Ó Tuathaigh, Gearóid, *Ireland before the Famine, 1798–1848* (Dublin: Gill & Macmillan, 2007)

Parke, William Thomas, *Musical Memoirs; comprising an Account of the General State of Music in England, from the first Commemoration of Handel, in the year 1784, to the year 1830*, 2 vols (London: Colburn & Bentley, 1830)

Parker, Lisa, 'Samuel J. Pigott', *EMIR*, vol. 2, p. 840

_____, 'Thomas Richard Gonzalvez Jozé', *EMIR*, vol. 1, pp. 550–1

Patterson, Annie, 'Musicians of the Day: Herr Theodor Gmür', *Weekly Irish Times*, 27 April 1901

_____, 'Musicians of the Day: Herr Theodor Gmür', *Weekly Irish Times*, 4 May 1901

_____, 'Musicians of the Day: Joseph Seymour', *Weekly Irish Times*, 1 September 1900

Pigot's City of Dublin and Hibernian Provincial Directory (London and Manchester: J. Pigot, 1824)

Pine, Richard, and Charles Acton (eds), *To Talent Alone: the Royal Irish Academy of Music, 1848–1998* (Dublin: Gill & Macmillan, 1998)

Pleasants, Virginia, 'The Early Piano in Britain (*c.* 1760–1800)', *Early Music*, vol. 13, no. 1, 1985, pp. 39–44

Plumb, J.H., *The Commercialisation of Leisure in Eighteenth-Century England* (Reading: University of Reading, 1973)

_____, 'The New World of Children in Eighteenth-Century England', *Past and Present*, vol. 67, no. 1, 1975, pp. 64–95

Powell, Martyn J., 'Beef, Claret and Communication: convivial clubs in the public sphere, 1750–1800', in James Kelly and Martyn J. Powell (eds), *Clubs and Societies in Eighteenth Century Ireland* (Dublin: Four Courts Press, 2010)

Pritchard, Brian, 'Some Festival Programmes of the Eighteenth and Nineteenth Centuries, 3: Liverpool and Manchester', *RMA Research Chronicle*, vol. 7, 1969, pp. 1–25

_____, 'The Provincial Festivals of the Ashley Family', *The Galpin Society Journal*, vol. 22, 1969, pp. 58–77

_____, 'The Musical Festival and the Choral Society in England in the Eighteenth and Nineteenth Centuries: a social history', 2 vols. unpublished PhD dissertation (University of Birmingham, 1968)

Provincial Grand Lodge of Munster/Hibernian Lodge, No 95, Cork http://www munsterfreemason.com/craft-lodges/hibernian-lodge-no-95-cork/ accessed 16 October 2016.

Quinn, John F., *Father Mathew's Crusade: temperance in nineteenth-century Ireland and Irish America* (Amherst, MA: University of Massachusetts Press, 2002)

Rafferty, Oliver P., *The Catholic Church and the Protestant State: nineteenth century realities* (Dublin: Four Courts Press, 2008)

Rainbow, Bernarr, 'Guillaume Louis Bocquillon Wilhem', *NGrove2*, vol. 27, p. 387

_____, 'The Rise of Popular Music Education in Nineteenth-Century England', *Victorian Studies*, vol. 30, no. 1, 1986, pp. 25–49

_____, 'Johann Bernhard Logier and the Chiroplast Controversy', *The Musical Times*, vol. 131, no. 1766, 1990, pp. 193–6

_____, with Gordon Cox, *Music in Educational Thought and Practice: a survey from 800 BC* (London: Boydell, 2007)

Reid, Douglas J., 'Some Festival Programmes of the Eighteenth and Nineteenth Centuries, 1: Salisbury and Winchester', *RMA Research Chronicle*, vol. 5, 1965, pp. 51–79

Rhodes, David J. 'Arne Family', *EMIR*, vol. 1, pp. 31–3

_____, 'Passerini Family', *EMIR*, vol. 2, p. 823

Rice, Paul F., *Venanzio Rauzzini in Britain: castrato, composer, and cultural leader* (Rochester: University of Rochester Press, 2015)

Ricks, Robert, 'Russian Horn Bands', *The Musical Quarterly*, vol. 55, no 3, 1969, pp. 364–71

Robins, Brian, 'The Catch and Glee in Eighteenth-Century Provincial England', in Susan Wollenberg and Simon McVeigh (eds), *Concert Life in Eighteenth-Century Britain* (Aldershot: Ashgate, 2004)

Robinson, Audrey, 'Anglo-Irish Music in Cork, 1750–1800', unpublished MA thesis (St Patrick's College, Maynooth, 1996)

Robinson, H.W., *A History of Accountants in Ireland* (Dublin: Institute of Chartered Accountants in Ireland, 1983)

Rocque, J., *An Exact Survey of the City and Suburbs of the City and County of Cork* (London: J. Rocque, 1759)

Rodmell, Paul (ed.), *Music and Institutions in Nineteenth-Century Britain* (Farnham: Ashgate, 2012)

_____, 'The Society of Antient Concerts, Dublin, 1834–64', in Michael Murphy and Jan Smaczny (eds), *Music in Nineteenth-Century Ireland* (Dublin: Four Courts Press, 2007)

Rohr, Deborah, *The Careers of British Musicians, 1750–1850: a profession of artisans* (Cambridge: Cambridge University Press, 2001)

Royal Academy of Music, *A List of Pupils Received into the Academy since Its Foundation in 1822–3* (London, Royal Academy of Music, 1838)

Royal Academy of Music, *The Musical Directory, Register and Almanack, and Royal Academy of Music Calendar for the Years 1853–1862* (London: Royal Academy of Music, 1853–62)

Russell, Dave, *Popular Music in England, 1840–1914: a social history*, 2nd edition (Montreal: McGill-Queen's University Press, 1987)

Russell, David, 'Provincial Concerts in England, 1865–1914: a case-study of Bradford', *Journal of the Royal Musical Association*, vol. 114, no. 1, 1989, pp. 43–55

Sainsbury, John S., *A Dictionary of Musicians from the Earliest Times*, 2 vols (New York: Da Capo Press, 1966, reprint of 1825 edition)

Sadie, Stanley, and John Tyrell (eds), *NGrove2*, 29 vols (London: Macmillan, 2001)

Scholes, Percy A., *The Mirror of Music, 1844–1944,* 2 vols (London: Novello, 1947)

Schott, Howard, 'From Harpsichord to Pianoforte, a Chronology and Commentary', *Early Music*, vol. 13, 1985, pp. 28–38

Sharpe, Richard, 'Tadhg Gaelach Ó Súilleabháin's *Pious Miscellany*: editions of the Munster bestseller of the early nineteenth century', *Proceedings of the Royal Irish Academy*, vol. 114C, 2014, pp. 1–59

Sheldon, Esther K., *Thomas Sheridan of Smock Alley* (Princeton: Princeton University Press, 1967)

Silburn, Muriel, 'The Most Extraordinary Creature in Europe', *Music and Letters*, vol. 3, no. 2, 1922, pp. 200–5

Sillard, Robert M., *Barry Sullivan and his Contemporaries: a histrionic record*, 2 vols (London: Fisher Unwin, 1901)

Slater's *National Commercial Directory of Ireland, 1846* (London and Manchester: Slater, 1846)

Slater's *National Commercial Directory of Ireland, 1870* (London and Manchester: Slater, 1870)

Slater's *Royal National Commercial Directory of Ireland, 1881* (Manchester: Slater, 1881)

Smith, Charles, *The Ancient and Present State of the County and City of Cork*, 2 vols (Dublin: Wilson, 1774)

Smither, Howard E., *A History of the Oratorio: the oratorio in the nineteenth and twentieth centuries* (Chapel Hill, NC: University of North Carolina Press, 2000)

Smith, Victor E., 'Organ in Christ Church, Cork', *JCHAS*, vol. 33, 1928, p. 105.

Smyth, W.J., 'Territorial, social and settlement hierarchies in seventeenth century Kilkenny', in William Nolan and Kevin Whelan (eds), *Kilkenny: History and Society* (Dublin: Geography Publications, 1990).

Snowman, Daniel, *The Gilded Stage: a social history of opera* (London: Atlantic Books, 2009)

Southey, Rosemary, 'Commercial Music-Making in Eighteenth-Century North-East England: a pale reflection of London?', 2 vols, unpublished PhD dissertation (University of Newcastle, 2001)

Southey, Roz, 'Competition and Collaboration: concert promotion in Newcastle and Durham, 1752–1772', in Susan Wollenberg and Simon McVeigh (eds), *Concert Life in Eighteenth-Century Britain* (Aldershot: Ashgate, 2004)

Squire, W.B. (rev. Clive Brown), 'William Richard Bexfield (1824–1853)', in H.C.G. Mullan and Brian Harrison (eds), *Oxford Dictionary of National Biography*, 60 vols (Oxford: Oxford University Press, 2004), vol. 5, pp. 626–7

Stockwell, La Tourette, *Dublin Theatres and Theatre Customs, 1637–1820* (Kingsport, TN: Kingsport Press, 1938)

Strickland, Walter G., *A Dictionary of Irish Artists*, 2 vols (Dublin: Maunsell, 1913)

Taylor, Ian, *Music in London and the Myth of Decline: from Haydn to the Philharmonic* (Cambridge: Cambridge University Press, 2010)

Teahan, John, 'A List of Irish Instrument Makers', *Galpin Society Journal*, vol. 16, 1963, pp. 28–32

Tenducci, Dorothea, *A True and Genuine Narrative of Mr and Mrs Tenducci. In a Letter to a Friend at Bath. Giving a full Account. From their Marriage to the present Time* (London: Pridden, 1768)

Thackeray, William M., *The Irish Sketchbook 1842, with numerous engravings on wood drawn by the author* (London: Sutton, 1990)

The City of Cork Directory, with which is incorporated the Commercial Directory of Queenstown (Liverpool: Fulton, 1871)

The Commercial Directory of Ireland, Scotland for the Years 1820, 1821, 1822 (Manchester: J. Pigot, 1820)

The County and City of Cork Almanac, calculated and adapted by C. Thompson (Cork: F. Jackson, 1843)

The County and City of Cork Post Office General Directory, 1842–3 (Cork: Jackson, 1842)

The First Dublin Grand Musical Festival, 1831 (Dublin: Underwood, 1831), NLI Ir 780941 d 1

The First Number of the Reports of the Society in Dublin for Promoting the Comforts of the Poor (London, W. Bulmer, 1800)

The Present State of the Charitable Infirmary of Corke for the Year 1750 (Cork: G. Harrison, 1750) [NLI I 6551]

'The Royal Academy of Music', *Quarterly Musical Magazine and Review*, vol. 7, no. 16, 1825, pp. 143–69

The Vocal Magazine or Compleat Songster, consisting of such English, Scotch and Irish Songs, Catches, Glees, Cantatas, Airs, Ballads, as are deemed most worthy of being transmitted to posterity, 3 vols (Cork: William Flyn, 1782)

Thomas, R., 'Boleyne Reeves', *Notes and Queries*, vol. s10–IX, no. 222, 28 March 1908, pp. 241–60

Thompson, Michael, 'Church of Ireland', *EMIR*, vol. 1, pp. 195–7

Tilmouth, Michael, 'The Beginnings of Provincial Concert Life in England', in Christopher Hogwood and Richard Luckett (eds), *Music in England: essays in memory of Charles Cudworth* (Cambridge: Cambridge University Press, 1983)

'Townshend's Comment on Musgrave's Memoirs', *The Critical Review, or Annals of Literature*, vol. 36, October 1802 (London: S. Hamilton, 1802), pp. 184–6

Troubridge, St Vincent, *The Benefit System in the British Theatre* (London: The Society for Theatre Research, 1967)

Tuckey, Francis H., *The County and City of Cork Remembrancer or Annals of the County and City of Cork* (Cork: Osborne Savage, 1837)

Vaughan, W.E. (ed.), *A New History of Ireland VI: Ireland under the Union II, 1870–1921* (Oxford: Oxford University Press, 2010)

W.G. 'Music in Cork', *The Musical World*, vol. 20, 1845, pp. 98–9

Walker, Alan, *Franz Liszt: I: The Virtuoso Years 1811–1847* (Ithaca, NY: Cornell University Press, 1987)

Wall, Maureen, 'The Rise of a Catholic Middle Class in Eighteenth-Century Ireland', *Irish Historical Studies*, vol. 11, no. 42, 1958, pp. 91–115

Walsh, Patrick, 'Club Life in Late Seventeenth and Early Eighteenth-Century Ireland', in James Kelly and Martyn J. Powell (eds), *Clubs and Societies in Eighteenth-Century Ireland* (Dublin: Four Courts Press, 2010)

Walsh, Rev. T.J., *In the Tradition of St Finbarr* (Cork: Guy, 1951)

_____, 'St Mary's Pro-Cathedral, Cork', *The Fold*, May 1964, pp. 13–21

_____, 'Francis Moylan, Bishop of Cork, 1735–1815', *JCHAS*, vol. 55, no. 182, 1950, pp. 98–110

Walsh, T.J., *Opera in Dublin, 1705–1797: the social scene* (Dublin: Allen Figgis, 1973)

_____, *Opera in Dublin, 1798–1820: Frederick Jones and the Crow Street Theatre* (Oxford: Oxford University Press, 1993)

_____, *Opera in Old Dublin, 1819–1838* (Wexford: The Wexford Festival, 1952)

Wangermée, Robert, 'Sigismond Thalberg', *NGrove2*, vol. 25, pp. 337–8

Waterhouse, William, 'The Double Flageolet: made in England', *The Galpin Society Journal*, vol. 52, 1999, pp. 172–82

Watmough, James H., 'Letters of James H. Watmough to his Wife, 1785', *The Pennsylvania Magazine of History and Biography*, vol. 29, no. 1, 1905, pp. 31–43

Weber, William, 'Mass Culture and the Reshaping of European Musical Taste, 1770–1870', *International Journal of the Aesthetics and Sociology of Music*, vol. 25, nos 1–2, 1994, pp. 175–90

_____, *The Rise of Musical Classics in Eighteenth-Century England: a study in canon, ritual, and ideology* (Oxford: Clarendon, 1996)

_____, 'The Contemporaneity of Eighteenth-Century Musical Taste', *The Musical Quarterly*, vol. 70, no. 2, 1984, pp. 175–94

_____, *Music and the Middle Class: the social structure of concert life in London, Paris and Vienna between 1830 and 1848*, 2nd edition (Aldershot: Ashgate, 2004)

_____, *The Great Transformation of Musical Taste: concert programming from Haydn to Brahms* (Cambridge: Cambridge University Press, 2008)

_____, 'Redefining the Status of Opera: London and Leipzig, 1800–1848', *The Journal of Interdisciplinary History*, vol. 36, no. 3, 2006, pp. 507–32

_____ (ed.), *The Musician as Enterpreneur, 1700–1914: managers, charlatans, and idealists* (Bloomington: Indiana University Press, 2004)

Webster, Bernard (ed.), *The Acting National Drama, Comprising every new Play, Farce, Melodrama, Opera, Burletta etc.*, vol 4 (London: Chapman & Hall, 1838)

Webster, Charles A., *The Diocese of Cork* (Cork: Guy, 1920)

Webster, James, and George Feder, *The New Grove Haydn* (London: Macmillan, 2002)

West, William, *A Directory and Picture of Cork and Its Environs* (Cork: West, 1810)

White, Eric Walter, *A History of English Opera* (London: Faber & Faber, 1983)

White, Harry, 'Carolan and the Dislocation of Music in Ireland', *Eighteenth-Century Ireland/Iris an Dá Chultúir*, vol. 4, 1989, pp. 55–64

_____, *The Keeper's Recital: music and cultural history in Ireland, 1770–1970* (Cork: Cork University Press, 1998)

_____, and Barra Boydell (eds), *The Enclyclopaedia of Music in Ireland*, 2 vols (Dublin: UCD Press, 2013)

_____, and Nicholas Lawrence (eds), 'Towards a History of the Cecilian Movement in Ireland', in Gerard Gillen and Harry White (eds), *Music and the Church* (Dublin: Irish Academic Press, 1993)

Wilkie's Cork City Directory 1872 (Cork: Wilkie, 1871)

Willes, Chief Justice (Baron) Edward, *A Tour through Ireland in Several Entertaining Letters* [BM Additional MS 29252]

Williams, Adrian, *Portrait of Liszt by Himself and His Contemporaries* (Oxford: Clarendon, 1990)

Windele, John, *Historical and Descriptive Notices of the City of Cork and Its Vicinity* (Cork: Bolster, 1846)

Wollenberg, Susan, *Music at Oxford in the Eighteenth and Nineteenth Centuries* (Oxford: Oxford University Press, 2001)

_____, and Simon McVeigh (eds), *Concert Life in Eighteenth-Century Britain* (Aldershot: Ashgate, 2004)

Wright, E.H., *Andre Besnard: a tale of old Cork with drawings by Grogan* (Cork: J. Mahony, 1889)

Yates, Nigel, *The Religious Condition of Ireland, 1770–1850* (Oxford: Oxford University Press, 2006)

Young, Percy M., *The English Glee* (Oxford: Oxford University Press, 1990)

Zingel, Hans Joachim, *Harp Music in the Nineteenth Century* (Bloomington: Indiana University Press, 1992)

Zon, Bennett (ed.), *Performance Culture in Nineteenth-Century Britain* (Farnham: Ashgate, 2013)

Zuk, Patrick, 'Words for Music, Perhaps? Irishness, criticism and the art tradition', *Irish Studies Review*, vol. 12, no. 1, 2004, pp. 11–27

Index

Note: illustrations are indicated by page numbers in **bold**. All individual buildings, streets and locations are in Cork unless otherwise specified.